THE MUSICAL EXPERIENCE

The Musical Experience

RETHINKING MUSIC TEACHING AND LEARNING

Edited by Janet R. Barrett and
Peter R. Webster

OXFORD
UNIVERSITY PRESS

OXFORD
UNIVERSITY PRESS

Oxford University Press is a department of the University of
Oxford. It furthers the University's objective of excellence in research,
scholarship, and education by publishing worldwide.

Oxford   New York
Auckland   Cape Town   Dar es Salaam   Hong Kong   Karachi
Kuala Lumpur   Madrid   Melbourne   Mexico City   Nairobi
New Delhi   Shanghai   Taipei   Toronto

With offices in
Argentina   Austria   Brazil   Chile   Czech Republic   France   Greece
Guatemala   Hungary   Italy   Japan   Poland   Portugal   Singapore
South Korea   Switzerland   Thailand   Turkey   Ukraine   Vietnam

Oxford is a registered trade mark of Oxford University Press
in the UK and certain other countries.

Published in the United States of America by
Oxford University Press
198 Madison Avenue, New York, NY 10016

Library of Congress Cataloging-in-Publication Data
The musical experience : rethinking music teaching and learning / edited by Janet R. Barrett
and Peter R. Webster.
    pages cm
Includes bibliographical references and index.
ISBN 978-0-19-936303-2 (hardcover : alk. paper)—ISBN 978-0-19-936304-9 (pbk. : alk. paper)
1. Music—Instruction and study.   I. Barrett, Janet R., editor of compilation.   II. Webster, Peter R.,
editor of compilation.
MT1.M987365 2014
780.71—dc23
2013044970

9 8 7 6 5 4 3 2 1
Printed in the United States of America
on acid-free paper

To Bennett Reimer
(1932–2013)

Late in our work with this volume, the editors learned of the passing of Bennett Reimer. Bennett was the founder of the Center for the Study of Education and the Music Experience at Northwestern University and a world figure in music education philosophy. The editors were close colleagues of Bennett at Northwestern. Each scholar whose work appears herein has been deeply affected by his writing, his teaching, or both. We dedicate this book to his memory and to his lasting legacy as a premier scholar in music teaching and learning.

Contents

Acknowlegments ix
About the Contributors xi

1. *New Thinking for the Study of Music Teaching and Learning* 1
     Janet R. Barrett and Peter R. Webster, editors

SECTION ONE | PHILOSOPHY 11
2. *Philosophical Musings: Reflections and Directions* 13
     Betty Anne Younker
3. *Escaping versus Confronting Reality: Politics and Music Education in the Age of Entertainment* 25
     Paul Woodford

SECTION TWO | LISTENING 43
4. *Music Listening Vistas, Visions, and Vim* 45
     Jody L. Kerchner
5. *Life Music as a Beginning Point: Connecting with the Intuitive Listener* 63
     Rob E. Dunn
6. *Music Listening Spaces* 88
     Carlos Xavier Rodriguez

SECTION THREE | CULTURAL DIMENSIONS OF MUSIC TEACHING AND LEARNING 103
7. *Finding Middle Ground: Music Education in Urban Settings* 105
     Catherine Larsen
8. *Framing Approaches to World Music Pedagogy in a Local Music Culture* 128
     Valerie R. Peters

9. *Spaces for Student Voices: Composition in Schools and Issues of Social Justice* 149
  Janice P. Smith

SECTION FOUR | CREATIVITY 167

10. *Is a Virtual Composer in Residence an Oxymoron?* 169
  Bruce Carter

11. *Creative Application: A Way to Include Music Composition and Improvisation in the General Music Curriculum* 183
  Lois Veenhoven Guderian

12. *Fostering Creativity in the Performance Ensemble* 205
  Kate Fitzpatrick

SECTION FIVE | EVOLVING ROLES 221

13. *Reframing Leadership and the Musical Experience: The Conductor as Servant Leader* 223
  Ramona M. Wis

14. *Reconsidering the Performing Ensemble Class and the Role of the Conductor/Teacher in Music Education* 243
  David S. Zerull

SECTION SIX | RECONCEPTUALIZING MUSIC TEACHER EDUCATION 259

15. *Preservice Music Teacher Preparation for the Conductor-Educator Role* 261
  Margaret H. Berg

16. *Music Education: Relevant and Meaningful* 284
  David A. Williams

17. *"No Actual Teaching": Expanding Preservice Music Teachers' Imaginaries of Teaching* 294
  Teryl L. Dobbs

18. *Building Bridges to Solve Puzzles: Strategic Curriculum Design in Music Teacher Education* 309
  Michele Kaschub

INDEX 333

Acknowledgments

The editors wish to acknowledge the valuable contributions of members of the Center for the Study of Education and the Musical Experience at the Bienen School of Music, Northwestern University, 2010–2012: Carlos Abril, Bernard Dobroski, Maud Hickey, Bennett Reimer (emeritus) and Center Fellows Linda Aicher, Kimberly Lansinger Ankney, Julie Bannerman, Kenneth Elpus, Donna Gallo, Jonathan Harnum, Sara Jones, Nasim Niknafs, Julia Shaw, Jason Thompson, and Richard Webb. Thank you for your collaborative work on this project.

About the Contributors

Janet R. Barrett, Marilyn Pflederer Zimmerman Scholar in Music Education and Professor of Music Education, University of Illinois at Urbana-Champaign

Margaret H. Berg, Associate Professor of Instrumental (String) Music Education, University of Colorado at Boulder

Bruce Carter, Independent Scholar

Teryl L. Dobbs, Associate Professor of Music Education, University of Wisconsin-Madison

Rob E. Dunn, Professor of Music Education, Brigham Young University

Kate Fitzpatrick, Assistant Professor of Music Education, University of Michigan

Lois Veenhoven Guderian, Assistant Professor of Music, University of Wisconsin-Superior

Michele Kaschub, Professor of Music and Coordinator of Music Teacher Education, University of Southern Maine

Jody Kerchner, Professor of Music Education and Director of the Division of Music Education, Oberlin Conservatory of Music

Catherine Larsen, Assistant Professor of Teacher Education, DePaul University

Valerie Peters, Professor of Music Education, Université Laval

Carlos Xavier Rodriguez, Associate Professor and Chair of Music Education, University of Michigan

Janice Smith, Associate Professor of Music Education, Queens College, City University of New York

Peter R. Webster, Scholar-in-Residence, University of Southern California; Professor Emeritus, Northwestern University

David A. Williams, Associate Professor and Director of Music Education, University of South Florida

Ramona M. Wis, Mimi Rolland Distinguished Professor in the Fine Arts, Chair of the Department of Music, North Central College

Paul Woodford, Professor of Music Education, University of Western Ontario

Betty Anne Younker, Professor of Music Education and Dean of the Don Wright Faculty of Music, University of Western Ontario

David S. Zerull, Professor of Music Education, Shenandoah Conservatory

THE MUSICAL EXPERIENCE

1

NEW THINKING FOR THE STUDY OF MUSIC

TEACHING AND LEARNING

Janet R. Barrett and Peter R. Webster, editors

CHANGE IS A contemporary watchword in the field of music education just as it is in education at large. Proposals for reform are plentiful—from teachers in the field, school communities, professional associations, policy makers, and the academy. Every era in the history of music teaching has presented significant opportunities and challenges, and this time is no exception. We live in a fast-paced, highly connected society in which music has never been more evident in the lives of children and adults of all ages; however, much of how we formally teach this music has remained stuck in age-old theories and practices that do not serve us well. What is desperately needed are new ways to conceptualize and execute music teaching that respect past achievements but also look forward to new paradigms for our field. The chapters in *The Musical Experience: Rethinking Music Teaching and Learning* examine these calls for change and offer productive avenues for action related to music teaching and learning in contemporary class-rooms. The authors in this collection situate musical experience at the center of a dynamic conversation about artistic values and visions and the nature of well-informed teaching and learning. They critically examine long-standing prac-tices in the field and suggest new avenues for engaging students in the compre-hensive study of music.

The notion of "music experience" is a complicated construct that has engaged the thinking of philosophers, aestheticians, and musicians over the centuries (Reimer & Wright, 1992). Music itself is often considered an inherently human construction of sound, unfolding in time, intentionally designed to be expressive.

Those engaged in the teaching of music consider four human behaviors as fundamental to its understanding: (1) performance of the music of others, (2) performance of one's own music (improvisation in its many forms), (3) composition of music, and (4) music listening. Authors in this volume would hold that these behaviors are at the center of music experience and, as such, are subject to continued scrutiny in the context of the teaching and learning process. Music experience, as it is conceived here in praxis, is the result of active engagement in the construction of music in its many forms. It includes the development of skills, knowledge, attitudes, and values that lead to deeper understandings of music as art. At its core are the intrinsic and affective quality of sounds and the construction of personal meaning that comes from the creative engagement with musical experiences themselves. Authors in this volume are also keenly aware of the social context of musical experience, as all music experience is inherently and fundamentally a product of the social interactions of time and place.

The chapters are grouped into sections that capture various dimensions of this scholarly discourse that strongly implicates practice. The authors describe, interpret, and synthesize central issues related to the changing needs of schools and society; expanded views of the creative, critical, and experiential nature of music listening; evolving roles of performers and conductors; deeper understanding of creative thinking in composition and improvisation; and shifting intersections of music and culture. Informed by scholarly inquiry and educational practice, the book concludes with a number of chapters that challenge traditional assumptions and pathways, re-envisioning local and systemic changes in elementary and secondary music education, as well as the forward-thinking preparation of music teachers.

The book was developed as part of a collaborative process that serves as a model of scholarly integration and synthesis. As editors, we asked past graduates of the doctoral program at Northwestern University to return to Evanston, Illinois, in June of 2010 to attend a symposium on change in music teaching and learning. Attendees were asked to contribute papers related to six key themes: (1) Philosophical Considerations for a Changing Time, (2) New Vistas in Music Listening, (3) Issues of Culture in Music Education, (4) Composition and Improvisation, (5) The Conductor/Performer as Leader, and (6) Curricular Reform for Schools and Music Teacher Education. Those who agreed were asked to draft manuscripts and submit them in advance to be compiled in a "print on demand" volume that was made available for participants to read before they arrived for the symposium. Each participant was charged to stand back and then look forward, prompting broad perspectives on the trajectory of scholarly research in their topic themes. During the event, authors responded to the other papers in their topical "set," followed by questions and discussion from the floor. In this manner, we set out to capture the constructive spirit of collegial exchange that invited deep thought and focused discussion. Seventeen papers were chosen for this book; each was edited extensively by the authors and current faculty and students to arrive at the chapters herein. In addition, all the rich and complicated discussions during the symposium were recorded and transcribed. Selected excerpts from these transcriptions serve as the interludes between sections in this volume. Inspired by the spirit and substance of twenty-five years of research completed by faculty and doctoral graduates of the music education program at Northwestern University, authors represented here reflect on new thinking about the complexities of teaching music at the beginning of the twenty-first century.

CHAPTER OVERVIEWS

For the opening theme of philosophical connections, Betty Anne Younker draws our attention to philosophical inquiry and the ongoing relevance of systematic appraisal of the foundational underpinnings of music education. She challenges us to engage in this work for the clarity of purpose it brings to us as individual practitioners, as well as the substantive aims it provides for our collective dia-logue. Dewey's writings on the nature of experience and education provide a historical platform, as well as a catalyst for contemporary applications of Deweyan ideas. After grappling with the task of defining music and musical experience, Younker provides a brief overview of some of the main streams of philosophical inquiry within music education in the last century. Her discussion of critical thinking, spirituality, social justice, and democratic values leads to provocative questions that invite further reflection and critical debate to prompt dynamic consideration of beliefs and practices.

In his chapter, Paul Woodford situates music education within current political and economic realities in Western democracies as neoliberal thought has taken hold as the dominant governing philosophy in many of these nations. Of particular concern for Woodford is the demotion of music in the schools from an educative endeavor to the pursuit of entertainment. He questions how music education policy and music educators have responded to the growing influence of commercial music, which seeks to, in his words, "infantilize rather than provoke or otherwise encourage thought." For Woodford, the ideal music education would encourage students to rethink the realities of life by confronting rather than escaping its difficulties, ultimately leading to critical self-awareness.

The theme of music listening follows. In her discussion of how music listening might be addressed with renewed vim and vigor in music education research, Jody Kerchner traces the influence of behaviorism, developmental theorists, cognitive science, and constructivism on the nature of musical listening. She describes twelve key principles of music listening and their implications for practice. Kerchner provides two categories of music research to augment the current understanding of the musical listening experience: (1) inclusion and diversity in the music listening experience and (2) the collective social consciousness and construction of meaning that occurs during music listening. Kerchner considers diversity in terms of both diverse learners and diverse styles and genres of music, suggesting that research and pedagogical tools must be as diverse as each of our listeners. To facilitate renewed listening experiences, Kerchner proposes a shift from teacher-directed listening experiences to those in which students construct their own meaning.

Listening is integral to all forms of musical experience. Rob E. Dunn suggests, however, that music educators have defined music listening so narrowly that it has been relegated to the shadows. Dunn portrays the dissonance between the ways that music listening has been taught in schools and the way that most individuals weave music listening into the fabric of their lives as intuitive listeners. After reviewing research from these two perspectives, Dunn provides models that represent key areas of contrast in formal and intuitive listening experiences. He places these on a continuum of experience rather than dichotomizing types of listening; he also provides principles for both guiding the incorporation of students' intuitive listening experiences into music education and revising common strategies and practices to embrace a more holistic and complementary view. Finally, Dunn describes several of these strategies and research studies that have investigated capacious views of music listening and its impact on listeners.

Carlos Xavier Rodriguez concludes the listening theme by discussing the concept of music listening space from a variety of angles, considering space as a conceptual tool with which to examine and understand music listening both historically and in the present. Citing scholarship from varied fields, Rodriguez reflects upon space in multiple dimensions—as spatial orientation of sound waves, as metaphor in understanding and describing musical materials and structures, as temporal and physical action, and as an arena for social interaction. Through this exploration, Rodriguez argues that the notion of listening space is complex and multidimensional, more so than has been examined in discussions of listening *contexts*. In a historical sweep, Rodriguez provides examples of diverse manifestations of listening spaces from ragtime to the popularization of radio, culminating with modern listening spaces including the Internet and digital media. He asserts that students produce unique listening spaces through these modern technologies and therefore have unique needs and interests. His chapter concludes with suggestions for music teacher education. Rodriguez calls for a focus on emerging music listening spaces to transform and enrich music education through student perspectives on musical experience.

Beginning the theme of cultural context, Catherine Larsen asserts that the arts are an integral component to a complete education and are particularly valuable for students in urban schools. She notes that opportunities to study arts in schools have become increasingly limited, especially in urban settings. This problem is thought to stem from budget issues and increased pressures to improve student achievement on standardized tests. Larsen suggests that arts integration—envisioned as a collaboration among classroom teachers, arts specialists, and external organizations—might offer a solution to these challenges. Establishing professional community collaborations and professional development programs for teachers is fundamental to establishing and maintaining arts integration programs that provide meaningful learning experiences for children.

One vital component of education is the intersection of theory and practice. Teachers hoping to find practical applications based on theories of culture and multiculturalism will be rewarded by Valerie Peters from her chapter, "Framing Approaches to Multicultural Music Education in a Local Culture." This chapter presents a number of conceptions of music and culture from the perspectives of influential theorists in music education, anthropology, and ethnomusicology. These perspectives provide a conceptual framework for a project Peters designed to help her students "understand music as a human behavior, embedded in social and historical contexts, encompassing a web of socially constructed meanings." This field-based project, which involved the study of a local music culture, was informed by David Elliott's insular and dynamic models of multicultural music education. In describing the results of this project, Peters demonstrates an effective means of promoting awareness and sensitivity in students who are examining a musical culture.

Inspired in part by the need for teachers to give students a sense of musical freedom and a place to practice their own musical thinking, Janice P. Smith provides both a philosophical base for music composition in schools and practical examples of how to achieve it. The emerging literature on social justice provides a framework for considering how the goals for culturally responsive classrooms intersect with goals for developing compositional thinking, particularly in the way that both projects honor the individual voices of students from varying backgrounds. Smith draws heavily from her years of public school teaching and from her base as a professor teaching in an urban setting to describe principles and practices for culturally responsive and creative work in music classrooms. The development of independent critical thinking on the part of students is stressed. Practical examples include the formation of composer clubs and guitar classes as entry points for teachers.

Turning to the important theme of composition and improvisation in schools, Bruce Carter, in his chapter on the role of a "composer in residence," reflects on his own personal experience as a "virtual composer in residence" at an urban middle school located two hundred miles from his home, thanks to advances in technology. To answer his question "Is a virtual composer in residence an oxymoron?" Carter focuses on his conception of the role of the virtual composer. He discusses the difficulties of how to teach composition in a middle school, noting four major themes that significantly shaped his instructional strategies: (1) task structures, (2) group instruction, (3) obstacles to teaching composition, and (4) compositional practices of eminent composers. He concludes that this type of virtual composition program could play an important role in linking students with a larger musical community.

Lois Veenhoven Guderian presents evidence for the lack of attention music teachers have given for engaging students in compositional creative experiences. A case is made for including improvisation and composition experiences in general music settings by using a process of integration called creative application. She argues that improvisation and compositional experiences engage students in learning and can enhance their understanding of traditional curricular content. Guderian offers examples of such integration, including teaching the recorder, music listening, music theory teaching, and exploring nontraditional notation. The use of computer-assisted composition is noted as a particularly creative way to teach about form. Throughout the chapter, Guderian offers several bases for composition and improvisation in the schools by citing writings that stress constructivism, schema theory, and sequential curriculum. The need for composition and improvisation instruction in teacher education is also noted.

Kate Fitzpatrick observes that while the act of performing is often perceived to be creative, performers in an ensemble are often not engaged in the creative process. She reframes the role of the conductor as a facilitator in a democratic classroom and offers strategies for fostering creative thinking in a large ensemble setting. This move encourages conductors to "step off the podium" and more fully involve students in making interpretive decisions. Fitzpatrick believes that when given the opportunity to shape interpretation, performers are engaged in creative thought by drawing upon their knowledge of conventions and upsetting these conventions to create an emotional response. Fitzpatrick explores contributions by researchers who suggest that composition and improvisation are fundamental to performers' understandings of the creative process and, therefore, are essential ingredients in performance classrooms. She offers practical strategies for fostering creative thinking such as borrowing chamber music techniques, setting long-term goals for success, using expressive gestures rather than conducting "beats," and making interpretive decisions transparent to students in a process she calls "opening up the score."

Ramona M. Wis challenges the traditional philosophy of conductor as autocratic leader, forwarding instead a model of the conductor as servant-leader. Her chapter is grounded in research within music education, business, and her own self-reflection on the meaning of leadership through years of practice. Wis expands readers' assumptions of conductors to cast them as servant-leaders while helping define the characteristics that mark a leader who constantly considers the needs of ensemble members. Her chapter also highlights the benefits that accrue when a conductor is willing to embrace the philosophy of conductor as servant-leader.

David S. Zerull also invites readers to reconsider the roles of conductors and performers in the context of school music programs and to consider how they often misalign with the aims of music education. By providing examples of normative behaviors—of conductors at work and conductors in training—he suggests that the directive, product-centered conducting paradigm is so pervasive that it permeates large ensembles in secondary schools. Zerull challenges the traditional model of ensemble performance classes, claiming that they may not provide the most valuable and complete musical experience. He suggests that this model does not challenge students' imagination and leads to an incomplete musical education. To support his argument, Zerull depicts two vignettes—a high school band rehearsal and a professional orchestra concert—in which creative listening was essential to the aesthetic experience. He delineates sixteen roles and four major functions of the imagination, contending that they are fundamental to music listening. According to Zerull, conductors of instrumental ensembles can engage students in a more comprehensive and meaningful approach to music by encouraging them to listen discriminately for sounds while also listening for musical gratification.

In coming years, the responsibilities of music teachers in primary and secondary schools will intensify beyond traditional foci on the rehearsal and performance of a musical score. The classic role of the conductor as the primary decision maker for musical performance is changing to include the role of conductor as a facilitator of discussion, collaboration, and constructed knowledge of the music in a more comprehensive sense. In her chapter on the conductor-leader, Margaret H. Berg argues for this more complex view. Citing research on the development of socially constructed identity as a function of early role model influences before college and then interaction with other experts and social settings that may alter beliefs about role and self during college and beyond, Berg challenges the reader to consider ways for teacher educators to foster conceptual change in preservice teachers' views of the conductor role. She raises several pertinent questions that music teacher educators should consider when planning methods courses. Suggestions from the literature include the use of visualization and metaphoric thinking as a way to encourage future teachers to expand their paradigm of "conductor" and their impact on preservice teachers' beliefs and practices.

Beginning the final section of the book devoted to school reform, David A. Williams calls into question the dominant large ensemble model of music education as outdated and irrelevant to the present musical culture. He implicates both K-12 school music programs and the structure of music teacher education programs in current controversies about the relevance of the music curriculum. He lists ten "experiences" that manifest themselves in the traditional ensemble classroom and how they might be transformed to encourage more lifelong learning on the part of the student. He suggests reorienting both of these elements around the development of lifelong music making and away from the large ensemble programs through the development of three new courses incorporated into collegiate music teacher education programs. Williams details these courses and proposes syllabi with objectives and content.

The next chapter represents a critical analysis of a common feature of life in academe—interpreting students' comments on course evaluations at the end of a term. Teryl L. Dobbs's puzzlement over a student's comment that her methods course was useful but there was "no actual teaching" set her on a quest to understand the embedded beliefs, values, and assumptions about teaching that constitute students' imaginaries. Often tacit comments such as these reveal disparate gaps in understanding and experience from one side of the teaching/learning dyad to the other. Dobbs was prompted by the student's entry to examine the demographic characteristics of public school teachers, contrasting those with the elite students who are likely to enroll in select schools of music. She contrasts these disparities with the characteristics of elementary and secondary school students, which further widens the potential for miscommunication and misinterpretation. Drawing on the analysis of prominent images of teachers and teaching from media studies, gender studies, and critical theory, she reminds us of the pervasive and robust presence of classism, racism, heteronormativity, and ableism in our classrooms and professional discourse. In closing, she challenges music teacher educators to act as catalysts for more holistic, culturally relevant, and dialogic practices.

Finally, Michele Kaschub offers a case study of curricular redesign as she and her colleagues substantially revised a curriculum leading to K-12 music certification at the University of Southern Maine. Although the chapter ends with details about the particular scope and sequence that represent this four-year, eight-semester model, her contribution is more focused on the steps necessary to create such a redesign. After an introduction that calls for starting afresh rather than tinkering around the edges of a curriculum, Kaschub outlines principles to guide the process of curricular redesign. Key questions included (1) What is believed to be central to music teacher education? (2) What are the institutional contexts? (3) In what contexts are the students liking to accomplish their practice? and (4) What do students need to know and be able to do? Eight additional principles celebrate the musical experiences of singing, playing, composing, improvising, and listening across the K-12 curriculum and in rehearsal halls and classrooms. The development of a personal philosophy of music education is stressed, as is the ability to employ reflective and independent thinking. The chapter ends with a display of the new curriculum that grew out of these guiding principles while engaging with the broader community. Recommendations are offered for how to accomplish such sweeping changes as a collaborative or "in collaboration" with fellow colleagues.

In a 1985 essay, Bennett Reimer observed, "Research can be and should be an intensely humane and cooperative endeavor, in which individuals, while doing their own work, are attached conceptually to a larger issue than their own and socially to a community of like-minded scholars" (1985, p. 18). The chapters in this book are examples of this potent blend of individual contributions and conceptual affiliation. Bound by powerful and complex questions, the authors employ diverse methodologies and perspectives to create a dialogic community. Music education is a dynamic and sophisticated field with robust traditions, evolving practices, and significant challenges to forward comprehensive and relevant programs. Meaningful musical experiences—engaging students fully and deeply in the generous satisfactions that music has to offer—ground these curricular and programmatic initiatives. In the spirit of scholarly discourse that has characterized the Center for the Study of Education and the Musical Experience in the past quarter century, we encourage you to read, debate, discuss, and consider the impact and influence of these ideas on research and practice in the field. The chapters reflect the long-standing and current intellectual interactions of a vibrant professional community and a desire to prompt dialogue and reflection about avenues of change in music education.

REFERENCES

Reimer, B. (1985). Toward a more scientific approach to music education research. *Bulletin of the Council for Research in Music Education, 83*, 1–22.

Reimer, B., & Wright, J. (1992). *On the nature of musical experience.* Niwot, CO: University Press of Colorado.

Section One

Philosophy

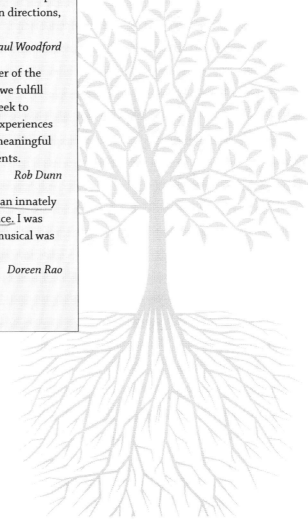

Do we encourage students to ask—
What are some of the forces that shape
our tastes, push us in certain directions,
and influence our lives?

Paul Woodford

The individual is at the center of the
educational experience and we fulfill
the role of facilitators. We seek to
enhance students' holistic experiences
in a way that is personally meaningful
and motivating to our students.

Rob Dunn

Conducting and teaching is an innately
personal and political practice. I was
taught early on that being musical was
being musical.

Doreen Rao

2

PHILOSOPHICAL MUSINGS

Reflections and Directions

Betty Anne Younker

PHILOSOPHY IS A systematic, precise reflection about values, ideas, beliefs, and meanings (Reimer, 2003). To think philosophically is to investigate, criticize, and reflect in a coherent, clear, and precise manner while answering questions like "What does it mean?" and "Is it true?" (Bedau, 1996). This thinking is presented in verbal and written prose as arguments are presented, rationalized, and evaluated. It also implies identifying and defining what "it" is and then determining the validity as it is defined and acted upon.

Some would suggest that investigating a philosophy of music education needs to begin with a systematic, precise reflection about values, ideas, beliefs, and meanings of music (and education), which would then provide direction for the field at the individual and collective levels for whom, with what, and when to engage, as well as how to construct the where, so that educative experiences are felt (Dewey, 1938; Reimer, 2003).[1] Such a foundation is not an ideological "cement block" but rather a malleable, fluid "solid" that is examined and solidified for implementation. Further reflection informs us about how we respond to new understandings as we engage with diverse populations who have constructed different meanings. This malleable, fluid consistent act of reflection shows the ethical responsibility of examining tradition and determining what is retained and maintained and what is in need of transformation (Bowman, 2002).

When reflecting on the values, defining, for some, is part of that process. For others, the investigation is focused on the feasibility of defining. Can music be defined as "it" and thus serve as a definition for music in all of its styles, genres, forms, and contexts, culturally, politically, socially, and, last but not least, musically? Or might a definition be musically bound or experientially bound, culturally bound or contextually bound? Might there be multiple definitions as opposed to a definition?

Blacking (1973) defined music as "humanly organized sound," which in part resonates with Reimer's (2003) description of music (with homage to Langer, 1953): "sounds organized to be inherently meaningful, in which the inherence can incorporate a great variety of additional meanings" (p. 133). Bowman (2002) purported that any attempt to define music/music education is fruitless because the definition lies in the context of the music making and thus the definition is defined through the experience; "it" is articulated (defined) and felt in the making or the doing. Small (1998) regarded music not as a thing but as a human activity, something that people do—the doing of music—which he referred to as "musicking." The search to identify and define music reflects attempts to articulate how music is meaningful, to capture "it" in words for further reflection and evaluation. For some it is an attempt to discern not whether music is meaningful, but where the meaning resides—"in musical materials themselves" or as "ascribed to musical materials by someone for some particular reason" (Wade, 2004, p. 10). The similarity across these writers is that the meaning is in the experience of making music—the experiencing, the doing, all of which is an active and engaged process. The difference is that some have attempted to capture that experience in a definition so that we can reflect on the experience *and* a conceptual definition of the experience; others consider the attempt to "conceptualize about" a moot point.

For some cultures, definitions are tied to the function of music, while for others, there is no verbal definition, only that which is defined while experiencing the making in context; meaning is constructed within the experience—it is embodied. For those who identify and define values of music within political, social, and cultural contexts, there is an understanding that meaning cannot transcend these contexts and that values are inextricably intertwined and situated in each context. Some would argue that values are as diverse as the cultures of the world, with artistic and functional judgments being determined by those who live within the particular cultures.

Elliott (1995, 2005), among others, suggested that the context provides meaning within the many miniworlds of music making; thus, musical experiences are situated within contexts that are influenced by cultural and social expectations and characteristics. Reimer (2003) purported that music "means" what is articulated affectively within the experience as one performs, conducts, composes, improvises, and listens. Our understanding is enhanced through past experiences brought to the situation and that which is experienced immediately, or what Dewey (1938) referred to as a "fund of experience."

Wade (2004) reminded us that the highest value of music for many people is placed on the affect (i.e., music's expressive capacity); thus, the value resides in the affect that is evoked through agencies of performing, conducting, improvising, composing, and listening to music. The focus, then, is not just on the meaning of the music but on the meaning of music as experienced affectively, a felt experience that articulates a part of our human condition. It is contextual and intertwined and understood with all that we know as individuals and as a community.

Fiske (1990) suggested that, when listening, understanding music is a product of enculturation and being aware of the rules that are culturally specific. While we as humans have the potential to understand music, the understanding is culturally specific (Serafine, 1988; Bamberger, 1991/1995; Gardner, 1983).

Therefore, when defining music making, interconnectedness is emphasized between process and product within a context, all of which informs the other. Words used to describe the process include engaging, active, and intentional. Reimer (2003) drew directly from Dewey (1934, 1938) when describing the musical experience. Throughout, the musician "works" on the music while the music "works" on the musician as the music is being shaped through critical and creative decision-making processes. This engagement is not bound by age or level of musical education, but can be experienced by children and adults alike at varying levels of breadth and depth. As students acquire knowledge and skills (which occurs in formal and informal settings), they should be immediately involved in the making of music, utilizing that which has been acquired. Throughout, the student is active and persistent, thinking musically while identifying, formulating, evaluating, and solving musical problems (e.g., Burnard & Younker, 2002; Webster, 2002). Meaning is constructed throughout as the student creates and re-creates music in various contexts. This intense musical involvement enables students to deepen and broaden their musical understanding, experience a vital part of being human, and gain insights about functions of music from political, social, and cultural perspectives. To further examine these ideas and others, I will provide a brief reflection on the philosophical field in music education and focus on dimensions that continue to inform us about the value of who we are and what we do, and that in turn affect decisions within our field.

REFLECTIONS

We have much to reflect as we ponder critical points in the field of philosophy of music education. Philosophy, as a discipline, has been a part of education and music for centuries and as a result has evolved, transformed, maintained, and returned in multiple forms and variations. Philosophical musings about why music should have a place in public education have occurred since Lowell Mason provided support for such inclusion.

Historically, we are familiar with how music became included in the public school system and early influences on the value of such inclusion. From military bands, singing schools, competitions, and the industry to Frances Clark's work with LP materials to guide listening experiences, music has served a variety of masters, including itself, through various permutations as students engaged in musical experiences for a variety of reasons.

During the 1950s and 1960s, the University of Illinois became a place of action within the philosophical world. Broudy, Reimer, Leonhard, and Bowman, to name a few, did critical work in examining the value of music education through the lens of the musical experience, which was articulated as a core value for education in music. This value of the musical experience was viewed as the reason for including music in education; to heighten students' musical experience through direct engagement with the music in a mindful way was the goal. To engage in a mindful way, one attends to the musical elements while listening, performing, composing, and improvising with attention to analyzing how the elements are organized to be meaningful. This can heighten students' perception and response to music, thus heightening the musical experience.

One could view this as a continuation of Francis Clark's work, which was in response to the growing performance, competition-based music education directed by utilitarian values, much of which was supported by the industry. This call back to the intrinsic nature of music as a foundation for value directed attention to Dewey's 1934 *Art as Experience* and his 1938 *Experience and Education*. Dewey's thinking about experience and the aesthetic (musical) experience was represented as one that is engaged and interactive, as the music works on the musician and the musician on the music. This focus, known as aesthetic education, continued on into the 1980s with the value of music education focused on broadening and deepening students' experiences to enhance their "knowing" of their subjectivity, to articulate a part of their human condition.

At the center of Dewey's thinking on learning is "experienced-based education": experiences that are meaningful and engaged. His work informed and influenced multiple educational thinkers who came after him (e.g., Bruner, 1960, 1996; Eisner, 1998). Teaching and learning is viewed as "a continuous reconstruction of experience," in which students are involved in educative experiences (i.e., experiences that generate as opposed to impede growth). Educative experiences produce sensitivity and responsiveness, connect with past and future, provide challenges that are accessible and yet evoke reflection, involve active and persistent inquiry that is mindful, and are organic as experiences are constructed and reconstructed (Bransford, Brown, & Cocking, 2000; Bruner, 1996; Noddings, 2004; Vygotsky, 1978).

The 1990s saw a diversification of philosophical thinking, with ethnomusicology, sociology, anthropology, and women's studies gaining more room in our spaces of thinking. Feminist theory, with a conference on music education at the University of Minnesota in the spring of 1991, became a lens through which to view the value of music making, as well as the politics of musical environments and what that meant across contexts and in multiple lives. Questions about whose voices were heard, whose music was played, who held the baton, and how experiences liberated or oppressed were examined. In the early 1990s, a new Special Research Interest Group (SRIG) was born in what was then the *Music Educators National Conference* (MENC), now *National Association for Music Education* (NAfME), Gender Issues in Music Education, which served as a platform for issues related to place, space, voice, power, and oppression. Theoretical frameworks within the field of social justice and constructed by ideals of democratic principles provided multiple spaces for relevant viewpoints to be examined and evaluated.

Praxialism via David Elliott (1995) called for musicking and the practice of music to be considered as the focal point for why and how we engage students. This was in response to aesthetic education; his definition was based on the eighteenth-century notions of contemplation and objective experiences of art, a definition that reflected formalistic thinking about music. Elliott regarded music making as practice, and drawing from the works of Schön (1987), whose dissertation was based on Dewey's work, he suggested that we engage students in reflective practice as they experience self-growth while accomplishing challenges that meet their abilities. Interestingly enough, I have always thought there were more similarities than differences between Elliott's and Reimer's thinking, particularly if you begin with Dewey, but that paper has been written and presented—so onward!

Since meetings such as Tanglewood in the late 1960s, debates about what is "proper" music for instruction have occurred. These conversations have required us to expand our thinking about how we define good or quality music. Can we evaluate music across cultures, genres, and styles with the same criteria? Is the meaning, intent, role, and function of music the same across cultures, genres, and styles? Must musical experiences and music be consistently defined across contexts, or can there be diversity of musical experiences and definitions depending on the culture and context? Might we enter communities with

FEMINISM

CULTURES

MUSIC ACROSS

expectations to learn "new" and engage others in "new"? Should the underlying approach to "other" be based on reciprocity, in which learning and teaching are shared as deemed possible and appropriate? For this disposition to develop, what changes are needed in the undergraduate curriculum? What can we do to broaden students' understanding of music outside of the Western European art music tradition? How can we ensure that students are not limited by a method or an approach, or by the notion of methodologies? How can we broaden their engagement with music beyond the performance mode of experience? How might experiences that involve composing, improvising, critiquing, and listening be meaningful for our students? They understand performing, but many of their students will experience music in multiple ways. Finally, what changes are needed in the undergraduate curriculum to ensure that students are able to construct environments of musical learning and utilize what they know and enable others to share what they are able to do?

CRITICAL THINKING/REFLECTIVE PRACTICE

With the growth of philosophical thinking in the field came a continued examination on how students are engaged with learning. As the 1900s progressed, however, a focus on content and observable behaviors dominated the field, and instead of a continued focus on the how of learning, a focus on content (the what) and sequencing of that content took center stage. Resurgence in the 1960s occurred but was diminished as the economy was challenged and a back-to the basic subject areas, now referred to as Science, Technology, Engineering and Math (STEM) took over educational thinking in the 1980s. From a variety of places during the 1990s there appeared to be a return to focusing on the process of learning, thus a return to a progressive view as educators stated that learning involves students being transformed through active engagement with content. This engagement includes flexibility, adaptability, curiosity, and imagination (e.g., Bransford et al., 2000; Dewey, 1938; Eisner, 1998; Goodlad, 2004). To learn and grow, experiences must be educative and involve critical inquiry that includes reflective practice.

Integral to educative experiences is the acceptance that (1) learners come to the classroom with much to offer and construct new understandings with habits of minds that are curious and critical; (2) the focus is not just the method or theory, but the student; and (3) both teacher and learner shift on a continuum between being a teacher and being a learner as reflective practitioners within a practice.

The process of critical inquiry, which contributes to reflective judgment, goes beyond simple logic or formulas (both of which involve types of critical thinking), in that one identifies relevant facts, formulas, and theories and generates solutions to bring closure to situations that are uncertain, are controversial, and involve doubt (Dewey, 1933/1991, 1938; King, P. M., & Kitchener, K. S. (1994). One would not accept formulaic and logical solutions that are uncontroversial and lack doubt, nor would one accept absolute and preconceived assumptions. Accepting absolutism allows for the generation of truths and pervasiveness of dogmatic thinking. Dogmatic thinking has no space for "messiness" found in reflective judgment, as examination of assumptions is continuous. In the continuous, messy, constructive world of critical inquiry, beliefs are always questioned within social and cultural situated settings (Bowman, 2005; Bruner, 1996; Jorgensen, 2003; Lave & Wenger, 1991; Vygotsky, 1978, Wiggins, 2001).

There continues to be a call to educate and not (just) train, to prepare future teachers for these paradoxical worlds, and to inculcate habits of mind to think (Bowman, 2002, 2005). Jorgensen (2001) reminded us of the importance of inculcating habits of mind to think critically (reflectively) and thus to experience a practice that requires analysis and criticism of one's own situations. Instead of training teachers to be technicians, that is, to realize specific practices and theories in a "recipe" fashion, we need to ensure that they are reflective practitioners (Schön, 1987) who are required to reason through options before choosing and to justify choices made. Reflective practice permits for openings to be found and choices to be a critical aspect of teaching and learning (Greene, 1995) and for spaces where ambiguity, doubt, and dissonances reside. In such dialectical worlds (Jorgensen, 2001), options are less clear-cut, and thus the habit to think critically is necessary as teachers embrace ambivalence, vulnerability, surprise, and joy as challenges are met with open-mindedness and reasoned thinking. Requiring students to question and inquire and providing communities that value curiosity should constitute foundational aspects of education, including music education (e.g., Allsup, 2003; Jorgensen, 2003; Woodford, 2005).

CONTINUING ON

We continue to experience an expanding philosophical world and one that provides guidance as decisions are made about issues that affect the field, including those related to democratic principles, disposition and attributes, spirituality, and sustainability. The notion of traveling along a continuum, turning to the past to make sense of the present and speculate about the future, is recognized as writers turn our attention (back) to democracy in music education (Woodford, 2005) while examining democratic principles and evidence of democratic practices in our communities of music making.

The role of informed, critical thinking is again emphasized as decisions are made about roles of students and teachers, and consumption and curriculum. Issues of inclusion, access, rights and responsibilities, ethics, fairness, trust, and respect are examined at conferences that are focused on social justice. Inclusiveness and access continue to require our attention as we reflect on the reaction to the lesbian, gay, bisexual, and transgender (LGBT) music education conference that was just held at the University of Illinois; are inclusion and access for some still a distant reality? Do we value musical experiences in spaces that recognize rights and require responsibility, reflect ethical considerations, are fair, and promote trust and respect? Are the musical environments educative, thus promoting growth? Are diversities of music making, each with its own context, culture, and place in history, recognized and afforded spaces in our music programs? If not, do we understand how and why choices are made? And for those who are afforded spaces, do we understand the layers of ethical issues as we live the musical experience and celebrate the human condition?

And what of those who enter the profession of music teaching? Are we mindful of the dispositions and attributes that are valued in educational circles? Have we identified them and nurtured them? Bowman (2002), Colwell (2007), Jones (2007), Jorgensen (2008), and Younker (2009) reminded us about dispositions and attributes that characterize those we want in the classroom—those who are fair, just, respectful, thoughtful, empathetic, inclusive, ethical, and trustworthy.

Related to dispositions and attributes is the role of spirituality as students' and teachers' personhoods are shaped. McCarthy (2007) brought to us notions about the "spiritual dimensions of music pedagogy" within the context of observing and interpreting college musicians and their leaders in a group musical improvisation setting. Her basic assumption for this study was that "contemplation is a foundation of both spiritual practice and musical improvisation" (p. 1). For her, it is the continuing work of making connections with the education of future music teachers while examining foundational relationships between qualities of contemplation and improvisation, and the shaping of teachers' personhood.

McCarthy (2007) noted that during her observations of the musicians and their leaders in improvisatory activities, the words "contemplation, mindfulness, playfulness, and deep engagement" (p. 6) became central to the reflective process. She noted that terms such as "heightening awareness, nurturing mindfulness, and developing the ability to engage musically with others" represent parallel processes in music teaching. This caused her to examine possible guidance from her observations and reflections when examining the spiritual formation of teachers. As well, she identified similarities experienced in improvisation and characteristics as found by those who examined the "soul of education" (Kessler, 2000) and "eight principles of spiritual leadership" (Sokolow, 2002). She found that the combined themes were central to the experiences of group improvisation. She then grouped them around four principal patterns: "attention, intention, relationship, and community" (p. 8). For her, these four patterns are critical to the shaping of future music educators. Attention to details and to the dynamics of a class, making intentions transparent, understanding inter- and intrapersonal relationships, and shaping communities for learning to occur are critical processes as we engage students in learning.

McCarthy's work reflects an increased interest in the role of spirituality in human development, particularly in the last ten years. This, coupled with the writings of those who have examined teaching with spiritual foundations to guide practice and reflection (e.g., Kessler, 2000; O'Reilley, 1998; Palmer, 1998), is making an impact in the field of education, and now in music education.

In terms of sustainability, our ability to nourish the arts is only possible if we have a clear vision and understanding of the value for musical experiences. The richness of the music making, with its context, situatedness, history, and culture; in all of its forms and genres; and with the multiple intentions of the engagement, can be sustained if we continue to articulate why. We are reminded of the importance to embody the arts as part of our existence, to sustain artistic expression and experiences in all of its rich contexts and knowing *because* we are human beings.

In relation to sustainability, we need to recognize the balance of supply, demand, and access to the arts (Zakaras & Lowell, 2008). If we value music as part of our communities, if we believe that it is a vital part of the human condition, individually and collectively, then we need to examine the following questions: What role does music play in the cultivation of demand? What does the current support infrastructure for demand look like, and does it contribute to the understanding that is needed to stimulate and sustain participation in music? What is the balance between performance-based and sensibility-based experiences in school-based music programs, or, as Eisner (1998) would state, connoisseurship? What roles do critiquing and listening play in students' experiences? Do our values and beliefs resonate with questions we ask about the kinds of musical experiences we desire for our students? Should we re-examine those values and beliefs and think about the demand of music by those students who experience our programs? Are they involved critically and creatively while constructing, inquiring, expressing, comparing, contrasting, analyzing and synthesizing, and critiquing?

CONCLUSIONS

As we move forward, we need to continue our examination of the values of music making, music in education, and educative experiences in music. The roles music plays at the individual and collective levels, the kinds of thinking that are required for the practice to be reflective in democratic spaces, the dispositions and attributes of those who should teach, the notions of ethics and spirituality, and continuing to sustain the arts are areas of concern as we continue to experience who we are and what we do, individually and collectively.

NOTE

1. For the purposes of this chapter, I will use the term *values* with the understanding that it is inclusive of ideas, beliefs, and meanings.

REFERENCES

Allsup, R. (2003). Mutual learning and democratic action in instrumental music education. *Journal of Research in Music Education, 51*(1), 24–37.

Bamberger, J. (1991/1995). *The mind behind the musical ear.* Cambridge, MA: Harvard University Press.

Bedau, H. (1996). *Thinking and writing about philosophy.* Boston, MA: Bedford Books of St. Martin's Press.

Blacking, J. (1973). *How musical is man?* Seattle, WA: University of Washington Press.

Bowman, W. (2002). Educating musically. In R. Colwell & C. P. Richardson (Eds.), *The new handbook of research for music teaching and learning* (2nd ed., pp. 63–84). New York, NY: Oxford University Press.

Bowman, W. (2005, April). *More cogent questions, more provisional answers: The need to theorize music education.* Keynote address given at the Fourth International Research in Music Education Conference. University of Exeter, School of Education and Life Long Learning, Exeter, England.

Bransford, J. D., Brown, A. L., & Cocking, R. R. (Eds.). (2000). *How people learn: Brain, mind, experience, and school.* Washington, DC: National Academy Press.

Bruner, J. (1960). *The process of education.* Cambridge, MA: Harvard University Press.

Bruner, J. (1996). *The culture of education.* Cambridge, MA: Harvard University Press.

Burnard, P., & Younker, B. A. (2002). Mapping pathways: Fostering creativity in composition. *Music Education Research, 4*(2), 245–261.

Colwell, R. (2007). Data, beliefs, and vacuity in music teacher education. In R. R. Rideout (Ed.), *Policies and practices: Rethinking music teacher preparation in the 21st century* (pp. 1–23). Amherst, MA: University of Massachusetts.

Dewey, J. (1933/1991). *How we think.* Buffalo, NY: Prometheus Books.

Dewey, J. (1934). *Art as experience.* New York, NY: Perigee Books.

Dewey, J. (1938). *Experience and education.* New York, NY: Collier Books, Macmillan Publishing Company.

Eisner, E. (1998). *The kind of schools we need.* Portsmouth, NH: Heinemann.

Elliott, D. J. (1995). *Music matters.* New York, NY: Oxford University Press.

Elliott, D. J. (2005). Introduction. In D. Elliott (Ed.), *Praxial music education: Reflections and dialogues* (pp. 3–18). New York, NY: Oxford University Press.

Fiske, H. (1990). *Music and mind: Philosophical essays on the cognition and meaning of music.* Lewiston, NY: Edwin Mellen Press.

Gardner, H. (1983). *Frames of mind: The theory of multiple intelligences.* New York, NY: Basic Books.

Goodlad, J. I. (2004). *Romances with schools.* New York, NY: McGraw-Hill.

Greene, M. (1995). *Releasing the imagination: Essays on education, the arts, and social change.* San Francisco, CA: Jossey-Bass.

Jones, P. (2007). Developing strategic thinkers through music teacher education: A "Best Practice" for overcoming professional myopia and transforming music education. In R. R. Rideout (Ed.), *Policies and practices: Rethinking music teacher preparation in the 21st century* (pp. 227-244), Amherst, MA: University of Massachusetts.

Jorgensen, E. R. (2001). A dialectical view of theory and practice. *Journal of Research in Music Education, 49*(4), 343–359.

Jorgensen, E. R. (2003). *Transforming music education.* Bloomington, IN: Indiana University Press:

Jorgensen, E. R. (2008). *The art of teaching music.* Bloomington, IN: Indiana University Press.

Kessler, R. (2000). *The soul of education: Helping students find connection, compassion, and character at school.* Alexandria, VA: ASCD.

King, P. M., & Kitchener, K. S. (1994). *Developing reflective judgment.* San Francisco, CA: Jossey-Bass.

Langer, S. (1953). *Feeling and form: A theory of art.* Upper Saddle River, NJ: Prentice-Hall.

Lave, J., & Wenger, E. (1991). *Situated learning: Legitimate peripheral participation.* Cambridge, MA: Cambridge University Press.

McCarthy, M. (2007, May). *Exploring the spiritual in music teacher education: Group musical improvisation points the way.* Paper presented at the Mountain Lake Colloquium for Teachers of General Music, Mountain Lake, VA.

Noddings, N. (2004). War, critical thinking, and self-understanding. *Phi Delta Kappan, 85*(7), 489–495.

O'Reilley, M. R. (1998). *Radical presence: Teaching as contemplative practice.* Portsmouth, NH: Boynton/Cook Publishers.

Palmer, P. (1998). *The courage to teach.* San Francisco, CA: Jossey-Bass.

Reimer, B. (2003). *A philosophy of music education: Advancing the vision* (3rd ed.). Englewood Cliffs, NJ: Prentice-Hall.

Schön, D. (1987). *Educating the reflective practitioner.* San Francisco, CA: Jossey-Bass.

Serafine, M. L. (1988). *Music as cognition: The development of thought in sound.* New York, NY: Columbia University Press.

Small, C. (1998). *Musicking: The meanings of performing and listening.* Hanover, NH: Wesleyan University Press.

Sokolow, S. L. (2002). Enlightened leadership. *The School Administrator, 59*(8), 32–33, 35–36.

Vygotsky, L. S. (1978). *Mind in society: The development of higher psychological processes* (M. Cole, V. John-Steiner, S. Scribner, & E. Souberman, Eds. and trans.). Cambridge, MA: Harvard University Press.

Wade, B. C. (2004). *Thinking musically.* New York, NY: Oxford University Press.

Webster, P. W. (2002). Creative thinking in music: Advancing a model. In T. Sullivan & L. Willingham (Eds.), Creativity and music education (pp. 16–34). Edmonton, AB: Canadian Music Educators Association National Office.

Wiggins, J. H. (2001). *Teaching for musical understanding*. Boston, MA: McGraw-Hill.

— Woodford, P. G. (2005). *Democracy and music education*. Bloomington, IN: Indiana University Press.

Younker, B. A. (2009, June). *Transforming undergraduate music education: The need for systemic changes*. Paper presented at the MayDay Group Colloquium XXI, USC Thornton School of Music, Los Angeles, CA.

Zakaras, L., & Lowell, J. F. (2008). *Cultivating demand for the arts: Arts learning, arts engagement, and state arts policy*. Santa Monica, CA: RAND Corporation.

3

ESCAPING VERSUS CONFRONTING REALITY

Politics and Music Education in an Age of Entertainment

Paul Woodford

INTRODUCTION: ON DEMOCRACY, FREEDOM, AND EQUALITY

THERE HAS BEEN a renewed interest of late among Western music educators in promoting democratic ideas and practices in school, university, and community programs (e.g., Allsup, 2003, 2007, 2010; Kelly, 2009; Reimer, 2003; Younker, 2003). At a commonsense level, most music teachers associate democracy with the pursuit of equality of educational opportunity so that all children are free to develop their own talents, abilities, and musical interests. But few music education scholars thus far have seriously attempted to define the term. Nor, in consequence, has there been much appreciation of the difficulties, paradoxes, and contradictions inherent in the concept of democracy, such as how allowing children unconstrained freedom to develop their interests and abilities will almost inevitably lead to inequality as privileged and so-called talented or gifted students outstrip their peers, and how the concepts of freedom and equality themselves are often thought to conflict. Equality, after all, usually implies some curtailment of people's freedoms and a redistribution of the collective wealth so that the rich and the privileged do not just monopolize power and resources. There are also different notions of equality that sometimes conflict and that demand different courses of action. For example, there is often a world of difference between equality of opportunity and equality of result, each of which presents different implications for the treatment of individuals and groups.

Freedom, too, has different meanings. There is freedom of mind, speech, ownership, association, and assembly, not to mention economic freedom. There are also negative and positive conceptions of freedom. Whereas negative freedom refers merely to the "absence of restriction or coercion," positive freedom involves the application of reason and conscience as means of exerting some modicum of control over life. And the best way of exercising this control is "through active involvement in the life of a society," including its politics (Norman, 1995, p. 291). Expressed in slightly different terms, positive freedom implies moral agency insomuch as it "is related to the power to do as one should," rather than, as with negative freedom, "to do as one likes" (Dimova-Cookson, 2004, p. 559). It is this former understanding of freedom as moral agency that underlies the notion of participatory democracy outlined in my book *Democracy and Music Education* (2005). As is explained therein, this capacity is not something that emerges naturally. Rather, it needs to be inculcated and nurtured in children "through various processes involving educational, social, and personal resources" (Christman, 2005, p. 87). The role of government in this political scheme is as an enabling agency charged with ensuring what philosopher John Rawls calls "fair equality of opportunity," meaning that the state should attempt to provide a more level playing field by compensating children for "deprived" backgrounds (Nagel, 2003, pp. 68–69; Rawls, 1999).

From this political perspective, the state is not limited to providing well-funded and equipped schools or to making traditional music programs and lessons available and accessible to all children, as that might only amount to negative freedom and thus better serve the privileged. In any event, as traditionally conceived and taught, those programs are just as likely to serve authoritarian as democratic ends (Leonhard & House, 1959/1972). No doubt some music educators will reply that their school choirs and concert bands promote democratic citizenship because they encourage the pursuit of excellence and the development of various qualities in children, including personal responsibility, loyalty, and obedience, all of which are important to creating a law-abiding citizenry and sense of community. But those traits are also valued by totalitarian regimes (Westheimer & Kahne, 2004). They are not necessarily democratic values. Nor is it necessarily true that the best school ensemble experiences are inherently egalitarian in nature because individuals are assigned parts according to ability and effort (Battisti, 2006; Hopkins, 2009). For now it will suffice to simply observe that those kinds of self-serving educational justifications are based on a "pedagogy of lies" that provides a convenient deficit rationale for failure and social ranking (Zinn & Macedo, 2005, p. 36).

Equality of opportunity to access school and community music programs is thus only potentially a first step toward helping children succeed in school and to eventually participate as moral agents in democratic society. Also required are the right kinds of educational policies and curricula and informed and socially engaged teachers who can stimulate critical thinking in their charges while inculcating in them a desire to develop and exercise their intelligence as moral agents; otherwise, the masses of children, and particularly those from deprived backgrounds, will remain overly susceptible to political and other forms of manipulation and domination. When lacking this kind of education, children may not realize that they are being coerced, that their freedom may only be an illusion, or that the language of freedom and democracy itself can all too easily become "an instrument of disguised oppression" (Green, 1986, quoted in Dimova-Cookson, 2004, p. 555). Nor will they necessarily acknowledge their own moral obligation and responsibility to the less fortunate and understand how the exercising of their own positive freedom in the service of others might contribute "to a better society from which they too benefit" (p. 559).

"LET THEM EAT CAKE"

As was explained in *Democracy and Music Education* (2005) and elsewhere (e.g., Woodford, 2009a), much of the recent political history of the Western world can be characterized as a struggle between those on the political Far Right who claim to be on the side of negative freedom and laissez-faire democracy versus social democrats on the political Left (most of whom are in reality just to the right of center along the political continuum) who place a higher premium on positive freedom and equality. Both sides of this political schism represent somewhat different understandings of democracy and of the purposes and value of education in Western society. It matters which conception and model of democracy one applies to educational practice, as each one will likely result in different social outcomes (Habermas, 2005). That is why it is important for scholars and music teachers to clarify what they mean when calling for freedom and democracy in music education lest they end up with something quite different from what they intended for the music classroom or rehearsal room. A neoliberal conception of democracy with its emphases on rugged individualism and free market economics, for example, would lead to a Darwinian "survival of the fittest" model of music education, such as has already happened to some extent in the United States and England, where the primary aim of music education is to inculcate in the children the skills and knowledge needed to compete globally.

Distinguishing features of the neoliberal model for education include an authoritarian emphasis on discipline and accountability as assessed with reference to national curricula and standards and a stated commitment to increased diversity and consumer choice (Seldon, Snowdon, & Collings, 2007). Discipline, according to this populist capitalist view, is something that must be imposed on children, teachers, and the citizenry, the vast majority of whom are considered fundamentally lazy and in need of domestication. Strangely enough, many voters like this tough talk about educational accountability because they admire strong and charismatic leaders—regardless of whatever political agenda they might have—and also because parents are often quick to blame teachers and others for their children's problems. Choice has more to do with corporate desires with respect to the relentless pursuit of increased profits through outsourcing and marketing strategies than it does with consumer autonomy and freedom. In fact, many economic policies and marketing strategies of those on the political Right may actually limit individuals' choices and are bad for the economies of individual countries because they result in huge job losses or reductions in pay and benefits as more workers are forced to accept part-time work (Stiglitz, 2010; Saul, 2005). Nor are corporations generally held accountable for severe economic problems caused by them. The 2008 collapse of the markets that necessitated huge government financial bailouts of many banks and corporations showed "how capitalism privatizes profits and socializes costs" (Albritton, 2009, p. 14). In the end, it is the public that pays the true cost of corporate freedom.

In this economic scheme, and because capitalism depends on inequality, the "rich get richer while the poor get poorer." This accounts for the apparent contradiction in neoliberal educational rhetoric between freedom of choice on the one hand and discipline and accountability on the other. The real aim of those on the extreme political Right is not to seek the freedom and improvement of the masses—who are regarded as incorrigible (the poor will not only always be with us but also are essential to the success of capitalism) and, when properly educated as democratic citizens, a threat to capitalism—but to create a permanent sense of crisis and a culture of fear so as to discourage them from becoming politically involved in the first place (Ginsberg & Lyche, 2008). This leads to the obsession among those on the political Far Right with educational standards, economic comparisons, and competition among different schools, regions, and countries (and their lack of attention to issues relating to actual quality of life) and their corresponding emphasis on the so-called educational basics. Their purposes are to create the impression that countries should be on a permanent economic war footing and to convince the masses that their children are only entitled to a minimal education (because they are always failing to meet national and/or international standards in the so-called educational basics such as mathematics and science).

This helps to explain why newly elected neoliberal governments are usually the first to call for tax cuts and for corresponding reductions in public funding for education and social programs—those tax cuts primarily benefit business and the rich—and why they typically have little interest in the arts and humanities except how they contribute to the "expansion of the Gross National Product" (Burgess, 1998, p. 147). In war, democracy and the arts and humanities are usually among the first victims, except of course when the latter can be usefully employed in the war effort as propaganda or as distractions from the problems of life. In those respects, music and the arts are actually quite useful to governments and other organizations wishing to manipulate the citizenry, making them "perpetually responsive" to the whims of politicians, corporate leaders, and the needs of the marketplace (Apple, 2003, p. 9).

Throughout the Western democracies, freedom and choice are for the rich and the powerful who can afford them, while the masses are to be entertained and distracted from their plight with a plethora of cheap food, music, and goods. Albritton (2009) helps to explain this point in his book *Let Them Eat Junk,* in which he outlines how the corporate world's lust for profit has contributed to an exponential growth in obesity in the Western democracies as more and more working- and lower-class people and their children are addicted to emotionally comforting but ill-nourishing junk food. The business media like to describe the looming health care crisis as an epidemic, because it suggests that it is a natural disaster for which no one should be held accountable, but in reality it is a man-made catastrophe.

The parallels with music are many and ominous. So much of the ubiquitous mainstream commercial music inundating today's world and often expressly marketed to children both at home and in school is intended to infantilize rather than to provoke or otherwise encourage thought. As Albritton (2009) warned, "We live in an age of fear, of powerful interests that spread misinformation, and of forms of consumerism that deflect the citizenry away from politics" (p. xii). This begins very early in life because the corporate world realizes that it is during childhood that lifetime tastes and habits of thought are formed. School music programs are implicated in this undermining of democracy because they rely overmuch on movie, commercial, and educational music that is intended primarily as entertainment and advertising, and because they generally fail to relate music education to the wider world and its problems. Children in school seldom learn of music's potential as distraction and propaganda and how it is often implicated in the abuse of their own freedoms, let alone how they might resist musical or other imposition. Nor do they typically learn of music's potential for confronting reality and thereby contributing to the reshaping of the world. According to Chomsky (1987), this is deliberate, as one of the primary functions of our educational and other institutions is to preserve the status quo by protecting "us from seeing what we observe, from knowledge and understanding of the world in which we live" (p. 136). Because the public education system operates almost as a "subsidiary of the state-corporate system," children in school music programs never learn how to distinguish truth from propaganda, needs from wants, and the real from the merely illusionary because that would be perceived as a threat to the music industry and to the consumer society on which it is based (Chomsky, 2006, p. 238).

For most people, and whether in politics, the commercial music and food industries, education, or health care, the neoliberal (and in the United States neoconservative) mantra of freedom and choice is only intended as rhetoric and propaganda to lull them into accepting social, economic, political, and educational reforms that may be contrary to their own and to their children's best interests. Stiglitz (2010) helped to explain this latter point in his recent book *Freefall: America, Free Markets, and the Sinking of the World Economy.* Many of the social and economic and other reforms advanced by corporate elites in America during the past thirty years, and especially leading up to the 2008 economic collapse, were intended to exploit the poor and middle class as the rights of corporations were given precedence over basic individual rights to "access to health care or to housing or to education" (p. 287). What those corporate elites wanted was freedom from the financial regulation and corporate taxation that were put in place after the Great Depression to provide the kinds of social programs that would protect the masses from the vicissitudes of unbridled capitalism. The combined result of those more recent reforms has been a reduction in the quality of life for the majority as most Americans work longer hours for less pay and job security. Median household income in America has fallen 4 percent over the past decade at the same time as the gross domestic product per capita has risen 10 percent, and this despite the fact that Americans are working longer hours than was the case thirty years ago. As Stiglitz observed, "A larger pie doesn't mean that everyone—or even most people—gets a larger slice" (p. 284). During the recession that began in 2008, and while many Americans were suffering economically, the ranks and collective wealth of the rich grew by 17 percent and 18 percent, respectively.

Music education suffered from those reforms as school programs were eliminated, teacher resources spread too thinly to properly maintain programs, and individual teachers and schools burdened with increased responsibility for fundraising as government money was redirected to the so-called educational basics, often at the behest of corporate leaders (Koza, 2002a, 2002b). One consequence of the reduction in public funding of school music programs is that teachers and their professional organizations are now more dependent on business partnerships for financial support, which leaves them even more vulnerable to corporate manipulation and control (Apple, 2004; Bakan, 2004; Woodford, 2009b).

As Hitler (1925/1999) understood, the keys to successful propaganda are emotional appeal and endless repetition. This is a lesson that has been well learned by leaders on the political Far Right who have long understood the emotional appeal of the words *freedom* and *choice* and their potential as tools for masking what some critics (e.g., Zinn & Macedo, 2005; Chomsky, 2006) describe as an Orwellian agenda for society and public education. A classic example of the repetitive nature of propaganda, and which also represents a misuse of the language of democracy, is found in country musician Lloyd Marcus's popular "Tea Party Anthem," which repetitively hammers home the slogans "freedom" and "liberty" while warning that President Obama's economic stimulus program is "just a socialistic scheme" (for a video clip of a performance of this tune at a political rally, see www.youtube.com/watch?v=z2H8xHFXC8U). Like all good propaganda, this song deliberately and simplistically distorts the truth while appealing to people's prejudices. Those who fail to achieve are simplistically described as lazy and a burden to society.

"IT'S SHOWTIME": MUSIC EDUCATION AS VOCATIONAL TRAINING AND ENTERTAINMENT

The neoliberal worldview has many serious implications for music education. Reimer (1989) and other professional leaders have long warned of the dangers of elitism in music education, although few scholars in our field have made this explicit linkage between elitism in music education and unbridled capitalism. One of the reasons for this is that capitalism remains political dogma in the United States, a country in which, as we have already seen, many people remain wary of anything that even hints of socialism (e.g., national health care) and in which growing media consolidation and corporate intrusion into schools and universities have led to an increasing blurring of lines among education, vocational training, and entertainment (Postman, 1985; Zinn & Macedo, 2005). Throughout much of today's world, capitalism is now the state religion in providing an "unstated framework for thinkable thought" (Chomsky, 1987, p. 132). And within that system of thought the highly educated are "typically the most profoundly indoctrinated and in a deep sense the most ignorant group, the victims as well as the purveyors of the doctrines of the faith" (p. 126). This is a sobering thought with which some readers may take umbrage, but it is only to be expected that many music teachers and teacher educators would tend to take capitalism for granted, since they have by now been subject to decades of neoliberal propaganda. That propaganda is more refined and subtle than the agitprop employed in the former Soviet Union, but it is equally pervasive. Most music teachers have also been trained within a technocratic educational culture that tends to discourage provocative ideas that might be perceived as threatening to the status quo (West, 2004). Given this understanding, it is not surprising that music teachers and their professional organizations appear unconcerned about—and even welcome—corporate intrusion into music education in ways that might potentially undermine its democratic purpose.

For reasons that are explained later, school music programs are probably more vulnerable than most to the blurring of lines among education, vocational training, and entertainment. In England, for example, the 2004 government and industry-sponsored Music Manifesto educational initiative aimed at children was intended to ensure the country's pre-eminence in the global music entertainment industry. An equally important aim of the Manifesto's writers and signatories as expressed in the document *The Music Manifesto: More Music for More People* was to "deliver an exciting range of musical experiences to all young people, helping to create the soundtrack to their lives" (document available at www.musikk.no/sfiles/3/83/50/66/5/file/music-manifesto.pdf, para. 4).

This was a revealing expression that showed that, for the majority of children and adults, music was only intended as background and a pleasant pastime and not as something warranting intellectual scrutiny or serious study. Ultimately, and while acknowledging music's potential for personal fulfillment, the Manifesto's writers conceived of children as either future entertainers or as passive consumers in training. Evidence in support of this contention was readily found on the Manifesto's website, which was liberally sprinkled with industry news, advertisements, and personal testimonies of representatives from the music, entertainment, and private education industries.

Not surprisingly, given all the industry hype on its website, the Manifesto's first chief executive had previously worked in the media entertainment industry. As stated by this individual, the Manifesto sought to "bring the education sector happily together with the music industry" by making music education more "vocationally orientated" while also catering more to children's tastes (Poole, 2008, para. 2). Nowhere, at least that I could find, was there any acknowledgment in Music Manifesto documents of the potential dangers of catering to children's tastes, which are largely shaped by powerful corporate or populist interests, and how this kind of music education would likely fail to adequately prepare children to participate in "the life of society" beyond their own immediate peers and the needs of the market. Nor would an overemphasis on vocational training prepare children for democratic musical citizenship. There was also the matter of how, or whether, government intended to regulate businesses and groups involved in Manifesto projects to ensure quality and fairness of educational opportunities for all children. This should have been cause for concern among music teachers given the apparent belief of the Manifesto's writers that virtually anyone engaged in the music industry could teach! Without that regulation to ensure accessibility, quality, accountability, and social justice (e.g., fair redistribution of resources), much of the funding for the Manifesto might just have amounted to corporate welfare while primarily benefiting privileged children.

The music industry's involvement in the Music Manifesto and other publicly funded educational initiatives was consistent with then Prime Minister Tony Blair's encouragement of the private sector in public education. Blair also believed that state schools should be more "entrepreneurial and business-like" in their operation (Seldon et al., 2007, p. 420). Since Margaret Thatcher's election to office in 1979, these beliefs in the desirability of educational entrepreneurship and of allowing business a greater and entrepreneurial role in public education have been dogma among those on the political Right who think that virtually all public spaces and institutions, including public schools, should eventually be privatized, or at the very least that school programs should be operated by business with government functioning as a kind of general contractor or overseer.

From the perspective of many corporate executives of educational management organizations (EMOs), the opportunities for private investment and profit in public education are enormous. To quote one prominent American EMO executive, "Education is bigger than defense, bigger than the whole domestic auto industry....In fact, only health care has a larger segment of the American marketplace" (quoted in Bakan, 2004, p. 115). It is thus to be expected that business should think of education as a growth industry. What is surprising is that right-wing or other politicians should be willing to entrust state schools or programs to an often ethically challenged corporate world that is "legally required" to pursue self-interest and profit over all else and that has yet to demonstrate convincingly that private schools and programs on the whole actually do outperform public ones (p. 118). This is not to say that some corporate-owned or -operated schools cannot outperform public ones on some measures and in certain contexts (such as may happen when private schools are selective or are populated by the privileged). It is only that placing state schools and educational programs in the hands of corporate executives is poor public policy because it will almost inevitably contribute to greater social inequality.

In England, it appears that EMOs have already made significant inroads into music education in state schools. One such EMO is the Education Group, which, as of 2010, controlled and operated music programs in more than one hundred primary schools in London. As described on its website, this company provides primary schools with qualified music teachers, most of whom are from commonwealth countries and employed on a part-time basis (www.educationgroup. com). The economic and political advantages to state schools of outsourcing educational programs and teaching are obvious and substantial. Administrators can streamline costs (because they are no longer responsible for health care and pension benefits) while simultaneously undermining teachers' unions. That was another aim of both the Thatcher and Blair governments.

The problem with this kind of policy, aside from the obvious one of making it more difficult to attract university graduates to lifelong careers in music education, is that it makes it difficult for schools to achieve long-term stability and program consistency. Schools can meet day-to-day minimum requirements for planning and assessment, but the teaching cohort consists of mostly temporary and relatively inexperienced part-time workers who return home after a year or two of teaching and touring in England. These kinds of stop gap and ad hoc employment policies and practices are thus hardly going to contribute to the long-term viability and success of those programs. Nor are they likely to help raise musical standards or to reverse the decline of interest in folk and classical music in school and society. Most likely they are just window dressing from governments that do not really believe in the importance of music and art in public education except as training, entertainment for the masses, and economic stimulus (by providing more opportunities for private business).

Among the dangers of allowing business too much say in public music education is that it becomes utilitarian and thus primarily concerned with vocational training and entertainment and less so with teaching children how to think. The warning about schools failing to teach children to think was broached earlier and also in *Democracy and Music Education* (2005), where it was observed that too many music teachers seem to agree with businesspeople that music should be taught primarily for its vocational and entertainment value. They seem to have little appreciation of the value of music education beyond performance and entertainment. It is an old and stubborn idea that gained new currency among populist capitalist governments such as Blair's, which sought to win and retain office by blaming teachers, local educational authorities, and academics for many of the country's economic woes while simultaneously pandering to the masses.

Many school music programs no longer seem to have an intellectual purpose beyond entertaining children and teaching them practical skills and knowledge (Eklund-Koza, 2002b). Nor are universities immune to this thinking, as they increasingly rely on corporate donors for research funding, and thus also for direction, while catering to students' interests.

Ever since Margaret Thatcher's directive to British universities that they should operate like corporations and be subject to market conditions, there has been an increased emphasis on accountability and competition among the rank and file of those institutions, not so much in terms of *proven* quality of programs as in terms of commercial value and popular appeal to students (Bruneau & Savage, 2002). One consequence of Thatcher's reforms, and which has long since spread to other Western countries, is that the mission of public universities has changed. Whereas my own university in Canada, for example, once boasted of creating an intellectual environment "in which critical thinking was cultivated and sustained," it now seeks to provide "the best student experience" (http://communications.uwo.ca/about/waywewere.htm). This, in combination with government pressure on universities to provide "more scholar for its dollar," has contributed to grade inflation because both high school and university students now view themselves as customers (Cote & Allahar, 2010, p. 5; 2011). Throughout today's Anglo-American university system, the language of upper administration is now of corporate branding, business partnerships, and consumer satisfaction. Just a few years ago in England, the chief executive of the Music Manifesto program even called for the tailoring of university music education programs to suit the "passions and interests of young people ... [and] the industry" (Poole, 2008, para. 3).

School music programs are by no means the only ones subject to corporate intrusion. However, they are probably more vulnerable than most other school programs because music teachers are dependent on the music and entertainment industries for virtually all of their repertoire, material, and equipment and much of their conference funding (and thus also planning), and because, as already suggested, corporate advertisers have long recognized their potential for indoctrinating children and their families to consumer culture. But, as Giroux (1994) and Barber (1996) reminded us, unless teachers consider the intent of the entertainment industry, which is all too often to sap children's intelligence by creating a fantasy theme park in which they can retreat from the world and its problems, then they might be abdicating their responsibility to educate. They should instead be teaching children to distinguish fact from fantasy and to identify and decipher the ideologies and political forces at play in the world in which they live, including in entertainment, politics, religion, education, music, and culture in general. Hedges (2009) similarly warned in his book *Empire of Illusion* that an education that favors escapism over reality and skills over values will result in a citizenry that is overly susceptible to manipulation by demagogues and the rich and powerful via the now ubiquitous media.

MUSIC EDUCATION AFTER AUSCHWITZ

Hedges is indebted for this point to Theodor Adorno's essay "Education after Auschwitz," in which the latter argued that the primary goal of all education should be to prevent future holocausts. All education should serve a moral purpose! The best way to accomplish that goal was by preparing children to confront reality while learning how to engage in critical self-reflection (Adorno, 1997). Teachers should help children learn about the real history and current state of their own country and of the world so that they are better informed, but children also need to have their consciousness raised with respect to the myriad ways that we are all potentially subject to manipulation and to what political or other ends. Only then can children learn from the lessons of the past, such as how the recent world economic collapse shared many similarities and causes with the Great Depression and how so much of what is presented to them about history, politics, education, music, and current events via the ubiquitous media is distorted or "make-believe" (Wolf, 2008, p. 35). Only then can children have any hope of intellectually defending themselves and democratic society from ideologues and would-be tyrants and thereby exercising any significant degree of musical or other freedom.

This admonishment applies as much to music teacher education as it does to school music, and perhaps more so given the profession's complicity in the passivization and Nazification of Germany during the Third Reich. Adorno knew from personal experience that music teachers are vulnerable to, and sometimes implicated in, political and other forms of manipulation and abuse (Kertz-Welzel, 2005). German music teachers welcomed Hitler's policy of music education as Nazi propaganda because it strengthened their position in the schools relative to other subject teachers. Something similar happened in America during the early years of the Cold War when the military-industrial complex and prominent educational reformers on the political Right set the terms for all education, including music education, by calling for greater emphasis in schools on the development of intellectual and other forms of ability *over* democratic values and citizenship (Woodford, 2010). It was more important that schools prepare children to compete militarily, economically, and culturally with the Soviets for world dominance than it was to create politically informed and socially engaged citizens who might challenge authority. Prominent music educators agreed with those educational reformers in stating that music education should have nothing to do with politics and that teaching democratic or other extrinsic values in music classes would only result in "low musical standards" (Leonhard & House, 1959/1972, p. 113).

The purpose of music education became to develop children's aesthetic potential and abstract thinking ability through exposure to great music, thereby helping them to transcend the world. This was thought to be humanizing and an argument that would convince government that music was a *serious* subject because it developed children's intelligence. But it was a blind intelligence insomuch as their attention was directed away from societal problems in which music was implicated (e.g., music as distraction, repression, or a means of creating a docile citizenry). This was a politically correct philosophy for the time, as a more truly progressive philosophy of music education would have been labeled un-American and a threat to national security. Adorno (2006), however, would probably have regarded this idea of transcending reality as a form of escapism that better served authoritarian than democratic interests, as did nostalgic appeals to the classics and tradition as representing timeless values. While by no means against tradition, he cautioned that it warranted careful critical attention.

If Adorno had been alive during the past decade, and owing to his experiences with the Nazis, he would have been wary of the Music Manifesto's call for a national singing campaign culminating in the 2012 Olympics and also, in the United States, of the National Association for Music Education's national anthem project. He knew that performance programs and projects of these kinds can all too easily be used to indoctrinate children and the masses to potentially dangerous ideologies while promoting escapism. When performance is overemphasized at the expense of critical consciousness, it will likely have diversionary and tranquilizing effects (Kertz-Welzel, 2005, p. 2). Perhaps more than anything else today he would be deeply concerned about growing media consolidation and corporate intrusion into virtually all aspects of our lives, including music education programs, sports, politics, food, water, energy, and the military, and how they threaten to undermine democracy and the public good.

Take, for example, the January 2010 Winter Olympic Games held in British Columbia. Adorno would have been appalled at the increasing commercialization of the Olympics and its reconception as entertainment over sport. Whereas media coverage of the games traditionally focused more on the actual sporting events with some commentary and advertising, today's games are saturated with music, video, and advertising as television producers seek to increase ratings and advertising revenue by dramatizing events and programming. Music is no longer used primarily as introductory material but as a soundtrack to provoke emotional responses in viewers while gluing them to their seats. He would have been aghast at the pervasiveness of music in Canadian television programming of the Vancouver Winter Olympics, which prompted one newspaper columnist to wryly exclaim that the games are "a musical rather than an athletic event" (Smith, 2010, p. R1). He would have been even more troubled by the deliberate patriotic boosterism, in which music is of course heavily implicated, that almost inevitably accompanies the Olympic Games because it encourages a false sense of national pride and identity based on medal counts rather than on sportsmanship and humane values.

Perhaps more than anything else, these kinds of events, in which the entertainment media are now central, contribute to the hijacking of democracy either by distracting the public from important issues or by helping to shut down democratic debate altogether. This literally happened in Canada in late December 2009 when the minority governing federal Conservative Party used the approaching Winter Olympics as an excuse for suspending Parliament for more than two months. That government also appreciated music's potential as distraction. Strangely embedded in the federal finance minister's 2010 austerity budget released immediately after the conclusion of the Winter Olympics was a proposal to amend the lyrics of the national anthem, this just after several weeks of nationalistic boosterism in which the anthem figured prominently! The proposed changes were quickly dropped following an emotional public outcry, but the gambit had by then already served its purpose of dominating the news and directing the public's attention away from the budget, just as the tactic of proroguing Parliament had prevented opposition parties from asking embarrassing questions about a political scandal relating to Canadian military policy in Afghanistan.

In this age of entertainment, instant communication, and the neoliberal manipulated man, it is more important than ever that music and other teachers encourage and help children to read and listen to the world, and particularly the media, with a critical eye and ear (and all of their senses), since virtually all of the information about the world and history presented to the public is prepackaged and filtered through various corporate-owned and controlled media that are themselves vulnerable to manipulation by political think tanks, government, advertisers, and others wishing to shape public opinion and tastes or to divert the public's attention from controversial issues. As Gutstein (2009) cautioned, we ignore the media at our peril because the corporate world literally owns and controls our primary means of mass communication and as such it "is no longer just one voice, albeit an important one, in the democratic debate. It controls the debate" (pp. 11–12). Many of us tend to trust the media for our news and entertainment, but, as Orwell warned in his own time, many of today's mainstream media are owned and controlled by a relatively small group of media barons with distinctly conservative outlooks, or at least that is the case in Canada, where literally a handful of wealthy and politically conservative individuals controls most of the mainstream news media. It would be extremely naive to think that those corporate elites have no say over news policy and general programming. Those same media barons also tend to be well connected politically (p. 200). The point here is simply that all of us, including our students, should pay careful attention to our world and music's many roles therein (including how music and music education are themselves vulnerable to co-option by political and other forces) lest we become or remain passive spectators rather than active agents in its shaping. This was Dewey's message in *The Public and Its Problems* (1927/1946), in which he warned of the possible eclipse of the public by "powerful special interest groups ... [and] the threat to democracy that resulted from the growth and spread of the 'corporate mentality'—a mentality that has taken on global dimensions in our time" (Bernstein, 2005, p. 25).

Given music's ubiquity and impact on all of our lives, it would be irresponsible were school music programs to continue sending graduates out into the world with musical skills and perhaps a smattering of knowledge of music theory and history yet having no idea of how their perceptions, tastes, values, and understandings of history and current social and political *realities* are often deliberately shaped by other people, organizations, and institutions for their own ends and how music and music education are sometimes implicated in that process. To quote Chomsky (1987):

> For those who stubbornly seek freedom, there can be no more urgent task than to come to understand the mechanisms and practices of indoctrination. These are easier to perceive in the totalitarian societies, much less so in the system of "brainwashing under freedom" to which we are subjected and which all too often we serve as willing or unwitting instruments. (p. 136)

It would be equally irresponsible were music teacher programs to continue graduating students without introducing them to fundamental political principles and real-world problems, such as the ones included herein, that are important to understanding not just what a democratic purpose for music education might entail but also how past and current politics and events have literally shaped the profession. As Dworkin (2006) suggested, without this knowledge, which includes awareness of the complexities of "the most contentious political controversies of the day," graduates of those programs will be ill-prepared to participate in political life and thus unable to defend themselves and the profession against future encroachments by those who would pervert its purpose. While fraught with difficulty, he continues, we *cheat* our students if we fail to prepare them to live as democratic citizens (pp. 148–149). Finally, we also fail our students if we neglect to teach them how music can also be used as a powerful tool both for confronting reality and for prompting critical self-reflection so that they are better prepared not only to see through the veil of perception that causes them to mistake appearances for reality and truth but also to function as moral agents in protecting the public interest.

REFERENCES

Adorno, T. (1997). Education after Auschwitz. In H. Schreier & M. Heyl (Eds.), *Never again! The Holocaust's challenge for educators*. Hamburg, Germany: Kramer. (Original work published in German in 1967).

Adorno, T. W. (2006). *Philosophy of new music* (R. Hullot-Kentor, ed. & trans.). Minneapolis, MN: University of Minnesota Press.

Albritton, R. (2009). *Let them eat junk: How capitalism creates hunger and obesity*. Winnipeg, Canada: Arbeiter Ring Publishing.

Allsup, R. (2003). Mutual learning and democratic action in instrumental music education. *Journal of Research in Music Education, 51*(1), 24–37.

Allsup, R. (2007). Democracy and one hundred years of music education. *Music Educators Journal, 93*(5), 52–56.

Allsup, R. (2010). Choosing music literature. In H. F. Abeles & L. A. Custodero (Eds.), *Critical issues in music education: Contemporary theory and practice* (pp. 215–235). New York, NY: Oxford University Press.

Apple, M. (2003). Competition, knowledge and the loss of educational vision. *Philosophy of Music Education Review, 11*(1), 3–22.

Apple, M. (2004). Creating difference: Neo-liberalism, neo-conservatism and the politics of educational reform. *Educational Policy, 18*(1), 12–44.

Bakan, J. (2004). *The corporation: The pathological pursuit of profit and power*. Toronto, ON, Canada: Penguin Canada.

Barber, B. R. (1996). *Jihad vs. McWorld: How globalism and tribalism are reshaping the world*. New York, NY: Ballantine Books.

Battisti, F. (2006, July). Untitled lecture presented at a conducting symposium at Acadia University, Nova Scotia, Canada.

Bernstein, R. J. (2005). *The abuse of evil: The corruption of politics and religion since 9/11*. Cambridge, UK: Polity Press.

Bruneau, W., & Savage, D. (2002). *Counting out the scholars: How performance indicators undermine universities and colleges*. Toronto, ON, Canada: James Lorimer & Company.

Burgess, A. (1998). Thoughts on the Thatcher decade. In *One man's chorus: The uncollected writings* (pp. 146–151). New York, NY: Carroll and Graf Publishers.

Chomsky, N. (1987). The manufacture of consent. In J. Peck (Ed.), *The Chomsky reader* (pp. 121–136). New York, NY: Pantheon Books.

Chomsky, N. (2006). *Failed states: The abuse of power and the assault on democracy*. New York, NY: Henry Holt & Company.

Christman, J. (2005). Saving positive freedom. *Political Theory, 33*(1), 79–88.

Cote, J. E., & Allahar, A. L. (2010). Grade inflation goes to graduate school. *Western News, 46*(15), 5.

Cote, J. E., & Allahar, A. L. (2011). *Lowering higher education: The rise of corporate universities and the fall of liberal education*. Toronto, ON, Canada: University of Toronto Press.

Dewey, J. (1927/1946). *The public and its problems*. Chicago, IL: Gateway Books.

Dimova-Cookson, M. (2004). Conceptual clarity, freedom, and normative ideas: Reply to Blau. *Political Theory, 32*(4), 554–562.

Dworkin, R. (2006). *Is democracy possible here? Principles for a new political debate*. Princeton, NJ: Princeton University Press.

Ginsberg, R., & Lyche, L. F. (2008). The culture of fear and the politics of education. *Educational Policy, 22*(1), 10–27.

Giroux, H. A. (1994). *Disturbing pleasures: Learning popular culture*. New York, NY: Routledge.

Green, T. H. (1986). Lecture on 'liberal legislation and freedom of contract.' In P. Harris & J. Morrow (Eds.), *Lectures on principles of political obligation and other writings* (pp. 194–212). Cambridge, UK: Cambridge University Press.

Gutstein, D. (2009). *Not a conspiracy theory: How business propaganda hijacks democracy*. Toronto, ON, Canada: Key Porter Books.

Habermas, J. (2005). Three normative models of democracy. In S. M. Cahn (Ed.), *Political philosophy: The essential texts* (pp. 527–534). New York, NY: Oxford University Press.

Hedges, C. (2009). *Empire of illusion: The end of literacy and the triumph of spectacle*. Toronto, ON, Canada: Alfred A. Knopf.

Hitler, A. (1999). *Mein kampf* (R. Manheim, Trans.). Boston, MA: Houghton Mifflin. (Original work published 1925)

Hopkins, M. (2009, November). *Equilibrium: How successful music ensembles resemble and reflect democratic values*. Paper presented at the Ontario Music Educators Association Conference, Toronto, Canada.

Kelly, S. N. (2009). *Teaching music in American society: A social and cultural understanding of music education*. New York, NY: Routledge.

Kertz-Welzel, A. (2005). The pied piper of Hamelin: Adorno on music education. *Research Studies in Music Education, 25*(1), 1–12.

Koza, J. E. (2002a). Corporate profit at equity's expense: Codified standards and high-stakes assessment in music teacher preparation. *Bulletin of the Council for Research in Music Education, 152*, 1–16.

Koza, J. E. (2002b). A realm without angels: MENC's partnerships with Disney and other major corporations. *Philosophy of Music Education Review, 10*(2), 72–79.

Leonhard, C., & House, R. W. (1959/1972). *Foundations and principles of music education* (2nd ed.). New York, NY: McGraw-Hill Book Company.

Nagel, T. (2003). Rawls and liberalism. In S. Freeman (Ed.), *The Cambridge companion to Rawls* (pp. 62–85). Cambridge, UK: Cambridge University Press.

Norman, R. (1995). Freedom, political. In T. Honderich (Ed.), *Oxford companion to philosophy* (pp. 291–292). Oxford, UK: Oxford University Press.

Poole, D. (2008, June 26). Take some musical notes. *The Independent*. Retrieved from www. http//journalisted.com/article/btvm.

Postman, N. (1985). *Amusing ourselves to death: Public discourse in the age of show business*. New York, NY: Penguin Books.

Rawls, J. (1999). *A theory of justice* (Rev. ed.). Cambridge, MA: Belknap Press of Harvard University Press.

Reimer, B. (1989). *A philosophy of music education* (2nd ed.). Englewood Cliffs, NJ: Prentice Hall.

Reimer, B. (2003). *A philosophy of music education: Advancing the vision* (3rd ed.). Upper Saddle River, NJ: Prentice Hall.

Saul, J. R. (2005). *The collapse of globalism and the reinvention of the world*. Toronto, ON, Canada: Penguin Books.

Seldon, A., Snowdon, P., & Collings, D. (2007). *Blair unbound*. London, UK: Simon & Schuster.

Smith, R. (2010, February 18). Now, the Olympic grammar slalom. *The Globe and Mail*, pp. R1–R2.

Stiglitz, J. E. (2010). *Freefall: America, free markets, and the sinking of the world economy*. New York, NY: W. W. Norton & Company.

West, C. (2004). *Democracy matters: Winning the fight against imperialism*. New York, NY: Penguin Press.

Westheimer, J., & Kahne, J. (2004). What kind of citizen? The politics of educating for democracy. *American Educational Research Journal, 41*(2), 237–269.

Wolf, N. (2008). *Give me liberty: A handbook for American revolutionaries*. New York, NY: Simon & Schuster.

Woodford, P. (2005). *Democracy and music education: Liberalism, ethics and the politics of practice*. Bloomington, IN: Indiana University Press.

Woodford, P. (2009a). Two political models for music education and their implications for practice. In A. Lamont & H. Coll (Eds.), *Sound progress: Exploring musical development* (pp. 109–114). London, UK: Matlock. National Association of Music Educators.

Woodford, P. (2009b). Why Canada does not have national music education standards, or does it? *Canadian Music Educator, 51*(2), 34–39.

Woodford, P. (2010). Democratic elitism or democratic citizenship? The politics of music, meaning and music education in Cold-War America. *Eufonia. Didactica de la Musica, 50*, 23–33.

Younker, B. A. (2003). Philosophical underpinnings for music making in democratic spaces. *Canadian Music Educator, 45*(2), 20–22.

Zinn, H., & Macedo, D. (2005). *Howard Zinn on democratic education*. Boulder, CO: Paradigm Publishers.

Section Two

Listening

Music listening is a unique experience for each person. As teachers, we need to broaden our vistas to include students' life music in our curriculum through a range of musical styles including popular music and world music.

Rob Dunn

In teacher education, we tend to function in a very different way than our students do. There have been 10 billion songs downloaded on iTunes as of this February, and that's in 150 years of recorded music. And in that time, we haven't really changed in how we teach listening and how we exclude listening from the curriculum.

Judy Bundra

Are we so indoctrinated in what we call a music listening lesson that we don't feel safe expanding what that really means? Are we acting as gatekeepers to lock people out of the musical experience? Or are we truly trying to open that gate and bring in the masses to experience a wealth, a richness of music?

Jody Kerchner

4

MUSIC LISTENING VISTAS, VISIONS, AND VIM

Jody L. Kerchner

OUR LIFE DRAMAS unfold in theaters having "surround sound." Of the sound-scapes that accompany our daily life routines, we bring only portions of sound bytes into our immediate consciousness for consumption and consideration. Other sound patterns occur to us as mere sensory phenomena. Yet other sound streams pass us by without our awareness or acknowledgment. We hear, listen, and respond to organized sounds known as music. In formal and informal settings, we listen to myriad musical sounds and bring them into our set of present musical experiences upon which subsequent listening experiences are built.

Small (1998) considered music listening to be one of the many ways people "music," that is, engage in musical activity. The *National Standards for Arts Education* (Consortium of National Arts Education, 1994) music content standards and many states' fine arts standards urge music educators to include music listening among those skills vital in nurturing students' independent musicianship. Therefore, music listening should be a component of PK-12 general music and performance ensemble curricular experiences if we are to nurture lifelong music listeners and appreciators.

In this chapter, I reflect on research literature that served as foundations for my research, especially focusing on studies (Bundra, 1993; Dunn, 1994; Dura, 1998; Kerchner, 1996; Stokes, 1990) that stemmed from the Center for Study of Education and the Musical Experience at Northwestern University. From that research and my own research and teaching, I posit principles of music listening and future vistas and visions in order to revitalize the vim and vigor of music listening research and pedagogical agendas. Finally, I present a vignette about researching and facilitating student music listening skill development as one model for investigating music listening experiences among diverse student learners.

WHERE WE ARE

Over the past seventeen years, I have attempted to unearth multisensory tools with which students might gain access to music. To situate my research, I have drawn from literature in the areas of cognition, perception, and developmental and constructivist theories to investigate school-aged students' focus of attention and how they might use music listening maps, movement, and verbal responses to inform researchers and teachers of their music listening experiences. Additionally, I have explored the development of listeners' constructed and co-constructed meanings made manifest in maps, movements, and verbal descriptions that listeners generated over the course of repeated listening to musical excerpts (Kerchner, 1996, 2001, 2005, 2009).

From a historical perspective, there are several critical points that seem to have influenced the way teachers and researchers view the nature of people's music listening experience—behaviorism, developmental theorists, cognitive science, and constructivism. Implicit in behaviorist thinking, teachers ask students to listen to individual musical events at the most atomistic levels of sound. Numerous researchers have asked subjects of various ages to listen and respond to micro-music events and patterns in an attempt to measure their abilities to discriminate same and different pitches, tempi, rhythmic patterns, and melodic contour (Dowling, Tillman, & Ayers, 2001; Geringer, 1983; Geringer & Madsen, 1984; Hair, 1977; Madsen, 1979). Research also indicated that the brain does not merely copy incoming musical stimuli, but rather performs mental operations on that material. From that line of thinking and spilling over into the music classroom, music listening activity was (is?) primarily teacher directed—the teacher tells students what to listen for in music listening examples and is the director of what students "should" listen for in the music. This tactic, however, disregards the complexity of the music itself, the possibility that people simultaneously hear and process multiple musical events, and the listeners' abilities to create their own unique experience.

Following the stage development theory relative to music listening, we have witnessed certain styles of music and musical concepts reserved for presentation at younger grade levels and other, more sophisticated musics and musical concepts reserved for older students. Supporting these pedagogical notions were the Piagetian theories of centration and decentration: students can only focus on one thing at a time in music listening, and they gradually develop the skill to listen to more than one musical event simultaneously. However, Zimmerman (1981) found that children's music development did not strictly adhere to Piagetian invariant stage development.

Cognitive scientists challenged behaviorist tenets by purporting that aural stimuli in the form of tonal and rhythmic patterns (instead of isolated tones) are perceived through people's sensory modalities. Stokes (1990) stated that those cognitive operations include discrimination, comparison, classification, abstraction, organization, schema formation, problem setting and problem solving, synthesis, judgment, intuition, and interpretation. She further suggested that perception and affective responses are concomitant responses (i.e., operations) during music listening.

Miller (1992) described cognitive processing—particularly mental representation and schemata formation—as the creation of mental patterns, directions, or models. We listen to a piece of music, and schemes are activated. When the existing schemes are no longer sufficient in organizing and making sense of incoming stimuli, newer cognitive paths are explored (building on the previous paths that were taken in the listening). When an interruption occurs and arousal takes place, cognitive activity is triggered, searching for an interpretation of the novel event (p. 422). Mental schemata are confirmed according to a person's expectations or otherwise modified because those original expectations were denied (Heller & Campbell, 1982; Meyer, 1956).

The cognitive science revolution brought the human engagement to the forefront of music listening experiences. The idea of listener as a passive, uninvolved receiver of musical sound was replaced by notion of listener as a mental organizer and affective respondent to patterned musical sound. Bamberger (1991) suggested that listening is an active restructuring of heard material. Specifically, she noted that during repeated presentations of musical excerpts, listeners regroup musical stimuli, create new sectional forms, appropriate the focus of attention for selected musical elements, and open the mind to musical aspects that might not have been heard in previous listenings.

This information can be applied to music teaching and learning: repeated music listening experience assumed a prominent position in the facilitation and elaboration of students' perceptual acuity, musical concept formation, and affective response. The more students are exposed to a piece of music—regardless of style or genre—and attend to its aesthetic properties, the more detailed their schemata become.

Hints of constructivist ideology are evident as early as the sixth century BC with Lao Tzu and the Buddha and, later, in the writings of Kant and Schopenhauer. Similarly, constructivist thinking is at the core of educational theorists and pedagogy embraced by Maria Montessori (1946), John Dewey (1910/1977,

1933/1964), Jerome Bruner (1966), Donald Schön (1983), Lev Vygotsky (1978), and Goldberger, Tarule, Clinchy, and Belenky (1996). Bruner (1966) considered constructivism an active process in which learners construct new ideas or concepts based on their current/past knowledge. Tenets of constructivism include (1) students' active agency in learning, (2) mental ordering (patterning) of information, (3) development and involvement of students' self and personal identity, (4) social-symbolic relatedness of learning, and (5) life span development. Thus, constructivists value the holistic body-minds as active participants in creating musical meaning. Constructivists also acknowledge learning as a socially constructed occurrence that is a direct result of the cultural, historical, sociopolitical contexts in which listeners are situated. To that end, Bowman (2004) stated, "…The bodily-constituted knowledge of which music is a prime and precious instance is not different in kind from intellectual kinds of knowing. Rather, the two are continuous, deeply involved in each other's construction, and each in turn ecologically situated in the social world" (p. 29).

With the introduction of qualitative research designs, the profession found new paths for exploring music listening in naturalistic venues (i.e., concerts, classrooms) and within authentic cultural and/or social communities. Single case studies, interviews with individuals or focus groups, and narratives have provided the profession with glimpses of people's music listening experiences. Researchers have presented listeners with multisensory tasks that prompt them to represent externally that which they attend to during their music listening experiences. Verbal descriptions (Flowers, 2000; Jellison & Flowers, 1991) and protocols (Bundra, 1993; Kerchner, 1996, 2001, 2005), drawn representations (Blair, 2006; Dunn, 1994; Kerchner, 1996, 2001, 2005, 2009; Richards, 1980), invented notations (Bamberger, 1991; Barrett, 2005; Davidson, Scripp, & Welch, 1988; Upitis, 1985), and kinesthetic responses and dimensions (Cohen, 1980; Dura, 1998, 2002; Kerchner, 1996, 2001, 2005) have become tools researchers and educators use to capture important insights into children's abilities to perceive, organize, recall, compare, store, and affectively respond to incoming musical stimuli. While these tools have been primarily used to procure students' responses to Western classical music, they might also work with students listening to styles and genres outside of the classical canon.

Listeners' multisensory responses, including invented notations, verbal reports, and kinesthetic gestures, are cognitive "black boxes"—externalized representations indicative of students' focus of attention and other mental processes employed during the music listening experience. By experiencing music along various multisensory felt (i.e., cognitive) pathways (Blair, 2008), students might build metaphoric (verbal, visual, kinesthetic) frames for knowing music and constructing personal meaning. Subsequently, as Zimmerman (1981) noted, this perceptual knowing leads to concept formation. In fact, she claimed interdependence between perception and concept formation: "In any given perceptual field there must be a selective focus for one's attention. Then internal operations of labeling, categorizing, and organizing follow. It is here that concept formation takes place" (p. 52). In my research, I have considered students' multisensory responses to be reflective of conceptual construction—musical meaning making and learning.

Listeners' multisensory responses might be considered not only as responsive representations of musical thinking and processing (i.e., post hoc) but also as symbols of musical thinking and feeling in real time. Although these metaphoric representations of thinking and feeling in musical sound provide researchers and teachers with valuable insight into the music listening experience, they also provide only partial glimpses into students' music listening experience. We must remain mindful that students choose the features of the experience they want or might be able to share with us. At best, researchers and teachers can only infer from and interpret listeners' externalized representations and responses that they provide during music experiences.

WHERE WE MIGHT WANT TO GO

How, then, might an "old" and "traditional" activity be transplanted into the new millennial thinking and the world of new pedagogical and research vistas? As a community of researchers, we have heard students talk about musical elements they experience, watched them create movements and gestures, and observed them draw maps of their music listening experiences. Basal text series have sported beautiful designs, photographs, and music listening maps to accompany student exposure to a gamut of Western and world musics. And there are still the occasional music education professional conference sessions devoted to the topic of music listening skill development. We acknowledge that music listening, as musical experience, allows people to interact with musical sound in concert halls, outdoor community events, or the privacy of their own living spaces. What more is there to wonder about and imagine in terms of research and pedagogy, since music listening is hardly a current trend in music education? Is there still vim, vigor, and verve left in the investigation of teaching and learning music listening skills? In other words, who cares?

Principles of Music Learning

Scholars have spent time and energy researching music listening perception and cognition relative to specific musical elements and patterns. And teachers have pondered how they might design music listening lessons in the most efficient and effective ways for PK-12 students. From others' and my own research findings and teaching PK-12 students, I present what I consider key principles of music listening, each being the basis for how music listening might be experienced in music education settings (formal and informal). Perhaps these principles might serve as connective tissue between the worlds of research and teaching praxis as we currently understand them. These principles represent hybrids of musical, pedagogical, and research ideology, and they might be useful in forging new paths for how we teach music listening, design classroom and rehearsal experiences that facilitate the development of students' music listening skills, assess students' listening skill development, and imagine new horizons for research.

The principles of music listening are (Kerchner, 2013):

1. Music listening is a skill worth developing, as it is the foundation for musical behaviors, and attentive listening is key in human communication and interaction.
2. Each person has the capacity to develop music listening skills, regardless of her or his cognitive, physical, or musical abilities.
3. Each person creates unique music listening experiences that are influenced by past and present musical experiences.
4. Music listening can evoke internal and external responses to music's formal and aesthetic qualities.
5. Music listening requires creative and active participation.
6. Music listening pedagogical activities serve to focus students' attention on the music.
7. Masterful musical examples, regardless of style or genre, provide material for conceptual study in class and ensemble rehearsals.
8. Teaching strategies, not the music itself, suggest age suitability.
9. Repeatedly listening to musical examples, within a single class period and over the course of several classes, enables students to become intensely familiar with the musical "material" and to ascribe "deeper" levels of musical meaning.
10. Repeatedly listening to musical examples enables students to create, re-create, and sophisticate their constructed musical meaning.
11. Multisensory (kinesthetic, visual, aural, tactile) music listening tools can provide multiple access points into the music for diverse students (i.e., cognitive/intellectual abilities, style preferences, linguistic skills).
12. Student responses can serve as "springboards" for subsequent musical discussions and explorations of other musical behaviors.

In light of these principles, I pose two broad categories of research in an effort to impel the current understanding of the music listening experience. Areas that I believe are in need of investigation include (1) inclusion and diversity in the music listening experience and (2) the collective social consciousness and construction of meaning that occurs during music listening.

Inclusion and Diversity in Music

In this section, I consider inclusion and diversity on two fronts: (1) the music listening experience of diverse learners and (2) the music listening experience of learners listening to diverse musical styles and genres. Perhaps it is now time to pull back our professional microscope lenses and think more holistically about music processes and products proffered by those individuals who are listening to music. As teachers and researchers, we have investigated those "safe" musics (i.e., musics with which we teachers are most familiar) and "safe" students who are in the mainstream of our educational society—those students who participate in traditional music performance ensembles, are enrolled in general music classroom environments, and provide us easy investigational access. And yet, what do we really know about the music listening experience of those who are in alternative learning settings, who are on the periphery of our educational (and musical) communities, and who listen to musics not typically found in schools? The amalgam consists of individuals who bring a host of diverse life and musical experiences, different intelligence profiles and learning modality predilections, and a variety of music listening biases and preferences as they listen to music. How might we investigate the variables of a diverse listening and learning population in order to inform our teaching for music listening skill development?

The proposed principles of music listening acknowledge that music listening experiences are multisensory phenomena. We hear the music, but we also tend to move, or allow ourselves to be "moved" in terms of emotional responses and involuntary physiological responses (e.g., increased or decreased heart rate, increased excitation and activity in various lobes of the brain, and blood chemical changes). Listeners are also visually engaged as we observe others perform music or create images as we listen to music.

It seems obvious, then, that our research and pedagogical tools must be as diverse as each of our listeners if we truly wish to gain a depth of understanding about the perceptual and affective nature of music listening experiences across the life span. Listening maps, movement, and verbal descriptions might be only a few tools in which our diverse students come to access and know (i.e., mindfully and affectively engaging in) music listening as an active musical experience.

These multisensory tools might be useful in classrooms and performance ensembles as students discover soundscapes from cultures, styles, and genres worldwide. Perhaps these multisensory music listening tools (and others yet to be designed) in tandem with technological trends (i.e., music composition software, iPads, iPods, music production software) might lead the music education profession to uncover ways to connect with learners, individualize music listening experiences and instruction, and investigate tools that might be more concrete in their representation of students' music listening experiences.

Since brain research has given us some information about how a person receives, perceives, and responds to music, I call on neuroscientists and music researchers to investigate the nature of the music listening experience. Anecdotally, it seems that our bodies and brains are engaged in ways unique to music listening experiences, different than while performing, composing, and critiquing. Dare we collaborate with our medical and psychological colleagues so that the combinations of diverse expertise lead to the holistic understanding of the roles that individuality and commonality play within music listening experiences? Utilizing current and future technologies, might we even discover "music listening" as one of several subintelligences subsumed by Gardner's (1983) "musical intelligence"?

Diversity in our population of music listeners and learners also calls into question the nature of the music listening experience for those who function at intellectual, physical, and social levels not considered by our society to be "typical." The body of music education research is more or less devoid of studies that investigate music listening and exceptional learners—those who function at the highest and lowest levels of cognition, physical capability, and/or socioemotional interaction. If music is a type of intelligence, might this imply that people who are atypically functioning (i.e., gifted or disabled in some capacity) experience music differently from typically functioning people? Collecting and analyzing these types of data for report would be a contribution to our profession in and of itself; however, the more important contribution seems a pedagogical one. Studies of exceptional learners and their music listening experiences might inform educators of ways to bring those typically underserved and underrepresented into the mainstream of music listening development and learning.

Engaging "Other": Connecting Research and Pedagogy

To illustrate the power of (1) action research, (2) connecting research and pedagogy, and (3) engaging diverse student populations in the music listening experience in a community of learners (Wenger, 1998), I turn to a teaching experience and research project within a middle-school music class (Kerchner, 2009). For four years, I worked with at-risk adolescent students in a local middle school in a pseudo-general music class—the Music Workshop. Most of the fifteen students in each of three classes were students of color, nonnative English speakers, and low academically performing students who also had one if not multiple learning disabilities.

I will focus on Kyle. He was a child who demonstrated characteristics of (and was diagnosed with) attention-deficit hyperactivity disorder (ADHD). It was not uncommon for Kyle to be in perpetual motion, fall out of his chair, kick other students, appear dazed, or offer an astute musical comment about an activity in class. He also had difficulty reading at grade level; his reading aloud was slow and often inaccurate in deciphering words.

One day, the students and I discussed ways we represent speech and other sounds (i.e., alphabet letters, music notation, punctuation, drawing, moving). I placed a music listening map of the theme of Schubert's "Die Forelle" Piano Quintet. (N.B. Although I used various styles of musics in class, the vignette examples provided here happen to involve only musical excerpts from within the classical canon.)

"Hey, we made one of those early this year!" noticed Kyle before I had even mentioned the word "map." Kyle continued: "We did it [the map] to…da-dada-dadadada, da, dada, dadadada" [he sings the melody of the first theme of Bizet's *Carmen* "Overture"]. "Oh yeah!" chimed in several other students.

I instructed the students to follow along as I performed the map I had created. We followed the map, my finger being the visual guide for these young, attentive eyes. Before I played the music, I asked, "Where on the map do you think the phrases are indicated? Listen, watch, and we'll talk about it after the music stops." The music began. "Hey, you didn't draw the map right!" bellowed Austin, a precocious child who had a volatile temper. "Oh?" I asked. "What would your map look like, or how would you want to change mine?" "You pointed to parts of the map more than once. Did you forget about the parts that come back in the music when you were drawing?" Austin snickered, probably thinking he had caught me making a mistake. "Good observation of the repetition, Austin. Which symbols on the map would you repeat on your map?" He shrugged his shoulders and rolled his eyes.

As I was about to play the musical excerpt and perform the map again, Kyle walked toward me. He said in a baby, rather than his changing, voice, "Move over. I'm doing the map this time." Admittedly, I was a bit startled by his statement of intention. "Are you asking me to perform the map for us this time?" "Yeah. May I please do the map?" he mumbled sarcastically. I stood next to Kyle and told him that I would "be there" if he needed help. "I don't want your help," he snapped. And he did not need my assistance! Not only did Kyle accurately point to each of the symbols I had drawn to represent various features of the music, but also he remembered which symbols I had pointed to more than once to indicate musical repetition. The map was not a linear map. After only one listening and one viewing of my performance of the map, Kyle performed the listening map, seemingly without effort. Afterward, the class and I applauded his performance. "I have never seen a student point to my map with such precision after listening to the music only one time. Good for you, Kyle." "It was nothing," he said as he allowed a small, but significant, smile to cross his face. This was one of the few times that Kyle had ever volunteered to participate in class.

In most music classes, Kyle might have been viewed as "other," given his difficulty in focusing long enough to contribute positively and consistently in class. The visual component of the music listening task drew him into the music. He had heard the music, processed it, and translated my markings on the music listening map into the musical events as they occurred in real time. The mapping (visual) component of the music listening experience allowed Kyle to show me the extent to which he was focusing on the musical sound. In terms of the principles of music listening, the multisensory tasks (visual and kinesthetic) provided Kyle with entry points into the music from the classical world of music, while also focusing his attention. The repeated listening fostered ownership and familiarity of the musical formal structures and elements so he could perform the map with ease. Perhaps most importantly at this juncture of the class, however, was that Kyle actively participated in thinking about musical sound. The "other" was capable of demonstrating his musical understanding vis-à-vis non-verbal responses.

Continuing the Story

Frankly, I did not know where to begin with the students in the Music Workshop. For the first weeks, I was called "that mean white lady doctor." I desperately sought some inroad, some connection with these students. I did not look like them, I did not speak like them, and I did not have life experiences similar to theirs. It soon became obvious, per the students' instruction, that I was perceived as the "other" and that I had to begin with their musical agenda. They liked listening to music, and they told me what type of music they wanted to listen to in class. We made lists of favorites—styles, genres, performers, and instruments. It was a mutual surprise when we realized that we shared a preference for certain country music performers! But when I posed the question "What about the music do you like?" there was often a shrug of the shoulders or the statement "I don't know. I just do." "I just do"—what is it that they were hearing, no, listening to? What was tugging at them and pulling them into the music?

So I asked each student to bring in her or his favorite music for me to listen to. Of course, some students went right for the music they thought would shock me most—music with profanity, sexually explicit content, and blaring sounds. After I listened to each song, I sat with the students and, together, we listened to the music. The students actually seemed surprised that they were not being scolded or given detention for the music they had presented to me. During our one-on-one conversations, I heard the students' stories of their life happenings, dreams, musical engagement outside of school, and, in their own words, descriptions of the music they listened to. Students who had never offered any response in class spoke passionately about their music listening experiences. Although it was not "school appropriate" to play some of the students' music in class, I still felt a musical connection with them because I made an effort, without judgment, to look beyond my own musical vistas and to honor theirs. In subsequent lessons, the students seemed willing to listen to the music I offered, perhaps because I had started from their music listening "turf" and found ways to connect conceptually their and my music listening worlds.

In recent years, the music education profession has begun to learn about music preferences, not only among young children and collegiate students but also among adolescents (Lamont, Hargreaves, Marshall, & Tarrant, 2003; North, Colley, & Hargreaves, 2003; North, Hargreaves, & O'Neill, 2000). In an aging society, music education researchers will want to not only retool their investigations toward adolescents but also investigate music listening preferences of younger, middle, and older adults. A fascinating longitudinal study might be to investigate how people's musical preferences evolve over the life span.

When we as a profession understand our clientele's music listening preferences and interests, we can then design relevant music listening experiences in formal, nonformal, and informal educational settings. Further, we can honor these preferences by incorporating the listeners' "familiar" musics and then finding connections to their "less familiar" musics in our curricula. How might students' music listening experiences—perceptual and affective responses—differ when they are personally invested in the music and have a strong preference for and relationship to the music? How do their responses as they listen to familiar musics differ when they listen to unfamiliar musics of the Western and world traditions? Does the nature of their multisensory responses (externalized and internal, perceptual and affective) change, or do the listening processes themselves change?

Communities of Listeners

In the last section, I reviewed the investigation of individual listeners' experiences, but none of the individuals in the illustrations from the Music Workshop acted alone. Their individual music listening responses and experiences were situated in social settings—the classroom, the school, the local community, and so forth. What do we know about the effect of social interactions (i.e., communities) on how people listen to music? In an age of texting invisible receivers rather than communicating face to face, perhaps now it is especially important to create pedagogical opportunities for students to interact with each other in meaningful ways.

Wenger (1998) stated:

> Students go to school and, as they come together to deal in their own fashion with the agenda of the imposing institution and the unswerving mysteries of youth, communities of practice sprout everywhere in the classroom as well as on the playground, officially or in the cracks. And in spite of curriculum, discipline, and exhortation, the learning that is most personally transformative turns out to be the learning that involves membership in these communities of practice. (p. 6)

To embrace Wenger's perspective is to acknowledge that our students are initiators, creators of their own musical meaning, decision makers, and problem solvers. When teachers and researchers empower students to think independently about music and provide active music engagement, we create communities of learners, in which the student–teacher relationship becomes a partnership in learning and experiencing. This partnership debunks the teacher/researcher-control model within the music learning community. However, it also refutes the laissez-faire student-control model. Instead, social constructivism offers "a third perspective…that is not a compromise between models emphasizing adult control or children's freedom, but, rather, relies on the active involvement of adults and children together" (Rogoff, Turkanis, & Bartlett, 2001, p. 7).

Earlier in this chapter, I made a case for implementing music listening maps, movement, and verbal descriptions as research and pedagogical tools that, for a moment, freeze musical thinking for others to observe. These tools are often created and presented by teachers and researchers to direct music listeners' focus of attention. Aligned with the principles of music listening, these junior learners are creators of their musical understanding, so it would be useful for teachers and researchers to step aside and allow the listeners to generate their own versions of maps, movements, and verbal descriptions. In this way, listeners can inform us by showing those musical events that capture their attention. These tools, then, become the impetus for teachers' and researchers' subsequent prob- ing, researching, and guiding listeners to deeper levels of understanding rela- tive to their baseline listening experiences. What is the nature of co-constructed musical meaning during music listening as communities of learners grapple with deciphering and representing characteristics of musical sounds that capture their attention?

The final vignette from the middle-school Music Workshop represents my initial investigation into the nature of group music listening activity (Kerchner, 2009). It also illustrates at-risk students taking charge of their own small-group learning, collaboratively determining what they heard in the music, and negoti- ating what and how to represent that which they heard and felt as they repeat- edly listened to a two-minute excerpt of Copland's *Fanfare for a Common Man.* I asked the students to determine their own groups (each having three or four students) and create symbols, words, pictures, graphs, and markings of anything they heard, thought about, or felt as they listened to the two-minute *Fanfare* excerpt. During the first two days, the groups created a rough draft of their lis- tening maps, and on day three, they transferred their maps onto large pieces of plastic banquet-table covering. After practicing, the students then performed their maps on the last day of the project for each other and a few guest audience members.

I was struck by the groups' determination and focus; after all, these were the students for whom being on-task was a daily challenge. Without hesitation, the students selected their own communities of learners (small groups). Before most groups began creating the maps, the students focused their attention on three events: (1) who would be the first to draw the map, (2) who could hold pre- tend mallets in their hands and play the bass drum opening of the *Fanfare*, and (3) who could create the most interesting body gestures to accompany the music. Indeed, their music experience was active and multisensory.

As the students repeatedly listened to the music, it was evident that roles within the small groups had been clearly determined. Some students operated the audio equipment, some were the drawers, some led discussion, some edited by erasing the markings on the map, some created the final listening map, and some performed the music listening map for the class. The students reminded each other verbally, and with an occasional shove, when it was their turn to draw on the map. Students tended to perform the portions of the map they had contributed; in fact, they were quite territorial about "their parts" of the map. On the day of the mapping performance, a student was absent from one of the groups. The other students in the group insisted they could not perform that day, because Chris (the absentee) drew particular parts of the map and only he could perform those portions. I mentioned that, as a group, sometimes members had to assume others' responsibilities. The students grumbled, but they eventually practiced and performed Chris's mapping markings.

On the day of the music listening map performances, the students taped their maps onto the cafeteria walls and practiced performing them (a dress rehearsal). They decided where they would stand to perform, the order in which they would perform, whether or not they would use a pencil or other object to point to the map, and who would be the stereo and video operators. Typically one person in each group emerged as the organizer of the performance. During the performances, students seemed comfortable assisting those who did not point accurately to the group's map; they gave each other verbal instructions and, at times, pointed to the map in order to get the performing student back on track. In some cases, the maps consisted of stacked, vertical representations that required two or three students to perform the map simultaneously. One group created a skit to accompany its music listening map.

The students found creative ways to depict some of the musical events, stories or referential associations, and emotional-intuitive-feelingful import experienced as they listened repeatedly to *Fanfare*. By trusting these students and serving as a guide only upon the students' request, I observed the small group communities within the larger class community become full of energy, motivation, and discovery. Because the students enjoyed working collaboratively, at their own pace, and on a divergent musical task, students invested in and owned their music listening experiences and products (the group maps). The students taught me to trust in the learning partnership of junior and senior learners in the classroom.

To any skeptics in our music education profession, I acknowledge that creating communities of learners (small groups, classes, ensembles) has its practical challenges. Teachers need to learn how to establish communities of learners and how to balance the time and energy of music classes and ensembles so that student collaboration might occur. Additionally, understanding the group dynamics within communities of learners involves dealing with changing cultural dynamics in our schools, learners of diverse abilities and interests, complex human interactions, and a variety of personal communication styles. Yet, working collaboratively on a common goal and leading and learning from others are skills that transcend our assisting students in developing their music listening skills. These skills are performance skills, critiquing skills, analytical skills, and . . . life skills.

For the profession to become more informed about co-constructed music listening experiences within communities of learners, I call on researchers to investigate the social constructivist and constructionist perspectives related to music learning, especially small group, class, and ensemble music listening experiences. Those specific areas for investigation might include (1) the effect of group listeners' past experiences on repeated listenings to the same musical excerpt and on listening encounters with unfamiliar musics, (2) the nature of group responses to listening to various styles and genres of music, (3) the nature of group listeners' problem-solving/ordering/organizing processes when presented with new musical information, and (4) the nature of group listeners' reflective thinking about their music listening experiences and refining their knowledge about and feeling with the music.

CONCLUSION

When we listen to music, we listen as a member of a community, whether we listen alone or in the company of others. We hear music, have emotional responses, and intuitively feel what the music offers us, in large part because we are influenced by sociocultural values and rules for musical interpretation and response. We come as diverse individuals listening to diverse musical sounds, yet we are deeply connected by shared and personally constructed musical meaning.

The student listeners in the vignettes demonstrated several of the principles of teaching and learning that I proposed earlier in this chapter: (1) the musical familiarity and ownership students gain by repeatedly listening to a musical excerpt or piece, (2) the role of focusing students' attention by having them actively engaged in multisensory music listening tasks, and (3) the propensity for our students (even those with hearing impairments or other learning disabilities) to develop their music listening skills and experience the joy of music. A missing piece, however, from this vignette was the use of non-Western music as the piece with which they repeatedly interacted. How might that affect their group dynamic? Their multisensory responses?

The possibilities for our profession to unearth the complexity of perception, emotion, feeling, and intuition during music listening are endless. What is it about musical sounds that capture our attention, shape our imaginations, excite our emotions and feelings, incite interpretations, and connect us as social and musical beings? There is much yet to investigate and apply to music listening pedagogy. As a music education profession, we deal with humans and their unique interactions with other humans and musical soundscapes. And that might be reason enough to renew our vim and verve toward music listening research and pedagogy.

REFERENCES

Bamberger, J. (1991). *The mind behind the musical ear: How children develop musical intelligence*. Cambridge, MA: Harvard University Press.

Barrett, M. (2005). Invented notation in children's musical communication. In D. Miell, R. MacDonald, & D. Hargreaves (Eds.), *Musical communication* (pp. 117–142). Oxford, UK: Oxford University Press.

Blair, D. (2008, August). Do you hear what I hear? Musical maps and felt pathways of musical understanding. *Visions of Research in Music Education, 11*, Retrieved September 29, 2011, from http://www-usr.rider.edu~vrme/

Blair, D. V. (2006). *Look at what I heard! Music listening and student-created musical maps* (Unpublished doctoral dissertation). Oakland University.

Bowman, W. (2004). Cognition and the body: Perspectives from music education. In L. Bresler (Ed.), *Knowing bodies, moving minds: Toward embodied teaching and learning* (pp. 29–50). Dordrecht, The Netherlands: Kluwer.

Bruner, J. (1966). *Toward a theory of instruction*. Cambridge, MA: Harvard University Press.

Bundra, J. (1993). *A study of music listening processes through the verbal reports of school-aged children* (Unpublished doctoral dissertation). Northwestern University.

Cohen, V. (1980). *The emergence of musical gestures in kindergarten children* (Unpublished doctoral dissertation). University of Illinois, Urbana-Champaign.

Consortium of National Arts Education (1994). *National Standards for Arts Education: What Every Young American Should Know and Be Able to Do in the Arts*. Reston, VA: Music Educators National Conference.

Davidson, L., Scripp, L., & Welch, P. (1988). "Happy Birthday": Evidence for conflicts of perceptual knowledge and conceptual understanding. *Journal of Aesthetic Education, 22*(1), 65–74.

Dewey, J. (1910/1997). *How we think*. New York, NY: Dover Publications.

Dewey, J. (1933/1964). School conditions and the training of thought. In R. D. Archambault (Ed.), *John Dewey on education*. Chicago, IL: University of Chicago Press.

Dowling, W. J., Tillman, B., & Ayers, D. (2001). Memory and the experience of hearing music. *Music Perception, 19*, 249–276.

Dunn, R. (1994). *Perceptual modalities in music listening among third-grade students* (Unpublished doctoral dissertation). Northwestern University.

Dura, M. (1998). *The kinesthetic dimension of the music listening experience* (Unpublished doctoral dissertation). Northwestern University.

Dura, M. (2002). *Music education and the music listening experience*. Lewiston, NY: Edwin Mellen Press.

Flowers, P. (2000). The match between music excerpts and written descriptions by fifth and sixth graders. *Journal of Research in Music Education, 48*(3), 262–277.

Gardner, H. (1983). *Frames of mind*. New York, NY: Basic Books.

Geringer, J. (1983). The relationship of pitch-matching and pitch-discrimination abilities of preschool and fourth-grade students. *Journal of Research in Music Education, 31*(2), 93–99.

Geringer, J., & Madsen, C. (1984). Pitch and tempo discrimination in recorded orchestral music among musicians and nonmusicians. *Journal of Research in Music Education, 32*(3), 195–204.

Goldberger, N., Tarule, J., Clinchy, B., & Belenky, M. (Eds.). (1996). *Knowledge, difference, and power*. New York, NY: Basic Books.

Hair, H. (1977). Discrimination of tonal direction on verbal and nonverbal tasks by first grade children. *Journal of Research in Music Education, 25*(3), 197–210.

Heller, J., & Campbell, W. (1982). Music communication and cognition. *Bulletin of the Council for Research in Music Education, 72*, 1–15.

Jellison, J., & Flowers, P. (1991). Music interviews with disabled and nondisabled children. *Journal of Research in Music Education, 39*(4), 322–333.

Kerchner, J. L. (1996). *Perceptual and affective components of music listening experience as manifested in children's verbal, visual, and kinesthetic representations* (Unpublished doctoral dissertation). Northwestern University.

Kerchner, J. L. (2001). Children's verbal, visual, and kinesthetic responses: Insight into their music listening experience. *Bulletin for the Council of Research in Music Education, 146*, 35–51.

Kerchner, J. L. (2005). A world of sound to know and feel: Exploring children's verbal, visual, and kinesthetic responses to music. In M. Mans & B. W. Leung (Eds.), *Music in schools for all children: From research to effective practice* (pp. 21–33). Granada, Spain: University of Granada.

Kerchner, J. L. (2009). Drawing middle-schoolers' attention to music. In J. Kerchner & C. Abril (Eds.), *Musical experience in our lives: Things we learn and meanings we make* (pp. 183–198). Lanham, MD: Rowman & Littlefield.

Kerchner, J. L. (2013). *Music across the senses: Listening, learning, and making meaning*. New York, NY: Oxford University Press.

Lamont, A. M., Hargreaves, D. J., Marshall, N., & Tarrant, M. (2003). Young people's music in and out of school. *British Journal of Music Education, 20*(3), 1–13.

Madsen, C. K. (1979). Modulated beat discrimination among musicians and nonmusicians. *Journal of Research in Music Education, 27*(2), 57–67.

Meyer, L. (1956). *Emotion and meaning in music*. Chicago, IL: University of Chicago Press.

Miller, R. (1992). Affective response. In R. Colwell (Ed.), *Handbook of research on music teaching and learning* (pp. 414–424). New York, NY: Schirmer.

Montessori, M. (1946). *Education for a new world*. Madras, India: Kalakshetra Publications.

North, A., Hargreaves, D., & O'Neill, S. (2000). The importance of music to adolescents. *British Journal of Educational Psychology, 70*, 255–272.

North, A. C., Colley, A. M., & Hargreaves, D. J. (2003). Adolescents' perceptions of the music of male and female composers. *Psychology of Music, 31*(2), 139–154.

Richards, M. H. (1980). *Aesthetic foundations for thinking: Part 3—The ETM process*. Portola Valley, CA: Richards Institute of Music Education and Research.

Rogoff, B., Turkanis, C., & Bartlett, L. (Eds.). (2001). *Learning together: Children and adults in a school community*. New York, NY: Oxford University Press.

Schön, D. (1983). *The reflective practitioner: How professionals think in action*. London, UK: Temple Smith.

Small, C. (1998). *Musicking: The meanings of performing and listening*. Middletown, CT: Wesleyan University Press.

Stokes, W. A. (1990). *Intelligence and feeling: A philosophical examination of these concepts as interdependent factors in musical experience and music education* (Unpublished doctoral dissertation). Northwestern University.

Upitis, R. (1985). *Children's understanding of rhythm: The relationship between development and music training* (Unpublished doctoral dissertation). Harvard University.

Vygotsky, L. S. (1978). *Mind in society*. Cambridge, MA: Harvard University Press.

Wenger, E. (1998). *Communities of practice: Learning, meaning, and identity*. New York, NY: Cambridge University Press.

Zimmerman, M. (1981). Child development and music education. In *Documentary Report of the Ann Arbor Symposium: National Symposium on the Applications of Psychology to the Teaching and Learning of Music*. Reston, VA: MENC.

5

LIFE MUSIC AS A BEGINNING POINT

Connecting with the Intuitive Listener

Rob E. Dunn

IN THE UNITED STATES, most school systems provide elementary music experiences for all students and call for some music or art requirement in middle or junior high school. From that point on, the majority of music courses that are available are most often elective ensembles or theory courses. This sequence of courses does not fit every student, as evidenced by the falling numbers of enrollment in higher grades. It is questionable whether these music courses address everyday music listening skills as students pass through their schooling years and whether they have prepared students for lifelong listening when they leave.

For us to make music listening a more effective part of the music curriculum, we need to understand two important aspects of our students more fully: how they intuitively listen to music and how they use music in their everyday lives. Based on a deeper understanding of these two aspects, we may be able to design learning encounters with music listening that will be more immediately relevant and have a lifelong impact on our students.

DISSONANCE BETWEEN LIFE MUSIC AND SCHOOL MUSIC LISTENING

Woody (2004) stated, "Since the primary purpose of music—and the arts in general—is the communication of expression and emotion, teaching to improve sensitivities in students' listening skills can provide lifelong benefits to students" (p. 32). He describes what is sometimes called the traditional music appreciation model of music listening, combining a study of musical recordings (most often of classical music), historical and cultural facts, and musical elements. "The problem with this approach may be that it requires people to listen to music in a way that is very different from how they normally do it outside of a formal education setting" (p. 32). I think many educators recognize this disjunction as a rift between what might be called "school music" and what I will call "life music."

Researchers examining music in everyday life have documented evidence of this disjunction in school music listening and life music listening. For example, in their comparison of home and school music listening, Boal-Palheiros and Hargreaves (2001, 2004) found that home listening was by far preferred by preteens and teens. Compared to home listening, school listening offered them few opportunities to make choices; it was very structured and usually involved formal learning activities. The authors state, "Enjoyment and emotion are neglected in school music listening, yet they are among the most important functions of music for children and therefore deserve more attention at school. The cultural dissonance between school and home listening deserves greater attention" (2001, p. 116).

After questioning nearly 2,500 thirteen- to fourteen-year-olds, North, Hargreaves, and O'Neill (2000) concluded that there is little doubt that music is a vital part of life for most teenagers outside of school. But they too found a "disjunction" between music at home and school, including listening, which appears to widen in early adolescence, that needs to be addressed (p. 256).

A compelling example of the dissonance between school music and life music listening comes from Williamson's (2005) study examining music listening and music-making experiences of students not enrolled in music ensembles. She designed and taught an informal class called "My Music" as a substitute for the school's "Study Skills" course for twenty-one seventh and eighth graders. She found that school music experiences were associated with conceptual learning (perhaps, one might say, not relating to life music), which was cited as the main reason for not continuing to be in an ensemble. She begins the study with a telling personal example from one of the students:

> Victorio walked into my classroom on the first day of middle school general music class and announced, "I just want you to know, I hate music."...As an experienced teacher, I replied, "thank you for being honest. Now, I have a question for you. Do you hate music, or do you hate music class?"
>
> I learned some of the answers to my question as the semester advanced. Victorio did not *hate* music at all and was an avid fan of several local and nationally known rock bands. He was an active music listener and spent hours in his room memorizing song words and polishing fantastic air guitar

licks. On listening days, he enthusiastically brought in Nirvana recordings and provided insightful information concerning his musical choices to his peers. He also exhibited a strong sense of musical identity; while he was not currently performing…he saw himself as a very musical person. His peers viewed him as a musical guru, whose knowledge and opinions were frequently consulted and infrequently challenged. He did, however, hate school music, due to his conflict with his previous elementary general music teacher and the exclusion of his favorite genres in the music curriculum. (Williamson, 2005, pp. 1–2, emphasis in the original)

In the conclusion of their cross-sectional study of the musical activities and attitudes of eight- to fourteen-year-olds, Lamont, Hargreaves, Marshall, and Tarrant (2003) challenged school music programs to find ways to enhance the musical experience of all students, not just the musically gifted, and "to help all those who show an additional interest in music beyond the classroom to develop that, recognizing the value of their own contributions, developing their individual skills through valuable social, cultural, and primarily *musical* experiences and activities, and providing the confidence to partake in musical activities in whatever personal or social context they choose" (pp. 22–23, emphasis in the original). Bridging the gap between school music and life music listening is a challenge that we need to take seriously as a profession.

MUSIC LISTENING IN EVERYDAY LIFE

If bridging the cultural dissonance between life music and school music listening is crucial, we must ask ourselves this question: What do we know about how people listen to music in their everyday lives?

According to North, Hargreaves, and Hargreaves (2004), "The value of music in people's everyday lives depends on the uses they make of it and the degree to which they engage with it, which are in turn dependent on the contexts in which they hear it" (p. 41). Various researchers have examined music listening in everyday life in different ways and at different ages in an effort to tease out and better understand the complexities of people's music listening patterns.

From birth, listening to music is linked with affective expression, embedded in a social context, and may provide the beginnings of self-identity (Trehub & Nakata, 2001/2002), trends that appear to continue through life. A child entering preschool or kindergarten already has a relationship with his or her own life music and, more than we perhaps have understood, has already begun filling a personal mental library of intuitive musical knowing and is ready for more

(Sims, 2001). As children age, their affective sensitivity appears to increase, while their responses become more global and less simplistic (Rodriguez & Webster, 1997). There appear to be wide differences in individual listening patterns and responses to music listening that begin early and continue through later life (Sims, 2004; Woody & Burns, 2001).

Preteens and teens like listening to music at home because it can be done in private, they are able to exercise choice in what they listen to, and home offers shared enjoyment in significant social interactions (Boal-Palheiros & Hargreaves, 2001). Home listening is preferred over school music listening because it is less structured, often accompanies doing something else, and appears to serve primarily emotional functions (Boal-Palheiros & Hargreaves, 2004) embedded in a cultural and social fabric.

Music listening is an important part of students' lives in general, but more so outside of school. Listening to music outside of school increases with age. The reasons students give for listening to music include allowing them to explore their emotions or to change them (Lamont et al., 2003).

A study of more than two thousand adolescents (North et al., 2000) indicated teens listen to popular music "in order to enjoy the music; to be creative/use their imagination; to relieve boredom; to help get through difficult times; to be trendy/cool; to relieve tension/stress; to create an image for him/herself; to please friends; and to reduce loneliness" (p. 263). On the other hand, they felt that teens would choose to listen to classical music rather than popular music "in order to please parents and to please teachers" (p. 263). More females reported use of music as a means of mood regulation, while more males reported use of music as a means of creating an impression with others.

Looking at an older population, Sloboda, O'Neill, and Ivaldi (2001) wanted to move beyond retrospective reports by testing the Experience Sampling Method (ESM) to investigate music listening in real-life episodes. Eight nonmusicians, ages eighteen to forty, were given pagers for a week and were asked to complete self-report forms with scaled and open-ended questions each time the pager was activated. Music was present in 44 percent of the episodes, but few involved listening as the primary focus. When music was involved, participants were more positive, alert, and focused on the situation, more so if they had a choice over the music. In most cases, music was an accompaniment to doing something else. A major result of the study was that moderation of mood was greater when persons had power over the listening choices. The researchers noted DeNora's (1999) study where "only those few respondents who were over the age of 70 and those who were trained musicians tended to consider it antithetical to conceive of music as 'background' to anything.... This has major theoretical implications for how we conceptualize music use. The focused attentive and 'respectful' listening of the 'music lover' figures hardly at all in our present sample of non-musicians" (pp. 22–23).

An exploratory study with a naturalistic approach to music listening in everyday life was undertaken by North et al. (2004). More than three hundred cell phone owners (ages thirteen to seventy-eight, M = 25.96) received one text message each day for fourteen days, which prompted them to fill out a questionnaire about what they were hearing at the moment (or had heard); where they were, with whom, and why; and their emotional responses at the moment. Results included a high incidence of experiencing music. Contrary to similar previous studies, the majority of listening episodes were in social settings, taking place in the presence of other people rather than alone. The latter result may be due to increases in ease of access to music due to technological changes. When listeners were able to choose what they heard, they chose different styles for different reasons (e.g., *It helped me to concentrate, It helped me to create the right atmosphere, I enjoyed it*, etc.). Only 11.9 percent of responses involved what might be thought of as focused listening (*At home deliberately listening to music, Concert*). When asked if listening to music was the main task they were engaged in (no matter what category they had selected), 26.4 percent said yes. When asked to rate their level of attention to the music at the moment (0 = no attention, 10 = complete attention), the mean was 4.87 (standard deviation [SD] = 2.74), indicating that music was not the central focus. The most common reasons for listening were *enjoyment, pass the time, habit*, and *create the right atmosphere*, indicating that when respondents could choose, they seemed to do so "with little thought, and seemed to opt deliberately to be subjected to a form of 'sonic wallpaper'" (p. 72). Overall, the results indicated that these subjects consciously and actively employed music listening in their lives in different social and interpersonal contexts, engaging at different levels and psychological states.

Juslin and Laukka's (2004) study of 141 "ordinary" listeners (as opposed to "musician" listeners) between the ages of seventeen and seventy-four confirmed their hypothesis that emotion is strongly related to the main reasons people listen to music. In their discussion, they presented this summary of the ordinary listener:

From these findings emerges a picture of the ordinary music listener as someone who listens to music many times a day, often in mundane everyday contexts where music listening is not the primary activity. It's a listener who chooses to listen to music to a large extent because of the valued emotional experiences it offers. Music is used to enhance or change emotions (to relax, to arouse, to comfort) or to evoke emotional memories. The strongest emotional experiences often occur while listening alone (while listening attentively to the music), but it may also occur in social and emotionally charged situations. Positive emotions dominate in people's responses to music, with some of the most common emotions appearing to be feeling happy, relaxed, calm, moved, nostalgic, pleasurable, loving, sad, longing, or tender. (p. 232)

These studies indicate that humans appear to seek musical experiences on a daily basis. Behne (1997) investigated the development of *Musikerleben*, a German term without a simple English translation. He defined it as "the sum of psychic processes which accompany the experience of music in situations when music is in the focus of interest: When a person is not only hearing, but listening to and appreciating music" (p. 143). Behne cautions that this is not to be confused with music appreciation, a term often associated with more cognitive noticing. It is involved with aesthetic experiencing but does not need to be an intense, subjective experience, as it is sometimes viewed. It must be thought of as having many varying degrees of intensity and attention.

To investigate *Musikerleben*, Behne developed a questionnaire that asked subjects to rate a series of statements on a five-point scale. Each statement began, "When I listen to music" followed by a statement such as "it changes my mood" or "I like to hum and sing." A variable cluster analysis of data from several studies grouped test items into a list of nine listening styles that are worthy of note (Behne, 1997, p. 147):

- Compensating (e.g., it changes my mood; it really calms me down if I was excited before)
- Concentrated (e.g., I like to close my eyes; I like to follow the various themes)
- Emotional (e.g., I pay attention to what types of feelings are expressed through the music)
- Distancing (e.g., I like to identify the music style; I try to understand the words of the vocal part)
- Vegetative (e.g., it really gets under my skin; I sometimes feel my heart beat faster)
- Sentimental (e.g., I like to dream; I remember things of the past)
- Associative (e.g., I invent a story)
- Stimulative (e.g., I like to play it very loud; it makes me feel very aggressive)

- Diffuse (e.g., my attention is divided; I like to do other things besides just listening)

It should be noted that Behne's "compensating listening style" corresponds with allusions to mood regulation seen in other studies. His "diffuse listening style" corresponds with listening while doing something else.

That human beings may experience an emotional response when interacting with music would appear to be undeniable, likely from our own personal experiences. It is not surprising that a common manifestation of emotional response to music listening would be selecting music for the purposes of mood regulation, perhaps to lift, calm, excite, or match one's mood; to help one cope with profound feelings of loss; or even to make the time pass more quickly. Researchers are compiling evidence of people making deliberate musical listening choices to explore emotions or change them (Lamont et al., 2003; Juslin & Laukka, 2004); to match their emotions (Woody & Burns, 2001); to relieve boredom, to help get through difficult times, to relieve tension/stress, or to relieve loneliness (North et al., 2000); to evoke emotional memories (Juslin & Laukka, 2004); and to create the right atmosphere, as in a social situation, or to help concentration (North et al., 2004).

Sometimes musicians, music educators, or other musical experts may devalue the use of music to regulate our moods. Behne (1997) strongly disagreed with this view. He said:

> Musical experts tend to think of a "compensating" listening style [mood regulation] as an inappropriate behavior towards a piece of music as a work of art. As members of a cultural upper class they think of such a plebeian way of using music as a misuse which should be restricted to trivial music, to pop-songs, "Schlager", musical "Kitsch" and to products of low culture in general. But there is no empirical support for this attitude. In a study of concert audiences in Germany, Dollase, Rüsenberg and Stollenwerk (1986) found that visitors of so-called high-culture concerts (classics by Beethoven or serious entertainment) reported having more problems in their everyday lives than those who attended more popular events. The first rated themselves higher than the latter for using music as a means of consolation. Our own results support this view: having problems seems to enhance the intensity of *Musikerleben*. Adolescents use *Musikerleben* to help them cope with their problems and this, perhaps, is why for very many adolescents music is one of the most important things in the world. (p. 157)

Studies of everyday listening are necessarily based on self-reported data. Juslin and Laukka (2004) rightly reminded us to be cautious about such data, especially in the difficult area of processes involved in emotional responses to music; however, they believed ordinary listeners seem more qualified than musicologists or philosophers to resolve issues such as the experience and uses of music in everyday life and are capable of giving us reasonably valid data. Furthermore:

> The neglect of the social context of music listening (e.g., the way that listeners actually use music and experience it in real-life) might easily lead to a musicological view that emphasizes sublime, "aesthetic" emotions to "works of art". While this view may be popular with musicians, no doubt, it has limited validity in terms of fully accounting for how most *listeners* actually relate to music. The consequence might be theories of musical emotion that overly emphasize musical structures, and sources of emotion related to structure (e.g., expectancy, iconic sources) at the expense of the rich personal associations listeners have to music, and that may involve a wider variety of human emotions. Hence, we argue that a move to extend research on music and emotion to everyday life contexts represents one of the most promising avenues towards a more accurate understanding of how human beings experience emotions in connection with music. (p. 233, emphasis in the original)

While there may be extant musicological views that fit Juslin and Laukka's viewpoint, I would argue that views of philosophy of music education have moved in a direction seeking to more fully account for all aspects of a listener's experience. However, the importance of seeking to understand the music listening experience from the ordinary listener's viewpoint is an important one, particularly with the goal of bridging the gap between school music and life music listening in mind.

Intuitive Music Listening

Juslin and Laukka (2004) stressed the importance of coming to understand the ordinary listener. I believe the ordinary listener is an intuitive listener. Children's music listening lives begin before birth (Lacanuet, 1996), blossom in a mother's arms (Trehub & Nakata, 2001/2002), and branch out from there. The studies of music in everyday life (e.g., Behne, 1997; North et al., 2000) show that people engage with music without the aid of formal musical training nearly every day of their lives in some way that is meaningful to them within their own social and cultural context that is a part of natural, intuitive human experience. Intuitive musical knowing (Bamberger, 1978; Theiss, 1990) is a result of intuitive music listening and experiencing.

What is intuitive music listening? I define it as an active, innate, human process by which we meaningfully engage music through listening that enables us to create mental representations of the music, the creative "product" of intuitive listening. Mental representations, as an idea, can be traced back to Piaget, who believed that "children develop cognitive schemas through interaction with the environment and other persons" (Gruhn & Rauscher, 2002, p. 446) that help explain experienced phenomena, which can be further refined or altered through additional experiences. The term *mental representations* is common in many fields, including cognitive psychology, brain research, and constructivist learning theory, and is considered a key component of musical learning and skill development (Lehman & Davidson, 2002). One definition of mental representation is "the internal representation in memory" of interactions with an object or event (Lehman & Davidson, 2002, p. 545), including concepts and ideas.

Such mental representations create a holistic framework that becomes our vehicle for remembering, making sense of, and finding meaning in a given listening experience. In repeated listenings, this mental representation allows us to recognize the piece; to recall objective, subjective, imaginative, contextual, and emotional information about it; and to make adjustments and additions to the framework with each new encounter. It involves an individual's unique cognitive and affective responses to music that extend beyond the listener's technical understanding of the music. It is intuitive because no formal instruction is necessary for this to occur as far as we know, at least in healthy individuals. Focus of attention to some degree in some aspect must be present for the intuitive listening process to occur (Behne, 1997).

What might the intuitive music listening process look like? Let me suggest a model for discussion.

In the model of the intuitive listening process (see Figure 5.1), the listening experience begins with the *listener* and is filtered through *past experiences*, including cultural and social influences, beliefs, and attitudes (cf., Woody & Burns, 2001). The listener's well-being and mood state have a primary impact, especially on focus. Two external factors precede the intuitive listening experience. First, the specific *context* of the listening experience may have a small or profound effect (e.g., social factors, cultural factors, physical surroundings, time of day, events preceding or following) and may include motivational factors (e.g., listening for an assignment, listening to figure out a lead guitar part for a garage band, or listening for mood regulation). Second, the music itself is an external factor

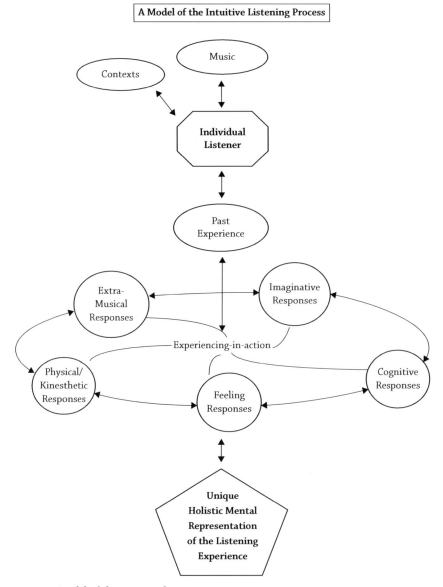

FIGURE 5.1   Model of the intuitive listening process.

(live or recorded), the result of the interaction between the specific musicians and the music (the musicians' particular "take" on the music, their skill level, incidental things that may happen during that performance such as a particularly great musical moment or an unanticipated misstep). The contexts, music, and past experiences combine with the following five types of responses: *extra-musical responses* (associations that are not music related can attach themselves to the music, e.g., "they're playing our song"); *imaginative responses* (more than passively experiencing the music, the person cocreates the experience along with the performers, making it come to life for herself or himself); *cognitive responses* (formal or factual noticing and responding to specific or overall aspects of or about the music); *affective responses* (affect or feeling is aroused, created, remembered); and *physical/kinesthetic responses* (the body responds to the music through outward motion, internal physiological response, or imagined/remembered kinesthetic motion). These different types of responses were documented in verbal reports of students of different ages in several studies (e.g., Bundra, 1994; Rodriguez & Webster, 1997; Dunn, 2008).

All of these factors come together in the listening experience through *experiencing in action*, a constant flux of experiencing during the event where we also interact with expectations of what may come and what does come and does not come as the music unfolds over time. The model in Figure 5.1 shows the interrelatedness of this holistic experience with arrows going in all directions for all the factors. The unlimited possibilities for interaction of the different factors suggest a possible explanation for the uniqueness of every individual listening experience, even for a piece one has heard multiple times from the same recording. All of this interaction results in an *inner mental representation* embodied with meaning, as known by the listener, and forms the basis for reflection, remembering and differentiating listening experiences. Further, as a result of this process, each listener's mental representation will be unique from other individuals', at least to some degree. As one ages and encounters new experiences, it is assumed that developmental growth occurs in all aspects of the model, although this remains to be demonstrated.

The question of musical meaning is too complex to be treated here (cf., Almén & Pearsall, 2006), but one possible view is that for musical meaning to occur, there must be enough focus of attention for the mental representation to gain some clarity and definition. Contrary to formal listening, however, the focus of attention may be minimal, as when music is playing in the background while doing something else. If the listener is still engaged with the music in a way that a mental representation is being created, the intuitive listening process is still engaged, although it may be at a minimal level (Lineburgh, 1994). If a person is listening to the music but responding mostly by reminiscing about the last time she heard "our song," the process is still engaged. The same would be true of someone working in the yard while listening and taking two sticks and beating rhythms on trash cans to the music. In a car full of teens talking over the blaring radio, someone may say, "Turn it up; this is my favorite part!" even though it seemed no one was paying attention. If asked, it's possible that none of these people could tell you anything about the instrumentation or meter or form; yet, they may still be engaged in ways that are personally meaningful, that allow them to recognize the music when they hear it again, and they are quite possibly adding response information to their holistic mental representations. It may also be that there are times when they are not noticing the music at all; in this case, the process is mute.

It is how we interact with all these aspects of the musical listening experience that make it special to us. It is more than just notes on a page. It is more than just sounds in the air. It is the listener interacting with context, musicians, past experience, and experiencing in action that have made it a part of every human culture in recorded history and personally important to us today.

INTUITIVE LISTENING CONTRASTED WITH FORMAL LISTENING

In school music, we have generally followed a more formal approach to music listening, reinforcing a dichotomy between life music and school music. When we teach formal music listening, the listener is no longer in charge of making all the decisions, or at least most of them, so the possible responses become somewhat limited as well. As we saw earlier, children preferred listening to music at home over school because they were able to exercise choice (Boal-Palheiros & Hargreaves, 2001), and when adults have control over selecting the music they hear, they were found to be more alert, positive, and focused (e.g., Sloboda et al., 2001). Teaching formal listening takes the listener out of the central role and puts someone else in charge—music listening becomes teacher directed.

In thinking about the typical kinds of teacher-directed listening experiences in schools and colleges for both general and music students, when contrasted with the intuitive listening model, what changes? For discussion, and in very simplistic terms, it appears that the focus of such formal learning would fall under cognitive responses, that is, spending most of the listening time and energy in having students looking for, identifying, and responding to things about the formal aspects and facts of the music (see Figure 5.2). The cognitive responses are experienced through teacher-directed activities and experiences. In so doing, what may often occur is a separation of the other types of responses from the cognitive response, perhaps a consideration of the "parts," or of one "part" (cognitive response), to the extent that one never really gets back to the "whole" of musical experience while in the classroom. Inherent, too, may be a devaluing of these other responses involved in the intuitive music listening experience. Perhaps it is here that school music and life music begin to diverge. If school music becomes this one-dimensional, it is not only about formal learning; it is

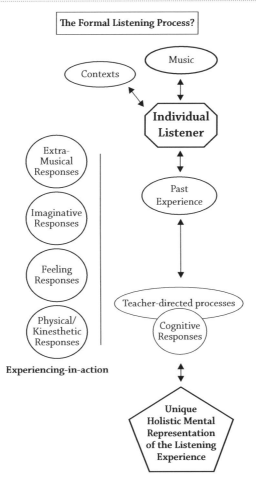

FIGURE 5.2 The formal listening process?

also about loss—of any aspect of choice, of music one can relate to, and of the musical experience as one knows how to relate with it and loves it.

Certainly, teacher-directed learning has been the model for music teaching for hundreds of years and has been fundamental to music education in the schools. Many aspects of effective teaching and learning can take place in the teacher-directed model. However, it is incumbent on educators to be reflective about practice and to focus on the most important outcome: What is best for enhancing our students' lifelong ability to meaningfully engage with music independently, in this case, with music listening? Should only teacher-directed learning be involved? Of course not.

In our quest to promote only formalized music learning in school, we may cause children to lose touch with their intuitive musical sense or "knowing"

(Bamberger, 1978). Bamberger (1982) observed that as students gained in their ability to read and write music, they lost their ability to be sensitive to their intuitive figural sense of rhythm; she termed this the "wipe-out" phenomenon. Perhaps many of us have experienced this with lessons on our instruments, where striving for better technique or tone led to a loss of musicality, hopefully only temporarily. In listening to music, perhaps this wipe-out phenomenon is a factor as well. In a music theory course, this could easily happen. Being taught and tested for a semester to listen for form in Mozart symphonies could cause one to miss listening for the "music" outside of class as well, for example.

TWO TYPES OF LISTENING

To sum up this section on the listening process, perhaps we can contrast the two types of listening, intuitive and formal, by envisioning each of them on a separate continuum (see Figure 5.3). Notice that each continuum moves from left to right, indicating progression in age and experience. As represented by the Intuitive Listening Continuum, the listening life of intuitive listeners begins certainly from birth (Trehub & Nakata, 2001/2002) and likely before (Lacanuet, 1996). They are immediately *beginning listeners*, with the intuitive musical listening process engaged as they come to know their life music. By the time they enter preschool or kindergarten, might they be called *experienced listeners*? Not fully developed, no, but they are experienced in certain aspects of their musical lives, fully engaged in a lifelong development of intuitive musical knowing (Bamberger, 1978), including an ever-growing mental library of musical mental representations from past experience. We need to acknowledge that children have musical lives outside of school (hopefully rich ones) and that some teens may be *experienced listeners*, sometimes even *highly experienced listeners* who may have more sophisticated ears than some adults with formal training. As not all people may become highly experienced listeners (something that would require real focus and energy), I have placed that term in brackets in the intuitive listening continuum. Victorio, the young man in middle school cited earlier with such a vast knowledge of Nirvana who could perform complex guitar licks (Williamson, 2005), would be an example of a highly experienced listener. For intuitive listening, this can happen without formal training. Beyond the early years of childhood, I am not sure if there is a boundary for when one can become an experienced intuitive listener.

A major factor in becoming an experienced listener, especially in becoming a highly experienced listener, is focus. For a mental representation of the music listening experience to be created, a degree of focus must be present. It seems

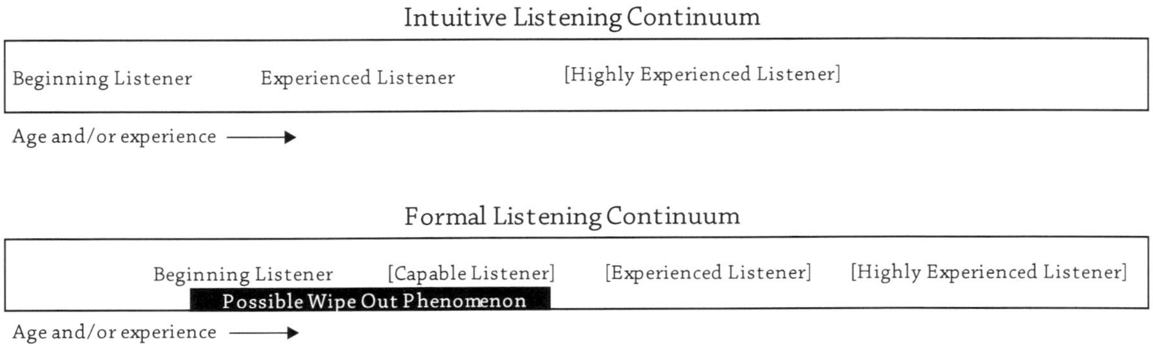

Intuitive Listening Continuum

Beginning Listener   Experienced Listener   [Highly Experienced Listener]

Age and/or experience ⟶

Formal Listening Continuum

Beginning Listener   [Capable Listener]   [Experienced Listener]   [Highly Experienced Listener]

Possible Wipe Out Phenomenon

Age and/or experience ⟶

FIGURE 5.3   Two listening continua contrasted.

logical that with a greater degree of focus on the listening experience, there will be more clarity and depth to the experience, giving more clarity and definition to the mental representation of the experience and making possible more connections with other such experiences.

On the Formal Listening Continuum, unless one is a gifted prodigy, it is unlikely that a child would become a beginning listener in a formal way until formal instruction begins. This is shown by placing *beginning listener* sometime after birth, depending on when formal instruction is encountered. Due to the length of time it takes to begin to perceive specific individual elements (beat, rhythm, melody, pitch, meter, dynamics, form, etc.), it may take quite some time to be able to hear elements combining (e.g., Sims's 1991 study of decentration) or hear them from a large-scale viewpoint. Cutietta's (e.g., 1985, 1993; see also Taetle & Cutietta, 2002) work suggests that this traditional musical element approach, common to many music curricula, is counter to the way the mind intuitively engages music. According to Cutietta, a more sound approach would be nonelemental, beginning by helping children make holistic categorizations based in musical moods or styles. The traditional focus on the cognitive aspects of music listening may lead to a wipe-out phenomenon (referred to earlier; Bamberger, 1982) as the intuitive experiencing of the music is lost to seeking formal understanding, hopefully only for a while. In formal listening, everyone is a beginning listener at some point. The brackets indicate that unless some training occurs, a person is unlikely to move toward becoming a *capable listener*. When one thinks about it, few become *experienced listeners* in formal listening, and even fewer become *highly experienced* in this kind of listening. This is cause to wonder why this is the case, and whether something can be done to change it.

HOW TO MOVE FORWARD

Is there no way to bridge the gap between intuitive listening and formal listening? In the broader picture, this question brings us to where we began, with the question of how to resolve the dissonance between life music and school music.

Discovering positive answers to these questions will require us to help students find relevance and meaning in music listening experiences in school. I suggest that resolving the dissonance between life music and school music will require moving away from the traditional formal listening model and toward a model more closely based on the intuitive listening model. This will involve the following:

1. Engaging and building upon the intuitive music listening process students have known since birth

2. Realizing that students are already experienced music listeners to some degree (perhaps even highly experienced listeners) when they enter our classrooms; while they may not have all the vocabulary for what they already know, they are often much more sophisticated listeners than we comprehend

3. Engaging students in ways that they find personally meaningful and motivating, including tasks that have real-world, even lifelong relevance

4. Either bringing their life music into the classroom or asking them to apply what they are learning using their own life music for class assignments as part of the curriculum

5. Involving students in self-constructed learning via listening experiences presented through problem solving, either in individual or group projects

Let me share a few ideas of ways these five principles may be put into practice to hopefully stimulate further discussion and action.

Musical Maps

Musical maps have sometimes been used as aids for guided listening in teacher-directed lessons and materials. More recently, they have been employed with success as a musical problem-solving task to aid in self-constructed learning in the classroom.

A musical map is an iconlike visual representation of an individual's intuitive, musical sense of a piece. The goal of creating a musical map is to have the map look like the music sounds to its creator. The intent of this style of mapping is to capture the figural musical gesture of each phrase rather than specific metric and pitch information. The figures in the drawings may be similar to the trace of an expressive conductor's conducting pattern with a few metric and melodic details. Information encoded in the figural maps may include groupings, motives, rhythms, form, energy, articulation, and dynamics (Dunn, 1997).

Working with students in a music listening course, I asked twenty-nine non-music majors to create their own individual musical maps (Dunn, 1997). Students were introduced to an existing map (Mozart, Symphony no. 41, movement 3), then asked to map the opening notes of "Eine Kleine Nachmusik," movement 2, and share the results with the group. Finally, they were given access to a recording of the first minute and forty seconds of Delibe's "Waltz" from *Coppelia*, a piece unfamiliar to them. They took it home over a weekend and brought their maps back to share with the class the following week. They reflected in writing on creating their maps, traced their maps for the group as the music played, then reflected on watching others' maps. Next, they were asked to trace several others' maps while the music played and reflect a final time. Their maps and verbal reports were analyzed. The maps appeared to be a successful vehicle for making an abstract listening experience concrete. Said one student, "It wasn't very hard to see that what I had on paper looked like what I was hearing" (p. 53). Several comments indicated students were thinking in sound as they worked to transform their inner listening experience into a visual representation.

More recently, a student taking the same course who was a musician with years of training responded to the assignment with this comment:

The idea of mapping has influenced the way I think about listening to music. Before this class I always knew music could mean something different to different people but I never realized people could listen to music differently. Through mapping I saw that people heard different things than I did. Their maps were tangible representations of the fact that though we listened to the same piece of music it actually sounded different to different people. Some heard sharp lines, others curves, and some mapped sounds I hadn't even noticed even though I listened to the piece at least twenty times. At first I looked at their maps and to be quite honest thought—wow they are wrong. But when they traced their own maps I realized that theirs were as right to them as mine was to me. It still baffles me that people can hear different things in the same piece of music but it makes me appreciate both music and the human brain all the more. It also turns one piece of music into fourteen when the class shares their maps as I see/hear things I did not before. Fascinating really. (Dunn, 2005).

After this initial mapping experience, students were asked to map a piece from their own music libraries, then bring a recording and share their maps with the class. This was a pattern for the course: any problem-solving listening strategy we explored in class, they were asked to apply to a piece from their own music library. Another mapping assignment had them create a background musical map, ignoring the melodic elements of the music. This was a challenge for most of the students, but it was an enlightening experience that led to a great deal of discussion after sharing their maps. One of the delightful outcomes was students telling me how many pieces they would go through before selecting just the right piece, sometimes taking hours of listening before they even started on the actual assignment.

As she considered the results of her mapping study observing small groups of fifth-grade students, Blair (2008) found a connection with Bamberger's term "felt paths" (Bamberger, 1991, p. 10), internalized sequences of actions, such as when one performs a well-learned piece on an instrument. Blair extended this term to "felt pathways" in the case of music listening, saying she believed "that through tools like creating musical maps, students can form pathways of knowing and feeling while *listening* to music, in addition to paths that Bamberger describes that are formed when performing music" (p. 11). They are internally created pathways, the result of imaginative response of mind and body as one listens. The maps provide a concrete, visual frame for reliving the listening experience, for further exploration of the experience, and for sharing the listening experience with others. Since the students all worked with the same piece, they were given an opportunity to view others' similar yet unique felt pathways when they shared their musical maps in the "performances."

Kerchner (2009) used a case study (Stake, 1995) to follow her experience introducing mapping as part of teaching a middle school general music class (grades six through eight) made up of mostly at-risk and a few gifted students not interested in participating in music ensembles. She documented the process of the students' first experience following another's map, being drawn into reworking parts of that map to make it look right, and eventually buying into a project of taking on a piece and finding a way to map it on their own or in small groups. The presentation day became a big event in their lives, both musically and socially. Said Kerchner: "I wondered how many times in their schooling these adolescents would encounter situations that invited creative problem-solving, in which their unique solutions would be accepted and celebrated because they were meaningful to *them,* instead of fitting a construct imposed by a teacher" (p. 28). She makes the connection with Vygotsky (1978) that learning is internalized through a contextualized process involving past and present experiences, cultural artifacts, and interaction with peers and adults. This study makes a strong case for self-constructed listening experiences in the school and using problem-solving tasks such as mapping to give students control over the outcome of a music listening learning task. Particularly compelling is the success she finds with the type of student who does not typically respond to the traditional model of general music or ensemble curriculum.

Creating Soundtracks for Film Clips

Students can find personal meaning and relevance when real-world problem-solving tasks involving music are brought into the classroom. As one example,

Greher (2001, 2002) found putting music to film clips was a real-world activity middle school students could relate to. "Having students experiment with putting music and sound effects against film to see how different moods, rhythms and melodies affect the pacing and feel of a film, [put] them at the center of their learning" (Greher, 2002, p. 21). Despite working through a number of challenges, students moved from skepticism to being willing participants, engrossed in the project and passionate about what they were creating. Students became active listeners, engaged a variety of genres they may not have willingly listened to before, and did so in a supportive social environment. This type of problem-solving approach to music listening is worthy of emulation in other types of real-world activities.

Listening Literacy

Another idea that may help us bridge the gap between life music and school music is an expanded idea of music literacy. Borrowing from the world of literacy, Broomhead (2008) applied the concept of multiliteracies (Cope & Kalantzis, 2000) to music education. In the expanded view of multiliteracies, literacy is no longer limited to drawing meaning from written texts. Texts are understood to be multimodal representations of meaning, such as visual, aural, gestural/kinesthetic, tactile, oral, and spatial. For example, to understand an event in history, texts might include a personal history, photographs, memorabilia, visiting where it took place, films, a visit from a participant, and writing about the experience.

Using this approach, Broomhead similarly takes music literacy beyond reading and writing music. He defines music literacy as the ability to act appropriately with and make meaning from a variety of musical texts. A musical text can be anything that a creator has intentionally embodied with meaning, such as musical scores, a conductor's movements, an instrument, a performance, and even listening to a recording.

Music *listening* literacy, according to Broomhead, is "the ability to negotiate listening-oriented texts such as live performances, recordings on CD, radio and other media, and fellow ensemble members" (Broomhead, 2008, p. 1). Some of the listening literacies that can be taught include those we would expect: the ability to match sounds with symbols, recognize form and patterns, and recognize instruments. Some are more unexpected: being open to new sounds, connecting music with our inner life, connecting our personal experience to those of others through music, and feeling comfort through music. He believed that a comprehensive list is probably not possible; once a text is chosen, the literacies within that text may be identified and explored.

The idea of music listening literacy in this expanded view of interpreting texts has some interesting implications. Exploring the topics of connecting music to our inner life and connecting our personal experience to those of others through music, for example, may be ways to address more of the intuitive listening process, as well as a way to access students' life music experiences.

The Role of Roles

Reimer (2003) proposed that different roles in music require interrelated and varied aspects of intelligence: composing, performing, improvising, listening, music theory, musicology, and music teaching. It seems useful to apply the idea of roles to the listener and wonder if there is any effect on the listening experience when the role is changed. Approached from the intuitive music listening process, how does one listen as a performer? Does one listen differently as an ensemble conductor? Does that have an effect on a person's listening experience? Would that be something worthwhile to develop in our students? How would one do that?

One might adapt the ensemble critique form developed by the *Arts Propel* Project (Winner, Davidson, & Scripp, 1992) to put students in the role of thinking and listening as an ensemble director (Bauer, 2008). Using this form, students are asked to record and listen to their own performance. They use the form to critique their own individual performance, as well as the ensemble's performance, and to list suggestions for remedying problems they may have heard. This can be the departure point for student-led activities, including discussion, small and large group rehearsal, informed individual practice, and further recording for critique. Putting students into the role normally held by the teacher, designed to include the different aspects of intuitive listening, may have a long-term impact.

Obviously, a high-level conductor does much more than find and correct simple errors; the ensemble critique form may be a way to begin to address what a truly fine conductor does as he or she listens and shapes a wonderfully musical performance. Another approach might be to buy two scores for each piece, and each day, have one student sit by the director in an ensemble and simply follow along with the extra score, then hold a brief discussion after class. Would that make a long-term difference? Would a percussionist's listening experience be different from the one she has had in the back of the room since sixth-grade band? Would that be important? Of course, one hopes the director is providing a model worth listening to/watching.

What other listening roles might be important to be explored? Using Reimer's list, a composer, an improviser, a music theorist, a musicologist (perhaps an ethnomusicologist?), even a music teacher? Perhaps a record producer, an American

Idol judge, a music critic? It seems likely that there is potential for exploration and study here as well.

New Courses

New courses for the "general student" in secondary schools need to be developed focusing on or including music listening as a primary element. Courses for highly experienced listeners—or to help develop skills to become highly developed listeners—that are not based on the typical music training model could be developed. What might a listening course that focuses on self-constructed learning using the intuitive listening process look like? Popular music, music from local culture, or music from many cultures might be included, as guided and selected by the teacher and the students. Perhaps a course could be organized simply around what makes a piece of music "great," sampling from the vast array of available musics, current and bygone, popular and classical and world music, but ignoring labels that have divided styles and periods in the past. Hargreaves, Marshall, and North (2003) noted that in this time of globalization and the Internet, people have nearly instant access to and unlimited choice of any kind of music in many different venues, and they make up their own minds; determining what is "serious" music and what is "popular" music is less important or meaningful than the music itself. And we have yet to explore all the possibilities technology has to offer for music listening learning experiences as well.

CONCLUSION

As we look forward, music listening needs to move from the shadows to a focus of music instruction that is meaningful to students. Finding ways to narrow or eradicate the gap between school music and life music is crucial. Effective learning experiences in music listening will involve the full range of the intuitive listening process and will recognize and build upon the musical listening experience of the individual. I have provided just a few suggestions of how this may be done, but the opportunities for exploration in this area are tremendous, especially as we seek to more clearly define and connect with the ways people use music in everyday life.

ACKNOWLEDGMENT

Portions of this chapter appeared in: Dunn, Robert E. (2011). Contemporary Research on Music Listening: A Holistic View. In R. Colwell and P. Webster (Eds.), *The MENC Research Handbook on Music Learning, Volume 2: Applications*. New York: Oxford University Press.

REFERENCES

Almén, B., & Pearsall, E. (Eds.). (2006). *Approaches to meaning in music*. Bloomington, IN: Indiana University Press.

Bamberger, J. (1978). Intuitive and formal musical knowing: Parables of cognitive dissonance. In S. S. Madeja (Ed.), *The arts, cognition and basic skills* (pp. 173–209). St. Louis, MO: CEMREL.

Bamberger, J. (1982). Revisiting children's descriptions of simple rhythms: A function for reflection-in-action. In S. Strauss (Ed.), *U-shaped behavioural growth* (pp. 191–226). New York, NY: Academic Press.

Bamberger, J. (1991). *The mind behind the musical ear: How children develop musical intelligence*. Cambridge, MA: Harvard University Press.

Bauer, W. I. (2008). Metacognition and middle school band students. *Journal of Band Research*, 43, 50–63.

Behne, K. (1997). The development of 'Musikerleben' in adolescence: How and why young people listen to music. In I. Deliège & J. Sloboda (Eds.), *Perception and cognition of music* (pp. 143–159). Hove, UK: Psychology Press.

Blair, D. V. (2008). Do you hear what I hear?: Musical maps and felt pathways of musical understanding. *Visions of Research in Music Education*, 11. doi:10.1117/12.850319

Boal-Palheiros, G. M., & Hargreaves, D. J. (2001). Listening to music at home and at school. *British Journal of Music Education*, 18(2), 103–118. doi:10.1017/S0265051701000213

Boal-Palheiros, G. M., & Hargreaves, D. J. (2004). Children's modes of listening to music at home and at school (in England and Portugal). *Bulletin of the Council for Research in Music Education*, 161/162, 39–46.

Broomhead, P. (2008, February). *Literacy in the content area: It means teach music*. Paper presented at the meeting of the Utah Music Educators Association, St. George, UT.

Bundra, J. I. (1994). *A study of music listening processes through the verbal reports of school-aged children* (Unpublished doctoral dissertation). Northwestern University, Evanston, IL.

Cope, B., & Kalantzis, M. (Eds.). (2000). *Multiliteracies: Literacy learning and the design of social futures*. New York, NY: Routledge.

Cutietta, R. A. (1985). An analysis of musical hypotheses created by the 11-16 year-old recall of familiar learner. *Bulletin of the Council for Research in Music Education*, 84, 1–13.

Cutietta, R. A. (1993). The musical elements: Who said they're right? *Music Educators Journal*, 79(9), 48–53.

DeNora, T. (1999). Music as a technology of the self. *Poetics*, 27(1), 31–56.

Dollase, R., Rüsenberg, M., & Stollenwerk, H. (1986). *Demoskopie im konzertsaal*. Mainz, Germany: Schott.

Dunn, R. E. (1997). Creative thinking and music listening. *Research Studies in Music Education*, 8(1), 42–55.

Dunn, R. E. (2005). [Written comment]. Unpublished raw data.

Dunn, R. E. (2008). The effect of auditory, visual or kinesthetic perceptual strengths on music listening. *Contributions to Music Education*, 35, 47–78.

Greher, G. R. (2001). Lessons in analytical listening from the reel world. *General Music Today*, 15(9), 9–15. doi:10.1177/10483713010150010104

Greher, G. R. (2002). *"Picture This!" (c)1997: An interactive listening environment for middle school general music* (Unpublished doctoral dissertation). Columbia University Teachers College, New York, NY.

Gruhn, W., & Rauscher, F. H. (2002). The neurobiology of music cognition and learning. In R. Colwell & C. Richardson (Eds.), *The new handbook of research on music teaching and learning* (pp. 445–460). New York, NY: Oxford University Press.

Hargreaves, D. J., Marshall, N. A., & North, A. C. (2003). Music education in the twenty-first century: A psychological perspective. *British Journal of Music Education, 20*(2), 147–163. doi:10.1017/S0265051703005357

Juslin, P. N., & Laukka, P. (2004). Expression, perception, and induction of musical emotions: A review and a questionnaire study of everyday listening. *Journal of New Music Research, 33*(3), 217–238. doi:10.1080/0929821042000317813

Kerchner, J. L. (2009). Drawing middle-schoolers' attention to music. In J. L. Kerchner & C. R. Abril (Eds.), *Music experience throughout our lives: Things we learn and meanings we make* (pp. 183–198). Lanham, MD: Rowman & Littlefield.

Lacanuet, J. (1996). Prenatal auditory experience. In L. Deliege & J. Sloboda (Eds.), *Musical beginnings: Origins and development of musical competence* (pp. 3–34). Oxford, UK: Oxford University Press.

Lamont, A., Hargreaves, D. J., Marshall, N. A., & Tarrant, M. (2003). Young people's music in and out of school. *British Journal of Music Education, 20*(3), 229–241. doi:10.1017/S0265051703005412

Lehman, A. C., & Davidson, J. W. (2002). Taking an acquired skills perspective on music performance. In R. Colwell & C. Richardson (Eds.), *The new handbook of research on music teaching and learning* (pp. 445–460). New York, NY: Oxford University Press.

Lineburgh, N. E. (1994). *The effects of exposure to musical prototypes on the stylistic discrimination ability of kindergarten and second-grade children* (Unpublished doctoral dissertation). Kent State University, Kent, OH.

North, A. C., Hargreaves, D. J., & Hargreaves, J. J. (2004). Uses of music in everyday life. *Music Perception, 22*(1), 41–77. doi:10.1525/mp.2004.22.1.41

North, A. C., Hargreaves, D. J., & O'Neill, S. A. (2000). The importance of music to adolescents. *British Journal of Educational Psychology, 70*(2), 255–272. doi:10.1348/00709900158083

Reimer, B. (2003). *A philosophy of music education: Advancing the vision* (3rd ed.). Upper Saddle River, NJ: Prentice Hall.

Rodriguez, C. X., & Webster, P. R. (1997). Development of children's verbal interpretative responses to music listening. *Bulletin of the Council for Research in Music Education, 134,* 9–30.

Sims, W. L. (1991). Effects of instruction and task format on preschool children's ability to demonstrate single and combined music concept discrimination. *Journal of Research in Music Education, 39*(4), 298–310.

Sims, W. L. (2001). Characteristics of preschool children's individual music listening during free choice time. *Bulletin of the Council for Research in Music Education, 149,* 53–63.

Sims, W. L. (2004). What I've learned about research from young children. *Update: Applications of Research in Music Education, 23*(1), 4–13.

Sloboda, J. A., O'Neill, S. A., & Ivaldi, A. (2001). Functions of music in everyday life: An exploratory study using the Experience Sampling Method. *Musicae Scientiae, 5*(1), 9–32.

Stake, R. E. (1995). *The art of case study research.* Thousand Oaks, CA: Sage Publications.

Taetle, L., & Cutietta, R. A. (2002). Learning theories as roots of current musical practice. In R. Colwell & C. Richardson (Eds.), *The new handbook of research on music teaching and learning* (pp. 279–298). New York, NY: Oxford University Press.

Theiss, J. A. (1990). *The relationship of tonal and human phenomena in the musical experience of fourth-grade children* (Unpublished doctoral dissertation). University of Maryland, College Park, MD.

Trehub, S. E., & Nakata, T. (2001/2002). Emotion and music in infancy. *Musicae Scientiae, Special Issue*, 37–61.

Vygotsky, L. S. (1978). *Mind in society: The development of higher psychological processes.* Cambridge, MA: Harvard University Press.

Williamson, S. J. (2005). *"My music": The music making and listening experiences of seventh and eighth graders not enrolled in school music ensembles* (Unpublished doctoral dissertation). University of Washington, Seattle, WA.

Winner, E., Davidson, L., & Scripp, L. (Eds.). (1992). *Arts Propel: A handbook for music.* Princeton, NJ: Educational Testing Service.

Woody, R. H. (2004). Reality-based music listening in the classroom: Considering students' natural responses to music. *General Music Today, 17*(2), 32–39.

Woody, R. H., & Burns, K. J. (2001). Predicting music appreciation with past emotional responses to music. *Journal of Research in Music Education, 49*(1), 57–70.

6

MUSIC LISTENING SPACES

Carlos Xavier Rodriguez

IN AN ERA characterized by rapid, inexorable change, it is challenging to account for all the reasons why and ways in which music listening activity has changed during these past twenty-five years. Music education researchers have borrowed perspectives from music theory, psychology, philosophy, and sociology to study the nature of the music listening experience. For this reason, I focus on describing music listening in a manner that relates to each of these areas and holds great potential for helping us understand how and why people listen to music. It is the music listening "space," an experiential artifact in which the orientation of oneself in relation to the musical sounds, the environment, and other people is understood. In this chapter I illustrate musical spaces by exploring some of their contributing influences. I then suggest how musical listening spaces have been shaped by various events in American music history and describe current and emerging attributes of listening spaces. Finally, I propose some ways we might use the idea of music listening spaces in music teacher education programs.

The previously indicated contributing influences represent a diverse range of scholarly literature. Some of these studies are *psychoacoustical,* establishing the parameters for human auditory perception. *Cognitive* studies concern the patterned use of elements in musical works and the role of musical structure in the listening experience. Other studies concern the *social* aspects of listening, an area for which we have accumulated much new information in the past decade. Finally, there are *psychological* aspects of listening that must be considered, which take into consideration the interconnected mental reference points that coordinate multiple facets of the listening experience.

DEFINING MUSIC LISTENING SPACES

There is compelling evidence that humans rely on knowing where a sound is coming from to make sense of it. Bregman (1990) described "auditory scene analysis" as the ability to segregate streams of sound amidst numerous competing elements. Paramount to this segregation skill is determining the sound location, allowing the listener to focus and lock in on an auditory stream emanating from that point. This so-called "cocktail party effect" (Cherry, 1953) requires normal hearing in both ears to quickly and accurately detect sound location. Broadbent (1954) investigated hearing tasks involving both ears and found that spatial delineation of auditory signals led to more accurate attention and memory. He further found that subjects in his dichotic listening paradigm, which simultaneously presented different sets of digits to each ear, reported digits heard in one ear first, followed by digits heard in the other ear, indicating that spatial differentiation influences the perceptual mechanism to temporally reorder sounds in memory. These studies support the conclusion that sound location mediates hearing and memory, suggesting that the spatial orientation of musical sound is probably more influential to the listening experience than we typically acknowledge.

In contrast to studies that define spatial attributes in terms of sound localization, others assert it arises from musical materials; that is, the musical sounds themselves have space, irrespective of their origination point. This seemingly implausible statement was defended by McDermott (1972):

> Simply said, the idea of a musical space needs an apology, for the space of the everyday world of touch, vision, objects, movements, etc. tends to be made by ordinary discourse into a rigid conceptual edifice. Indeed, musical space is a patent nonsense to some people I have talked with. For them, space is a safe, secure, well-ordered, and self-evident domain, which will not suffer an association with impalpable sounds moving in time.... This objection proves unreasonable. Philosophers and scientists who attempt to define physical space—and there have been many—find that the logical underpinnings of our conception of the space around us are often hazy and furtive, and indeed do not possess the stability ascribed to them in daily life. (p. 489)

To support McDermott's justification for conceptualizing musical space, I have noticed that teaching pitch concepts requires spatial reasoning: we anticipate patterns of pitches to "ascend" and "descend." Alternatively, we may say pitches move "up and down," the latter perhaps more relevant to space than the former. It is quite challenging to derive any explanation of pitch that does not invoke space. However, different instruments produce their own spatial nomenclatures. For example, pianists conceptualize pitch space on a left-to-right continuum, harpists on a near-to-far continuum, and guitarists on an inverse high–low continuum (i.e., higher notes are closer to the ground and lower notes are further from the ground, perhaps giving guitarists little in common, pitch space–wise, with singers, and suggesting that multiple nomenclatures are tolerated and even interdependent, such as when playing guitar and singing simultaneously). Levitin (2006) claimed that these spatial dimensions were relatively salient to the human auditory system, with the left–right continuum most sensitive, the forward–back continuum next sensitive, and the up–down continuum least sensitive.

If space is related to pitch, it then might well also apply to texture. For example, homophony is melody and accompaniment, streams of melodic and harmonic material spatially separated, with melody occupying a space "above" the accompaniment (that it is notated this way strengthens this spatial relationship). Counterpoint is defined by the space between notes, the various species articulated by the relative movement of independent lines. Monophony suggests open space around a single stream of notes. Heterophony extends monophonic space horizontally, by presenting multiple, subtle timing variations of sound, and vertically, since octaves result from natural differences in instruments and/or voice types.

Langer (1953) acknowledged musical space conceptually as it relates to tonality but viewed it as conflicting with her conception of virtual time in music and quite different from what we generally mean by "space":

> The frequent references to "musical space" in the technical literature are not purely metaphorical; there are definitely spatial illusions created in music, quite apart from the phenomenon of volume, which is literally spatial, and the fact that movement logically involves space, which may be taking movement too literally. "Tonal space" is a different thing, a genuine semblance of distance and scope. It derives from harmony rather than from either movement or fullness of tone. The reason is, I believe, that harmonic structure gives our hearing an *orientation* in the tonal system, from which we perceive musical elements as holding *places* in an ideal range. But the space of music is never made wholly perceptible, as the fabric of musical time is; it is really an attribute of musical time, an appearance that serves to develop the temporal realm in more than one dimension. Space, in music, is a *secondary illusion*. But primary or secondary, it is thoroughly "virtual," i.e., unrelated to the space of actual experience. (p. 117)

In an opposing view, Sager (2006), in her analysis of John Blacking's writings on the Venda, asserted that Blacking's "virtual time" was analogous to her "musical space" (p. 143), both supporting the transcendent state of "other self," which Sager and Blacking believed humans need to ensure personal development and social well-being.

Space relates to other aspects of music as well, such as its structure and analysis. Morgan (1980) described the spatiality of musical compositions from the theorist's perspective:

> ... The spatial model is useful primarily with respect to the "aggregate" quality of musical relationships viewed as a totality, a quality that is admittedly conditioned by the specific order in which these relationships occur. The music analyst, then, is not only concerned with defining the relevant musical space of a composition—that is, its total set of relationships—but with the way these relationships occur sequentially. For a musical composition not only defines its own space, but does so by moving through this space in its own unique manner. Musical space is thus inseparable from musical time, just as musical time is inseparable from musical space. Indeed, the most salient characteristic of musical time, as distinct from ordinary, "psychological" time, is precisely its pronounced spatial—that is, structured— quality. Musical space is the framework within which, and through which, the actual sequence of musical events is shaped. (p. 529)

Morgan's explanation suggests temporal aspects are more critical than tonal aspects in creating musical space, and there is empirical evidence to support this view. Monahan and Carterette (1985) assessed the dimensional properties of musical space by asking subjects to make similarity judgments on pairs of brief melodies with slightly altered pitches and rhythms. Five dimensions emerged from multidimensional scaling and cluster analyses, including (in order of strength) rhythm, accent, duration patterns, high versus low pitch, and pitch contours. The authors claimed these dimensions accounted for the subjects' perceptual space, concluding, "Our study has shown the primacy of traditional rhythmic variables over pitch variables when the two were varied simultaneously" (p. 26).

The influence of temporal parameters in the listening experience has been investigated using another approach as well. Halpern (1988) presented subjects with a lyric, then a second one, and asked if they were from the same song. She then repeated the task using the pitches corresponding to the lyrics. Results showed longer reaction time as a function of distance in beats between the two lyrics, which is strong evidence that listeners encode a song with the appropriate temporal span the performance requires.

Kinesthetic relationships to music have also been found to be fundamental to listeners' responses to music. Adopting an "ecological" approach to studying music listening, Clarke (2005) proposed three reasons why physical motion is fundamental to the experience: (1) sound is created by requisite action in the natural world, (2) there is recent evidence of neuronal connections between perception and action, and (3) musical sound requires performer actions that listeners recognize and understand. Clarke believed these attributes remain influential even while (especially Western European) cultural and instructional norms tended to minimize the relationship between perception and action.

There are also shared aspects of music listening spaces. While individuals may uniquely experience music, they simultaneously achieve social bonds with friends and identify with desirable subcultures. As Cross (2006) stated:

> Music's floating intentionality allows participants to interpret a flow of musical behaviors and sounds in individual terms while the temporal regularities of the framework that it provides act to co-ordinate their behaviors and attentional foci (Cross, 2005). Hence participants in a collective musical act—and I include dance and ostensibly passive listening in this category—may each experience that musical act as bearing personal and potentially quite different, though determinate, significances without the integrity of the collective musical act being undermined. Music can be construed as guaranteeing the success of social interaction by creating conditions for minimisation of conflict through its semantic open-ness while simultaneously enabling a joint sense of shared action that is oriented around commonly experienced temporal regularities. (p. 8)

The idea of psychologically constructed and socially shared space in human experience is frequently attributed to Foucault's (1997) essay, originally written in 1967, on his distinction between *utopias*, which are idealized spaces, and *heterotopias*, which are socially constructed and differentiated counter sites. Humans create heterotopias as substitutes for utopias by constructing and inhabiting convenient and desirable surroundings for certain types of human activity. These surroundings, or spaces, have physical and psychological parameters, and while some are actual (e.g., movie theaters) and others virtual (e.g., mental states), both serve the function of protecting a person from outside distractions or constraints in order to optimally focus on present experiences. Applied to music listening, spaces reflect one's music listening habits, which are variously influenced and transformed by evolving musical styles and delivery systems for music consumption.

Most popular music listening experiences involve lyrics, which usually tell stories. Narrative storytelling invokes spatial and temporal thinking, which carries over into the listening experience in the form of lyrics. Turner (1996) described the interplay of spatial and temporal thinking in his book *The Literary Mind*:

> By projecting the basic abstract story of spatial perceiving onto the basic abstract story of temporal perceiving, we understand ourselves as able to focus on one or another temporal space from one or another temporal "location" or "viewpoint." We can "focus" on the temporal space of "yesterday" from the viewpoint of "today": "I did it yesterday." We can "focus" on the temporal space of 1066 from the temporal "viewpoint" of 1066: "It's raining as William lands on English shores." We can "focus" on the temporal space of the day after tomorrow from the temporal space of today, and in the space of the day after tomorrow, there can be someone who is focusing on his yesterday (our tomorrow) from the viewpoint of our day after tomorrow, as in "He will come home tomorrow night and *we will ask him the following morning whether he has made the phone call, but he will say he did it as soon as he came home*." (pp. 119–120)

Turner's explanation is surely applicable to music lyrics, raising the question of whether lyric complexity (having multiple spaces and viewpoints) is uniformly more appealing in certain genres or for certain types of listeners. Consider Bob Dylan's "Like a Rolling Stone", a song voted by *Rolling Stone* as number one on its list of "The 500 Greatest Songs of All Time," first in 2004, and again 2011, and by Dylan's own account, the best song he ever wrote. The opening lines contrast the setting in the past—"Once upon a time" and "you threw bums a dime in your prime"—and the present: "Now you don't.../Now you don't...." Turner might suggest that the warning "People'd call, say, 'beware doll, you're bound to fall'" focuses on a temporal space in the past from the temporal viewpoint of the future, while the final three lines:

> Now you don't talk so loud
> Now you don't seem so proud
> About having to be scrounging for your next meal
> (retrieved from http://www.elyrics.net/read/b/bob-dylan-lyrics/
> like-a-rolling-stone-lyrics.html, May 5, 2011)

with the repetitive insistence on "now" and the sudden switch to a complicated participle clause/gerund construction in the present tense ("having to be
scrounging") focus on the temporal space of the present from the temporal viewpoint of the present. Having described features of music listening spaces from
varied disciplines, I now offer a few examples that illustrate how spaces may have
formed and transformed throughout music history.

HISTORICAL EXAMPLES OF MUSIC LISTENING SPACES

Music in worship is considered multidimensional because it intensifies religious
beliefs yet is formed by natural materials such as humans and instruments
(Trotter, 1987), extending the potential spatiality of church music for listeners.
Early music education in the United States centered on worship long before the
inception of public school music. Church musicians and congregations created
environments that were essentially spiritual worship spaces, with assembled
participants singing hymns and reciting prayers shoulder to shoulder and face
to face. Organ pipes, choir lofts, and other conventions extended the location
and variety of sounds and maximized the architectural features of the church.
The musical spaces created in the context of church attendance consist of a rich
amalgam of sound, place, and function, which perhaps accounts for the sustained
success of contemporary music for worship.

Vaudeville became popular in the mid-nineteenth century, and audiences
influenced the success of each performance, extending the critical listening space
from the stage to the entire room (Kenrick, 1996). This arrangement activated
the chain of events in musical expression, a shared musical idea from composer
to performer to listener, to include audience reactions, which in turn influenced
performers to retain or revise their performance plans. Audience members thus
exerted formidable control over the parameters of their own listening spaces.

Ragtime was one of the most important developments in the history of
American music. Scott Joplin's *Maple Leaf Rag* was the first sheet music to sell a
million copies, which profoundly influenced the direction of parlor music across
the United States. In the ragtime style, listeners attended to two different playing techniques, one for each hand, with the right hand producing syncopated
melodies imbedded with cross-rhythms of the Deep South and the left hand
playing metrically in octaves, reminiscent of the then-popular Sousa marches
(Berlin, 1980). This novel addition of Southern vernacular music created a more
inclusive social listening space, allowing the music to be appreciated and understood by a larger percentage of American listeners while fundamentally changing
the experience for the middle-class listeners.

With the emergence of jazz in the early twentieth century, Americans were captivated by ensemble music. However, much of the work available to musicians was as solo performers. In New Orleans, the most resourceful pianists playing in the bars and brothels were dubbed "professors" because they possessed seemingly endless repertories and were able to "cover" the various instruments in an ensemble. This practice of emulating various instruments on a single instrument encouraged listeners to suspend disbelief while assessing the performer's rendition of various instrument parts. The piano style called "stride," which subsequently arose in Harlem, is an example of this technique, requiring that the left hand emulate the rhythm section of a full jazz ensemble, playing bass notes on the first and third beats, and jumping octaves to play chords on the second and fourth beats (Scaruffi, 2007). To the extent listeners recognized and appreciated the practice of covering instruments, rich musical spaces surely resulted. The ragtime and jazz examples demonstrate Clarke's (2005) aforementioned principles of the perception–action relationship, which explain why listeners typically "hear" the motion of others or themselves in music.

With the advent of radio broadcasting in the early 1920s, families fortunate enough to own a radio gathered together to listen, facing each other rather than the performer(s). The ability to hear an expansive repertory of sounds simultaneously broadcast coast to coast fundamentally changed the experience of music listening (Lewis, 1993), and even while the country suffered through the Great Depression, by the end of the 1930s over 90 percent of American households had radios. Over time, radios became smaller and wireless, but the social practice of music listening from a small device while facing others became increasingly common. The poor audio source provided little dimensionality itself, but access to the sounds in one's own home or other preferred place created a highly desirable social space. Some of my earliest listening memories occupy these same music listening spaces. During the 1960s, I first experienced the Beatles on a nine-volt transistor radio, roughly the size of a deck of cards. My older sister was seated opposite me, and my mother would stop cooking dinner to join us around the radio, such that I could read both their facial expressions. I identify these early listening spaces with the Beatles, which are invoked even when I now hear them on stereo headphones while staring into a computer screen.

Much of the subsequent history of rock music was a gradual process of creating larger spaces for experiencing music. Many of the most successful production techniques captured the essence of larger ensembles, much like the aforementioned techniques of ragtime and stride. A notable example was producer Phil Spector's "wall of sound" during the 1960s, which reproduced extremely well on transistor radios. Another example was the Leslie speaker, in which a large loudspeaker was set to rotate inside an enclosure to mechanically create a swirling sound. Jimi Hendrix used this device in his performance of the "Star Spangled Banner," which has been extensively analyzed as listening experience from multiple perspectives (Biamonte, 2007; Clarke, 2005). Yet another example was the mellotron, a keyboard instrument that played recordings of instruments from tape heads fixed under each key. It was first used by English groups—notably Cream and the Beatles—to produce lush arrangements of strings, brass, winds, and voice sounds. The sound became ubiquitous in the 1970s as listening tastes gravitated toward classical rock, multitrack recording technology advanced, and sound systems with stereophonic speakers became the norm.

The listening spaces implied in the preceding examples are directly analogous to "listening context," but a unique amalgam of knowledge, perception, intuition, interpersonal influence, personality, and beliefs about music that listeners bring with them to the activity. These influences comingle with external factors such as listening environment, as well as delivery medium characteristics. Indeed, what distinguishes the larger "space" from a smaller "context" is its integration of the sounds, the place, the listeners' personal dispositions, and social relationships. Perhaps music itself does not mediate listening spaces so much as listeners select and prefer music according to how well it resonates with the other elements of existing spaces.

Now that I have described some of the possible characteristics and manifestations of music listening spaces from a historical perspective, I will apply them to the contemporary world of digital music consumption in which students are so facile, and which is a primary concern for music education.

CHARACTERISTICS OF CURRENT AND EMERGING MUSIC LISTENING SPACES

The characteristics of digital music media have profound implications for music listening spaces. Portable music players and headphones effectively help listeners make spatial differentiations while sealing out competing perceptual elements, two critical attributes of musical space. Digital music is much more convenient than previous linear storage systems, so there is no delay of access such as "skipping the needle forward" on records, "fast-forwarding" or "rewinding" tapes, and so forth. With all points of the music instantly accessible, listeners have more control over what and how they hear.

In many ways, the Internet is the ultimate music listening space. It is rich with possibilities and flexible to use. By offering three-dimensional attributes, precise navigational control, and an endless supply of instantly available music, it helps users create music listening spaces efficiently. However, easy access to unlimited music has affected the attentional characteristics of listeners. Many listeners, especially younger ones, do not listen to any selection for very long, and typically do not listen to any piece in its entirety. The architecture of sites such as YouTube supports the tendency to sample music only briefly. In comparison, several decades ago, listening to extended songs was a gesture of allegiance to a performer or group. For example, in 1965, Arlo Guthrie's "Alice's Restaurant" lasted almost twenty minutes and occupied one entire side of his album, and offered a sing-along opportunity near the end to bond listeners further. In 1966, Bob Dylan's final song "Sad Eyed Lady of the Lowlands" from the album *Blonde on Blonde,* considered by many as the greatest album of all time, lasted over eleven minutes and also occupied an album side. In 1970, Pink Floyd recorded "Atom Heart Mother," which lasted almost twenty-four minutes, and in 1975 recorded "Shine On You Crazy Diamond," which lasted just over twenty-six minutes. These pieces were decidedly group activities, with listeners intent on imaginatively capturing the atmosphere of live performance and spending time together engrossed in collaborative activity. Music listening spaces have gradually become more temporary refuges from everyday life: today's average listeners sample more selections of music within a given listening span. This phenomenon can be witnessed by sharing a car trip with young people and observing them incessantly flipping through songs on an iPod.

Jourdain (1997) made the argument that melody is the focal element for most listeners, since it is connected with language, and popular music is sufficiently entwined with lyrics that most listeners have difficulty recalling song melodies without first retrieving words. A familiar protocol for writing songs begins with a melodic/rhythmic idea, which is then repeated and elaborated into coordinated sections, composing the song structure. As Jordain commented, "This orientation has meant that popular music is a world of three-minute compositions, since simple melodic writing generally can't be stretched out much farther" (p. 256). Thus, a contemporary listener's tendency to sample just the first few moments of a song is perhaps an astute strategy for popular music, much like a cook who samples a teaspoon of sauce to determine the quality of the entire pot. Assuming that listening spaces are partly formed by perceived cues and meanings in the music, this confluence of sonic and semantic information can be ascertained remarkably quickly, given the structure of much popular music.

In addition to listening for shorter periods, many young people prefer to listen alone. Music listening remained a primarily communal experience until Beyerdynamic invented headphones in the late 1930s. From that point forward, music listening has become increasingly privatized. Similar to Foucault's (1997) example of a mirror being partly a utopia (because it is not real, but a reflection) and partly a heterotopia (the reflection is real in the sense that one can see it), headphones create the illusion of being alone even when one is not alone. To again use the car trip example, we have probably all experienced someone in the back seat with earphones on, completely oblivious to all outside conversations and occurrences, yet sitting shoulder to shoulder with others doing the same thing in the back seat. The music listening conditions acquired with handheld digital music players and headphones thus provide privacy in nonprivate places, making them portable heterotopias. Present-day musical concerts, whether they feature "serious" or popular music, have become increasingly superfluous because listeners must travel farther than the computer or iPod, relinquish control over music selection and listening duration, pay money for tickets, and interact with an audience of mostly strangers. The music listening space is drastically different from what most listeners are used to; that is, it is much larger, overly inhabited, and much more vulnerable to the influence of others.

The content of music listening is also changing with the rise of user-generated content (UGC) on the Internet. Whereas exceptionally skilled or talented musicians may have previously held sway on recordings and airwaves, today quite literally any-one who wants to create music can find an audience. Listeners and musicians have interchangeable roles, and the availability and user-friendliness of digital music instruments and software make possible compositions that are neither complex nor time consuming. Young listeners embrace music made by amateurs, and this trend is abundantly present in the latest pop stars. For instance, in a recent *Time* magazine interview, Taylor Swift claims to have written the song "Love Story" on her bedroom floor in about twenty minutes (*Time*, 2009). I know many middle and high school students who regard it as the best song ever written; it is the most downloaded country music song in history; and based largely on the strength of this hit, Swift became the best-selling artist of 2008 in the United States (*Time*, 2009). New pop sensation Justin Bieber launched his career with informal YouTube performances and chatting with fans. A phenomenally popular new development exemplified by YouTube user "Kutiman," who meticulously cut and pasted preex-isting YouTube videos into new composite works, represents UGC based on UGC. Young listeners favor music made by peers, using entry-level musicianship and lyr-ics, and of a structure that can be apprehended in only a few minutes of listening time (i.e., music in a repetitive form). These are the qualities that resonate with young listeners and for which they readily build music listening spaces. They want to listen to each other and share the unique and idiosyncratic musical spaces they build for themselves with their own compositions and performances.

I propose the foregoing analyses to characterize changes in the ways today's students consume and participate in music. I hope it promotes inquiries regarding how we might best situate prospective music educators to meaningfully serve today's students, and what follows is an attempt to generate some questions and possible answers.

IMPLICATIONS FOR MUSIC TEACHER EDUCATION

Is the concept of a music listening space helpful to preparing music educators? Does it support existing curricular goals and objectives for music listening? I have some suggestions based on the ideas presented in this chapter, experience teaching music methods and leading internship programs, and discussions with colleagues. My suggestions are stated as dispositions and habits we should nurture, rather than as specific activities.

Developing Personal Musicianship

There is no more critical measure we can take than to insist that future music teachers use their total personal musicianship. Traditional university-level music programs tend to de-emphasize what students bring to the program from outside their experiences in traditional school ensembles and private study, yet their accumulated musical skills and insights are critical to their success as public school music teachers. These skills and insights are what bind them experientially to a larger student constituency: not all students, and not enough students, play orchestral or band instruments or sing in choirs, but many more students listen to music, want to make their own music, and have self-defining favorites. In my experience, music education students must discover, then nurture, and finally embrace their total personal musicianship—what they have been musically, what they are musically, and what they are becoming musically—and we must encourage them to do so. Progress toward this goal may involve preservice music educators remembering, assessing, and sharing the many ways they have created, consumed, and cherished music in the past. Music listening spaces are the most abundant and revealing artifacts of our musical lives, so we might well expect students to explore, define, and share their own. There are numerous intersections between classically trained and vernacular musicians: these compose the most important work preservice music educators can accomplish.

Embracing Popular Music and Culture

What can be learned through the Western European canon that cannot also be learned through popular music seems to be the reason for preserving the former in public schools. However, this statement is becoming increasingly less of an issue with time—it is not so much whether popular music serves just as well as art music in teaching music fundamentals, but whether what we consider "fundamental" is changing, or should change. It is quite pointless to teach public school students about classical music without helping them first develop listening spaces for it: most young people have no use or need for classical music for this reason. I suggest that preservice music educators must focus on understanding listening spaces as they currently exist in their students, meaning they should accept popular music as a vital, indispensable learning medium and prepare themselves for the imminent instructional difficulties that are every bit as complex and inhibitive as they are for teaching Western European classical music. Being well versed in popular music is beginning to serve teachers quite as well as being well versed in classical music.

Redefining the Role of the Teacher

In my experience, most preservice music educators have spent a greater part of their lives thinking of themselves as musicians than teachers, which is clearly disadvantageous to their future success. Additionally, undergraduates are at a level of intellectual development in which they seek and value "correct" answers (Perry, 1970) and thus envision teaching as a process of transferring correct knowledge to their students, another disadvantage. These attitudes present formidable challenges to young teachers, since they might be better served to accept themselves as educators and commit to facilitating rather than dictating learning. The idea of a musical space is relevant here, not merely as a way of diversifying the teachable curriculum, but as a new way of seeing the musical world through the eyes of their students, one which transcends transmission of facts, has potential to fully engage students and teachers in creative learning, and is consistent with best practices in education.

The proliferation and availability of information in the digital world signals our collective inability to base future instruction on conscious retelling of knowledge and demonstration of skills. We must now recognize a new priority in music teaching—to "become experts in helping students make things happen for themselves" (Rodriguez, 2009, p. 39). This challenge requires a rethinking of the core curriculum in general music, which is the basis for all music instruction in the schools. Again, music listening spaces are relevant here. What would music instruction look like if we viewed it primarily from the needs (i.e., the spaces) of our students? Perhaps it would look much like what we would teach ourselves as students in our classes, since our own total personal musicianship is our greatest asset.

CONCLUSION

In conclusion, I propose here that music listening spaces are relevant to musical experiences in tomorrow's classrooms. They take into account the broadest range of potential influences on music listening and represent how listeners orient themselves in relation to these influences. Music listening spaces serve as a metaphor for the mental world constructed by the listener to meaningfully link what is heard to what is felt, thus serving as a bridge between musical perception, cognition, and affect. A future challenge for music educators is to help their students explore and understand this bridge so that we, and our students, better understand the nature of music listening.

REFERENCES

Berlin, E. (1980). *Ragtime: A musical and cultural history*. Berkeley, CA: University of California Press.

Biamonte, N. (2007). *Wordless rhetoric in Jimi Hendrix's versions of the Star Spangled Banner*. Paper presented at the International Conference for Music Since 1900, University of York, United Kingdom.

Bregman, A. (1990). *Auditory scene analysis*. Cambridge, MA: MIT Press.

Broadbent, D. (1954). The role of auditory localization in attention and memory span. *Journal of Experimental Psychology, 47*(3), 191–196.

Cherry, E. (1953). Some experiments on the recognition of speech, with one and with two ears. *Journal of Acoustical Society of America, 25*(5), 975–979.

Clarke, E. (2005). *Ways of listening: An ecological approach to the perception of musical meaning*. New York, NY: Oxford University Press.

Cross, I. (2005). Music and meaning, ambiguity and evolution. In D. Miell, R. MacDonald, & D. Hargreaves (Eds.), *Musical communication* (pp. 27–43). Oxford, UK: Oxford University Press.

Cross, I. (2006). *Music and social being*. Retrieved from http://www.mus.cam.ac.uk/~ic108/PDF/Mus_Aust_paper06.pdf

Foucault, M. (1997). Of other spaces: Utopias and heterotopias. In E. Leach (Ed.), *Rethinking architecture* (pp. 350–356). London, UK: Routledge.

Halpern, A. (1988). Mental scanning in auditory imagery for songs. *Journal of Experimental Psychology: Learning, Memory, and Cognition, 14*(3), 434–443.

Jourdain, R. (1997). *Music, the brain, and ecstasy: How music captures our imagination*. New York, NY: Harper Perennial.

Kenrick, J. (1996). *A history of the musical: Vaudeville: Part II*. Retrieved from http://www.musicals101.com/vaude2.htm

Langer, S. (1953). *Feeling and form: A theory of art*. New York, NY: Scribner.

Levitin, D. (2006). *This is your brain on music*. London, UK: Penguin Books.

Lewis, T. (1993). *Empire of the air: The men who made radio*. New York, NY: Harper Perennial.

McDermott, V. (1972). A conceptual musical space. *Journal of Aesthetics and Art Criticism, 30*(4), 489–494.

Monahan, C., & Carterette, E. (1985). Pitch and duration as determinants of musical space. *Music Perception, 3*(1), 1–32.

Morgan, R. (1980). Musical time/musical space. *Critical Inquiry, 6*(3), 527–538.

Perry, W. (1970). *Forms of intellectual and ethical development in the college years: A scheme.* New York, NY: Holt, Rinehart, and Winston.

Rodriguez, C. (2009). Informal learning in music: Emerging roles of teachers and students. *Action, Criticism, and Theory for Music Education, 8*(2), 36–45.

Sager, R. (2006). Creating a musical space for experiencing the other-self within. In S. A. Reily (Ed.), *The musical human: Rethinking John Blacking's ethnomusicology in the twenty-first century* (pp. 143–169). Burlington, VT: Ashgate Publishing.

Scaruffi, P. (2007). *A history of jazz music.* London, UK: Omniware Perfect Paperback.

Time. (2009, April). Ten questions for Taylor Swift. Retrieved from http://www.time.com/time/video/player/0,32068,20867219001_1893645,00.html

Trotter, F. T. (1987). *Loving God with one's mind.* Nashville, TN: Board of Higher Education and Ministry of the United Methodist Church.

Turner, M. (1996). *The literary mind.* New York, NY: Oxford University Press.

Section Three

Cultural Dimensions of Music Teaching and Learning

In every culture the musical aspect that goes on is like a laboratory. Music educators in every culture should take responsibility to learn from the laboratory.

Isaac Amuah

Disability theory is now asking us: is disability located in the environment? It is located in the social interactions. It is located in attitude. What I'm asking people to do is to reframe where disability is.

Teryl Dobbs

Whether it's African drumming or Italian traditional music or French Canadian music, our children don't know anything about their own music culture. Let's interrogate that assumption. Perhaps *that*'s the world culture that needs to be present.

Valerie Peters

7

FINDING MIDDLE GROUND

Music Education in Urban Settings

Catherine Larsen

RECENT EVIDENCE FROM across the country indicates that a different kind of conversation is occurring relative to the inclusion of the arts in the educational lives of children. States as diverse as California, Michigan, Rhode Island, Kentucky, Washington, Illinois, Minnesota, and New Jersey have engaged in survey research, gathering evidence to assist state policy makers in decision making (Governor's Commission on the Arts in Education: Findings and Recommendations, 2006; Ruppert & Nelson, 2006). These authors noted that the data-free climate of decision making among arts educators decried by the Arts Education Partnership in 2004 is starting to change, as collaborative efforts document the amount of time students spend studying the arts, who is providing arts instruction and under what conditions, how much money is being spent on arts programs, and available funding sources. These surveys are beginning to produce measureable results in some states, including data about increased graduation requirements, additional budget lines, and favorable policy development.

In the report "The Art of Collaboration: Promising Practices for Integrating the Arts and School Reform," Nelson (2008) reported the work of eight large school–community or school–university collaboratives in Baltimore, Maryland; Cleveland, Ohio; St. Louis, Missouri; Dallas, Texas; Washington, DC; Jackson, Mississippi; and Alameda County, California. Strategies were identified for the creation and maintenance of collaborative organizations that work to integrate the arts into public education. Missing from this research and from the resulting reports is sustained inquiry into teacher preparation, certification, and professional development. Although the data are still incomplete, these efforts hold significant promise in guiding policy and practice in arts education, particularly in urban environments. They underscore the potential of efforts to generate arts integration in collaborative settings, and also reinforce the fact that while we do not have a completely clear picture of arts education opportunities in schools nationwide, it appears that the arts are often being squeezed out of the picture to make room for subjects found in high-stakes tests (CAAE Staff, 2013; DeBacker, Lombaerts, DeMette, Buffel, & Elias, 2012; Governor's Commission on the Arts in Education, 2006; Ruppert & Nelson, 2006).

CHALLENGES CONTINUE

The arts are recognized as an essential part of the curriculum in the Goals 2000: Educate America Act, visible evidence of the importance of the arts in standards-based education. State- and district-level standards have been added to the benchmarks initially set forth in the National Standards for Arts Education (1994). In spite of the acknowledged importance of the arts as an integral part of a complete education, the arts are in fact absent from the curriculum that serves many public school children (Burnaford, 2007; Governor's Commission on the Arts in Education, 2006; National Assembly of State Arts Agencies, 2006). A lack of meaningful arts education for a substantial number of children in public schools has been clearly documented in "Creative America," a report created by the President's Committee on the Arts and Humanities (1997). Funding for school arts programs continues to shrink, and specialist positions and arts experiences are cut back or eliminated altogether when economic recession plagues school systems (Cornett, 2007; Davis, 2008; Myers, 2003; President's Committee on the Arts and the Humanities, 2011).

Education in the arts can be particularly effective for young people in challenging urban school environments (Burnaford, Aprill, & Weiss, 2001; Catterall, Chapleau, & Iwanaga, 1999; Catterall & Waldorf, 1999; Fiske, 1999; Gelineau, 2004; Heath & Roach, 1999; Larsen, 2001; Nelson, 2008; Noblit, Corbett, Wilson, & McKinney, 2009; Rabkin & Redmond, 2004). However, severe budget cuts and pressure for academic instruction and improved student achievement on standardized tests have had a negative impact on arts education programs (Bresler, 1993; Deasy, 2002; Duncan, 2009; Governor's Commission on the Arts in Education, 2006; Ruppert, 2006). Instruction by arts specialists continues to decline (Myers, 2003; Nelson, 2008; Oreck, 2004). Arts education is increasingly being provided by a combination of arts specialists, classroom teachers, and external providers such as cultural institutions and arts agencies (Cornett, 2007;

Davis, 2008; McDonald, 2010; Myers, 2003; Ruppert & Nelson, 2006). This situation is particularly prevalent in large urban school systems with diverse student populations, districts that are frequently in the midst of school restructuring as an attempt to improve student performance (Deasy & Stevenson, 2005; Noblit et al., 2009; Ruppert, 2006). In these beleaguered urban environments, resources are diminishing, yet classroom teachers face the burden of increased expectations due to expanding curricular and accountability mandates (Ingram & Riedel, 2003; Jeanneret & DeGraffenreid, 2012).

Any absence of music, drama, dance, and visual art in the lives of schoolchildren and young adults represents a significant void in the quality and depth of experience schools provide for their students, in which the joyous creativity of art making is replaced by a profound educational silence (Eisner, 1985; Zastrow & Janc, 2004). Are the challenges, economic and otherwise, insurmountable? What possible solutions can be brought to bear to support sequential, ongoing arts education in schools?

ARTS INTEGRATION

Integration of the arts with other areas of the curriculum has been one way to confront the dilemma of mandates to improve student outcomes and teacher accountability at the same time that necessary resources are disappearing (Barrett & Veblen, 2012; Bresler, 1995, 1995/1996; Burnaford, 2007; Cornett, 2007; Davis, 2008; Deasy, 2002; Dunn, 1995; Gelineau, 2004; Goldberg, 2011; McDonald, 2010; Ruppert & Nelson, 2006; Russell-Bowie, 2009b, 2010). For these authors, arts integration is situated in the larger context of curriculum integration. The integration is based on shared or related concepts, respecting the integrity and uniqueness of each of the disciplines to be combined (Campbell & Scott-Kassner, 2013).

Labeling arts integration efforts as either "intrinsic" (art for art's sake) or instrumental (in service of other social or curricular learning) has created the perception of a contentious dichotomy of purpose among educators and arts advocates (Booth, 2013; Burnaford, 2007; McDonald, 2010). More recently, researchers have emphasized the importance of collaborative efforts among all educators in the implementation of arts curricula (Arts Education Partnership Task Force on Higher Education, 2007; Benton & Schillo, 2004; Breault & Breault, 2010; Burnaford et al., 2001; Fine and Performing Arts Magnet Cluster Program, Chicago Public Schools, 2010). However, classroom teachers often do not have the necessary background and experience to provide arts instruction, and existing arts integration programs often are not conceptually based, with authentic experiences and sequential instruction in the arts (Jeanneret & DeGraffenreid, 2012; Stake, Bresler, & Mabry, 1991; Wiggins & Wiggins, 2008). Classroom teachers require additional support in the form of staff development to participate in and facilitate effective arts integration (Gelineau, 2004; Goldberg, 2011; McDonald, 2010; President's Committee on the Arts and the Humanities, 2011).

The kinds of arts experiences young people are afforded are clearly impacted by who is providing the instruction (Larsen, 2001, 2008). If, indeed, this landscape is changing, we must expand the traditional model of specialist arts instruction in schools to encompass the classroom teacher as an important component of the equation. Especially in urban environments, where the challenges are great and resources are often severely diminished, the classroom teacher can become a significant player in providing authentic arts instruction for young people (McDonald, 2010; Rabkin & Redmond, 2006). Arts integration may be the middle ground we seek.

What, exactly, is meant by arts integration? Arts integration is here defined as instruction combining two or more content areas, wherein the arts (music, visual art, drama, and dance) constitute one or more of the integrated areas, and instruction in each content area has depth and integrity reflected by embedded assessments, standards, and objectives.

How can integration of the arts into classroom curricula and instruction, integration that honors the arts as discrete content areas, address the absence of arts instruction in today's schools? What role can arts educators play in facilitating this trend toward a stronger and more significant presence for the arts in culturally rich yet challenging urban school environments? To answer these questions, consideration must be given to issues in urban school reform, arts education in the urban context, teacher professionalization and development of communities of practice, and the possibilities inherent in collaborative partnerships.

URBAN SCHOOL REFORM

The challenges facing proponents of increased arts education in schools must be considered within the larger context of school reform. School reform issues and initiatives have generated an unprecedented level of public attention for the past three decades. Panels, commissions, research reports, and policy analyses have noted numerous problems in American educational systems, and a wide array of remedies have been proposed. Every aspect of school organization and classroom practice has been challenged (Bryk, Sebring, Kerbow, Rollow, & Easton, 1998; Bryk, Sebring, Allensworth, Luppescu, & Easton, 2010; Darling-Hammond & Bransford, 2005; Darling-Hammond, Wei, Andree, Richardson, & Ophanos, 2009).

Many different school reform configurations have been developed and implemented, some more successfully than others. The demands for accountability that accompany each new reform strategy are often issued without the support necessary for change efforts, especially support for the teachers who bear the burden of responsibility in most school reform initiatives (Breault & Breault, 2010; Damore & Kapustka, 2007; Damore, Kapustka, & McDevitt, 2008; Darling-Hammond & Bransford, 2005; Johnston-Parsons, 2012; Zeichner, 2007). Calls for accountability in school reform have engendered increasing efforts at national, state, and local levels to codify curricular content and assess student progress, as evidenced by the Goals 2000 Initiative; the development of national achievement standards in several subjects, including the arts disciplines (Lewis, 1989, 1995; National Standards for Arts Education, 1994); and, more recently, the No Child Left Behind Act (NCLB) (2001), Elementary and Secondary Education Act (ESEA) (n.d.), and American Recovery and Reinvestment Act (ARRA) (2009), which includes the current "Race to the Top." In this latest iteration of federal support, states complete for resources to develop enhanced teacher preparation and programs that demonstrate promise in enhancing student performance on standardized tests.

The 2001 passage of the No Child Left Behind Act exacerbated educators' concerns about a narrowing of the curriculum in the wake of high-stakes testing and external accountability. The American Recovery and Reinvestment Act of 2009 has educators scrambling to compete in a "Race to the Top" in which accountability mandates are now also accompanied by a focus on preparing American children for the workplace of tomorrow. These federal directives have had significant negative impact on curricular offerings and teacher delivery of the curricula (Darling-Hammond, 2010; President's Committee on the Arts and the Humanities, 2011; C. Weiss & Lichtenstein, 2008; Zastrow & Janc, 2004).

Along with accountability emphases, current trends in urban school reform have focused on fundamental restructuring of the system that delivers education. An important aspect of school restructuring is increased and ongoing professional development for teachers in order to support teachers in the change process (Darling-Hammond, 2010; Teitel, 2008). One prevalent restructuring strategy, school-based management, devolves authority to determine the program of a local school to administrators and community personnel. The school-based management movement holds particular promise for addressing numerous problems that stem from the extraordinarily pluralistic character of large urban school districts, including the lack of education in the arts (Bryk et al., 1998; Bryk et al., 2010; Hess, 2005; Nathan, 2008).

Educators involved in urban reform efforts are attempting to reinvent schools in the most difficult of environments, endeavoring to create something vital and engaging in the midst of a status quo that presents enormous challenge. In *Spinning Wheels: The Politics of Urban School Reform*, Frederick M. Hess asserted that reform has indeed become the status quo in troubled urban school systems (1998). Waves of reform sweep through these school districts, producing limited sustained change. What results is a dizzying progression of reforms, constantly modified or recycled, which teachers are left to implement, generally with marginal support. Hess (1998, 2003, 2005) labeled this phenomenon of ceaseless unsupported change "policy churn," in which schools are attempting to do a number of things in a stop-and-start, chaotic fashion that is not part of a clear strategy to improve specific elements of schooling. This disorganized and often tumultuous approach to school improvement continues to be reported by researchers in urban centers in San Diego (Hess, 2005), New York (O'Day, Bitter, & Gomez 2011), Los Angeles (Kerchner, Meneffee-Libey, Mulfinger, & Clayton, 2008), and Chicago (Bryk et al., 2010).

Large urban school districts are particularly apt to evidence a decline in arts education opportunities (Nathan, 2008) due to pressures for improved student achievement in cash-strapped systems. This decrease cannot be separated from the issues of school reform that are often characteristic of urban educational settings. Changing demographics in urban areas and state funding formulas based on property tax both serve to underscore the fact that all schools are not created equal (Bryk et al., 2010; Payne, 2008; Sirotnik, 1991). An enormous number of disadvantaged youth attend troubled urban schools, districts where the tax base is quite low and the problems are diverse and persistent.

What happens when local control meets escalating performance standards and high-profile student and teacher assessments in a large urban school system? The manifold pressures inherent in school reform combine with the documented absence of arts education to create a critical juncture of need and opportunity for arts educators and policy makers. This intersection of opportunity can enable the individual school to develop creative solutions to local needs, empowering teachers, students, and parents to participate as decision makers. Noteworthy in this scenario are opportunities to create arts programs to address the particular needs of each school, supporting teachers in acquiring necessary content knowledge and pedagogical skill, and capitalizing on the resources available in the community.

THE ARTS IN URBAN SCHOOL REFORM

While education in the arts is important for every child, a substantial amount of research has indicated that arts experiences may be particularly important for children who are at risk of academic failure (Catterall et al., 1999; Catterall

& Waldorf, 1999; Fiske, 1999; Goldberg, 2011; Heath & Roach, 1999; McDonald, 2010; Rabkin & Redmond, 2006; Stevenson & Deasy, 2005). The children who fit this descriptor often attend school in large urban school systems, systems that are unwieldy in size and depersonalized, systems beleaguered by problems of poverty, race, scarcity of resources, transience, and often violence. Traditional forms of arts education are frequently in short supply in the urban environment due to serious financial restrictions and the chaos and disorder brought about by policy churn. Although the arts present a potentially powerful ally in combating the challenges of urban education, they are often missing in an area where they could be particularly effective (CAEE Staff, 2013; President's Committee on the Arts and the Humanities, 2011; National Assembly of State Arts Agencies, 2006; C. Weiss & Lichtenstein, 2008).

Ironically, urban environments can be rich in arts resources that could help to address this problem and offer interesting alternatives to traditional arts education. Many potentially vibrant opportunities exist for collaborative efforts among school districts and universities, museums, cultural institutions, and performing groups of many cultures and disciplines. Unfortunately, the presence of arts specialists within a school district does not ensure any collaboration with external resources such as cultural institutions or arts in education organizations (Larsen, 2001; Nardo, Custodero, Persellin, & Fox, 2006). Arts specialists are often unable to work effectively outside the parameters of their traditional role at the center of school-based arts programs, perhaps because their specialist training may not facilitate skill in the development of such collaborative structures (Dretzke & Rickers, 2011). School administrators and classroom teachers are frequently even less well equipped for this collaborative task (Arts Education Partnership Task Force on Higher Education, 2007; Cobb, 2000; Davis, 2008; Gates, 2010; Larsen, 2008; Lind, 2007). Interestingly, educational and cultural institutions may also be unskilled in the processes of collaboration with public schools.

Many administrators, policy makers, researchers, and education personnel are in strong accord regarding the importance of the arts in the core curriculum. There is less agreement as to who should provide arts instruction: arts specialists, classroom teachers, or external providers (Arts Education Partnership, 1997; Barrett & Veblen, 2012; Hope, 1997, 2002; Myers, 2003; McDonald, 2010; Russell-Bowie, 2009a, 2010; Wiggins & Wiggins, 2008). Due to the funding constraints endemic to urban school systems, arts specialist positions are frequently eliminated or are seriously underfunded. As a result, classroom teachers often become the primary vehicle for arts instruction and arts integration, whether or not they have the necessary arts background, training, or teaching experience (Jeanneret & DeGraffenreid, 2012; Russell-Bowie, 2010).

The increasing emphasis on curricular integration and theme-based curricula noted earlier has therefore often shifted the responsibility for arts instruction from specialists to general classroom teachers, although in some settings, assistance and direction from arts specialists and/or visiting professional artists are still available to classroom teachers. Many authors supported this type of collaborative effort (Barrett, McCoy, & Veblen, 1997; Barrett & Veblen, 2012; Cornett, 2007; Gelineau, 2004), arguing that students' educational experiences were strengthened when both generalists and specialists attended to the potential of disciplines within the curriculum to connect and cohere. However, in systems where arts specialist staff reductions have been dictated by budget cuts, classroom teachers may be required to provide arts instruction on their own (Booth, 2003; Bresler, 1995; Burnaford, 2007; Cornett, 2007; DeBacker et al., 2012). As a result, local needs and challenges can hamper the implementation of national standards, state goals for learning, and assessment in the arts, especially in instances where resources have been cut (CAAE 2013; Noblit et al., 2009).

Classroom teachers who are required to provide arts instruction and experiences for their students have a strong need for professional development in the arts that can better prepare them to teach arts concepts and skills (Larsen, 2001, 2008). Themes in the literature on teacher professionalization point to the need for such training to (1) be site based and long term, (2) involve collaboration with an outside partner, (3) combine a mixture of content and methodology, (4) provide opportunities for collegial interchange and teacher input, and (5) have a design that evolves over time in response to expressed teacher need (Ball & Cohen, 1999; Darling-Hammond et al., 2009; Sahlberg, 2011; Zeichner, 2007). Educational and cultural institutions are uniquely positioned to advance such professional development opportunities for teachers. Carefully designed and implemented staff development programs can have a significant impact on the quality and quantity of arts instruction and effective arts integration in troubled urban schools (O'Day et al., 2011; Rabkin & Redmond, 2004).

The transformation of teacher practice in arts education and arts integration requires long-term attention, particularly in an urban environment where there may be minimal arts instruction by specialists and little is done to help teachers learn to integrate the arts with regular classroom instruction (Lind, 2007; Nelson, 2008; Noblit et al., 2009; Oreck, 2004). Researchers note a decided lack of detailed studies examining long-term comprehensive design and implementation of professional development programs supporting more complex forms of teaching such as arts integration (Deasy, 2002, 2005; Nelson, 2008; New Opportunities for Research, Arts Education Partnership, 2004; Ruppert & Nelson, 2006). Staff development is needed that can empower classroom teachers to change the ways they think about their teaching practice and that provides the multiple kinds of support that can enable change (Oreck, 2004; Russell-Bowie, 2009a, 2009b, 2010; Sahlberg, 2011; Schussler, 2006).

TEACHER PROFESSIONALIZATION AND COMMUNITIES OF PRACTICE

Teacher professionalization initiatives are central to school reform efforts. Among them, professional development has been vital in supporting and facilitating the far-reaching changes in teachers' beliefs, knowledge, and habits of practice required for effective implementation of school reform. Professional development is considered to be a key ingredient in improving US schools (Benton & Schillo, 2004; Bredeson & Scribner, 1999; Fullan, 2011; Gates, 2010; Oreck, 2004; Sykes & Darling-Hammond, 1999; Teitel 2008). Education reform reports, legislative mandates, and contemporary educational literature uniformly cite professional development as one of the primary mechanisms for achieving the goals of school reform. Researchers and policy makers are careful to note that the professional development of teachers, while it is not a silver bullet, can function as a primary educational reform strategy intended to help schools and teachers develop more rigorous curriculum standards, design meaningful educational assessments, facilitate organizational change, guide school improvement plans, and improve teachers' knowledge and skills to enhance student learning outcomes (Breault & Breault, 2012; Bredeson & Scribner, 1999; Cobb, 2000; Darling-Hammond, 2005; Darling-Hammond & Bransford, 2005; Dretzke & Rickers, 2011; Gates, 2010; Teitel, 2008; Vernon-Dotson & Floyd, 2012).

Several issues are important in consideration of staff development initiatives. Teachers' sense of professional community must be developed and sustained (O'Day et al., 2011). We know that teachers prefer staff development opportunities that provide collegial involvement; therefore, staff development program structure should be collaborative and evolutionary in design, reflecting the teachers' unique perspectives. Changes in teachers' habits of practice also require instruction in both content and pedagogy (Cobb, 2000; Darling-Hammond & Bransford, 2005; Gates, 2010; Goldberg, 2011). To facilitate transfer of this instruction into the classroom, teachers must have long-term, ongoing support in the form of observation, coaching, feedback, and reflection, all of which should occur in the context of the school and the classroom (Rabkin & Redmond, 2006; Vernon-Dotson & Floyd, 2012). External partners are essential to staff development initiatives, especially in urban school districts (Breault & Breault, 2010). These partnerships can provide resources, ideas, program coherence, and levels of support not available in the school environment (Gates, 2010; Larsen, 2001; Rieckhoff & Larsen, 2012; Teitel, 2008).

In recent years, staff development program design has been moving away from more traditional context-free workshops and university-sponsored courses toward an emerging paradigm that is a site-specific and recursive design process (Breault & Breault, 2010, 2012; Damore et al., 2011; Sahlberg, 2011). In this new paradigm, creation, implementation, reflection, and modification occur in ongoing cycles. The kind of learning that will be required of all teachers, many of whom were taught and learned to teach under a different paradigm of instruction and learning, has been described as transformative, necessitating wholesale changes in deeply held beliefs, knowledge, and habits of individual practice (Gates, 2010; Ingram & Riedel, 2003; Kerchner et al., 2008; O'Day et al., 2011; Oreck, 2004; Yendol-Silva & Dana, 2004). Examples of this kind of cyclical professional development can be found in the A+ Schools Program (Noblit et al., 2009), the Urban Professional Development School (PDS) (Damore, Kapustka, & McDevitt, 2011), the FACETS program in Minneapolis Public Schools (Dretzke & Rickers, 2011), and Project AIM (C. Weiss & Lichtenstein, 2008).

While the enhancement of individual professionalism is desirable, active work as a part of a professional group is also important in efforts to increase both teachers' sense of craft and their overall commitment to work contexts that are increasingly difficult and demanding. Sustained efforts to improve practice must include attention to the development of professional community and teachers' collective engagement in reform efforts. This shared commitment to a fundamental change of teaching practice requires a school-wide focus on professional community, so that empowerment works to the advantage of students and teachers (Damore & Kapustka, 2007; Johnston-Parsons, 2012; Larsen, 2001, 2008; Larsen & Rieckhoff, in press; Lieberman, 1990; Leiberman & Miller, 2001; Reickhoff & Larsen, 2012). Research by Hess (2005) and Bryk et al. (2010) suggested that while an emphasis on professional community would be beneficial for all students, it is particularly pressing for urban schools where other resources for school reform are limited. Noblit et al. (2009) identified the need to teach the concept and practice of collegial environment, positing that dialogue is an approach that links teachers' professional development to school reform. Darling-Hammond and Bransford (2005) and Myers (2003) concurred, supporting the importance of collaborative efforts that can mitigate the negative effects of teacher isolation. Educators who have regularly scheduled planning time with selected teams of teachers across grade levels or across curricular areas, for example, are much more able to address complex inquiry questions relative to curricula or teaching practice (Dretzke & Rickers, 2011). This is a common function in several Chicago Public Schools Arts Magnet schools and in many PDS partnerships.

Shared decision making, a primary component of site-based management, is one form of school restructuring that is strengthened by the development of teachers' professional community (Clark, 1999; Damore & Kapustka, 2007; Larsen, 2001, 2008; Noblit et al., 2009). Stein, Smith, and Silver (1999) found that in an environment of shared decision making, the most effective and long-lasting changes have been evolutionary, rather than revolutionary. Reflection is also emphasized as a necessary component of staff development (Darling-Hammond et al., 2009; Vernon-Dotson & Floyd, 2012; C. Weiss & Lichtenstein, 2008; Yendol-Silva & Dana, 2004). The need for long-term support for teachers has been clearly documented by many researchers (Bryk, Easton, Kerbow, Rollow, & Sebring, 1993; Bryk et al., 2010; Catterall & Waldorf, 1999; Fullan, 2011; Schussler, 2006; Teitel, 2008), who note that a motivated group of teachers can serve as pioneers and gradually seed the rest of the group until most of the teachers are enthusiastic participants.

The development of this type of professional community is essential in efforts to improve teachers' habits of practice, especially in urban schools where other resources for school reform are limited. Teachers need, and prefer, sustained professional contact with colleagues (Fullan, 2011; Ruppert, 2006). The shared decision making that is a hallmark of more recent reform initiatives also requires professional development that is collaborative and evolutionary in design and informed by the teachers' unique perspectives (Benton & Schillo, 2004; Breault & Breault, 2010; Burnaford, 2007; Burnaford et al., 2001; Darling-Hammond, 2005; Deasy & Stevenson, 2005; Vernon-Dotson & Floyd, 2012).

An example of the potential long-term impact of shared decision making in professional teacher communities can be found in one Chicago elementary school that partnered with a major university to enhance professional development and student achievement. The school leadership team, composed of several teacher leaders, implemented a restructured day that added enough instructional minutes to the school schedule to facilitate early dismissal one day each week. Filling this weekly "extra time" with professional development (two and one-half hours) enabled several whole-school changes to be researched, piloted, successfully implemented, and evaluated. Teacher teams determined the topics, participated in presenting and "training," and enthusiastically embraced the opportunity to work in focused and supported ways over time with colleagues.

Teacher professionalization is a hallmark of collaborative partnerships in education. Recent research documents the emergence of this effective paradigm shift for teacher professional education (Ball & Cohen, 1999; Darling-Hammond,

2005; Darling-Hammond & McLaughlin, 1995; Hiebert & Morris, 2012; Zeichner, 2007). Based on the depth of relearning required of teachers engaged in school reform and an assessment of what has not been effective to date, this paradigm encompasses the following features: (1) teacher assistance that *directly focuses on an individual teacher's practice*, such as coaching, coteaching, assistance with planning, and reflection on actual lessons, in order to enhance teacher planning and decision-making processes; (2) teacher assistance *grounded in the content of teaching and learning*, so the teachers encounter the discipline as learners before grappling with how to teach it; (3) *development of communities of professional practice* by working with organizationally intact groups of teachers, to develop teacher leaders and teachers' capacities to explain, challenge, and critique the work of peers; (4) *collaboration with experts outside the teaching community*, who can bring fresh perspectives, ideas about what has proven effective elsewhere, and an analytic stance toward the school improvement process; and (5) *consideration of organizational context*, to align the multiple contexts in which teachers perform their work and to provide the support of organizational values and operating procedures (Gates, 2010; Goldberg, 2011; Hiebert & Morris, 2012; Johnston-Parsons, 2012; Larsen & Reickhoff, in press; Lind, 2007; Nelson, 2008; Teitel, 2008).

Researchers have proposed that implementation of this emerging staff development paradigm should be approached as a design process (Clark, 1999; Darling-Hammond, 2005; Darling-Hammond et al., 2009; Johnston-Parsons, 2012; Lind, 2007). They advocate a process of thoughtful, conscious decision making in staff development design. This process of creation, implementation, reflection, and modification of approaches and programs is preferable to importing an externally predetermined model or formula. Central to this process is a planning sequence that incorporates goal setting, planning, doing, and reflecting (Johnston-Parsons, 2012). Key components of this planning process include knowledge about teacher learning, consideration of context, and attention to issues of sustainability, leadership, and professional culture. Noteworthy in this design process is the incorporation of information from many fields of inquiry, including content issues, organizational context, research on teaching and learning, school change, and staff development issues. This information informs the design of transformative staff development for teachers and is supportive of a school culture congenial to teachers' newly learned knowledge and skills (Larsen & Reickhoff, in press; Teitel, 2008).

Studies of teacher learning also suggest that teachers interpreted new ideas and practices through the lens of their existing beliefs and habits of practice (Cohen & Ball, 1990), as well as through cultural images of what teaching should look like (Darling-Hammond et al., 2009). When a clear vision of the new teaching practices was lacking, teachers filled in with knowledge from their past experience. Implementation of successful professional development programs, therefore, requires clarity of objectives, individualized support, and the development of professional community (Nelson, 2008). PDS partnerships, like the one described in the following paragraphs, are uniquely suited to addressing these issues.

COLLABORATIVE PARTNERSHIPS

Collaborative efforts between schools, universities, and cultural organizations can effectively address the absence of the arts in schooling for urban students. Partnerships are indeed receiving increasing attention from policy makers, researchers, and funders. School reform analysts have documented the value of strong connections to resources outside the school system in reform implementation efforts, especially in urban environments (Breault & Breault, 2012; Bryk et al., 1993; Bryk et al., 1998; Bryk et al., 2010; Hess, 2003, 2005). Researchers also noted the value of strong connections to external partners in the implementation of effective arts integration programs (Bresler, 1995; Burnaford, 2007; Catterall et al., 1999; Dretzke & Rickers, 2011; Fiske, 1999; Myers, 2003; Stake et al., 1991; Stevenson & Deasy, 2005). Partnerships with cultural and educational institutions can be especially effective in leveraging scarce resources, facilitating school-wide enthusiasm for change efforts, maintaining design flexibility, and operating effectively outside the constraints of current school system policy. The "insider/outsider" perspective can also enable the long-term commitment so necessary to change efforts (Breault & Breault, 2010, 2012; Burnaford, 2007; CAEE Staff, 2013; Fine and Performing Arts Magnet Cluster Program, Chicago Public Schools, 2010; Larsen, 2001, 2008; McDonald, 2010; Oreck 2004).

The effectiveness of partnerships in furthering the goals of staff development represents a common thread throughout the teacher professionalization literature, including reports from the Rockefeller Foundation's Collaboratives for Humanities and Arts Teaching, the Consortium on Chicago School Research, the Chicago Annenberg Challenge, the Holmes Group Teachers for a New Era Initiatives, the President's Committee on the Arts and Education, and the Professional Development School model.

University–school partnerships, in particular the PDS, have demonstrated promise as collaborative partnership models that can incorporate the recommended supports for teachers in content learning and acquisition of new teaching methodologies into site-specific and long-term change efforts. Documented effects of effective PDSs included a heightened feeling of empowerment and efficacy (Benton & Schillo, 2004), increased collegiality and a greater sense of professional responsibility (Breault & Breault, 2010), greater decision-making authority (Schussler, 2006), and ability to impact policy (Yendol-Silva & Dana, 2004). The cognitive goals outlined by the Holmes Group (1990) include new content area learning, increased reflection on teaching and learning, more opportunities to be creative, greater decision-making authority, and the ability to impact policy. The Holmes Group reported that teachers also need both support and time as they learn to navigate the newly created decision-making space (1990, 1995).

The Arts Education Resources Initiative of the Washington State Arts Commission describes elements of effective, sustainable arts education in six areas—curriculum, assessment, teaching capacity, collaboration, scheduling, and funding (Arts for Every Student, 2006). Notable are the recommendations in the areas of collaboration and teacher capacity. Michael Fullan (2011), noted education and management theorist, posited that current school reform efforts are utilizing policy and strategy levers (he called them "drivers") that have the least chance of driving successful reform. He stated, rather, that teachers must engage in collective work that fosters continuous improvement of instruction and learning. He identified capacity building through partnerships, group work, and systemic solutions as effective drivers of successful reform.

In "The Art of Collaboration: Promising Practices for Integrating the Arts and School Reform," Nelson (2008) reported on the Integrating the Arts and Education Reform Initiative, a roundtable of school–community collaboratives and school–university collaboratives. The report documents sixteen strategies for collaboratively integrating the arts into public schools and building community support for arts education. In addition to guidance relative to establishing and maintaining collaborative partnerships, partnership participants identified specific strategies for designing and delivering high-quality integrated arts instruction. Strategies included (1) developing a theory of arts integration and a plan for delivering it to the classroom; (2) aligning arts education programming with state or district standards; (3) using professional development to build strong relationships among classroom teachers, arts specialists, and teaching artists; and (4) collecting data to measure progress and then documenting the work (Nelson, 2008, p. 10). These stated goals offer clear indication that arts integration in this environment is focused on conceptually sound arts curricula and benefits from the multiple perspectives the partnership provides.

Another example of collaborative arts curricula in an urban setting can be found in the Fine and Performing Arts Magnet Cluster Program (FPAMCP), a network of arts-focused elementary schools in the Chicago Public Schools. Arts teachers at FPAMCP schools work with students and classroom teachers to provide intensive and integrated instruction in the arts. Students attending FPAMCP schools (1) learn and grow in multiple art forms: dance, drama, media arts, music, and/or visual art; (2) develop cultural awareness and understanding; (3) make connections between arts learning and other subject areas (curriculum integration); and (4) are exposed to arts opportunities and environments, both in and out of the Chicago community, whether through visiting artist partnerships, going to performances, or going on museum trips.

A long-term study in teacher change and the arts in a large urban school system (Larsen, 2001) noted that collaborative inquiry and the development of professional communities of practice were key elements of successful arts integration and teacher change efforts. The process of teacher change in this longitudinal study was slow, characterized by forward-then-backward movement. Partnerships with external institutions can provide valuable support and stability in the creation and delivery of professional development that is long term, site specific, and site supported; is composed of content knowledge and methodology; is desired by teachers who are convinced of the importance and/or necessity of the proposed changes; fosters collaboration and collegiality (change occurs at the individual level but requires group support); and features some sort of external pressure or urgency to galvanize teachers to move past fear into the risk taking that is necessary for change. In the instance of collaborative arts integration, pedagogical content knowledge was also a key requirement.

Teacher leadership has been noted to foster site-specific curriculum development, authentic arts integration, and investigation of the notion that learning in the arts, and its relationship to other learning, is complex and interactive (Deasy, 2001). A notable exemplar of this approach, the Urban Professional Development School Network described by Damore, Kapustka, and McDevitt (2011), also demonstrated the power of collaborative teacher change efforts involving urban elementary and high schools and an urban university.

IN SEARCH OF MIDDLE GROUND: ARTS INTEGRATION

Arts integration efforts can clearly benefit from current thinking about urban school reform, teacher professional development and communities of practice, and collaborative partnerships. A definition for arts integration proposed by the Southeast Center for Education in the Arts (SCEA) situates arts integration in the larger context of curriculum integration:

> Integrated instruction is often designed, implemented, and evaluated in collaboration with other teachers, arts specialists, community artists,

and institutions; and delivered, experienced, and assessed through a variety of modalities: artistic processes, inquiry methods, and intelligences. (Burnaford, 2007, p. 18)

When this kind of integration is planned and implemented within the context of ongoing and supported collegial teacher communities, situated in contexts rich with cultural resources, enabled by collaborative partnerships, assessed by trained teacher teams, and connected to school-wide curricula, the results can be compelling. The following paragraphs describe arts experiences from urban settings where partnerships are thriving.

In a middle school radio script project, students and teachers engaged in mystery genre writing. A university professor guided understanding of historical and cultural perspectives represented in film noir. Students wrote their own radio script, researched music related to the genre, and visited the campus radio station to record and produce the scripts.

In a visual arts multimedia and science unit, students and teachers explored the skeletal system, circulatory system, organs, and functions of the human body through a variety of media—silhouettes, bone drawings, "blood" painting, organ cutouts, skeleton "pop-up books," and poetry. The unit culminated in a larger-than-life multimedia body installation, where students performed original poems and created an accompanying "orchestra" of body sound effects.

Through dance, upper-grade students explored electricity and Chicago history, organized around the idea of flow. Kindergarten students investigated shapes and patterns, exploring geometric shapes with body shapes through movement. Fifth graders used technology to investigate ritual dance and integrated their findings into a personal historically themed dance piece with cultural facts and artifacts to reinforce the concept.

Community artists, classroom teachers, and arts specialists collaborated to create a Tree of Life, a large-scale installation project involving grades one through eight. Featured were West African mud cloths, Andinkra symbols from Ghana, Chinese silk paintings, Dutch wax cloths, Indonesian batiks, and Native American totem symbols. The integrated curricula developed through the project explored different textile arts on silk cotton and paper using paint, dye, and wax and investigated geography and cultures associated with each art form. Students led an exhibition featuring interactive experiences and mini-workshops for parents, students, and community.

In each of these examples, collaborative relationships developed over time facilitated the development of context-specific standards-based arts curricula. Shared leadership and relationships created through partnerships enabled the provision of time needed to plan, implement, and assess the efficacy of the units described. Cultural and artistic resources from the community were engaged. Teachers were given time to work together. Students from challenging urban environments experienced meaningful arts instruction with direct connections to core classroom subjects.

One partnership school principal described it this way:

> Partnerships have an exponential effect on our resources. Our partnership with an urban university provides access to a university-level faculty talent pool, potential teacher candidates, and on-campus resources. This increases our capacity to serve each child, as arts opportunities expand in number and quality. This also elevates the role of our school in the community, as a long-standing academic institution helps us connect to other public and private schools, artists, and the vibrant Chicago arts community. These diverse connections bring energy, skill sets, experiences, and perspectives. The infusion of human capital also provides a model of cooperation, collaboration, and consensus building for our parents and students. (interview transcript, 2010)

It must be noted that professional communities of practice that emerge from long-term partnership efforts require sustained time to develop, resources to maintain, and administrative vision and support to enable and to encourage. Human capital is the engine, supported by insider/outsider relationships with cultural and education organizations. Proactive inclusion of the classroom teacher in the community of arts integration professionals can support changes in classroom practice to include the arts, enable more effective use of resources, and expand the potential for students to experience authentic and meaningful arts instruction.

CONCLUSION

What is necessary to enable schools and teachers to provide the kind of rich arts integration described in this chapter? Teacher professional development efforts in the arts should provide teachers the opportunity to develop pedagogical content knowledge in the arts, in collaborative environments that encourage action and reflection. Classroom observation, individual coaching, and peer support should reinforce work in these content areas. Partnerships with outside organizations can facilitate such opportunities, working collaboratively with school personnel so that programs available to teachers address individual school goals, as well as district and state mandates. Long-term planning and involvement in staff development can be effective ways to facilitate classroom teachers' acquisition of the knowledge and skill necessary for effective arts integration.

Also needed are programs designed to enable sustained coherent collaboration among arts specialists, classroom teachers, and external partners. There is consensus among policy makers and researchers that effective teaching and student learning in the classroom are not guaranteed by structural changes alone. Staff development for all participants, classroom teachers and arts specialists alike, must focus on subject content, pedagogical knowledge, and methodology to facilitate changes in teachers' habits of practice.

Professional development programs should be flexible in design, to counter the negative effects of urban policy churn, and should provide long-term support for teachers who are engaged in efforts to change beliefs and habits of practice as they learn to include the arts in the curriculum (Damore & Kapustka, 2007; Damore et al., 2008; Larsen, 2001, 2008). It is clear that classroom teachers faced with district and state mandates to provide arts instruction must personally experience meaningful artistic growth to provide effective arts instruction. Content knowledge and pedagogical skill in teaching that content are also required. Collaborative partnerships can provide powerful impetus, long-term vision, necessary resources, and important leadership in making effective arts integration curricula a reality in urban schools.

REFERENCES

American Recovery and Reinvestment Act. (2009). Retrieved from http://www.recovery.gov/About/Pages/The_Act.aspx

Arts Education Partnership Task Force on Higher Education. (2007). *Working partnerships: Professional development of the arts teaching workforce.* Retrieved from http://209.59.135.52/files/partnership/AEP%20WorkingPartnerships.pdf?PHPSESSID=119 5e48c51c20a3ef72c63393579ecf9

Arts for Every Student. (2006). Retrieved from http://www.arts.wa.gov/education/AERI/Arts-Education-Resources-Initative-Booklet.pdf

Ball, D. L., & Cohen, D. K. (1999). Developing practice, developing practitioners: Towards a practice-based theory of professional education. In G. Sykes & L. Darling-Hammond (Eds.), *Teaching as the learning profession: Handbook of policy and practice* (pp. 3–32). San Francisco, CA: Jossey-Bass.

Barrett, J., & Veblen, K. (2012). Meaningful connections in a comprehensive approach to the music curriculum. In G. McPherson & G. Welch (Eds.), *The Oxford handbook of music education* (Vol. I, pp. 361–380). New York, NY: Oxford University Press.

Barrett, J. R., McCoy, C., & Veblen, K. (1997). *Sound ways of knowing: Music in the interdisciplinary curriculum.* Belmont, CA: Wadsworth.

Benton, C. J., & Schillo, J. M. (2004). School and university collaboration partners: A model for collegial support of literacy and professional development. *Action in Teacher Education*, 24(4), 30–37.

Booth, E. (2013). Arts for art's sake and art as a learning tool: Achieving a balance. *Journal for Learning Through Music, 2,* 19–22.

Breault, R., & Breault, D. (2010). Partnerships for preparing leaders: What can we learn from PDS research? *International Journal of Leadership in Education, 13*(40), 437–454.

Breault, R., & Breault, D. A., (2012). *Professional development schools: Researching lessons from the field.* Lanham, MD: Rowman and Littlefield.

Bredeson, P. V., & Scribner, J. P. (1999). Learning about performance assessment: Some observations on teacher professional development. Paper presented at the annual meeting of the American Educational Research Association, Montreal, Canada.

Bresler, L. (1993). Music in a double-bind: Instruction by non-specialists in elementary schools. *Bulletin for the Council on Research in Music Education, 115,* 1–13.

Bresler, L. (1995). The subservient, co-equal, affective, and social styles of integration and their implications for the arts. *Arts Education Policy Review, 96*(5), 31–37.

Bresler, L. (1995/1996). Curricular orientations in elementary school music: Roles, pedagogies, and values. *Bulletin for the Council on Research in Music Education, 127,* 22–27.

Bryk, A. S., Easton, J. Q., Kerbow, D., Rollow, S. G., & Sebring, P. A. (1993). *A view from the elementary school: The state of reform in Chicago.* Consortium on Chicago School Research. Retrieved from http://ccsr.uchicago.edu/publications/AViewFromTheElementarySchools_TheStateOfReformInChicago.pdf

Bryk, A., Sebring, P., Allensworth, E., Luppescu, S., & Easton, J., (2010). *Organizing schools for improvement: Lessons from Chicago.* Chicago, IL: University of Chicago Press.

Bryk, A., Sebring, P., Kerbow, D., Rollow, S., & Easton, J. (1998). *Charting Chicago school reform: Democratic localism as a lever for change.* Boulder, CO: Westview Press.

Burnaford, G. (2007). *Arts integration frameworks, research, and practice.* Washington, DC: Arts Education Partnership.

Burnaford, G., Aprill, A., & Weiss, C. (Eds.). (2001). *Renaissance in the classroom: Arts integration and meaningful learning.* Mahwah, NJ: Lawrence Erlbaum.

CAAE Staff. (2013). *A policy pathway: Embracing arts education to achieve title 1 goals* (white paper). Retrieved from http://www.artsed411.org/blog/2013/04/embracing_arts_education_achieve_title_1_goals

Campbell, P. S., & Scott-Kassner, C. (2013). *Music in childhood: From preschool through the elementary grades.* Boston, MA: Schirmer.

Catterall, J. S., Chapleau, R., & Iwanaga, J. (1999). Involvement in the arts and human development: General involvement and intensive involvement in music and theater arts. In E. Fiske (Ed.), *Champions of change: The impact of the arts on learning* (pp. 1–18). Washington, DC: The Arts Education Partnership.

Catterall, J. S., & Waldorf, L. (1999). Chicago Arts Partnerships in Education summary evaluation. In E. B. Fiske (Ed.), *Champions of change: The impact of the arts on learning* (pp. 47–62). Washington, DC: The Arts Education Partnership.

Clark, R. W. (1999). *Effective professional development schools.* San Francisco, CA: Jossey-Bass.

Cobb, J. (2000). The impact of a professional development school on preservice teacher preparation, inservice teachers' professionalism, and children's achievement: Perceptions of inservice teachers. *Action in Teacher Education, 22*(3), 63–75.

Cohen, D. K., & Ball, D. L. (1990). Relations between policy and practice: An overview. *Educational Evaluation and Policy Analysis, 12,* 347–353.

Cornett, C. (2007). *Creating meaning through literature and the arts.* Boston, MA: Pearson Education.

Creative America: A report to the President by the President's Committee on the Arts and the Humanities. (1997). President's Committee on the Arts and Humanities. Retrieved from www.eric.ed.gov/ERICWebPortal/record Detail?accno=ED413276

Damore, S., & Kapustka, K. (2007). Using research to inform fledgling professional development schools: Data-driven decision making. *Mid-western Education Researcher, 20*(4), 2–11.

Damore, S., Kapustka, K., & McDevitt, P. (2011). The urban professional development network: Assessing the partnership's impact on initial teacher education. *The Teacher Educator, 46*(3), 182–207.

Darling-Hammond, L. (Ed.). (2005). *Professional development schools: Schools for developing a profession* (2nd ed.). New York, NY: Teachers College Press.

Darling-Hammond, L. (2010). *The flat world and education: How America's commitment to equity will determine our future.* New York, NY: Teachers College Press.

Darling-Hammond, L., & Bransford, J. (Eds.). (2005). *Preparing teachers for a changing world: What teachers should learn and be able to do.* San Francisco, CA: Jossey-Bass.

Darling-Hammond, L., & McLaughlin, M. W. (1995). Policies that support professional development in an era of reform. *Phi Delta Kappan, 76*(8),597–604.

Darling-Hammond, L., Wei, R. C., Andree, A., Richardson, N., & Ophanos, S. (2009). *Professional learning in the learning profession: A status report on teacher development in the United States and abroad.* Dallas, TX: National Staff Development Council.

Davis, J. H. (2008). *Why our schools need the arts.* New York, NY: Teachers College Press.

Deasy, R. (Ed.). (2002). *Critical links: Learning in the arts and student academic and social development.* Washington, DC: Arts Education Partnership.

Deasy, R., & Stevenson, L. (2005). *The third space: When learning matters.* Washington, DC: Arts Education Partnership.

DeBacker, F., Lombaerts, K., DeMette, T., Buffel, T., & Elias, W. (2012). Creativity in artistic education: Introducing artists into primary schools. *International Journal of Art and Design Education, 31*(1) 53–66.

Dretzke, B. D., & Rickers, S. (2011). FACETS: Focus on arts, culture, and excellence for teachers and students. Center for Applied Research and Educational Improvement, University of Minnesota, Twin Cities.

Duncan, A. (2009). Retrieved from http://www2.ed.gov/news/pressreleases/2009/08/08182009a.pdf

Dunn, P.C. (1995). Integrating the arts: Renaissance and reformation in arts education. *Arts Education Policy Review, 96*(4), 32-37.

Elementary and Secondary Education Act (ESEA). (n.d.). Retrieved from http://www2.ed.gov/policy/elsec/leg/esea02/107-110.pdf

Eisner, E. (1985). Why art in education and why art education? In Beyond creating: The place for art in America's schools. Los Angeles, CA: Getty Trust.

Fine and Performing Arts Magnet Cluster Program, Chicago Public Schools. (2010). Retrieved from http://www.cpsoae.org/apps/pages/index.jsp?uREC_ID=72699&type=d&termREC_ID=&pREC_ID=151365

Fiske, E. (Ed.). (1999). *Champions of change: The impact of the arts on learning.* Washington, DC: The Arts Education Partnership and the President's Committee on the Arts.

Fullan, M. (2011). *Choosing the wrong drivers for whole system reform.* Centre for Strategic Education Seminar Series. Retrieved from http://www.cse.edu.au/content/choosing-wrong-drivers-whole-system-reform

Gates, L. (2010). Professional development through collaborative inquiry for an arts education archipelago. *Studies in Art Education, 52*(1), 6–17.

Gelineau, P. (2004). *Integrating the arts across the elementary school curriculum.* Belmont, CA: Wadsworth.

Goldberg, M. (2011). *Arts integration: Teaching subject matter through the arts in multicultural settings* (4th ed.). Boston, MA: Pearson,

Governor's Commission on the Arts in Education: Findings and Recommendations (2006). Education Commission of the States. Denver, CO.

Heath, S. B., & Roach, A. (1999). Imaginative actuality learning in the arts during the non-school hours. In E. B Fiske (Ed.), *Champions of change: The impact of the arts on learning.* The Washington, DC: The Arts Education Partnership.

Hess, F. (1998). *Spinning wheels: The politics of urban school reform.* Washington, DC: Brookings Institution Press.

Hess, F. (2003). *The spinning wheels of urban school reform.* National Charter School Community. Retrieved from http://www.aei.org/docLib/20030717_Journal_three.pdf

Hess, F. (2005). *Urban school reform: Lessons from San Diego.* Cambridge, MA: Harvard Education Press.

Hiebert, J., & Morris, A. K. (2012). Teaching, rather than teachers, as a path toward improving classroom instruction. *Journal of Teacher Education, 63*(2), 92–102.

Holmes Group. (1990). *Tomorrow's schools: Principles for the design of professional development schools.* East Lansing, MI: Author.

Holmes Group. (1995). *Tomorrow's schools of education.* East Lansing, MI: Author.

Hope, S. (1997). Support systems for preK-12 music education: The roles of education agencies, arts agencies, and NASM Schools. NASM Annual Meeting.

Ingram, D., & Riedel, E. (2003). *What does arts integration do for students?* Center for Applied Research and Educational Improvement. Minneapolis, MN: University of Minnesota.

Jeanneret, N., & DeGraffenreid, G. (2012). Music education in the generalist classroom. In G. McPherson & G. Welch (Eds.), *The Oxford handbook of music education* (Vol. I, pp. 399–416). New York, NY: Oxford University Press.

Johnston-Parsons, M. (2012). *Dialogue and difference in a teacher education program: A 16-year study of a professional development school.* Charlotte, NC: Information Age Publishing.

Kerchner, C. T., Meneffee-Libey, D. J., Mulfinger, L. S., & Clayton, S. E. (2008). *Learning from L.A.: Institutional change in American public education.* Cambridge, MA: Harvard Education Press.

Larsen, C. (2001). *Complex silences: Exploring the relationship between teacher change and staff development and the arts* (Unpublished doctoral dissertation). Northwestern University, Evanston, IL.

Larsen, C. (2008). *Teacher education across the lifespan: What does our network-wide research tell us about the network's impact on preservice candidate preparation and inservice educator capabilities?* Paper presented at the AACTE Annual Conference, Chicago, IL.

Larsen, C., & Rieckhoff, B. (2013). Distributed leadership roles in a PDS. *International Journal of Leadership in Education.* (1-23). DOI:10.1080/13603124.2013.774051

Lewis, A.C (1989). *Restructuring America's schools.* American Association of School Administrators. Arlington, VA.

Lewis, A.C. (1995) An overview of the standards movement. *Phi Delta Kappan, 76*(10), 744-750.

Lieberman, A. (1990). *Schools as collaborative cultures: Creating the future now.* New York: Falmer.

Lieberman, A., & Miller, L. (2001). *Teachers caught in the action: Professional development that matters*. New York, NY: Teachers College Press.

Lind, V. R. (2007). High quality professional development: An investigation of the supports for and barriers to professional development in arts education. *International Journal of Education & the Arts, 8*(2). Retrieved from http://ijea.asu.edu.

McDonald, N. L. (2010). *Handbook for K-8 arts integration: Purposeful planning across the curriculum*. Boston, MA: Pearson Education.

Myers, D. E. (2003). Quest for excellence: The transforming role of university-community collaboration in music teaching and learning. *Arts Education Policy Review, 105*(1), 5–12.

Nardo, R. L., Custodero, L. A., Persellin, D. C., & Fox, D. B. (2006). Looking back, looking forward: A report on early childhood music education in accredited American preschools. *Journal of Research in Music Education, 54*(4), 278–292.

Nathan, L. (2008). Why the arts make sense in education: The Boston Arts Academy demonstrates the value of incorporating the arts into academics, rather than segregating education into two separate spheres of learning. *Phi Delta Kappan, 90*(3), 177–181.

National Assembly of State Arts Agencies. (2006). *Critical evidence: How the arts benefit student achievement*. Retrieved from http://www.nasaa-arts.org/Research/Key-Topics/Arts-Education/critical-evidence.pdf

National Standards for Arts Education (1994). Music Educators National Conference (MENC).

Nelson, A. (2008). *The art of collaboration: Promising practices for integrating the arts and school reform*. Washington, DC: Arts Education Partnership.

No Child Left Behind. (2001). Public Law print of PL 107-110, the No Child Left Behind Act of 2001.

Noblit, G., Corbett, H. D., Wilson, B. L., & McKinney, M. B. (2009). Sustaining change: The difference the arts make in schools. In *Creating and sustaining arts-based school reform: The A+ program* (pp.138–162). New York, NY: Routledge.

O'Day, J. A., Bitter, C. S., & Gomez, L. M. (2011). *Education reform in New York City ambitious change in the nation's most complex school system*. Cambridge, MA: Harvard Education Press.

Oreck, B. (2004). The artistic and professional development of teachers. *Journal of Teacher Education, 55*(1), 55–69.

Payne, C. (2008). *So much reform so little change: The persistence of failure in urban schools*. Cambridge, MA: Harvard Education Press.

President's Committee on the Arts and the Humanities. (2011). *Reinvesting in arts education: Winning America's future through creative schools*. President's Committee on the Arts and the Humanities.

Rabkin, N., & Redmond, R. (Eds.). (2004). *Putting the arts in the picture: Reframing education in the 21st century*. Chicago, IL: Columbia College.

Rabkin, N., & Redmond, R. (2006). The arts make a difference. *Educational Leadership, 63*(5) 60–65.

Rieckhoff, B., & Larsen, C. (2012). The impact of a professional development school network on leadership development and school improvement goals. *School University Partnerships, 15*(1), 57–73.

Ruppert, S., & Nelson, A. (2006). *From anecdote to evidence: Assessing the status and condition of arts education at the state level*. Washington, DC: Arts Education Partnership.

Russell-Bowie, D. (2009a). Syntegration or disintegration? Models of integrating the arts across the primary curriculum. *International Journal of Education and the Arts, 10*(28). Retrieved from http://www.ijea.org/v10n28/

Russell-Bowie, D. (2009b). What me? Teach music to my primary class? Challenges to teaching music in primary schools in five countries. *Music Education Research, 11*(1), 23–36.

Russell-Bowie, D. (2010). A ten year follow-up investigation of preservice generalist primary teachers' background and confidence in teaching music. *Australian Journal of Music Education, 2*, 76–86.

Sahlberg, P. (2011). *Finnish lessons: What can the world learn from educational change in Finland?* New York, NY: Teachers College Press.

Schussler, D. L. (2006). The altered role of experienced teachers in professional development schools: The present and its possibilities. *Issues in Teacher Education, 15*(2), 61–75.

Sirotnik, K. A. (1991). Improving schools in the age of "restructuring." *Education and Urban Society, 23*(3), 256–269.

Stake, R., Bresler, L., & Mabry, L. (1991). *Custom and cherishing: The arts in elementary schools.* Urbana, IL: Council for Research in Music Education.

Stein, M. K., Smith, M. S., & Silver, E. A. (1999). The development of professional developers: Learning to assist teachers in new settings. *Harvard Educational Review, 69*(3), 237–269.

Stevenson, L. M., & Deasy, R. J. (2005). *Third space: When learning matters.* Washington, DC: Arts Education Partnership.

Sykes, G., & Darling-Hammond, L. (Eds.). (1999). *Teaching as the learning profession: Handbook of policy and practice.* San Francisco, CA: Jossey-Bass.

Teitel, L. (2008). School university collaboration: The power of transformative partnerships. *Childhood Education, 85*(2), 75–80.

Vernon-Dotson, L.J., & Floyd, L.O. (2012). Building leadership capacity via school partnerships and teacher teams. *The Clearing House: A Journal of Educational Strategies, Ideas, and Issues, 85*(1), 38–49. Doi: 1080/00098655.2011.607477.

Weiss, C., & Lichtenstein, A. C. (Eds.). (2008). *Aimprint: New relationships in the arts and learning.* Chicago: IL: Columbia College Chicago.

Wiggins, R., & Wiggins, J. (2008). Primary music education in the absence of specialists. *International Journal of Education and the Arts, 9*(12). Retrieved from http://www.ijea.org/v9n12/

Yendol-Silva, D., & Dana, N. F. (2004). Encountering new spaces: Teachers developing voice within a professional development school. *Journal of Teacher Education, 55*(2), 128–140.

Zastrow, C. V., & Janc, H. (2004). *Academic atrophy: The condition of liberal arts in American's public schools.* Washington, DC: Council for Basic Education.

Zeichner, K. (2007). Professional development schools in a culture of evidence and accountability. *School-University Partnership, 1*(1), 9–17.

KEY WORDS

handwritten annotations:

KEY WORDS _(underlined)_

• Culture
• Intersection of { music / culture }
• Dynamic multiculturalism

poßles indígenes del Canadà

Cree culture, for native teens and young adults, is very important....It's good to have people who still want to learn the old ways of their ancestors.

SERENA, REPRESENTING OTHERS, DATABASE, MAY 24, 2011[1]

8

FRAMING APPROACHES TO WORLD MUSIC PEDAGOGY IN A LOCAL MUSIC CULTURE

Valerie R. Peters

WHAT CONSTITUTES CULTURE and how it is best described and interpreted is a matter of much debate. There is little overall consensus on its precise meaning, although there is general agreement that culture (a) is not an objectified, self-enclosed, coherent thing or object and (b) is not something that is learned by observing and documenting but something that is inferred; culture is portrayed, written, or inscribed in the acts of representation of the inquirer. In ethnography, culture is used as an analytic and not as a descriptive term. In other words, the term does not describe a set of traits of a group but refers to a form or pattern abstracted from observed behavior. Currently, that pattern is most often spoke of as an ideational system—that is, a kind of knowledge and understanding that members of a given group share.

Schwandt (2001, p. 50)

(margin text, vertical:) CULTURE

INTRODUCTION

Schools today find themselves surrounded by the richness of diverse music cultures. By adopting an anthropological perspective and ethnographic research approaches, it is possible for students to embark on a journey of inquiry to discover or rediscover a music culture in their community. This approach to learning about different world musics engages students in research about cultural beliefs and values embedded in a local community's musical practices. Students come to

128

understand <u>music as a human behavior, embedded in social and historical con-</u>
<u>texts, encompassing a web of socially constructed meanings.</u>

   This chapter will examine several theoretical perspectives that may be useful in framing curricular approaches to the study of local music cultures. These theoretical frameworks were used as a guide to conceptualize three case studies about the teaching and learning of local music cultures. The first case study was conducted with a group of thirteen students (fifteen to seventeen years old) selected from an upper-level music performance class in a multiethnic high school in Montreal (Peters, 2007). The goal of the other two case studies was to study the impact of the same world music curricular innovation used in the original study with different populations, a homogeneous grade nine music performance classroom of French Canadian students in Quebec City (Peters & Bilodeau, 2012, November) and a small group of Cree students in a French language classroom in Chisasibi (James Bay, Northern Quebec) (Peters & Bilodeau, 2012, July). My hope is that the findings of these multiple case studies with different populations will provide rich information that will inform and orient pedagogical approaches to world music pedagogy in particular cultural contexts.

   One of the objectives of the case studies was to describe the phenomenon of secondary music students using <u>the tools of inquiry of ethnographers</u> (participant observation, interviewing and transcribing) to construct and represent their understanding of a local traditional music culture including concepts, beliefs, and values embedded in musical/cultural practices. Students became "researchers" of a local music culture, acting as participant observers during local cultural events, experiencing visits from culture bearers, interviewing local musicians or family members, transcribing interviews in a communal database, and subsequently theorizing about music, culture, and society based on their fieldwork.

   The goal of this chapter is not to describe these case students in detail. The first case study is well documented (Peters, 2007, 2009), and articles describing the other two studies are in preparation. Data from the studies will be used to exemplify the theoretical frameworks that guided the conception of these studies. While theoretical frameworks are helpful in guiding the work of music educators, I believe that empirical evidence from the field needs to validate theoretical claims, as well as exemplify how these claims might be translated into practice.

   I will begin by exposing the different theoretical frameworks related to the intersection of music and culture from philosophy, anthropology, and ethnomusicology. I will weave in examples from the three case studies to illustrate how these frameworks are exemplified in practice. Literature and student interpretations of how music reflects cultural beliefs and values and how it functions as a culturally signifying practice will be presented. Finally, I will close the

METHODOLOGY

chapter with a discussion of what it means to educate musically in culturally relevant ways.

THEORETICAL PERSPECTIVES: STRUCTURING CURRICULA
Music as Culture

Elliott (1989, 1990) proposed a multicultural conception of arts education and several models of multicultural music education. He began by exploring the concept of music as culture rather than music as an isolated activity in culture. Music as culture defines music as a form of human activity that requires active doing, a doer, something done, and a context. "Music is, in essence, something that people make or do, a people's music is something that they are, both during and after the making of music and the experiencing of music.... The essential values of a culture are often reflected in the way music is learned and taught" (Elliott, 1989, pp. 12–13). Therefore, Elliott contended that music is embedded in context, and that sounds are part of a web of socially defined meaning. Music is a human activity mediated by concepts and expectations that are determined socially and historically.

Elliott (1990) conceptualized culture as both local and contextualized and music as a form of social practice in cultural context. "Music (conceived as a dynamic system), regardless of the form or level it takes, is an ongoing social practice into which new members (potential makers, audiences, critics, teachers, etc.) are constantly being inducted" (Elliott, 1990, p. 155). Elliott insisted that we must understand music as a human reality embedded in the social practices of art and not exclusively as a work of art. "In music (as in culture), the fruits ('works') produced by a particular musical practice are inseparable from their roots (an underlying network of beliefs)" (Elliott, 1990, p. 154).

> Culture, therefore, is not something that people have, it is something that people do. Culture is generated by the interplay between a group's beliefs about their physical, social, and metaphysical circumstances and the linked bodies of skills and knowledge they develop, standardize, preserve, and modify to meet the intrinsic and extrinsic needs of the group. (p. 149)

Therefore, music exists as a multidimensional phenomenon in a particular culture, as well as *constituting* a web of human activity, a music culture.

> If the nature of music lies in its multidimensionality "as culture," then encouraging insight into the meaning and use of one's own or another person's "music culture" requires us to engage students in the interplay of

concepts, actions, and outcomes that comprise the essence of a given music culture. (Elliott, 1990, pp. 157–158)

In other words, an approach to studying a music culture should encourage students to interact with the concepts in order to understand the essence and core values of the culture. Students who participated in the different case studies were able to gain insight into the meaning and use of traditional musics as an essential aspect of a local community culture. Subsequently, they were engaged in discussions about the concepts and values embedded in a community's cultural practices. For the Cree students, traditional music embodies such values as intergenerational contact, mutual aid, passion, fun, family (welcoming, getting together, pride), respect for elders, language, spirituality, and healing (Peters & Bilodeau, 2012, July).

Elliott (1990), in forming a multicultural concept of arts education, asked how one can develop a disposition for understanding and insight into one's own art or another person's art. According to Elliott, the goal of multicultural education is to develop insight into one's own self, to explore the relationship between one's self and one's culture, subsequently "moving out," trying to understand other music cultures. The starting point for all three case studies was the students' own music culture (for the most part). Given that most students know very little about their own musical heritages, it seems that world music pedagogy might begin with the "self" in order to move more empathetically and with greater understanding toward the "other."

Because in venturing forth and "living in" the inherent and delineated meanings of an unfamiliar musical context, all students gain what only such "moving out" can provide: insight into one's "self" (musical and otherwise) and the relationship of one's self to one's own and other music cultures. Accompanying all such risk taking, disorientation, and eventual musical "acculturation" is self-examination and the personal reconstruction of one's relationships, assumptions, and preferences. (Elliott, 1990, pp. 160–161)

Elliott's (1989, 1990) description of music as a local and contextualized social practice encouraged me to design a study where students could observe musical practices in an authentic cultural context and bring the cultural practices to the classroom via culture bearers. I wanted the students to think about music as culture and how the musical practices they were observing or asking about in interviews embodied concepts that represented a local culture.

Elliot (1989) proposed six curriculum models of multicultural music education: (1) assimilation, (2) amalgamation, (3) open society, (4) insular multiculturalism, (5) modified multiculturalism, and (6) dynamic multicultur-alism. The last three models are concerned with the preservation of cultural diversity. *Insular multiculturalism* is a curriculum based on one or two minority cultures that are represented in the school community. Each musical tradition is highlighted, but there is little musical sharing between communities. *Modified multiculturalism* selects musics based on regional or national boundaries and compares and contrasts different approaches to musical elements or roles of music in society. The accepted teaching method for a particular culture is used when presenting its music. While this approach presents a culturally diverse rep-ertoire, with a concern for equality, authenticity, breadth, and values of different musical expressions, Elliott felt that its weakness is the reliance on a conceptual approach to music learning. Elliott considered *dynamic multiculturalism*, based on a "pan-human" perspective, to be conceptually superior to the other models. This model asks students to interact with topics and concepts that are original to a particular culture's music. Ideas about music are developed inductively, from the bottom up.

I designed the curriculum in the case studies to incorporate aspects of the insular and the dynamic models. I wanted students to observe music situated and practiced in a local cultural context and to experience the "depth and breadth of human expression through music" (Campbell, 1992, p. 38). The students focused on one minority culture represented in the school community. They also inter-acted with topics and concepts original to the culture such as music and the other arts and the function and value of music in culture.

Dynamic multiculturalism illustrates Elliott's concern that students develop a world perspective that can be applied to a variety of musics. Quesada and Volk (1997) also emphasized the need to understand a variety of musical cultures and perspectives. They advocated for research to examine bimusicality if it is to be considered a goal of a world music curriculum. Studies should focus on how bimusicality influences attitudes, the process by which it can be achieved, and its relationship to bilingual studies. According to Walker (1990b), the danger of studying many different musical cultures is that no music culture is learned in a profound way. Understanding and experiencing one music culture in depth is a challenge. It is questionable whether students can become proficient in several musical cultures during their time in school. Is it realistic to expect that students will truly become *bimusical* or *multimusical*?[2] I believe that immersion in a local music culture might be a place to start before engaging students in discourse between and among other musical traditions.

Given limited instruction time and resources in schools, teachers must make important choices about which music cultures they will focus on. Accordingly, in

(margin notes, handwritten)
CURRICULUM MODELS BY ELLIOTT

DYNAMIC MULTICULTURALISM

the case studies we chose to explore identity construction of students by examining a particular musical tradition in depth rather than seeking to represent the multiplicity of musical cultures. We privileged depth over breadth. These are difficult decisions for teachers, but I believe that local contexts can guide choices toward significant musical experiences that educate for cross-cultural understanding and sharing, goals that include but go beyond understanding music as comprising many diverse music cultures to educating students musically (W. Bowman, 2002).

Music Is Culture

While Elliott advocated for music *as* culture, Swanwick (1994) asserted that music *is* culture, a direct way in. "It is nonsense to say that we cannot understand music without understanding the culture from which it came. The music *is* the culture. We enter the minds of others through their products—the things they make, do and say" (Swanwick, 1994, p. 222). Therefore, he advocated for direct experiences with symbolic forms that articulate the history and elements of a culture, as well as the perceived feelings and actions of people as a way of experiencing the music of other cultures. Learning about the music of others involves meaningful discourse, consisting of knowledge construction by students. This is very different than reading a book or hearing the teacher talk about a music culture. "Understanding music is more like knowing a person than knowing a fact, it is knowledge by direct acquaintance; knowledge *of* rather than knowledge *about*" (Swanwick, 1994, p. 225). Students in the first case study believed they learned more from the interviews than from books regarding how Italians feel about their own music.

> A book you read it but interviewing a person your there at that moment sitting with them making eye contact and noticing their facial expressions, hand gestures, the way they interact with you. There is more of a connection with a person than a book. (Tina, Database, Virtual Discussions, June 27, 2003).

Campbell (1992) believed that rather than focusing on nonmusical goals such as prejudice reduction, the development of intercultural understanding, and the enhancement of self-esteem, which are often offshoots of teaching music from other cultures, teachers should concentrate on the musical sounds and their contexts. These contexts include information about the music makers such as where they live, how they dress, and their thoughts about the music they perform. The goal of world music pedagogy, according to Campbell, is to understand musical expression more fully.

> Teaching music with a multiethnic consciousness directs us to selecting the music of more than one ethnic group in delivering a fuller understanding of "what makes music tick" to our students, and in helping them to realize the depth and breadth of human expression through music. (Campbell, 1992, p. 38)

Walker (1990b) advocated a pan-cultural approach to music education, "treating the study of a single musical culture as a special unit within a broader definition of music education" (p. 220). This offers the students the advantage of knowing their own music culture, as well as other music cultures. Walker insisted that society should offer students a variety of cultural influences from a wide variety of sources. Therefore, he suggested two approaches that form the basis of a pan-cultural music education. The first approach proposes that students experience a wide variety of "culture-free" sounds, auditory gestalts as he defined them. These are sounds that have hints and elements of many cultures rather than sounds from one single music culture. The second approach is for students to experience cultural sounds as music in the context of their belief systems. Walker offered an example:

> Hearing the different musical sounds that different cultures use to express similar events (such as tragic ones) can highlight the uniqueness of each musical culture as well as indicate the significance of cultural uses of music and the role of theory in helping our understanding, as well as determining the nature, of musical expression. (Walker, 1990b, p. 226)

Walker stated that all cultures believe that their respective musical practices reflect and embody value systems.

> A new understanding of the role and function of music within society is emerging. Music is seen less and less as something hierarchical in terms of its adherence to qualitative values, and more and more as possessing unique information about the culture which nurtured it. For education this trend is particularly important. For music to be understood, in these terms, implies knowledge of the ways in which music can embody, signify, and represent cultural values, belief systems, traditions, and deeply felt emotions which are peculiar to each cultural system. (Walker, 1990a, p. 78)

PAN - CULTURAL APPROACH

There continues to be much debate in the literature about the goals and structuring of multicultural music education (Bradley, 2012; W. Bowman, 2002). In terms of recommendations for practice, Swanwick (1994) encouraged teachers to take advantage of the richness outside of school walls and bring this richness to the students in the classroom. Therefore, participation in local community activities and bringing culture bearers into the classroom can engage students in significant experiences with different music cultures. This raises some important questions regarding the structuring of world music pedagogy (WMP) in the music classroom.

For example, Campbell (personal communication, April 3, 2012) posed the following questions related to WMP: What to teach (or whether to teach)? When/where to teach? Who should teach what to whom? How to teach (or how to facilitate learning)? Regarding culture bearers, bringing young artists-musicians who play traditional music and have appropriated and reconceptualized particular features of traditional musics, as well as innovating and "updating" the music, may have a positive effect on student openness toward the cultural tradition. The traditional music, often exemplified by oral traditions, may be viewed less as a static object and more as a phenomenon that is moving, evolving, and changing, as is the case with all musical traditions (Schippers, 2010; Nettl, 1998). This idea of reconceptualized authenticity is important to consider in designing educational curricula in world musics: "A powerful piece of music presented 'inauthentically' out of context may engage learners more than an academically approved, representative traditional piece, especially if the connection with the learners is well conceived and carefully presented" (Schippers, 2010, p. 59). During the second case study in Quebec City, young, "hip" culture bearers were brought into the classroom to interact with students. The positive reaction of the students seems to confirm the viability of this approach with youth in this case study. One of the students wrote about how the culture bearers reinvented musical traditions: "I was really moved by the music....It is the same traditional music base, the same principles, just that they made the music their own, did it their way" (Gregory, June 7, 2011). Another student affirms that music of the young French Canadian groups is more accessible to young people and that these groups are trying to revive this music to reach as many people as possible and to continue to disseminate the culture (Alexandra, June 13, 2011).

My research assistant noted that the future of traditional musics in schools may be facilitated via these young, hip groups that know the history of the music and are able to capture its essence while also presenting it in a new way that is attractive to students. She affirmed that the students were moved by traditional music that sounds modern and rhythmic.

In the next two sections, I discuss how anthropological and ethnomusicological perspectives framed the studies. Students came to understand the role and function of music and how music is able to communicate unique information about the society in which it was created. The studies engaged students in critical discussions about how traditional musics represent cultural beliefs and values of a local community culture.

ANTHROPOLOGICAL PERSPECTIVES

The students in this study needed to adopt an anthropological point of view in order to understand a local music culture. The goal of an anthropological perspective is to grasp concepts that are *experience near* for members of a community, ideas that make sense to people within their world, as opposed to *experience distant* concepts that capture the general features of social life. According to Geertz (1983), experience-near concepts are ones that members of a local community naturally and effortlessly use to define what people feel, think, or imagine.

> People use experience-near concepts spontaneously, un-self-consciously, as it were colloquially; they do not, except fleetingly and on occasion, recognize that there are any "concepts" involved at all. That is what experience-near means—that ideas and the realities they inform are naturally and indissolubly bound up together. (Geertz, 1983, p. 58)

Therefore, cultural ethnographers employing a Geertzian type of anthropological perspective seek to identify and understand the experience-near concepts that underpin a local community's cultural practices (including their musical practices). Geertz (1983) insisted that the art systems of a culture "inscribe a communal sensibility, present locally to locals a local turn of mind" (p. 12). One important aspect of coming to understand the mind of a local community is interacting in settings where members share meanings through "signifiers" such as art systems.

Geertz (1983) viewed knowledge as situated in local contexts where it originates. "The shapes of knowledge are always ineluctably local, indivisible from their instruments and their encasements" (p. 4). During the first case study, the students perceived the music they were researching as reflecting a particular cultural context, prewar Italy, where life was "simpler" and "happier." The encasement of the music was described by one of the participants: "The songs we are studying are sort of like a time capsule for the pre-war times in Italy, when Italian people had simple happy lives, which is reflected in the music very much"

(Jimmy, Virtual Discussions, Database, June 23, 2003). While this statement may seem like an oversimplification, it does reflect the nostalgic perception of the past of many of the older Italian people who were interviewed. Learning, according to the anthropological perspective put forward by Geertz (1983), means interpreting culture, bringing to light the diversity of perspectives represented by different groups of people. Local cultures are repositories for accumulated cognitive resources, collective products that capture the emic perspectives[3] of a local community.

Geertz (1983) believed that art is a cultural system connected to collective life, and, therefore, it reflects a distinctive, local perspective and brings to light the role of a particular community within a larger society. The local contexts of art embody implicit meanings that arise from their use. For example, one of the students, Melissa, recounted her grandmother's perspective regarding the context and purpose associated with music and how the meanings arising from its use can be lost when music is separated from its original purposes.

> I was just gonna say that, um, both my grandmother and my grandfather, they used to tell me about how, in Italy, they didn't have radios. They didn't have the, you know, the recorder, tape machines, CD players. They had nothing, record players, nothing. So when they hear the song it was from the neighbor singing it from, you know, the kid down the street. And now, my grandmother keeps saying that on the radio, she listens to the Italian radio, she goes "On the radio I'm hearing all these new songs but, you know, I don't know what it means. Its just like some girl singing it. When I was little, there was whoever is singing to the daughter of so and so to get them to fall asleep because it was the song that the mother sang to them." Like, it had, it has a specific meaning. You don't know it anymore. (Melissa, Transcription, June 16, 2003)

"The arts reflect the culture 'out of which they come' and they embody ideas in cultural processes and products, reflecting the ways of thinking of a local community" (Geertz, 1983, p. 119). The arts, including music, communicate these ideas visibly, audibly, and tangibly. By analyzing symbolic art forms, a communicative system, we can interpret how a community thinks and uncover the cultural beliefs and values that are important to its members (Geertz, 1983).

ETHNOMUSICOLOGICAL PERSPECTIVES

Ethnomusicologists have contributed significantly to the conceptualization of world music pedagogy. In addition to their detailed studies of different music cultures, they have also enlightened the music education community by the research methods employed to study different musical and cultural practices, as well as illuminating the differences in teaching, learning, and cultural transmission from one practice to another. Nettl (1998) clarified the inclusive nature of ethnomusicology in the study of world musics:

> Ethnomusicology is <u>not</u> the study of ethnic musics.... Ethnomusicology is <u>not</u> the study of exotic musics, folk and tribal musics; or rather, not exclusively of such musics. It is not indeed, the study of any one group of musics but, ideally, the study of all of the world's music from particular perspectives. (p. 24)

One of the most important contributions of ethnomusicology to world music pedagogy is the affirmation that all musics reflect the culture and the values of a particular group of people. The scope of this chapter does not allow an exhaustive discussion of the related work of ethnomusicologists. Instead, significant literature that contributes to the conceptualization of world music pedagogy has been chosen.

Rice (1985) is one example of an ethnomusicologist who has made significant contributions. His study in Bulgaria revealed that music was integrated into everyday life, rather than existing as a separate entity. Music was a pastime in a preliterate and pre-Walkman society, and the person-to-person interaction, especially with older people, was an important part of preserving the music culture. These older people often act as bearers of culture and tradition, and, therefore, they are often good informants for younger people who may not know about a particular musical practice. In Bulgaria, music was learned informally rather than being taught as part of a sequential curriculum. This observation led Rice to question the common teaching practices of music educators in schools. "We teach our own version of musical knowledge and pretend that young people come in as blank slates" (Rice, 1985, p. 118). The paradigm of the conductor/teacher makes it difficult for some music educators to break with tradition and become facilitators of student learning, taking into account children's prior knowledge.

According to Nettl (1985), "ethnomusicology teaches that music reflects culture" (p. 75). "It has long been a basic assumption that the music of a society in some way reflects its values" (Nettl, 1985, p. 69). Nettl cited the work of David McAllester with the Navaho as pioneering an anthropological approach, connecting the values and characteristics of a culture with the uses and conceptions of music. Nettl's work in Iran focused on the study of music as a system of sound in addition to identifying central social values and behaviors of the Iranian people. His findings associate the values of hierarchy, individualism, surprise, and framing of events with the classical music system in Iran. This connection between musical practices and cultural values is an important aspect of Nettl's work. The symbolic nature of music means that learning music allows a person to understand what is important in a particular culture. Nettl illustrated how this is possible.

> The *radif* is a repertory of music in which the values of Iranian culture are particularly well reflected. But it is also the main teaching tool of classical music. In some ways it functions as professor and etude, exercises and theory text. And if Persian classical music is a reflection of cultural values, the *radif* must be a device for teaching not only the music but also these cultural values it symbolizes. Our ways of teaching our musical system inevitably are also ways in which we teach the values of our culture: and the more central the music, the more central their values to our culture. It is believed that some societies even more than the rest use music as a way of teaching their own culture. Thus we say that music is thought in some cultures to have primarily an enculturative function. It is possible that some societies actually make this explicit, saying, as it were, that the purpose of learning music is to learn what is really important about culture. But I would suggest that to some extent many or all societies use music for this purpose. . . . I believe, music is used more widely than we suspect to transmit important if not easily verbalized values of society. (pp. 69–70)

Music reinforces values, as well as representing and teaching the values and guiding principles of a culture. During the first study, the students focused on the cultural beliefs and values embedded in the musical practices of a local Italian community's music culture.

In the publication *Music of the World's Cultures*, Nettl (1998) described the contribution of ethnomusicology to the teaching of the music of the world's peoples. "It is ethnomusicologists who have grappled most with the difficulties inherent in looking at and listening to musics outside one's own background, with the problems of studying music both in its own cultural context and also from a comparative perspective, and with ways of seeing what it is that music does in culture" (p. 23). Nettl believed that one of the principle markers of a group's ethnicity is its music. "All musics are 'ethnic' in the sense that for each music, each style, repertory, or genre, there is a group of people who identify themselves with it and consider it their own" (p. 24). According to Nettl, to understand something about a world culture, it is necessary to understand something about its music because of the important connection of music to self-esteem and cultural integration. Music cannot be understood without knowledge of the social and cultural context of a people. I believe that understanding a world music culture means studying the music from a particular perspective, focusing on what the music does in the culture, its use and function.

Nettl (1998) described the different beliefs and approaches of ethnomusicologists. A "comparative perspective" views each musical culture as one of many and no music as superior to another. A person's existing knowledge is used as a point of departure to gaining new knowledge. "Relativism" is related to the comparative perspective in that each musical system is studied in its own context, revealing its own unique perspective. Anthropologists and ethnomusicologists employ insider and outsider perspectives[4] in their descriptions of musical phenomena. The goal of ethnomusicology is to understand the structure of the music, what the society thinks music is, what music can do, how music is used, and the kinds of events at which music is performed. Therefore, the roles of cultural identity, family units, and social organization, as well as political and economic life, are equally important to the understanding of music in culture. Nettl (1998) made the following suggestion as a way to understand music in culture:

> Some ethnomusicologists have suggested a three-part model of music as a guide for study: a) music sound (or the "music itself"); b) behavior (e.g., events, lessons, audience behavior, relationship of musicians to each other); and c) concept (i.e. the ideas and beliefs about music). This model has helped researchers; it is also sufficiently simple to be helpful even to young students. (p. 25)

The students in the case studies focused on behaviors and concepts about music. They were able to pursue their understanding of traditional musics through participant observation and ethnographic interviewing in the local community.

Fieldwork is the privileged way to understand how members of a society learn music and, subsequently, to reflect member perspectives in writing. Musical change and cultural change are related, and music should be understood as a process rather than simply a work or product. "It certainly seems desirable for the music teachers of the world's nations to present music everywhere as a constantly changing, constantly adjusting and evolving phenomenon" (Nettl, 1998, p. 27). Fieldwork allows the student researchers to experience aural forms of transmission and to explain them to readers, allowing a window into the deeper understanding of music.

Ethnomusicological perspectives framed how the students in my study researched a local music culture. Students were involved in case studies in order to represent the emic perspectives of the local community. They followed Nettl's (1998) suggestion of how to understand a local community's music by reflecting on how music is able to transmit concepts, values, and attitudes of a culture. The students experienced music in everyday life, and in many cases, they interviewed older people who acted as tradition bearers and who were good informants. The students experienced music as a principal marker of a group's ethnicity and focused on what music does in culture. They used their existing knowledge as a point of departure for new knowledge and studied music in the framework of a local music culture.

HOW MUSIC REFLECTS CULTURAL BELIEFS AND VALUES

In this section I will present data from the first case study as students were asked to identify cultural beliefs and values expressed by members of a local Italian community and observed in traditional musical practices (Peters, 2007). I asked the students the following questions during the online discussion that took place on June 27, 2003:

> Having read all the interview transcriptions and other notes in the database, what do you think are the most important common features of Italian traditional music? Why do you think this music is important to the culture? What is the value of music for a particular cultural group? What are the important cultural values and beliefs that are reflected in the interviews (please give examples—don't talk about your interview only—I would like you to show me what you have learned from other interviews). Do you think the music reflects the cultural beliefs and values of a people? How? (give examples) (Ms. Peters, Database, Virtual Discussions, Discussion – June 27 – 9-11 a.m., June 27, 2003)

I was asking students to identify the important cultural beliefs and values of a local community and to represent their understanding of the culture. This question is directly connected to my second research question: how does a selected group of secondary students represent[5] their understanding of a local music culture, including concepts and values embedded in cultural practices? In the following two citations, students describe how the lyrics and traditional Italian songs reflect the values of a local community:

> Music does reflect beliefs and values. Love in the songs reflects the love of the people. The harships [hardships] in some of the songs represents what the people went through. The music represents the hope and the love and

the faith and I think that is really important to realize. Most italian music is joyful and up lifting. (Nadine, Database, Virtual Discussions, Question 3, June 27, 2003)

Do I think the music reflects these beliefs? Yes, I most certainly do. Just by listening to the lyrics you can get an idea of the people's mentalities, the kind of people they are and how they act. (Victor, Database, Virtual Discussions, June 29, 2003)

The preceding citations reflect on how cultural beliefs and values can be deduced from song lyrics. In the first citation, the student describes traditional Italian music as generally uplifting, whether the songs talk about love or hardships. The student quoted next believes that music allows people to understand the mentality of a group of people and the way they act. In the following passage, a student describes in detail how music reflects the beliefs and values of a particular culture:

Folk music defenetally reflects the values and beliefs of that culture. In the "old days" in Italy, when the folk music was sung, it was about hard work, going to war, family, love...and as we've said in class, these are some of the values that Italians believe in. Just look at our society. We are very materialist and sexual. Our music relflects that! Shania Twain's Ka-Ching (she sings 'We live in a greedy little world'), Christina Agulera's Dirrty ('I need that-uuhh-to get me off, sweating till my clothes come off'). If you notice, in the late [lately], the message in music has changed so much throught [throughout] the years, as society's values change. From The Beatles' I Wanna Hold Your Hand, to Bryan Adams' Every Really Love A Woman, to the Bloodhound Gang's Bad Touch. These three songs are from three different eras and look at the love in three different ways. Same goes for Folk music; the songs from back the [then] represent how they felt, their beliefs, their values...their culture! (Melissa, Database, Virtual Discussions, June 27, 2003)

In the preceding quote, the student gives a chronological timeline of examples to illustrate changing beliefs and values of society as reflected in popular music. This student describes masterfully how music is a reflection of a time and place and is situated in a local culture.

MUSIC AS A CULTURALLY SIGNIFYING PRACTICE

Students in this study were asked to examine the distinctive characteristics of a local music culture and to describe the shared beliefs and values of members of a culture as exemplified by its musical practices. Students represented music as culture, part of a larger context of the way of life of a group of people.

Students in the different studies were able to comprehend traditional musics as signifying practices. This means that music and all other cultural practices are inscribed with particular cultural meanings (Hall, 1997). According to Merriam (1964), one of the important functions of music is "symbolic representation of other things, ideas, and behaviors" (p. 223). Musical practices are inseparable from the underlying beliefs and values of a particular cultural group.

Therefore, songs and musical elements such as sounds represent concepts, ideas, and feelings of a culture. They objectify culture by operating as symbols to construct and transmit meaning. Meanings and worldviews are shared by members of the same cultural group. "Members of the same culture must share sets of concepts, images and ideas which enable them to think and feel about the world, and thus to interpret the world, in roughly similar ways" (Hall, 1997, p. 4). Therefore, cultural products such as music reflect the mental processes, the way a group thinks, and the context of a local community culture. This is what Geertz (1983) referred to as the "local turn of mind" (p. 12). Musical performances act and embody cultural values (Stokes, 1994). "Music cultures transmit sets of concepts, values, and attitudes that are essential to producing and understanding the music.... In all societies, we venture to say, cultural values and guiding principles are to some extent transmitted through the music" (Nettl, 1998, p. 28).

THE VALUE OF MUSIC IN CULTURE

One of the significant student findings is the importance and value of traditional music in people's lives. Music is a fundamental need, a way of constructing and exchanging meaning, and its pervasiveness enriches our everyday lives. Music is a signifying practice that embodies, enacts, and communicates the beliefs and values of a culture.

Art and music meet a social need, and they are integral to the cultural practices of a community. While this may seem evident to many people in the profession, it becomes even more significant when students express this, echoing the literature in anthropology and ethnomusicology.

The importance of music, as judged by the sheer ubiquity of its presence, is enormous, and when it is considered that music is used both as a summatory mark of many activities and as an integral part of many others which could not be properly executed, or executed at all, without music, its importance is substantially magnified. There is probably no other human cultural activity which is so all-pervasive and which reaches into, shapes, and often controls so much of human behavior. (Merriam, 1964, p. 218)

The following two student database entries from the first case study articulate the importance of music within a local Italian cultural community. Music holds the key to memory and unites the members of the community. Music permeates their lives with meaning.

> I also learnt about the italian music culture and how it is one of the most valued and important things in ones life. They cherish it, because it holds a memory, a connection to something they once knew. (Nadine, Database, Virtual Discussions, Question 2, June 27, 2003)

> All in all, music, is one of the most important things in the Italian culture and others as well. It brings great significance to them. It has a connection with them that sometimes people may not even have. Simply put it is communication through the soul. (Nadine, Database, Virtual Discussions, Question 3, June 27, 2003)

The students in the different case studies were given the opportunity to study a local music culture. As a result of visits from culture bearers, participant observation at local events, and interviews with members of the community, students were able to identify the cultural beliefs and values of the community as embedded in musical and cultural practices. They were able to experience firsthand the community's attachment to its traditional music and the significant contribution of this music to members' everyday lives.

IMPLICATIONS FOR CULTURALLY RESPONSIVE TEACHING AND EDUCATING MUSICALLY

Ladson-Billings (1995) defined culturally relevant pedagogy in the following way:

> A theoretical model that not only addresses student achievement but also helps students to accept and affirm their cultural identity while developing critical perspectives that challenge inequities that schools (and other institutions) perpetuate. I term this pedagogy, *culturally relevant pedagogy*. (p. 469)

Culturally relevant pedagogies that affirm cultural identities and culturally responsive music education practices that view students as resources, taking into account their prior knowledge about music and culture, may guide teacher decisions related to curricular choices (Hookey, 1994; Ladson-Billings, 1995). In addition, the community must be viewed as a resource that helps the teacher to situate musical practices in cultural context. Culture bearers from the community can be brought into the classroom and students can also go out to meet culture bearers acting within communities of musical practice. This allows students to experience music authentically as cultural production in social context (Klinger, 1996).

Making connections with artists and members of the community was an enriching learning experience for me as a teacher. During all three case studies, I chose to become the outsider to a music culture that I knew very little about. I concur with Campbell (1996) and P. B. Bowman (1996) that teachers must continue to pursue their education through musical outreach in the local communities that surround the school and that students' music cultures should also be considered when designing music curricula. Students in the first case study appreciated learning about a local music culture in context and from "real people" in the community. I witnessed the rich exchanges that took place between students and members of the community during the interviews. I do not think that this type of "learning" could have been experienced in the classroom. The participant observation activities provided the students with context and situated them within cultural and social activities of the community.

During the case studies, many of the students were interested in finding out about their own cultural heritage or the cultural heritage of the other. However, we cannot assume that all students will react the same way. Youth may be very ambivalent regarding the making of their own cultural identities (Yon, 2000). Nonetheless I do believe that the pedagogical interventions described may help many students to deconstruct and reconstruct their identities (an ongoing process) in relation to their own race and culture and in relation to others. For many youth, this time in their lives is filled with changes. Music teachers can encourage students to explore connections to their past, present, and future musical traditions. By studying a local music culture, students can make connections to how music functions in their own lives and how it expresses and maintains their identity. Teachers can encourage students to explore these concepts related to music cultures of the world in order to move pedagogical practices toward a deeper understanding of how music functions in culture and in students' lives.

What is at stake for world music pedagogy given the results of these studies? The findings reiterate the importance of music programs in schools as places where the identity construction of students can take place. Students can learn deeply about themselves and others through engaging with local music cultures using the tools of anthropology and ethnography. Therefore, curricula need to reflect the students' cultures and the cultures of the local community as a starting point for the study of world musics.

Studying music cultures in their sociocultural contexts is essential to portraying music as an evolving human practice. These case studies sought to place students in the contexts of music cultures and to interact with culture bearers and interviewees who were able to exemplify cultural processes for students. The aims of the studies went beyond simply understanding the musical behavior for its own sake. Understanding how music cultures exemplify cultural beliefs and values of a community educates the students about their own humanity. As stated by Bradley (2012), "Multicultural music education is not a mode of practice or curricular orientation to be pursued for its own sake, without regard for its consequences. It has deep roots in philosophical assumptions about the nature and value of music, and about the aims and objectives of education" (p. 427). W. Bowman (2002) insisted that "inessential though music may be to life, it is indispensable to a life lived well, or to a life worth living. It can, taught and learned well, impart rich meaning and purpose to people's lives....Music teaches us things about our common humanity" (p. 63). Students were privileged to share in the understandings of how traditional musics provide meaning and purpose, and subsequently, these educational experiences taught them life lessons about our common humanity.

W. Bowman (2002) argued that education should be about whom one becomes through educational processes and experiences. "Education is clearly concerned with identity, the construction of selfhood of a certain kind, and the formation of fundamental dispositions" (p. 67). I believe that the educational activities that students in the case studies have engaged in have contributed to attitudes and dispositions that have impacted deeply and in a transformative way their understanding of self and the other.

NOTES

1. Pseudonyms will be used throughout the chapter to protect the identity of the participants. Citations from the database are quoted verbatim (including misspellings, grammatical errors, etc.). Out of respect for the students who contributed these important data and to retain their authentic "voice," such mistakes have not been corrected or identified. In some cases, I have edited the students' writing (square brackets) to ensure that the meaning is clear.

2. Able to function in two different music cultures or in multiple music cultures.

3. Originating in the field of linguistics, *emic* refers to terms that are indigenous to the specific culture such as local language, concepts, and expressions used by group members to name their experiences. Geertz (1983) describes an emic term as one used by people naturally to define how they think, feel, and imagine.

4. Emic and etic perspectives.

5. Students' utterances (class discussions) and their writings (contributions to the communal database).

REFERENCES

Bowman, P. B. (1996). Defining your commitment to multicultural music education. In M. McCarthy (Ed.), *Cross currents: Setting an agenda for music education in community culture* (pp. 60–69). College Park, MD: University of Maryland.

Bowman, W. (2002). Educating musically. In R. Colwell & C. Richardson (Eds.), *The new handbook of research on music teaching and learning* (pp. 63–84). Oxford, UK: Oxford University Press.

Bradley, D. (2012). Good for what, good for whom?: Decolonizing music education philosophies. In W. Bowman & A. L. Frega (Eds.), *The Oxford handbook of philosophy in music education* (pp. 409–433). New York, NY: Oxford University Press.

Campbell, P. S. (1992). *Bringing multicultural music to children.* Reston, VA: Music Educators National Conference.

Campbell, P. S. (1996). Music, education, and community in a multicultural society. In M. McCarthy (Ed.), *Cross currents: Setting an agenda for music education in community culture* (pp. 4–33). College Park, MD: University of Maryland.

Elliott, D. J. (1989). Key concepts in multicultural music education. *International Journal of Music Education, 13,* 11–18.

Elliott, D. J. (1990). Music as culture: Toward a multicultural concept of arts education. *Journal of Aesthetic Education, 24*(1), 147–166.

Geertz, C. (1983). *Local knowledge: Further essays in interpretive anthropology.* New York, NY: Basic Books.

Hall, S. (1997). Introduction. In S. Hall (Ed.), *Representation: Cultural representations and signifying practices* (pp. 1–11). London, UK: Sage.

Hookey, M. (1994). Culturally responsive music education: Implications for curriculum development and implementation. In H. Lees (Ed.), *Musical connections: Tradition and change. Proceedings of the 21st World Conference of the International Society for Music Education* (pp. 84–89). Auckland, New Zealand: ISME.

Klinger, R. (1996). Matters of compromise: An ethnographic study of culture-bearers in elementary music education (Doctoral dissertation, University of Washington, 1996). *Dissertation Abstracts International, 57/05,* 1987.

Ladson-Billings, G. (1995). Toward a theory of culturally relevant pedagogy. *American Educational Research Journal, 32*(3), 465–491.

Merriam, A. P. (1964). *The anthropology of music.* Chicago, IL: Northwestern University Press.

Nettl, B. (1985). Montana and Iran: Learning and teaching in the conception of music in two contrasting cultures. In D. McAllester (Ed.), *Becoming human through music: The Wesleyan Symposium on the Perspectives of Social Anthropology in the Teaching and Learning of Music* (pp. 69–76). Reston, VA: Music Educators National Conference.

Nettl, B. (1998). An ethnomusiciological perspective. In B. Lundquist & C. K. Szego (Eds.), *Music of the world's cultures: A source book for music educators* (pp. 23–28). Reading, UK: ISME/ CIRCME.

Peters, V., & Bilodeau, M. H. (2012, July). *Engaging youth as producers of knowledge about local music cultures.* Paper presented at the 30th ISME World Conference on Music Education, Thessaloniki, Greece.

Peters, V., & Bilodeau, M. H. (2012, November). *The implementation of an intercultural curricular innovation in music education: A case study in Quebec City*. Paper presented at the international conference Music Learning: Benefits for the 21st-Century Learner, Quebec City, Canada.

Peters, V. R. (2007). Collaborative knowledge building of ethnic musical communities in an urban high school: An ethnographic case study. *Dissertation Abstracts International, 68*(09), 3778. (UMI No. 3278066)

Peters, V. R. (2009). Youth identity construction through music education: Nurturing a sense of belonging in multi-ethnic communities. In E. Gould, C. Morton, J. Countryman, & L. Stewart Rose (Eds.), *Exploring social justice: How music education might matter* (pp. 217–230). Waterloo, ON, Canada: Canadian Music Education Association.

Quesada, M. A., & Volk, T. M. (1997). World musics and music education: A review of research, 1973-1993. *Bulletin of the Council for Research in Music Education, 131*, 44–66.

Rice, T. (1985). Music learned but not taught: The Bulgarian case. In D. McAllester (Ed.), *Becoming human through Music: The Wesleyan Symposium on the Perspectives of Social Anthropology in the Teaching and Learning of Music* (pp. 115–122). Reston, VA: Music Educators National Conference.

Schippers, H. (2010). *Facing the music: Shaping music education from a global perspective*. New York, NY: Oxford University Press.

Schwandt, T. A. (2001). *A dictionary of qualitative inquiry* (2nd ed.). Thousand Oaks, CA: Sage.

Stokes, M. (1994). *Ethnicity, identity, and music: The musical construction of place*. Oxford, UK: Berg.

Swanwick, K. (1994). *Musical knowledge: Intuition, analysis, and music education*. London, UK: Routledge.

Walker, R. (1990a). Multiculturalism in the teaching of music. In V. D'Oyley & S. M. Shapson (Eds.), *Innovative multicultural teaching* (pp. 72–91). Toronto, Canada: Kagan and Woo.

Walker, R. (1990b). *Musical beliefs: Psychoacoustic, mythical, and educational perspectives*. New York, NY: Teachers College Press.

Yon, D. A. (2000). *Elusive culture: Schooling, race, and identity in global times*. Albany, NY: State University of New York Press.

9

SPACES FOR STUDENT VOICES

Composition in Schools and Issues of Social Justice

Janice P. Smith

MY PERSPECTIVE ON teaching composition is partial and biased—as any teacher's view usually is. However, years of guiding compositional activities in elementary school settings, then with undergraduate and graduate music education students and with elementary education majors, have convinced me that (1) it can be done, and (2) it is a beneficial use of instruction time. Composition offers another way of creating spaces for students to own their learning and communicate in their individual voices if teachers and schools allow those voices to surface and become sonified.

Sadly, in the name of allowing students to experience successful first attempts, composition activities sometimes are reduced to theory exercises and "fill in the blank" creations that stifle not only expressivity but also individual student voices. While the skills of artistic craftsmanship deserve attention, they should be taught on a "need to know" basis to the students. More emphasis on intention and expressivity allows the voices of even the youngest composers to emerge in their works.

Clearly this change in emphasis requires a substantive change (Jorgensen, 2007) in how teachers view their roles in their classrooms. It also suggests that teachers have some experience with composing themselves and that this exposure focuses on intent and expressivity. We cannot teach what we do not understand. We teach better that which we have experienced.

Such change is rarely easy and often uncomfortable, and as Kumashiro (2009) points out, just because something represents common sense or common practice does not make it the best way for all students to learn. While the suggestions for educational change in this chapter will work for many teachers and their students, it cannot be assumed they will work for all. The balance of power and control in classrooms has to shift radically for students and their teachers to succeed with music composing. Many may be uncomfortable with those changes. "Trying something new, or even something familiar in a new way, is not an easy commitment within the confines of the educational enterprise" (Kaschub, 2009, p. 289).

However, to move education forward and create positive change, educators have to disrupt things to some extent. When done with goals of student independence and expressive freedom, composition allows students to claim their own voices. Composition can also accommodate culturally specific ways for creating and transmitting music. Students can work from their own cultural contexts and backgrounds—and that includes hip-hop and other urban and ethnic genres. Urban schools, even those without performance programs, can be good places to start composition programs. Composition can provide a view of the world from someone else's sonic perspective. This can foster interesting cultural overlaps, as well as contrasts, and possibly facilitate better cultural understanding. Much depends on how the music is shared and valued in the classroom.

Composition should be done *with* students, not *to* them. The teacher is a coach and a guide; the teacher should not be the one in charge of the emerging composition. This requires relinquishing control. Benedict and Schmidt (2007) acknowledged that relinquishing control leads to "the fearful discomfort of uncertainty" (p. 30), but really it is a willingness to let go of the way that much teaching has always been done while embracing new possibilities.

All this begins with knowing or getting to know the students. The students and their concerns, opinions, and musical preferences cannot be treated as incidental to the educational process. Teachers can "find ways to honor the unique perspectives of all members of the classroom" (Kaschub, 2009, p. 291) and to allow their voices to be heard not only in class but also in the wider world beyond. This chapter will explore some of the issues that impede or support this effort.

SOCIAL JUSTICE AND COMPOSING MUSIC

Social justice means many things to many people. Music—and especially songwriting—can give voice to the issues raised by social justice concerns. Music is always reflective of its cultural context. The context and the processes of composition are likewise situated. Students write from their own cultural milieu. Fortunately, music and the act of composition can draw people together around a common cause or issue. This creates and strengthens a sense of community and purpose and can sustain people in times of difficulty. Music is often the most effective way to communicate the very human emotional content of the issues being challenged.

Composition can be viewed as a form of social agency, as well as a means of personal expression. One need only think of the labor movement ("Bread and Roses") or the civil rights movement ("We Shall Overcome") or the antiwar movement ("Where Have All the Flowers Gone") to see how the music influenced the individuals, the groups, and eventually the wider culture of the United States. Examples from other times and places could be cited, but the point remains the same: music moves people. This is as true for students as it is for other groups and communities. What students need is the space, time, and encouragement to express themselves.

In this chapter, after a brief discussion of who can be a musician and how a musician acquires those skills, I will offer comments on the empowering possibilities of composition programs. This will lead to a reflection on culturally responsive pedagogy and its possible alliances with composition in schools. A few examples of school compositional activities that have a social justice or societal implications will be presented. The chapter will conclude with comments that address how teachers can be prepared to lead composition activities utilizing and creating socially relevant musics.

THEORETICAL BACKGROUND
Who Is a Musician and How Is Musicianship Defined?

If music educators are to re-envision school music curricula by including student composition, they will also need to examine their inherent beliefs about musicianship. Dictionaries usually define musicianship as skill at performing music, if they define that separately from what a musician is it at all. (See, for example, wordnetweb.princeton.edu/perl/webwn). Occasionally conductors and composers are also listed as having musicianship, but this is rare. If there is any hope of making music curricula more encompassing, this needs to change. Teachers are able to conceive of and promulgate a definition of musicianship that includes skills besides performance skill.

Reimer (2003) suggested a variety of musical intelligences (composing, performing, improvising, listening, music theory, musicology and criticism, music teaching). Each of these could be viewed as needing very different types of thinking, but also as ways of being musical. However, when performance is nearly the *only* option open to students, gifted composers may never be noticed; indeed, they are somewhat unlikely to ever emerge in many school settings because of lack of opportunity and encouragement. (I am deliberately ignoring the other intelligences here. Other whole chapters could expand on each of those.)

Some students will find their way outside of the usual school offerings. They may take guitar lessons and write songs, form their own ensembles, or even find a composition teacher (if they already have traditional instrumental training, particularly in piano). As computer and web-based composing applications become more and more available, other people might take up the task of composing for the pleasure of it *if someone suggested it might be a pleasant way to pass time and gave them some ideas on how to proceed.* These applications, too, can be found online. Even an audience can be located among the social networks available. Still, there is a role for the interaction between a guiding teacher and a live face-to-face audience.

It is difficult to imagine a school English/language arts curriculum that did not encourage students to write for the pleasure of it—even in these test-driven times. Letters, blogs, stories, poems, and many other kinds of writing are explained, assigned, encouraged, and published in some format. Even allowing for the time constraints and public expectations for school music programs, it would seem wise, and even necessary, to encourage informal music compositions for various occasions in people's lives. Examples from schools could include songs for special people (teacher, nurse, principal, custodian), for special occasions (birthdays, holidays, Earth Day, concerts), and for dealing with strong feelings (loss of pets, moving away from friends, grandparents coming to visit, new baby).

When students come to see composing as something everyone can do, some will continue to pursue it as an avocation and for personal expression in other areas of life. Students should be able to write a song or piece as easily as they construct an essay or research paper. However, music educators often lack the models, training, and experience to implement this aspect of the curriculum.

This leads students and others to believe that only special people can compose, when actually it is more a factor of exposure, experience, and effort. As people come to see themselves as composers, they often find their voices and use them. Granted, some will be much more talented at it than others; obviously, this is true of writers as well, but educators do not teach writing only to the gifted. Composition should not be the exclusive preserve of the gifted either.

Empowerment and Composition

Many times students seem to flourish as they take the risks associated with composing. This is similar to acquiring performance skills but seems to be of a much more personal nature when the young composer is trying to sonify his or her own feelings and opinions. When students learn they have something to say and how to begin to say it, composing can increase self-efficacy and self-esteem. Younker and Hickey (2007) pointed out two aspects of the self as articulated by Bruner (1996): agency and articulation. Agency is related to self-efficacy: can learners initiate, create, and complete a composition on their own? For this to occur, the students must have the power to make most of the decisions about the work themselves.

When all the power and control lies with the teacher, this ability is stifled. This is the problem with the compositional etudes that are overly prescriptive: very few choices remain for the students to make. While this supposedly guarantees success for most students, it also often guarantees cookie-cutter compositions with little to no expressivity. Teachers need to distinguish between etudes designed to teach, reinforce, or assess musical skills and concepts and those compositions designed to elicit student creativity and expression.

Second, Younker and Hickey commented on Bruner's idea of self-evaluation. Bruner felt that self-efficacy is directly related to people's ability and agency in evaluating themselves. This is where teachers and peers can play a powerful role in developing a student's confidence. Kaschub and Smith (2009) wrote elsewhere about the need for creating a supportive community of composers and how to structure that as a positive experience for all learners. Briefly, this is often done through remembering to ask many questions of the composer and making few suggestions. "Ask, don't tell" could be the mantra of the composition teacher in many instances. Younker and Hickey stated:

> Inviting inquiry into what is occurring, whether through musical decisions . . . or the running of the educational space provides all stakeholders opportunities for reflection on the choices and self-reflection of one's learning. Through such opportunities, ownership evolves, motivation increases, confidence emerges, and values are embraced. Students are given voices and spaces to think and evaluate. (p. 225)

If we truly want to encourage independence and freedom of musical thought, students need to have the space to develop those qualities.

Composition seems uniquely situated as a mode of musical engagement that can offer that creative space. Why has the music education profession largely overlooked this opportunity? As suggested in the introduction, two possibilities are (1) the lack of teacher models for guiding student composition and (2) an overarching resistance to change.

Often, once teachers begin providing space and time for composition, they find they cannot go back to teaching without including composition. Students begin to demand it. Once they have experienced "a participatory, democratic community, in which opportunities for opinions, informed decisions and justification are understood and accepted at the tacit level, and fairness and responsibilities are expected and practiced" (Younker & Hickey, 2007, p. 215), it can be difficult to get them to learn any other way.

Similarly, once teachers see the power and breadth of this approach to constructivist learning, directed instruction is never the same. Learning imposed by the teacher will cause many urban adolescent students to resist instruction because they are determined not to be what school is trying to make them into. If students are allowed the freedom to create, that resistance can fade somewhat. Adolescents need that freedom to express who they feel they are becoming. Composing, especially songwriting, can create a space for that.

Composing should be about personal ownership. Topics, genres, styles, and forms can be determined by the students. Teachers then can work to expand their students' sonic palettes so that there is an ever-increasing range of choices available to them. However, one begins with where the students are most comfortable. Even this will vary widely in the typical secondary school classroom. Teachers will want to carefully consider the needs of the students. Their interests, expectations, and connections to each other and to the world provide a foundation for collaboration. However, Vaugeois (2007) suggested, "Musical likes and dislikes are strongly associated with identity and, while musical identities are saturated with personal significance, they are also deeply connected to social and political relations" (p. 167). This can be a real challenge for teachers because they will need to study and learn new styles that are initially unfamiliar and often seemingly unpleasant. However, teachers who have mastered the intricacies of a Bach fugue, for example, have the necessary skills to analyze and absorb dubstep (or any other style of music). If we are truly interested in meeting our students where they are comfortable, we need to understand the music they enjoy. Only then can we begin to successfully expand their comfort zones to include composing.

This extends to the social groups and communities of which students are members. New music that resonates with the students will attract an audience if it is allowed a performance. (This does not mean necessarily that the composer performs the work, but that someone does.) Appreciation is a powerful reinforcement and can encourage continued effort. But all this must have a beginning. The next section will explore some possible beginnings.

COMPOSITION AND CULTURALLY RESPONSIVE PEDAGOGY

Vaugeois (2007) stated:

> Without tools to analyze how injustice is produced we are likely to adopt salvationist approaches that follow from an uncritical acceptance of liberal democratic ideals. Having the tools to ask a broader set of questions is particularly important to the field of music education when we consider that the demographic make-up of music educators is almost entirely middle class and white. (p. 190)

Culturally responsive practice can be one such tool and works especially well with compositional processes in schools not only for children of color but also for nearly all children. This section of this chapter will draw some parallels between composing classes, composers' workshops, and culturally responsive pedagogy.

Villegas and Lucas (2002) identified six traits of culturally responsive teachers. One way of considering the beginnings of a composition program in middle and secondary schools, particularly those with diverse populations, is to examine this framework as a model for teachers who want to encourage student composers. Here are the traits, as delineated in Butler, Lind, and McKoy (2007).

(1) Culturally responsive teachers are socioculturally conscious; they know that there are multiple ways of perceiving reality and that these ways are influenced by one's race, ethnicity, language, socioeconomic status, and place in the social order.

For young composers and their teachers, this reinforces the suggestion to start with the students where they are. Begin with the styles and genres that are familiar and let them struggle to come to terms with the techniques needed to work with them. Students bring into their classrooms musical content knowledge that is informed by their own cultural backgrounds and experiences. This clearly means the teachers must expand their knowledge of the music the students prefer and how it is organized and created. However, the teacher's task is to then take the students beyond their preferred styles and genres. Work by Green (2008) suggests one possible way to begin to expand the students' sonic palettes by having them attempt to learn aurally music that is unfamiliar to them and perform it. Creative teachers will be on the lookout for other teachable moments in their classes where unfamiliar music can be experienced.

(2) Culturally responsive teachers affirm the value of students from diverse backgrounds. Diversity is not a problem to be overcome.

This includes allowing students to work in their own preferred ways, some of which may be culturally based or influenced. Students may prefer to work alone, in pairs, or in small groups of their own choosing. Some may not have the group skills needed to work collaboratively and may need to be taught those techniques through modeling in whole-class activities and through role-playing situations. Many others will be well versed in collaborative working styles from their own cultural and academic backgrounds. While the social aspects of a composer's community cannot be taken for granted, those aspects can be expanded and enriched by the diverse perspectives brought to the setting.

All students deserve the opportunity to explore the creation of music in ways that support their learning styles and preferences, but they also benefit from other models and experiences. Teachers who have affirming attitudes about students culturally different from themselves and who have high expectations for student achievement will see their role as adding to what students bring to their learning, rather than replacing it. The possibilities for expanding their range of working styles are nearly as great as those for expanding their sonic palettes. Diversity is an opportunity—not a liability—for creative teachers and their students.

(3) **Culturally responsive teachers see themselves as educational change agents. They advocate for better ways of teaching and for bringing an inquiring mind and intellectual flexibility to the task of reaching all students.**

Allowing composition into the music education classroom can be a radical act both for the teacher and for the students. The topics explored, the ways of structuring the learning, and the appearance of chaos and lack of progress that can occur all disturb the quiet order of a classroom. Kaschub (2009) explained one project that addressed issues of social justice in a high school music appreciation described later in this chapter. Other ways of raising issues of concern to adolescents likely can be created. Once the students have a topic, there is often much to study and much to say. It is finding the artistic, musical, and often less obvious way to express themselves—finding their voices—that matters.

(4) **Culturally responsive teachers believe learners construct knowledge in numerous ways, many of which weave in and around each other.**

Learning styles and preferred musical styles are aspects of the composer's community, but so are the teachers' strengths and preferences and wider knowledge of the world of music. Composer workshops and group projects are not the only way of structuring a class. Composing classes can begin with a whole-group activity that shares something interesting, unfamiliar, or technical. This is often where issues of artistic craftsmanship can be addressed briefly before getting down to the work at hand.

It is also a good place to explore current issues and interesting side trips. National Public Radio's *The Composer's Datebook*, Minnesota Public Radio's *Song of the Day,* and *Indiefeed* are all podcasts that can be used for icebreakers like this. Similarly, these types of activities can end a class as a way of bringing closure to the day's efforts. They can also be student led with good effect.

Because different students learn in different ways, student-led mini-lessons can support those different approaches to learning. This can be especially important for students from traditions that value oral learning and literacy. While music classes in general can be used to facilitate this, the opportunity for oral presentation and discussion of new music seems particularly valuable for some students. This can be expanded to blogging about music for students who prefer to write rather than speak. Often students who are reluctant to offer opinions aloud in class will have very interesting observations and opinions on a composer's discussion board.

It seems wise to offer multiple ways for constructing and displaying knowledge in an ever more diverse and culturally rich world. Exploring alternative modes of learning can help students define who they are and how they learn. Doing things the same way over and over stifles learning—and all academic life. Teaching composition almost always mitigates this for both the teachers and the students. It is never an easy way to teach, but it is almost always an intellectual and artistic challenge.

(5) Culturally responsive teachers become very familiar with the background of their students inside and outside of school, and (6) Culturally responsive teachers use this background to design pedagogy that builds on what students already know and takes them beyond the familiar. These two points have been touched on previously, but some of the other aspects of planning composition work with students should also be considered. Effective composition teachers need to be aware of their own strengths and biases as well as, or better than, those of their students. They take into account the idea that their cultural identities and values may be quite different from their students and find it necessary to continually interrogate their own roles in a culturally diverse classroom. Such teachers acknowledge that their preferred teaching style may not be a good match for the majority of their students and that they will have to adjust accordingly. The teachers' preferences, experiences, and expectations are possibly very different from those of their students and their cultural communities.

For many people, anything unfamiliar is often not well liked at first. Becoming familiar with something can be an intellectually rigorous exercise for teachers and their students. Teachers need to model intellectual openness if they expect to expand their students' sonic palettes and frames of musical reference. This cross-fertilization of teacher and student learning is one of the great pleasures of music teaching. It only requires an invitation and an open mind to exist.

Creating communities of student composers is one way to bring that richness of experience into schools and other settings.

The conceptual model of Butler et al. (2007) of aspects of race, ethnicity, and culture that can serve as barriers to or supports for music learning among diverse student populations suggests other mediating dimensions of music teaching and learning that most educators would recognize: content, instruction, and context. In an adolescent composing workshop, the content needs to be negotiated. All parties need to have a say in what is to be done and how it might be accomplished. Blogs or other written assignments, as well as class discussion, can be included to allow for more voices to be heard. This sense of "buy in" to the process is necessary for success in the long term.

This does not mean that there is no planning or process structured by the teacher, but that these processes may simply be etudes leading to larger and longer work. Again, this style of teaching is more about asking questions and exploring possibilities than direct instruction. Done correctly, it leads to far greater student involvement and learning than is typical in secondary school music appreciation or general music classes.

Composing can also enhance performance classes, guitar classes, and keyboarding classes. These settings can be more challenging because of the typical size of an ensemble and its class structure. Setting aside some time once a week over the course of a year can yield results. Using the time after end-of-year concerts can also provide opportunities. Sectionals can be a convenient place to begin including composition and may provide a ready-made composer's sharing circle for works in progress.

Community expectations also play a role in this. When the pressure is there for performance after performance, there is often not time to teach anything else. However, if a teacher can find a way to have students create original compositions and to present them as one of the concerts, composing may take on a life of its own and become an accepted part of community expectations. Regardless of the recognition or lack thereof by the community, the students and the teachers will know the worth and value of the work they have done. Enabling the students' compositional voices is a very powerful thing and one they do not put aside lightly once they have experienced it.

Delorenzo's Places to Begin

Delorenzo (2003) pointed out:

Teaching music from a philosophy rooted in social justice has many complex issues, and one would dramatically shortchange the integrity of these ideas by suggesting that a democratic classroom can be attained quickly and simply. On the other hand, theory must be balanced with practice, and practice demands some concrete starting places. (p. 39)

She then suggested three ways to start a more democratic practice in our classrooms. These correspond well with the idea of a composing community of learners. First, she said we must "work with our students in a learning environment that promotes fairness, trust, and respect for others in the class" (p. 39). Of course, this is often much easier to espouse as a value than it is to implement in practice. However, it does begin with the values and attitudes of the teachers and how they handle issues of culture, race, religion, and sexual identity in their classrooms. It has a larger role in the school community and will be more difficult to implement if not encouraged elsewhere, but that does not excuse the music educator from acting equitably and responsibly.

This leads to Delorenzo's second suggestion: an emphasis on critical thinking. "This means critical examination not only of music and musical structures, but also of how democratic issues impact musical culture and personal freedom" (p. 40). Much has been written about the values and ways of teaching critical thinking since Richard Paul's 1990 book, *Critical Thinking: What Every Person Needs to Survive in a Rapidly Changing World*. The work of the Critical Thinking Foundation continues and readers needing more ideas for teaching students to think critically are referred to their website, http://www.criticalthinking.org, and also to their handy *Miniature Guide to Critical Thinking: Concepts and Tools* by Richard Paul and Linda Elder (2008). This booklet provides a wealth of pithy ideas for guiding discussion to support critical thought and commentary.

Third, Delorenzo suggested that students become involved in social justice issues and in advocacy in their schools, their communities, and the world beyond. The next section of this chapter briefly describes some compositional projects that implement this suggestion. These ideas are meant to inspire other creative ideas in educators that can encourage broader social justice involvement among their students via composition and the resulting performances.

EXAMPLES OF PRACTICE

First, here are a few reminders about coaching composition. Sonifying feelings is about organizing sound in expressive ways. It is not about using the tools of preservation (especially notation). Beginning with prescriptive etudes and exercises can stifle all but the most hardy individual voices. The examples presented to follow do not begin with notation, but with encouraging thinking and creating in sound, and then preserving it by whatever means seems appropriate. Most are designed for secondary-level students, but some can be adapted to younger students.

As stated before, composition should be something done with students, not to them. Teachers function as coaches and guides. They are collaborators in a process. Second, students benefit from repeating these experiences. The teachers become more comfortable with the process and the students become more polished in their skills and conceptual understanding. Students almost always benefit from the opportunity to do similar projects. While much can be accomplished in a one-time experience, and while some students will repeat the process on their own, second and third attempts usually lead to greater skills and to the exploration of other media and techniques. This is especially true if the students receive proper feedback and support.

Unfortunately, composition is a time-intensive process, and repetition is not always possible. One solution to this problem is the formation of a composer's ensemble class or a composer's club.

Forming a Composer's Club

One solution to the idea of being able to continue composing beyond in-class projects for those students who are interested in further explorations or for teachers without an appropriate space or time during classes is to form a composer's club. Ms. Margolis (a pseudonym) teaches in an urban school-within-a-school high school. She set aside Friday lunchtime as a space when students could bring their works in progress to the music room. Students brought their lunches and compositional products in process and sat in a circle taking turns sharing where they were in their compositional process and receiving questions and feedback from the other composers and the teacher. Five regulars appeared nearly every Friday and others came as they wished to share and listen. Most completed a piece before the end of the year, even though the group was not formed until November. Their works were presented at a Friday noontime concert for friends and any family members who could attend, and a recording was made.

Social Justice in Music Appreciation

Kaschub (2009) has described elsewhere a research project that she undertook in a diverse semiurban high school. This is a summary of that project, but readers are referred to the original article for further detail and for the insightful comments of the student participants in the process. The Critical Pedagogy for Creative Artists course was designed to empower students to "exercise a socially conscious musical voice within their communities" (p. 289). The class met daily for fifty minutes for eighteen weeks. There were eighteen students in the class. There was an introductory week, three units of study collaboratively designed by the class and the teacher, and a one-week reflection period.

The first unit was Understanding the Role of the Composer. The students collected pieces that focused on issues of social justice and explored their cultural contexts and the techniques the composer's used to create impact. This unit was also used by the teacher to build the confidence and self-reliance of the students. It took about four weeks.

The second unit was Identifying and Analyzing Issues of Social Justice and also took about four weeks. In this time the students identified issues, problematized approaches to collecting information on emotionally charged situations, and began to define their artistic intentions. Ultimately, several issues were selected and students formed groups to work on the pieces. The original intent had been that each student would create a work, but time constraints soon made that impractical. The work on unit two allowed common interests to emerge and these formed the basis of the group work.

The unit Projects in Musical Social Justice took approximately eight weeks and students created and performed their original compositions. Computers and available instruments played by some class members were used. Two performances occurred. The first performance was for the class and feedback on the performance and the piece was elicited. Several days of refinement and rehearsal then occurred before the official premiere. The premiere was attended by friends, parents, and some representatives of local agencies working to resolve some of the issues raised by the class or representing the victims affected by the issues.

Environmental Composition: City Sounds

Students in Mr. Perez's urban middle school beginning percussion class did a composition to raise their awareness of noise pollution and other acoustic hazards. Part of the class instruction time had included the necessity of using hearing protection while practicing and the hazards of loud continuous sounds. Students were asked to identify five examples of noise from their own usual acoustic environment and, if possible, to record them and bring them to class. At least one sound had to be of a quieter, more soothing variety. The class then spent part of the next period trying to identify and then classify the sounds. Some time was spent discussing which seemed the most intrusive and dangerous.

Mr. Perez then introduced the idea of environmental compositions: compositions that combine naturally occurring sounds with composed sounds. He played several examples for the students. He suggested that the students take what they knew about the dangers of sounds and the sounds they had brought in and create pieces using the sounds and the instruments they had been learning to play to raise awareness about hearing damage. Since there seemed to be several categories of sounds that had emerged in the classifying activities based on where the sounds occurred, some natural groupings occurred: sirens, airplanes, subways stops, traffic, and so forth. Most groups consisted of three students. Students in this project were also required to create a visual display of some type to accompany their piece and reinforce the hearing safety message. These were displayed in the music room for several weeks. The compositions were shared with the other instrumental ensembles in the school and included questions and comments for the composers.

Guitar Classes—"All They Want to Be Is Rock Stars"

This quote comes from an online twitter chat called *musedchat* in response to a suggestion that American music educators should be teaching guitar to every high school student who wants to learn. While the comment might have some surface validity, aspiring school guitarists also have voices that composing can enable. Teaching songwriting as part of guitar classes should be a natural part of instruction, but the focus is often on reading notation of various sorts and playing songs written by someone else.

It need not be this way. A quick Internet search on two chord songs can bring up a great many titles. Once the students know two chords, they can be encouraged to create songs. This may need to be modeled by the teacher in several different ways (lyrics first, music first, lyrics and music simultaneously, etc.). There are also several good songwriting websites that can assist the process. Additionally, once students begin writing songs, they often quickly expand their guitar-playing skills to keep up with their songwriting intentions.

This can lead to self-formed music ensembles. (Let us stop calling them garage bands.) Ideally, these would be facilitated in a supportive school setting by knowledgeable music educators who had a background in pop music. This is the case in some urban high schools where the teachers have side jobs as performers to augment their income and keep their hand in the business. These teachers often formed their own groups in college to play at events. Other teachers can learn these skills from these knowledgeable colleagues.

Encouraging the growth of pop music ensembles and laptop, tablet, and even cell phone ensembles can open new spaces for creative teachers and their students. It takes a willingness to explore, experiment, and allow new voices to arise from their own cultural milieus. While this acknowledges the students' musics and their cultural values, it also can expose them to musics beyond their frame of reference as they hear other composers and collaborative ensembles.

Unfortunately, many music educators lack the background or skills to coach these ensembles—and much of academia seems unwilling or unable to provide the background or skills needed except for the skills needed for traditional Western art music. Even students who enter college with a pop or non-Western music background are soon denied opportunities to express that understanding except outside the confines of their classes and ensembles. Bradley (2007) stated:

> Graduates of such programs may enter the classroom with broader knowledge about a greater number of musical practices, but their understanding, developed through and framed by colonialist representations, often remains constrained by racialized binaries: Western music and *"other"* music; "our" music and "their" music; "high art music" and "popular" music, and so on. (p. 150)

The time has already long passed where the traditional Western canon is sufficient to teach American students. Music educators need to see the field of music much more openly and less prejudicially. Students have other options for acquiring the skills they seek, but these are not always as satisfying as those that could be offered by an empathetic and skilled music educator.

Who Gets to Study Composition?

Earlier, Bradley (2006) also wrote:

> Music education has its own history of exclusion, a history that continues to self-perpetuate in part due to the imposition of colonial value judgments upon musical genres and practices. Rock musicians, West African drumming masters, North Indian classical musicians and many other specialists, unless they are also expert in Western art music, are not likely to find spots in North American university music education programs premised on Western classical music. (p. 24)

Thus stated, this is an obvious omission; a few higher education institutions have made efforts to recognize musicality other than in the context of Western classical performance. But the vast majority have not. Only jazz seems to have become an acceptable alternative in academe, and even that has struggled its way to acceptance.

Moreover, even where composition programs exist, they are not always available to music education students. These programs often are graduate-level studies and provide little background in composition pedagogy, let alone real guidance for implementing school programs. Where are music teachers to acquire the skills and conceptual understanding that will allow the voices of their students to emerge? Composition lessons can help them build their own skills and provide some conceptual guidance. It is not possible to teach well that which one cannot do. However, coaching students and developing their skills and understandings requires more than practical experience as a composer. Compositional skill is not the same as pedagogical skill. Both are needed in educational settings. Both can serve to release the voices of the teachers and their students. Unfortunately, as yet, this profession does not seem to embrace the need for this change. But change we must, because the musical world around us has changed radically.

CONCLUSION

Randall Allsup (2007), in the editorial section of a special focus issue of *Music Education Research,* wrote, "In times like today, the music educator is likely to ask herself, to what extent does my work impact the school I teach in and the larger problems I see around me? What remedy, if any, might I offer? Where can I do good?" (p. 167). Music educators might rephrase those questions to ask, "What impact can the work of students have? What remedies can we offer? What good can we do?" Allowing their voices to emerge and letting them define the issues and the contexts, as well as the forms, of musical expression may provide one pathway for them to define what is important to them, to define what their feelings are, and to sonify those feelings.

These changes and challenges will require courageous teachers who allow students to draw from their personal experiences and viewpoints to create meaningful sound. These educators will need to know themselves and their own creativity and perspectives very well in order to recognize the differences between their voices and those of their students—and to prevent teachers' voices from dominating. They must take the time to know their students' frames of musical and cultural reference well enough to support the students' nascent compositional projects. Those who embrace this approach to teaching will find themselves amazed and informed by the learning that will transpire in their classrooms and ensembles. The growth in the students often will be matched by a reciprocal growth in the teacher as all work together to find deeper understanding of the ways to sonify feelings—and life—into expressive music.

REFERENCES

Allsup, R. E. (2007). Editorial. *Music Education Research, 9*(2), 167–168. doi:10.1080/14613800701424841

Benedict, C., & Schmidt, P. (2007). From whence justice? Interrogating the improbable in music education. *Action, Criticism, and Theory for Music Education, 6*(4), 21–42. Retrieved from http://act.maydaygroup.org/articles/Benedict_Schmidt6_4.pdf

Bradley, D. (2006). Music education, multiculturalism, and anti-racism: 'Can we talk?' *Action, Criticism, and Theory for Music Education, 5*(2), 2–30. Retrieved from http://act.maydaygroup.org/articles/Bradley5_2.pdf

Bradley, D. (2007). The sounds of silence: Talking race in music education. *Action, Criticism, and Theory for Music Education, 6*(4), 132–162. Retrieved from http://act.maydaygroup.org/articles/Bradley6_4.pdf

Bruner, J. (1996). *The culture of education.* Cambridge, MA: Harvard University Press.

Butler, A., Lind, V., & McKoy, C. (2007). Equity and access in music education: Conceptualizing culture as barriers to and supports for music learning. *Music Education Research, 9*(2), 241–253. doi:10.1080/14613800701424841

Delorenzo, L. C. (2003). Teaching music as democratic practice. *Music Educators Journal, 90*(2), 35–40. doi:10.2307/3399932

Dunbar-Hall, P. (2005). Colliding perspectives? Music curriculum as cultural studies. *Music Educators Journal 91*(4), 33–37. doi:10.2307/3400156

Green, L. (2008). *Music, informal learning and the school: A new classroom pedagogy.* Burlington, VT: Ashgate Press.

Jorgensen, E. R. (2007). Concerning justice and music education. *Music Education Research, 9*(2), 169–189. doi:10.1080/14613800701411731

Kaschub, M. (2009). Critical pedagogy for creative artists: Inviting young composers to engage in artistic social action. In L. Bartel (Series Ed.) & E. Gould, J. Countryman, C. Morton, & L. Stewart Rose (Vol. Eds.), *Research to practice: Vol. 4. Exploring social justice: How music education might matter* (pp. 289–306). Canada: Canadian Music Educators Association.

Kaschub, M., & Smith, J. (2009). *Minds on music: Composition for creative and critical thinking.* Lanham, MD: R&L Education—A Division of Rowman & Littlefield Publishers.

Kumashiro, K. (2009). *Against common sense: Teaching and learning toward social justice.* New York, NY: Routledge Falmer.

Paul, R. (1990). *Critical thinking: What every person needs to survive in a rapidly changing world.* Tomales, CA: Foundation for Critical Thinking.

Paul, R. & Elder, L. (2008). *Miniature Guide to Critical Thinking: Concepts and Tools.* Tomales, CA: Foundation for Critical Thinking.

Reimer, B. (2003). *A philosophy of music education: Advancing the vision* (3rd ed.). Upper Saddle River, NJ: Prentice Hall.

Vaugeois, L. (2007). Social justice and music education: Claiming the space of music education as a site of postcolonial contestation. *Action, Criticism, and Theory for Music Education, 6*(4), 163–200. Retrieved from http://act.maydaygroup.org/articles/Vaugeois6_4.pdf

Villegas, A. M., & Lucas, T. (2002). Preparing culturally responsive teachers: Rethinking the curriculum. *Journal of Teacher Education, 53*, 20–32. doi:10.1177/0022487102053001003

Younker, B., & Hickey, M. (2007). Examining the profession through the lens of social justice: Two music educators' stories and their stark realizations. *Music Education Research, 9*(2), 215–227. doi:10.1080/14613800701384334

Section Four

Creativity

Although creative thought is usually considered in regard to the domain of the individual, Reimer encourages us to consider the intriguing dimension of group creativity. What is the nature of creative thinking in such a context?

Janice Smith

How are we able to give individuals opportunity for divergence when, obviously, the demands of an ensemble require convergence in many different ways to make sure that we have some type of a complete product or a complete musical expression? And I think that all of us can probably recall moments when we've been enabled or empowered to seek moments of divergence when we're going against what the typical expectations of a certain musical line, perhaps, might be. And we make our own decisions, even within a group setting.

Margaret Berg

10

IS A VIRTUAL COMPOSER IN RESIDENCE AN OXYMORON?

Bruce Carter

WHEN FIRST ASKED to serve as a composer in residence for a middle school two hundred miles away from my home, I almost immediately declined. At first there seemed to be more obstacles than advantages to working with students so far away. Although teaching composition to young people is a passion of mine, I feared that I would not have time to travel periodically to the school or provide adequate instruction to the band students. However, the director was insistent and persuasive in her argument, most notably stating that no other composer would agree to help. As it turned out, I was not her first choice as a composer in residence. I am unsure of how many composers she had asked before contacting me, but given her exasperation I assumed there were quite a few. Mrs. Finn, the long-time director of Braddock Oaks Middle School,[1] had heard of my experiences working with another middle school program from a colleague. She explained that most composers she contacted did not want to teach her students to compose, that "composers are only interested or capable of composing; they have no idea or interest in engaging students in the craft" (personal communication, March 3, 2008). Furthermore, because the school was located in an urban area known for high crime and poor-performing schools, outsiders were wary of visiting her program. After hearing Mrs. Finn's story, I agreed to help her introduce composition to her students by offhandedly stating, "I'll be your virtual composer in residence."

Although I have earned a master's degree in composition from a conservatory and completed several commissions for new music, I feel lost whenever teachers ask for advice concerning the composition process. My limited experience teaching composition in private settings and K-12 classrooms leads me to question my ability to teach composition, even in the most traditional settings. Given these uncertainties, the notion of teaching composition in a nontraditional way seemed a challenge I was not properly prepared to meet. However, upon deeper reflection, I realized that almost all of my composition instruction stemmed from improvisatory methods. Teaching composition to middle school students from a distance should be no different, just a different etude in the improvisatory craft.

THE VIRTUAL COMPOSER IN RESIDENCE

In this section, I address previous scholarship concerning models of compositional process in the classroom. Next, I discuss the ways technology was extensively utilized to engage the students and band directors throughout the compositional process. Last, I briefly address issues of group composition that are more social than technical in nature and how they meaningfully shaped my interactions with the students.

Looking for Guidance

Each of the band directors at the four middle schools I work with asked the same question before I arrived: "Exactly how do you teach composition to middle school students?" Truth is, very little is "exact" in either my own compositional process or the way I have taught group composition in the past. Therefore, before working with the students, I reviewed previous scholarship on composition pedagogy to gather ideas for developing an effective instructional design. In designing the curriculum for the four band ensembles, I intentionally did not consider possible limitations that might occur due to the distance learning. Four key themes emerged from the review that meaningfully shaped my teaching strategy: (1) task structures, (2) group instruction, (3) obstacles to teaching composition, and (4) compositional practices of eminent composers. The first category, *task structures,* describes well-formed, prescribed, or predetermined compositional experiences that clearly articulate a process for creating music. Three distinct themes emerged in this area: models of composition instruction in the classroom, extramusical associations, and free composition.

Models of Composition Instruction in the Classroom

Morin (2002) stated that teaching composition entails three distinct phases: expanding the compositional base, selecting aesthetic content, and finally composing music. To expand a student's compositional base, teachers must immerse the student in skills, contexts, styles, and rhythms to create a foundation of musical knowledge easily called upon when faced with a compositional task. Selecting aesthetic content concerns the student's ability to recognize an emotional element in his or her musical expression. To best engage the students, Morin suggested presenting material that is culturally relevant and accessible. In the final phase of composing music, the students begin by exploring sounds on their instrument and then are encouraged to improvise ideas that fit the compositional task. The key concept behind Morin's strategy is that students must have a large compositional base if they are to create meaningful and well-written compositions.

To scaffold students' individual decision making during the composition process, Hickey (1997) advocated for the use of the SCAMPER process when teaching students how to compose. SCAMPER is an acronym for substitute, combine, adapt or add, magnify, put to other uses, eliminate, and reverse or rearrange. The acronym is useful to students because it reminds them of things they can be doing in their composition if they arrive at a point where they cannot generate any ideas. Before beginning a compositional task, students are shown how each letter of the acronym works. This allows the student to experience various compositional devices before engaging in an individual task.

Extramusical Associations

Another common practice utilized to teach composition involves engaging the student's interest with extramusical associations. Extramusical associations provide students with ideas for their composition, as well as a basis for comparing composition with other familiar tasks (Berkley, 2004; Ginocchio, 2003; Kaschub, 1999; Tait, 1971; Wiggins, 1999). Ginocchio (2003) used extramusical associations by having the students create melodies based on impressions of literature, art, photography, or world events. As students become more advanced in their understanding of musical elements and composition, the compositional tasks also become more advanced and the students move from creating variations to adding expression, harmony, and even orchestrations. Kaschub (1997) also recommended using sources outside of music, such as poetry. Students use poetic subjects and the rhythm of the words to create either a melody that matches the words or an accompaniment that fits the reading of the poem. Kaschub emphasized that the subject of the composition must be interesting to students in order to generate maximum interest in the task.

Another composition task involving extramusical associations concerns the notion of a soundscape. A soundscape requires no knowledge of written notation or melodic structure. Students are simply given a scene to re-create through sound such as a city street, a jungle, or even a farm (Tait, 1971). With this activity, students are encouraged to create their own notation so the soundscape can be duplicated multiple times.

Using extramusical themes and soundscapes often involves creating a replicable composition with original notation and also relates composition and music to areas outside of the music classroom. Wiggins (1990) related the process of composition to the writing process that students learn in their language arts classes. Since students are already familiar with the concepts of brainstorming, organizing, editing, and publishing, these concepts easily transfer to the music classroom and help students understand that the two processes are quite similar. Berkley (2004) related the composition process to problem solving. Students using this comparison are taught to first recognize the problem, generate initial ideas, create a draft through development and revision, and then determine the final version through review and rehearsal. Goldberg (1990) suggested that during this process, students should be asked frequently how they are creating their composition. Asking students about their thought process not only helps them problem solve but also helps the teacher determine if the students fully understand the task.

Free Composition

While many researchers and teachers advocate for templates, limitations, and very specific guidelines to be used when composing with students, other researchers provide alternative views. Bauman (1972) and Wiggins (2003) both recommended providing students as much freedom as possible. Wiggins suggested that forcing too many constraints on the student is similar to telling students to write a story using only certain words. Both Bauman and Wiggins were concerned that compositional products resulting from too many constraints would be more contrived rather than a true expression of the student composer. For students to be able to truly express themselves and develop their unique voice, they must be allowed to compose whatever they want in whatever way they choose to do it.

Taken together, these studies provide meaningful viewpoints and strategies for teaching composition. The authors' work encouraged a compositional pedagogy that provided numerous approaches for students rather than a "one size fits all" method to learning. After reviewing the scholarship concerning composition, I was motivated to consistently provide highly prescriptive composition exercises juxtaposed with "free" composition. Examples of composition exercises that were prescriptive in nature included:

Find a friend's musical phrase that interests you. Can you think of two ways you would change the melody to make it sound like something you have written? Describe your new melody in words to someone who may never get to hear it. Notate the original melody and your new melody. Bonus Challenge: Notate your new melody in a way that looks completely different but sounds the same. How can you accomplish this?

Examples of composition that were more free and designed for students to explore various soundscapes included:

Select a piece of kite string that is almost as long as you are tall. Stand on the string with your left foot and after wrapping the string around your index finger a few times, place your finger gently into your ear. The sound you should hear when your pluck the string with your left hand should resemble a string bass. Can you make the string sound higher or lower? How? What happens if a friend touches the new "string bass" around the mid-way point? Next, using a metal coat hanger from your closet, loop the string around the hanger 5-6 times, wrap the ends around your index fingers, and gently place both fingers in your ears. The hanger should now be hanging around waist level in front of you. What happens when you swing the hanger and strike various elements around the room?

Each composition assignment the students were given included prescriptive elements coupled with "free" play. Other examples are provided later in the chapter and overlap themes presented in the next section.

GROUP INSTRUCTION

The second subgroup of research related to compositional pedagogy examines research involving composition instruction occurring within a group setting. Creating a composition in a small group or as an entire class is a strategy used by many teachers (Ginocchio, 2003; Hickey, 1997; Thoms, 1996; Wiggins, 2003). Small group compositions can range from creating short melodies as a group to creating a small ensemble piece to be performed at a concert. The importance of peer teaching is evident throughout the group composition process (Wiggins, 2003). Working toward a common understanding of the final product in a group setting encourages students to compromise and take on new perspectives. Sometimes, disagreements will produce new ideas and take the composition in a different direction.

In my experience, establishing a virtual residency where the majority of instruction occurred online presented many anxieties. For example, I worried that students would not have the opportunity to engage in unscripted, improvisatory musical play in fun social contexts. Early on I realized that group composition could provide students with a social outlet and the chance to interact musically with one another. Examples of group composition were largely influenced by the work of Green (2008) and her belief that informal learning is vital to the music experience.

Ask students to create small groups with no fewer than four in a group and no more than six. Next, ask the students to agree on a song they would like to learn and perform. Next, tell the students they that will not receive sheet music, but will have to learn the song from listening to the recording. Allow the students multiple days to work together to re-create the song on their instruments. After the students have performed for one another, ask each group to adapt their song in any way they wish. They can choose to change any one element of the song—the rhythm, harmony, texture, key, etc. After they have re-created their songs, ask the students to share their work, having the audience guess which musical element was changed.

OBSTACLES TO COMPOSITION INSTRUCTION IN THE CLASSROOM

Teachers unfamiliar or uncomfortable with the composition process are most likely to avoid incorporating composition in their classroom (Kennedy, 2002; Morin, 2002). Others admit that they feel such a large amount of stress from preparing for performances that they do not feel like they have time to fit in something else (Kennedy, 2002; Reid, 2002; Strand, 2006). Class sizes and complex schedules also play into the difficulty with incorporating composition because many teachers find it difficult to allow students to work on their own with too many kids, the noise factor, and a very short amount of time to teach (Strand, 2006). A lack of resources also contributes to this as many teachers may have the desire to use composition activities but do not have the instruments, space, software, or instructional guides to do so (Kennedy, 2002). Morin (2002) found that even if offered the training, funding, and resources to include composition, some teachers would still not incorporate it simply because they feel that creativity is more of a personal enterprise and that it should be developed individually and outside of the music classroom.

A variety of reasons and benefits exist for teachers to incorporate composition into the music classroom; however, a variety of obstacles stand in their way. According to Berkley (2004), one main reason teachers do not incorporate composition into the classroom is that there is a lack of publications about composition pedagogy and teaching strategies. However, recent texts such as *Minds on Music: Composition for Creative and Critical Thinking* (Kaschub & Smith, 2009) specifically address concerns and fears music teachers may have when incorporating composition instruction into classrooms.

Obviously, teacher involvement was not an issue in this project—each band director was excited about integrating composition instruction. However, all four band directors stated that time "taken away" from rehearsals was a significant source of stress. Additionally, the directors each discussed their own frustrations and feelings of uncertainty when attempting to help students in a process that was open-ended and foreign. Throughout the process, the teachers were encouraged to call or Skype so we could talk through their questions and address any anxieties. This consistent dialogue was key to the virtual residency. It was evident that the teachers enjoyed talking through their learning experience in addition to sharing the stories of their students' successes.

COMPOSITIONAL PRACTICES OF EMINENT COMPOSERS

A few books illuminate issues and concerns surrounding the compositional practices of eminent composers. However, the texts are often philosophical in nature, providing theoretical and abstract approaches to compositional practices at the college level (Adolphe, 1999; Ford, 1993; McCutchan, 1999; Piirto, 1992). In contrast, other textbooks written by eminent composers provide highly technical, prescriptive approaches to composition study (Hindemith, 1942; Persichetti, 1961; Piston; 1987). Besides these few sources, very little is known about the teaching practices of composer-teachers (Barrett, 2006).

In recent years, researchers have begun questioning eminent composers, focusing on issues of compositional pedagogy (Barrett & Ford, 2000; Barrett & Gromko, 2001). For example, Lapidaki (2007) interviewed eminent composers to view the ways they describe and analyze the composition process. Lapidaki had two goals in pursuing this study. The first was to obtain a better philosophical understanding of contemporary composers. She stated:

> With so many researchers of music education looking at the compositional processes of students in classrooms and music technology laboratories, it would be very helpful to acknowledge and draw philosophical implications for music composition in schools from recognized composers' voices and their individual composing realities. (p. 96)

The second goal of the study was to explore how a more philosophical understanding of composers could inform the practice of composition instruction at all ages. She stated, "A music teacher needs to indeed grasp how this creative process works in a real world context in order to foster and expand the student composer's craft of composition in educational settings at all levels" (p. 94).

After examining the lifestyles and compositional practices of the eminent composers, Lapidaki (2007) cited four prevalent themes: (1) the composer, the conscious, and the unconscious; (2) the beginning of the compositional process; (3) moving the compositional process forward; and (4) the composer between tradition and innovation. Lastly, Lapidaki stated that composer-teachers should strongly encourage students to write in styles and ways that differ from their own compositional practices. In this way, students are pressed to find their own voice and seek out new and original ways of expressing themselves.

Barrett (2006) provided one of the most recent and thorough research articles exploring compositional practice. Building on preliminary work, she investigated the ways composition instruction is taught, learned, and perceived within music programs. The participants in her study included an eminent composer-teacher, a composition student currently enrolled as an undergraduate major, and a composition major that had recently graduated but also studied with the same eminent composer. The following teaching strategies were observed during the lessons by the composer-teacher:

1. Extended thinking, provided possibilities
2. Referenced work to and beyond the tradition
3. Set parameters for identity as a composer
4. Provoked the student to describe and explain
5. Questioned purpose, probed intention
6. Shifted back and forth between micro and macro levels
7. Provided multiple alternatives for analysis of student work
8. Prompted the students to engage in self-analysis
9. Encouraged goal setting and task identification
10. Engaged in joint problem finding and problem solving
11. Provided reassurance
12. Gave license to change

For each of the teaching strategies listed, Barrett provided detailed examples of the dialogues between the composer-teacher and student. In addition to the teaching strategies, Barrett also noted three prevalent themes that emerged from her experiences with the three composers: composer model, enterprise, and composer voice. The theme of composer model refers to the ways the student-composers described their teacher's influence. Concerning the theme of enterprise, Barrett stated, "To be enterprising includes showing initiative and imagination, and taking risks in new endeavors" (p. 211). Lastly, the theme of composer voice emerged when Barrett noticed that the student composers all credited their teacher for helping find their own individualized style. When discussing the philosophy of his teacher, one of the student-composers remarked, "His style was not to be the grand composer-teacher and saying that the only way you can learn is by studying my works, you know the composer-teacher was allowing me to experience my own identity and my voice" (p. 211). Furthermore, the composer-teacher insists that young composers be provided with the opportunity to explore multiple types of writing styles to find a voice they feel is their own. Barrett concluded that eminence studies have the potential to inform the teaching and learning practices of music at all levels. She stated:

> Whilst the teaching of composition in school settings has few parallels structurally with the one-on-one tutoring employed in this study, the teaching strategies observed may be modified and adapted to accommodate these settings. (p. 214)

Similar to Barrett, I believe that reviewing the strategies of composers within the academy could foster greater understanding of compositional instruction. After reading the work of Lapidaki and Barrett, I was reminded of the importance of teacher affirmation and modeling. I was convinced then, and even more so now, that students desire feedback during the composition process. Consistent, constructive communication is needed to guide students' technical ability in addition to fostering meaningful social interactions. After reaching this conclusion, I again questioned whether a virtual residency was possible or, more specifically, effective.

TECHNOLOGY IN THE CLASSROOM

Educators have numerous technological resources available to them now that they did not have just five years ago. Faster Internet speeds, increased access to the Internet, increased availability of computers in schools, and larger percentages of students who have computers at home make the use of online learning experiences more widely available. In this section, I outline three ways technology was utilized during the virtual residency.

First, knowing communication is key, I designed a blog that allowed the students, directors, and myself to share ideas and files. Numerous companies provide spaces on the Internet for free blogs, such as Google (https://www.blogger.com/start?hl=en), and Blogger (http://www.blogspot.com). Communicating with students and directors through the blog was very effective during the residencies. Students were encouraged to ask questions about their work and review comments I had made about all of the compositions uploaded on the site. In addition to the blog, teachers and students were able to videoconference with me during their classes. Services like Skype, Elluminate, and iChat make video-conferencing easy to set up and use in the classroom. After the very first video exchange, it was evident that videoconferencing would profoundly impact the experience for everyone involved. Although socially awkward at first, students and directors quickly grew comfortable with me being "in the room" and within a few days were eager to interact and share their work.

Second, educators no longer need to rely on music notation software programs that are expensive and sometimes difficult to learn. Several online notation programs with no downloading requirements are now free and easy for young students to use. In these residencies I utilized Noteflight, a smartly designed pro-gram that allows individuals to create accounts and save their work. I selected Noteflight because it is easy to learn yet complex enough to allow users to write one or multiple parts, play them back, edit them, and post online for others to view. At the top left-hand side of the example in Figure 10.1, you can see the menu screen that allows the composer to easily touch the desired musical element and place it on the staff. Within one lesson, most students were able to use the notation system with ease. All four directors were surprised to see that students utilized the online notational system to not only write music but also teach them-selves unfamiliar rhythms and melodies found in their band literature. For the band directors, this was one of the clearest examples of the composition instruc-tion positively impacting the overall musical learning of the students.

As previously described, each composition lesson consisted of one prescriptive musical element. The online notational software allowed students to more easily con-front tasks that required standard notation. With the software, students could easily identify if a measure did not have the appropriate number of beats, readily transpose score and parts, and, most importantly, play music back to revise their work.

Technology did not just aid in communication and notation; several new pro-grams and websites were ideal for encouraging free composition. One example is

FIGURE 10.1   Noteflight example 1.

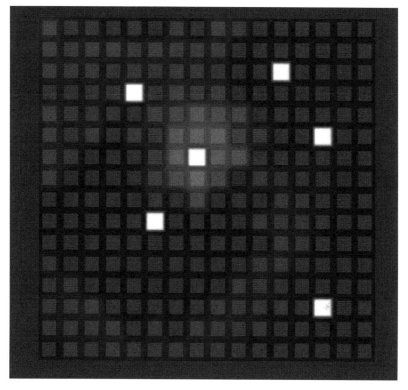

FIGURE 10.2 Example of a tone matrix.

the tone matrix available at http://tonematrix.audiotool.com/ (Figure 10.2). At this website, visitors can use the matrix to create musical loops. The matrix provides a powerful visual and aural tool for teaching basic musical elements. The simple but effective website served as a wonderful way to demonstrate the interaction between harmony and rhythm. Besides free play on the computer, students were asked to improvise on their instruments using their invented tone loop. Starting composition activities at the computer often provided students with opportunities for quick successes. Building upon these accomplishments, students were encouraged to create music on the computer that could be played along with their instrument. On the whole, students did not have to be prompted; they readily adapted musical experiences gained from computer-based instruction to their band instruments.

CONCLUSIONS AND IMPLICATIONS

In the introduction, I questioned whether a virtual composer in residence was an oxymoron. Although I am just beginning to reflect upon and analyze my two-year experience, all early data suggest that a virtual composer in residence not only is possible but is also effective. There exist numerous benefits for a composer-in-residence experience (Tsisserev, 1997). The opportunity to work with a composer and witness the perspective and process of a professional musician can be meaningful for numerous reasons. Students have the opportunity to interact with a musician without fear of consequences imposed by a grading system, freeing them to express themselves musically. Students might ask the composer questions not only about the creation of music itself but also of career and educational trajectories. Additionally, experiences working with living composers who help students to realize their creative music making and improvisation may bridge the gap between prior informal musical knowledge and formal musical knowledge.

Recent advances in technology make the "virtual" part of the residence less of an obstacle. New websites and programs allow students to easily create and communicate their music ideas. Recently developed online notational systems can assist students in the often-difficult experience of working with standard notation while providing the opportunity to hear their work and easily revise.

As I reviewed research and considered the instructional design for the middle school band students, I did not create lessons based on the knowledge that I would be teaching from a distance. I wondered if I could create the best composition experience possible for students and implement it "virtually." The biggest drawback in being away from the students occurred when I wanted to improvise with students, in time, to demonstrate a compositional technique or to just have fun with music. As the speed of the Internet increases, I hope to be able to make music with students without delay.

Although I worked with middle school band students, I believe this type of program could be effective in any K–12 classroom. Large, well-funded music programs may be able to continue to commission new works and welcome visiting composers, but the current economic climate limits opportunities for our students to gain the benefits described from these types of experiences. Additionally, geography continues to serve as an obstacle for many teachers who would otherwise plan for composition experiences linking their students with the larger musical community. Many rural schools are located too far from densely populated places with communities of professional artists or large universities with composition faculty. Other schools face the obstacle of outside perceptions of their neighborhoods as unsafe, keeping otherwise willing musicians away from working with wonderful students. I intend to continue working as a virtual composer in residence; the experience has been personally rewarding and musically educational. It is my hope that this chapter will encourage educators to consider bringing a composer to their classroom, even if at a distance.

NOTE

1. All references to people and places in this chapter are pseudonyms.

REFERENCES

Adolphe, B. (1999). *Of Mozart, parrots and cherry blossom in the wind: A composer explores mysteries of the musical mind*. New York, NY: Limelight Editions.

Barrett, M. (2006). 'Creative collaboration': An 'eminence' study of teaching and learning in music composition. *Psychology of Music, 34*(2), 195–215.

Barrett, M., & Ford, A. (2000). Seeking a key to the art of composing. *Australian Review, 23*, 10–11.

Barrett, M., & Gromko, J. (2001, January). *Scaffolding the creative process: Provoking the "muse that sings."* Paper presented at the Ninth International Conference on Thinking, Auckland, New Zealand.

Bauman, J. (1972). Pretend that you're a band: A composition performance project for general music classes. *Music Educators Journal, 58*(6), 58–59.

Berkley, R. (2004). Teaching composing as creative problem solving: Conceptualizing composing pedagogy. *British Journal of Music Education, 21*(3), 239–263.

Ford, A. (1993). *Composer to composer*. St. Leonards, Australia: Allen and Unwin.

Ginnochio, J. (2003). Making composition work in your music program. *Music Educators Journal, 90*(1), 51–55.

Goldberg, M. (1990). Teaching and learning: A collaborative process. *Music Educators Journal, 76*(5), 38–41.

Green, L. (2008). *Music on deaf ears: Musical meaning, ideology and education*. Bury St. Edmunds, UK: Abramis Publishing.

Hickey, M. (1997). The computer as a tool in creative music making. *Research Studies in Music Education, 8*(1), 56–70.

Hindemith, P. (1942). *The craft of musical composition*. New York, NY: Schott Publishing.

Kaschub, M. (1997). Composition in the choral rehearsal. *Music Educators Journal, 84*(1), 28–33.

Kaschub, M. (1999). *Sixth grade students' description of their individual and collaborative music composition processes and products initiated from prompted and unprompted task structures* (Unpublished doctoral dissertation). Northwestern University, Evanston, IL.

Kaschub, M., & Smith, J. (2009). *Minds on music: Composition for creative and critical thinking*. Lanham, MD: R&L Education—A Division of Rowman & Littlefield Publishers.

Kennedy, M. A. (2002). Listening to the music: Compositional processes of high school composers. *Journal of Research in Music Education, 50*(2), 94–110.

Lapidaki, E. (2007). Learning from masters of music creativity: Shaping compositional experience in music education. *Philosophy of Music Education Review, 15*(2), 91–110.

McCutchan, A. (1999). *The music that sings: Composers speak about their creative process*. New York, NY: Oxford University Press.

Morin, F. (2002). Finding the music 'within': An instructional model for composing with children. In T. Sullivan & L. Willingham (Eds.), *Creativity and music education* (pp. 152–177). Edmonton, AB, Canada: Canadian Music Educators Association.

Persichetti, V. (1961). *Harmony: Creative aspects and practice*. New York, NY: W. W. Norton.

Piirto, J. (1992). *Understanding those who create*. Dayton, OH: Ohio Psychology Press.

Piston, W. (1987). *Harmony* (5th ed.). New York, NY: W. W. Norton.

Reid, S. (2002). Creativity: A fundamental need of adolescent learners. In T. Sullivan & L. Willingham (Eds.), *Creativity and music education* (pp. 100–109). Edmonton, AB, Canada: Canadian Music Educators Association.

Strand, K. (2006). Survey of Indiana music teachers on using composition in the classroom. *Journal of Research in Music Education, 54*(2), 154–167.

Tait, M. (1971). Whispers, growls, screams and puffs…lead to composition. *Music Educators Journal, 57*(6), 33–34.

Tsisserev, A. (1997). *An ethnography of secondary school student composition in music—a study of personal involvement within the compositional process.* Ph.D. diss., University of British Columbia.

Thoms, M. (Speaker). (1996). *The well of creativity: A conversation with Mihalyi Csikszentmihalyi* (Tape #2578). Ukiah, CA: New Dimensions Audio Program.

Wiggins, J. (1990). *Composition in the classroom.* Reston, VA: Music Educators National Conference.

Wiggins, J. (1999). The nature of shared musical understanding and its role in empowering independent musical thinking. *Bulletin of the Council for Research in Music Education, 143*, 43–65.

Wiggins, J. (2003). A frame for understanding children's compositional processes. In M. Hickey (Ed.), *Why and how to teach music composition: A new horizon for music education* (pp. 141–165). Reston, VA: Music Educators National Conference.

11

CREATIVE APPLICATION

A Way to Include Music Composition and Improvisation

in the General Music Curriculum

Lois Veenhoven Guderian

CURRENT EDUCATIONAL TRENDS emphasize the importance of nurturing creative thinking abilities in children and youth. During the last twenty years, educators have seen the establishment of national and state standards and organizations that promote the reconfiguration of curriculum and lesson content to include the development of creative thinking (Education World, 1996; National Association for Music Education [MENC], 1994; National Association for Music Education [NAfME], 2013; Partnership for 21st Century Skills [P21], 2002). Educational systems and learning taxonomies such as Bloom's ("Bloom's Taxonomy," 1999) that underpin standards, goals, and curricula recognize creative thinking as involving the highest levels of cognitive learning processes and, therefore, something desirable to achieve. In preservice teacher education, the emphasis on developing understanding in how to nurture and develop creative thinking in children and youth is reflected in performance assessments such as the edTPA (Stanford Center for Assessment, Learning and Equity [SCALE], 2013). According to the *edTPA K-12 Performing Arts Assessment Handbook* (SCALE, 2013), preservice teachers' instructional plans should "build on each other to help students in creating, performing and responding to music" (p. 10), implying that developing the ability to nurture human creativity is part of what it means to be a good educator.

The present-day educational climate and reforms also include an emphasis on "best practices" and effective principles of instruction (Rosenshine, 2012); student engagement techniques (Barkley, 2010); differentiated instruction to meet the needs of all learners (Tomlinson, 1999; Smutny & von Fremd, 2004); new peda-gogies for better teaching and learning (Gurung, Chick, & Haynie, 2009); collab-orative and cooperative learning experiences toward the development of social skills necessary for present-day living and working (P21, 2002); and the design of learning environments that are conducive to fostering and achieving these ends (Bielaczyc & Collins, 1999; Brown & Campione, 1996; Rogoff, Turkanis, & Bartlett, 2001).

In music education, emphasis on the importance of nurturing creative think-ing in music is reflected in numerous ways within the profession: in the National Standards for Music Education content standard number 3 (improvising melo-dies, variations, and accompaniment) and content standard number 4 (com-posing and arranging music within specified guidelines) (MENC, 1994); in the establishment of state and national program opportunities in composition; in the newly formed National Council for Music Composition (NAfME, 2012); in a plethora of publications (Hickey, 2002, 2003; Kaschub & Smith, 2009; Webster, 1992), journal articles, and research studies that address creative thinking in music and how improvisation and composition can be taught; in an increase in conference sessions and interest in teaching and learning in improvisation and composition; and in a growing interest in models of comprehensive general music curricula that include these musical processes.

At all grade levels and in all areas of the general music education curriculum, teachers strive to design curriculum goals, desired student outcomes, instruc-tion, and assessments that align with national, state, and local curricula. Under the umbrella of established standards and goals, finding an approach to the logical sequencing of instructional materials and processes for classroom learn-ing that supports students' development in skills, knowledge, and creative thinking in music can be challenging. In Strand's (2006) survey of Indiana music teachers' beliefs and practices on inclusion of composing in classroom activities, teachers reported that there were too many musical skills and activi-ties to teach to include composition in the classroom (56.9 percent). Others reported a lack of technology (28.2 percent) and too few instruments for com-posing (26.5 percent). Others regarded composing as an inappropriate activity for the types of classes the teacher taught (19.9 percent). Some mentioned the restrictions of time for composing (9.1 percent) and the idea that composing was not a useful learning tool. Teachers mentioned concerns regarding stu-dents' behavior during composing activities and found it more important to spend their teaching and learning time on meeting the other seven content standards (p. 160).

Reimer (2003) recommended a comprehensive music curriculum to provide students with the opportunity to develop all of the multiple intelligences in music in support of individuals' aptitudes, various interests, and levels of desired involvement in music. He urged teachers to begin fostering applied creative thinking in students in the early stages of learning (1989, p. 191). Reimer also spoke to the potential for incorporating composition into general music in order for the curriculum to reflect all musical intelligences in interrelated ways (2003, p. 258).

In this chapter, I explore a way of thinking about teaching and learning in general music that could aid educators in realizing Reimer's idea of a comprehensive and interconnected curriculum. The idea addresses the challenges that teachers face in nurturing creative thinking in their students by trying to incorporate improvisation and composition into the curriculum and lesson content. It includes a learning environment and an approach to the curriculum—a teaching and learning pedagogy I refer to as *creative application*—that provides students with opportunities to apply what they are learning in creative ways (Guderian, 2008, 2009, 2012). In this approach, students are provided with creative problem-solving assignments, for the most part, in some form of applied music improvisation or composition, that foster the developing skills and understandings they have acquired as a result of music class activities and instruction. In essence, rather than through traditional practice methods, worksheets, or tests, students reinforce, deepen, and demonstrate ideas, their learning and understanding in music through assignments in improvisation and composition that require applied creative thinking.

Research on how individuals learn has shown that opportunities to teach others have an effect on student recall of information (Sousa, 2006). Pitcairn (2010) advised that students in music classes need to learn how to organize knowledge. "They need to practice explaining knowledge to others, and they need to hear diverse explanations. They need to write or represent their mental models visually. They need to use their organized knowledge to strengthen the neural connections, the networks or pathways of interconnected brain cells, through application and practice" (p. 21). In general music classrooms that include creative application, students work in various configurations of individual, paired, and collaborative groupings. As part of the teaching and learning process, students are given applied improvisation and composition exercises, activities, and assignments that are related to and reinforcing of curriculum and daily lesson content. Through an emphasis on inquiry, students are provided with opportunities to explore musical ideas and to experiment with and apply in creative ways the content, skills, and understandings that the teacher introduces, facilitates, and nurtures. When assignments in music improvisation and composition are embedded into the curriculum—designed as an outgrowth of sequentially ordered curriculum content and therefore directly related to conceptual and perceptual learning in music in the classroom—teachers can accomplish sequentially designed curriculum goals in all areas of the music curriculum: including, over time, the skills and understanding that are necessary for sophisticated levels of improvising and composing. There are numerous, student-centered practices that can be applied to attaining this goal, numerous ways to design experiences in music comprised of creative skill-building activities and holistic composition assignments that support students' development of musical skills, understanding, and creative thinking in music (Guderian, 2012).

There are many considerations in the design of an interrelated, interconnected, comprehensive curriculum for general music education that includes improvisation and composition. Content questions include why and what should be included in the determination of goals and desired student outcomes. Additional considerations include instructional strategies for accomplishing the desired student outcomes and how and when to assess students; determination of what kinds of student-centered teaching and learning practices will facilitate student learning; and establishment of a learning environment that is physically, educationally, and emotionally conducive to accomplishing the goals and the anticipated effects on student learning and well-being. With support from research and theory, this chapter addresses these considerations and explores the why and how of creative application pedagogy within a *learning communities* approach to the general music class environment.

THEORY AND PRACTICE: INFLUENCES IN THE DEVELOPMENT OF THE PEDAGOGY CREATIVE APPLICATION PEDAGOGY

Approaches to teaching and learning do not exist in a vacuum. Research in many areas of study such as psychology, sociology, philosophy, cognition, creativity, education, curriculum scholarship, and teaching experience is a necessary component in the groundwork for developing new approaches to the teaching and learning process. J. R. Barrett (2007) reported currents of change in music education practices as having an impact on curriculum design and propounded the value of "cross-fertilizations of perspectives from sociology and areas of study outside of music that inform traditional practice" (p. 147).

In part, the theories and educational practices of the twentieth-century psychologist, philosopher, and educator John Dewey influenced the development of creative application as a teaching practice for music education. Dewey

(1900/1990) believed in a learning environment where individuals were allowed to explore and pursue their interests and capabilities. The four characteristic interests of children were that of (1) conversation or communication, (2) inquiry, (3) construction or making things, and (4) artistic expression that should follow as a natural expression and outgrowth of the child's experiences (p. 47). The child's development was fluid and transitional, dependent on his or her experiences, interests, and emotional well-being and the adults in the child's environment who served as organizers and facilitators in the collaborative enterprise of teaching and learning. Sensitive educators who understood the learning goals per area of study were able to interpret where the child was in his or her learning/understanding and guide the child accordingly via learning experiences that would tap the child's interests and present level of development (Dewey, 1900/1990, pp. 181–195). Providing children with opportunities to "express themselves artistically" as natural outgrowths of their understandings of classroom learnings by "inquiring" within their thinking process in order to "make" compositions in "communicative" groups aligns with Dewey's four characteristics of children's learning and, in essence, describes creative application pedagogy in music teaching and learning.

Dewey's (1900/1990) aforementioned ideas about education blend with the ideas of the twentieth-century social psychologists Lev Vygotsky (1934/1986) and Jean Piaget (Myers, 2004, pp. 143–150). Using a synthesis of the ideas of the three theorists as a lens provides insight into understanding the potential merits of creative application as a pedagogical approach to the general music curriculum. All three believed that learning is socially and culturally situated, dependent on what humans had learned and experienced previously. During the process of constructing knowledge, the interplay of former knowledge and new knowledge was at work, resulting in new understanding. The learning process often required assistance from a knowledgeable individual who could guide the learner in the direction of new understandings.

Dewey (1916/1967) believed that the school should be a place of inquiry, where all members of the community had equal opportunity to realize their interests and potential. Educators in schools should simplify information so the child could grasp it, grow and develop, and "escape from the limitations under which he was born" (1916/1967, p. 20).

Vygotsky and Piaget also believed in the importance of a simple to complex organization of the learning process, experiences that would allow for connections between new knowledge and students' former knowledge. Thus, children could form new understandings constructed from a foundation of prior learning experiences. Outgrowths of the idea take current form in sequentially ordered curricular planning: the idea that knowledge should be arranged so that children are able to build upon their former knowledge and move from uncomplicated concepts to the complex (Boardman, 1988; Bransford, Brown, & Cocking, 2000; Bruner, 2006; Mark & Gary, 1999; Pitcairn, 2010).

In further support of this idea, Piaget believed that the human mind builds schemas of understanding from which new experiences are initially interpreted and then modified through assimilation, adaptation, and accommodation resulting in new understandings (as cited in Myers, 2004, pp. 143–150). Vygotsky (1934/1986) also wrote on how the child's mind works. Children's informal understandings learned in such places as the home combined with formal learning in the school creating new schemas of understanding: all of which were culturally situated. Children matured in their knowledge and understanding by interpreting new information based on what they understood from schemas they had already formed. Social interactions with teachers, adults, and peers played a significant role in the child's learning.

Under these theories, curriculum planning that allows students to build on their former knowledge is important to successful learning. When creative learning experiences such as improvising and composing are an outgrowth of a standards-based, sequentially ordered curriculum, understandings in content are reinforced and take on new meaning, and students experience growth in composition and notation skills in an organized way. Further research in cognition and the workings of the brain since Dewey, Vygotsky, and Piaget's time supports these ideas as to the importance of learning information in context and for drawing on students' current levels of understanding (Bransford et al., 2000). To advance knowledge and understanding, teachers can build on the knowledge students have acquired from their formal and informal learning experiences.

An example as applied to music education is Guderian's (2008) study, in which beginning recorder players, randomly assigned to an experimental group, experienced a creative application approach to teaching and learning in music. After the initial introduction to the soprano recorder, students in the experimental group began their studies with rote learning of patterns in order to develop playing ability and to learn fingerings and instrument technique. Rote learning preceded music reading activities. Improvisation activities preceded composition assignments. The composition assignments were related to the aforementioned improvisation activities and to the curriculum content. Assignments in music improvisation and composition were an outgrowth of class activities given in varied levels of structure and open-endedness as aligned to curriculum and instructional content.

In this study, the fifth graders experienced teaching and learning in music where the curriculum content was connected to the creative work and the creative work was an outgrowth of and support to the curriculum content. Neither the teaching of concepts nor nurturing of creative thinking was a "stand alone" activity. Each was situated within the organization of an interrelated plan of learning activities within a larger sequentially ordered curriculum plan. Teaching and learning in recorder playing, music theory, and sight reading were sequentially ordered and interrelated in support of the learning goals. Instruction was both child-centered and teacher-centered. Composing and improvising assignments were related to the aforementioned music learning activities. During the composing activities, students were given the option to work in pairs or groups and were encouraged to move about the room to share and play their pieces with one another. Results from the study revealed that allocating 50 percent of class time for creative application of curriculum content reinforced students' learning in music equally well with another group who spent 100 percent of class time learning and reinforcing skills and understanding in music through traditional teacher-directed instruction and practice. Both groups made significant gains in learning in musical skills and understanding. Posttest scores were remarkably similar. However, given the same amount of time for instruction, only one group experienced the opportunity to apply their understandings through composition. In a poststudy questionnaire that gave voice to the children regarding their learning experiences, seventeen of the twenty-four children in the experimental group wrote that composing was their favorite activity. In the control group of children, the most preferred activity was playing the recorder.

Creative application experiences are in line with Dewey's ideas of children's four characteristic interests, and the three psychologists' understanding of how children learn. Dewey's, Vygotsky's, and Piaget's influences are also evident in contemporary *learning community* approaches to the classroom environment.

THE LEARNING ENVIRONMENT FOR CREATIVE APPLICATION IN GENERAL MUSIC CLASSROOMS

In a creative application approach to the curriculum in general music, one of the goals is to help students to develop deep learning in musical understanding and skills for lifelong social music making. A *learning community* environment for general music facilitates the acquisition of deep learning and social music-making skills. The concept of an educational environment as a learning community evolved as a result of research in cognitive development in science and psychology (Bransford et al., 2000). In such an environment, students experience a variety and balance of student-centered and teacher-guided teaching and learning experiences that afford them many opportunities for constructing knowledge. Teaching and learning are integrative, cooperative, and collaborative, with emphasis on social interaction and distribution of resources and authority (Oakes, 1995; Resnick & Rusk, 1996; Rogoff et al., 2001). The curriculum is comprehensive, with employment of varied pedagogies and assessments (Oakes, 1995, p. 4). Research via technology and extended learning outside of the classroom is a hallmark of many learning community designs (Brown & Campione, 1996; Resnick & Rusk, 1996; Scardamilia & Bereiter, 1993). Differentiated teaching and learning practices are employed to serve children and youth in their learning development according to their interests, background experience, and learning profiles (Smutny & von Fremd, 2004; Tomlinson, 1999). Learning communities are based on the idea that people construct knowledge in a sociocultural context. The model is especially well suited to general music education classrooms where an educator might alternate whole-group music activities to establish context with small-group activities that require problem solving, such as applied music composition, or paired learning on skills or activities following listening experiences.

For example, during studies in form in a general music learning community with middle school or high school students, a variety of whole- and small-group, context and content knowledge-building student-centered activities that help students to start thinking, exploring, and experimenting creatively in and with sound can precede a holistic entry-level creative musical problem-solving activity. For purposes of learning in music and foundational for the creative work, class sessions would include integrated listening experiences followed up with a variety of student-centered formative assessments. Strategies of inquiry could also be incorporated before and following repeated listening experiences in a variety of classical, ethnic, and popular styles of music. Formative assessments might include whole- and small-group written listening comparison charts, individual short written descriptions, alternated paired and/or small- with whole-group discussions following repeated listening experiences, index cards where groups might hold up a card on which they had written what they determined as the form of a particular piece, and hands-on musical activities in instrument playing and singing to illustrate musical concepts or musical features in a particular style. Whole-group discussions would include comparisons across styles in the formal organization of pieces and possibly texture, instrumentation, harmonic or melodic structure, emotive content, and dynamics as integral to the whole piece regarding stylistic, expressive, and formal features in the music.

On the day of the applied creative assignment, references to previous classes would provide connection and the baseline context for the creative work followed by a "whole picture" context-setting experience: for example, a YouTube video performance of the group Stomp. Under large principles of understanding as to what constitutes music—form, style, and expression (Boardman, 1988, p. 4) that would have been established previously, the instructor could further develop context for the assignment by having a list of questions prepared to facilitate discussion. Consider, for example, a situation in which the teacher and students have viewed various pieces of music from both a broad lens view and, in some cases, a more specific view of the parts and features that constitute a piece of music. Using the Stomp performance for example, the class might be asked, "From the broader view, does the example of the Stomp performance we just saw and heard constitute what we think of as music?" The teacher might then encourage students to view the piece through the three principles of form, style, and expression. "Did the piece exemplify form, style, and expression?" "How, and in what ways?" "Did the piece strike you as being simple in organization or complex?" "Did you notice a particular form from only one hearing and viewing of the piece?" "Can we think of the piece in terms of the forms we have studied, like AB or ABA form or free form?" "Is it possible to determine form after only one hearing and viewing of the piece?" "If we were to write down the form or score for the piece, what do you think it would look like?" "Did the piece appear to be improvised or composed, composed meaning that someone had made decisions and worked out and practiced a plan for the performance?" "Why do you think so?" "Is it possible to separate the movement of the performing group members from the sound of the rhythm in this piece?" Differences in students' answers might warrant listening to the performance again to pay close attention to how the piece is organized. "What might help us to understand the form?" "Yes, thank you, looking for ideas that repeat and contrast would likely help us gain insight into the composer's or composers' ideas."

Discussion would follow each question. After the second listening/viewing experience, students would be assigned to or choose small groups in order to create their own compositions under an open-ended assignment framework that included options for their collaborative problem solving. Percussion instruments, plain paper, staff paper, a hard copy of the assignment, and hard copies of a sound composition chart that had metric markings would be available for the hands-on creative problem solving.

As a further example, consider how this assignment framework engages students in musical problem solving within the social environment of their classroom learning community.

Assignment Framework (one to two copies given to each group for planning and reference)

1. Assignment

Create a multilayered rhythm composition using traditional percussion instruments, found sounds, body percussion, or a combination of these. For your piece, compose two or more contrasting sections of music. Explore possible rhythmic/musical idea(s) and/or pattern(s) for your piece that will comprise the musical content of the two sections. Experiment with your ideas and see where they might lead regarding formal organization such as in some of the forms we have studied: binary (AB), ternary (ABA), free form, or others. You may find that you want to compose an introduction, bridge, or coda for your piece or that your piece seems to logically flow into a third idea. When you share a performance of your piece with the class, the rest of us will try to determine the form of the piece from the listening experience.

This assignment would include additional sections with options for generating musical ideas as experienced in class, for notating examples, and for sharing and performing the musical ideas with the whole class. There would also be optional, follow-up homework assignments which could be completed by individuals, pairs or small groups of students, inside or outside of class dependent on how the time would play out during the composing activity per group and the availability of electronic resources in the classroom.[1]

Rubrics could be used to assess the composition. Ongoing work could include additional group work using students' choices of pieces to analyze and prepare to share with the class in some kind of learning activity that the students could design in a group activity. As further reinforcement of studies in form and composition, providing students with an opportunity to apply their learning to a new situation could be an assignment to create a rondo or theme and variation using a looping program like Garage Band or Acid Pro 8. The opportunity would also include instruction in how to use the looping program.

As this example illustrates, a learning community approach to general music facilitates creative application as one of several pedagogies supporting an interconnected, comprehensive curriculum for teaching and learning in general music classrooms and the development of students' social, collaborative and cooperative skills. Creative problem solving in small groups helps to establish a sense of community in the classroom and lets students know early on that they are an integral part of that community.

Balancing Time for Teaching and Learning under Comprehensive Curricula

As given in the previous example, important to teaching and learning in creative activities like group composing is a balance in time devoted to teaching and learning activities that nurture content and skills and time for activities that allow for creative exploration, experimentation, and application of learned ideas and skills (Stephens, 2003; Webster, 1987). As given in the example with secondary music students, important to this endeavor is context setting via priming activities (Regelski, 2004) and whole-picture listening activities (M. S. Barrett, 2003) in order to provide students with a cognitive framework of understanding, or point of departure for their creative work. Use of inquiry often facilitates the process. Preparing a list of guiding questions for both the listening/priming example and subsequently the creative task that will follow as outgrowth from the priming experience can provide students with cognitive scaffolding for engaging in composing.

Consider an interdisciplinary four-day teaching and learning experience with fifth graders where the goals included development in understandings in musical and poetic forms. The learning outcomes included student-created original nature-themed Haiku poems and programmatic compositions to express the poetry (Guderian, 2011). Priming experiences began with examples in and discussion of various symbol systems followed by comparison and discussion of listening experiences: works based on nature themes such as Beethoven's 6th, movement 4; Enya's "Storms out of Africa"; and Vivaldi's *Four Seasons, movement 3, Summer.* Such examples provided students with beginning understandings in how music can be created to represent ideas from outside of music. To guide students' learning experience, inquiry preceded and followed the listening experiences with questions such as "What is it about this music that makes us associate it with a storm?" "Can you listen for the thunder in the music?" "Can you listen to the storm music to hear if the sun comes out?" "What instruments did Beethoven use to compose music that sounded like a storm?" "Could you tell what kind of an instrument ensemble played the piece?" "How do you know it was an orchestra?" "How did Beethoven use instruments, dynamics, and high and low pitch so that we were able to hear thunder in the music?" "How did Vivaldi and Enya express 'storm' ideas?" "Would we need to know that the music is about storms to enjoy it or to be affected by it?" "Could the music express a different story; for example, could we make up a different story for the pieces?"

Another context-building activity that preceded the creative work provided the children with opportunities for hands-on free improvisation to explore "sound" possibilities of mood words, sounds, and ideas from nature on percussion instruments. To model the activity before the students broke into groups, in a whole-group activity, the students learned and performed a pre-created Haiku poem-composition notated in the nontraditional notation format that was one of the options the students could use for their own compositions.

The formal aspects of teaching and learning in Haiku poetry were introduced first via experience with Haikus followed by a list of prepared questions to engage the children's thinking in and about the poetic form. After the whole-group priming activities, the children were assigned to small groups. After each group had generated two Haikus with contrasting themes, students engaged in the process of programmatic composing to express the Haikus through sound. Questions prepared in advance helped to steer the progress of group work in generating and organizing ideas and in the group playing/performance of the subsequent product.

Questions included:

1. Shall we go over and explore the instrument sounds to see what might be interesting choices to use for our composing?
2. What instruments might be good choices for the sounds of your piece?
3. How do you think you could show that idea using instruments or sounds?
4. Do you want other instruments playing at the same time?
5. How will you play your instruments?
6. Who will play the instruments?
7. What will the parts sound like?
8. How long do you want the sound or part to last?
9. Will one person play a part or more than one play a part at the same time?
10. How will you notate it on the chart?
11. Will this help you to remember your piece so you can perform it for the class?
12. How will you show others how to play your piece?
13. How can we write it down on the chart?
14. Would the piece sound good if we added an introduction or a bridge between the two Haiku ideas? A coda? When you have composed your piece, practice it and try to determine the form or decide on a form and compose the piece to represent that form.
15. If you finish early, you might want to explore the idea of making the piece longer or of extending the form, or you might want to create a new piece with a subject other than nature.

Some students needed very few questions to guide their learning process and others needed direction and organization for either the sound-making process and composing or the organizing of the group score writing and practicing in preparation of a sharing performance with their classmates. Ultimately, each group created two contrasting programmatic sections of music based on their original Haikus and determined a formal structure for their composition. Products included AABB form, ABA, and AB, some with introductions, codas, or bridge sections. After each group shared/performed their piece, the rest of the class tried to determine the form. A second performance followed in order for the audience members to "check their answers."

Rather than simply study Haiku form, program music, and interdisciplinary connections between the two processes of creative poetry writing and creative music writing, through creative application students were given the opportunity to apply their understandings in the two forms and experience the creative working out of ideas toward the goal of product and performance.

BALANCE IN DESIGN OF ASSIGNMENTS FOR IMPROVISING AND COMPOSING

As demonstrated in the examples given previously with the fifth graders and secondary students, balance in the *design* of assignments and instructional strategies for developing students' abilities in creative thinking and writing in music is another important consideration for music educators. Since each child is different in music aptitude, background in music education, informal musical experiences, learning styles, cognitive understandings, and learning profiles (Smutny & von Fremd, 2004), some will need more structure than others in approaching creative assignments. As demonstrated earlier, a priming activity such as a listening experience that draws students' attention to particular aspects of the music might be enough structure for some students to stimulate the generation of ideas for working out creative ideas. As given earlier in the example of fifth-grade recorder students (Guderian, 2008), assignment criteria linked to students' own active music making in singing, playing, and improvising provided students with structure, a starting point and framework for the working out of ideas and for reinforcing and demonstrating understanding of concepts. When assignments are open-ended and the criteria for an assignment are flexible, students are able to exercise creative freedom and explore the possibilities.

CONVERGENT AND DIVERGENT THINKING AS APPLIED TO CREATIVE APPLICATION

In support of the idea of balance in time spent on content-building activities designed to introduce and develop skills and understanding in music and time spent in creative music making is research in convergent and divergent thinking. Literature surrounding the study of creative thinking in music emphasizes the importance of the interplay between convergent thinking, which includes learning in culturally situated skills and understandings, and divergent thinking, which is diverse. Webster upholds "the importance of divergency of thought and imagination in context with the more convergent thinking that often involves just plain hard work" (Webster, 2002, p. 23). He believed creative thinking to be "a dynamic process of alternation between convergent and divergent thinking, moving in stages over time, enabled by certain skills (both innate and learned) and by certain conditions, all resulting in a final product" (p. 26). Related to this line of thinking, Amabile (1996) wrote of the interplay between innate abilities, learned knowledge, and creative tendencies and abilities as important to the creative process. Learned knowledge, or "domain relevant skills," was necessary in all levels of creative endeavors within a domain. Brophy (2000/2001) found substantial creative thinking and problem-solving ability demonstrated by individuals who were combination thinkers, that is, thinkers who were able to engage in the interplay of convergent and divergent thinking. According to these ideas, under the framework of curricular goals, teachers might work for balance in providing students with opportunities to practice skills and understanding followed by opportunities to creatively apply and further develop their skills and understanding through improvising and composing.

To support the development of interplay between thinking based on domain understandings and thinking based on creative possibilities, students need opportunities to develop and practice both. Reimer (2003) noted the importance of memory in the processes of improvising and composing. At times, practice of domain skills and understanding is necessary in order to acquire domain knowledge in support of fluid, creative thinking. As given in the fifth-grade examples provided earlier, interplay and synthesis of understanding are possible during guided learning experiences and applied creative problem solving.

For purposes of usefulness to elementary music and elementary classroom educators, an example that appears elsewhere is provided here (Guderian, 2008, 2009, 2012). To develop understandings in dynamics as applied to expression in music, at the kindergarten or first-grade level the teacher could facilitate the children's learning of a new song such as a lullaby and ask the children to show how they think the piece should be sung to help a baby fall asleep. When the children perform the song softly, the teacher could start to add aural word association "soft" and later, visuals—perhaps a picture of a baby sleeping or a baby kitten to represent singing or playing music softly. Thus far, the teacher has provided ways for the children to develop knowledge and understanding for dynamics in music by drawing on the informal knowledge the children would likely have acquired at home or in other informal learning settings. To deepen children's understanding, via creative application, children could be asked to create soft music on a barred instrument that could help a baby fall asleep. The content- and context-building prior to the assignment would likely provide enough cognitive framing and a point of departure for the child to enter the activity. "Can you find or make music on the instrument that would help a baby to fall asleep?" The question is open-ended enough, providing the children with freedom to explore the many possibilities for completing the assignment. Balance and design of activities in the classroom that include creative application support the development of interplay in convergent and divergent thinking (creative thinking) in students. Further teaching strategies involving inquiry regarding different associations (a thunder storm, a giant walking, etc.) and explorations on instruments would lead children to understand different concepts in music: additional dynamics, tempi, articulations, and form. "Can you make some music that would sound like a parade that is far, far away coming closer and closer to us? How do you think it would sound?" Eventually, the small cursive *p*—the musical symbol for playing or singing softly—and the other dynamic symbols would be incorporated into the learning activities (Guderian, 2008, 2009, 2012).

In this scenario, the teacher is helping students to both discover and add to conceptual knowledge and understandings that are necessary for ongoing levels of understanding in the domain for making and creating music and to practice creative thinking. The assumption here is that the interplay between convergent knowledge and thinking and divergent experimentation and thinking not only reinforces understandings and creative thinking ability but also expands them (Guderian, 2008, 2009, 2012).

TEACHER SCAFFOLDING AND CHILDREN'S COMPOSING

Educators' scaffolding during students' engagement in creative applied activities in the classroom can support students' understanding and provide the teacher with information regarding a child's learning development. Younker (1997) examined the thought processes and strategies of children that occurred while they composed with technology. She found that methods of inquiry in scaffolding provided her with valuable information as to where students were in their learning and "what knowledge support was needed and how it should be delivered" (1997, p. 376). Guderian (2008) found strategies of inquiry useful in targeting where students needed help in their learning and where there might be misconceptions or a lack of knowledge. M. S. Barrett's (2003) unobtrusive strategy to find out about children's thought processes while composing was to simply ask them to tell her about their piece. To help students move through a "block" they had reached in the composing process on a particular piece, Webster's (2003) strategy of inquiry included questions regarding length, dynamics, and additional tangible musical ways to generate students' ideas for moving forward. Scaffolding requires sensitivity in assessing where students are in the learning process and in determining what kind of help they need.

Students also need time to work on their own to try out and work through ideas that result from teachers' context building and scaffolding. Gromko (1996) engineered learning activities with children that made it possible for the children to experience and acquire understandings that allowed for the interplay of convergent and divergent thinking in completing a creative task. The purpose of her study "was to capture in the voice of children their understandings of inversion, retrograde, and retrograde inversion techniques used by composers to transform or transpose musical ideas" (p. 37). To begin, she provided the children with an activity that would help them to develop understanding in the concepts. She followed this with creative application of these concepts via a composing task. In preparation for the independent composing, Gromko worked one on one with each child. Both Gromko and the child had identical matrixes and colored disks. Through modeling and inquiry techniques, she helped each child to discover and learn how to use the aforementioned compositional techniques. The learning activity included enactive learning as the children answered Gromko's questions by moving the colored disks in the matrix and iconic representation of the disks and matrix as visual representation of the compositional strategies. When later given a five-note row to use in demonstrating the strategies through original composition, the visual and verbal cues the children had experienced during the priming process served as aids in direction and structure for exploration. Explorations and improvisations in sound influenced the children's decisions to finish the work. The working out of new concepts by way of the interactive "matrixing" and teacher inquiry provided enough grounding and structure for the children's engagement in the independent creative work. The newly acquired conceptual knowledge opened up new possibilities for creative opportunities—the interplay of convergent and divergent thinking, resulting in new understandings. Once the children were involved in the process of the composing, Gromko found that her scaffolding seemed to interrupt the children's thought process (Guderian, 2008).

IN SUMMARY

Perhaps the strongest argument for inclusion of improvisation and composition in music education in schools lies in the results from research findings that indicate improvising and composing strengthen students' understanding and skills in music learning and support the development of creative thinking. Many researchers have noted the benefits to children's learning and understanding in music when they are given opportunities to engage in creative explorations and experimentations in sound and the written representations of sound (Azzara, 1993; Bamberger, 1999; Christiansen, 1992; Coleman, 1922, 1926, 1931; Davis, 2005; De Lorenzo, 1989; Gamble, 1984; Gromko, 1996; Guderian, 2008; Hickey, 1995; Levi, 1991; Loane, 1984; Miller, 2004; Pond, 1981; Reimer, 1989, 2003; Smith, 2004; Stauffer, 2001; Upitis, 1992; Wiggins, 2003). As Pitcairn (2010) advised, students in music classes need to learn how to organize and practice knowledge. Providing students with opportunities to creatively apply their learning of curriculum content supports Pitcairn's ideas of organization, interconnectedness, and reinforcement of skills and understandings introduced in the classroom through instruction and activities.

As put forth in this chapter, even under the restrictions of the school setting, one way teachers can meet the demands of standards-based comprehensive teaching and learning in general music that promotes the development of musical skills, understanding, and creative thinking in students is through *creative application*: improvising and composing activities that are embedded in the curriculum and therefore interconnected, interrelated, and complementary to other areas of the curriculum.

The following recommendations may be considered: (1) Balance is necessary in the planning of curriculum goals and instruction. Time should be allocated for instruction that supports learning in domain knowledge and for exploring, experimenting with, and applying domain knowledge. (2) It is important to include a balance in the kinds of activities we give to students that require creative thinking and problem solving. The development of domain knowledge and understandings and opportunities to apply these learnings in creative ways help students to develop understanding and creative thinking in music. (3) The design of assignments is especially critical in trying to help children develop understanding and creative thinking in music and to make meaning in and through music. Students require varying levels of structure in assignment design in order to enter the creative activity. Both focused creative exercises and holistic open-ended composition assignments can support the development of students' musical skills, understanding, and creative thinking in music for improvisation and composition. (4) Composing activities and teacher scaffolding can provide teachers with valuable information regarding students' understanding in the teaching and learning experiences that take place in the classroom. Students' compositions often reveal where it is that children need help with their learning.

Teachers can differentiate instruction based on children's needs through scaffolding techniques that include inquiry and sensitivity to facilitate students' thinking and problem solving and that move their learning forward.

Music education and educational theories surrounding music education should not exist without connections and alignments to larger educational theories. As described in this chapter, student-centered approaches within a learning community environment can support music education that involves children's creative music making. At times, teacher-directed instruction can be useful for helping students to develop skills and awareness of domain knowledge in music. A balance and blend between student-centered and teacher-directed approaches within a learning community environment might work best in music education.

CONCLUSION

Under the restrictions of time afforded many general music programs in the schools, meeting all of the expectations as put forth in the National Standards for Music Education, including ways to nurture students' creative thinking in music and abilities to improvise and compose music, can present challenges for music educators. One way to approach the situation is to interconnect and interrelate improvisation and composition assignments in support of curriculum goals. Through creative application, offering children and young people experiences with a variety of "musics" in combination with and as related to formal learnings in music, followed by opportunities to apply what they have learned through assignments that require creative problem solving and creative expression, fulfills the needs for sequentially ordered, comprehensive music study and the nurturing of creative thinking in music in individuals. There are many meaningful, student-centered ways to establish general music communities of learning where the social, intellectual, musical, and creative needs of children and youth can be met and transformed.

NOTE

1. Research the group Stomp and find other examples on YouTube. Consider the following questions: How did the group get its start? Is there a leader of the group? Who composes the pieces for the group? Are the pieces written down? What is involved in the learning process before a performance? Generate additional questions and/or information to share during class discussion. Prepare a written document of your findings that you will hand in for a graded assignment.

Take a piece of music that is one of your favorite listening pieces. Listen to the music several times. Write down what you believe to be the form of the piece. If you can find the piece on YouTube, send the link to my e-mail with the results of your listening and analyzing of the form, a short description of why you believe the form to be what it is, and how you came to your conclusion. Be prepared to share your piece and findings with the class. If your piece has lyrics, be sure to choose examples that you can share in a public setting. Of course, no swearing or inappropriate content, please.

REFERENCES

Amabile, T. M. (1996). *Creativity in context: Update to the social psychology of creativity.* Boulder, CO: Westview Press.

Azzara, C. D. (1993). Audiation-based improvisation techniques and elementary instrumental students' music achievement. *Journal of Research in Music Education, 41*(4), 328–342.

Bamberger, J. (1999). Learning from the children we teach. *Bulletin of the Council for Research in Music Education, 142*, 48–74.

Barkley, E. F. (2010). *Student engagement techniques: A handbook for college faculty.* San Francisco, CA: Jossey-Bass.

Barrett, J. R. (2007). Currents of change in the music curriculum. In L. Bresler (Ed.), *International handbook of research in arts education, part 1* (pp. 147–161). Dordrecht, The Netherlands: Springer.

Barrett, M. S. (2003). Freedoms and constraints: Constructing musical worlds through the dialogue of composition. In M. Hickey (Ed.), *Why and how to teach music composition: A new horizon for music education* (pp. 3–30). Reston, VA: National Association for Music Education.

Bielaczyc, K., & Collins, A. (1999). Learning communities in classrooms: A reconceptualization of educational practice. In C. M. Reigeluth (Ed.), *Instructional-design theories and models: A new paradigm of instructional theory* (pp. 269–292). Mahwah, NJ: Lawrence Erlbaum Associates.

Bloom's taxonomy of learning domains. (1999). Retrieved from http://www.nwlink.com/~donclark/hrd/bloom.html

Boardman, E. (1988). Generative theory of music learning, part II. *General Music Today, 2*(2), 2–6, 28–31.

Bransford, J. D., Brown, A. L., & Cocking, R. R. (Eds.). (2000). *How people learn: Brain, mind, experience, and school.* Washington, DC: National Academy Press.

Brophy, D. R. (2000/2001). Comparing the attributes, activities, and performance of divergent, convergent, and combination thinkers. *Creativity Research Journal, 13*(3 & 4), 439–455.

Brown, A., & Campione, J. (1996). Psychological theory and the design of innovative learning environments: On procedures, principles, and systems. In L. Schauble & R. Glaser (Eds.), *Innovations in learning: New environments for education* (pp. 289–325). Mahway, NJ: Erlbaum.

Bruner, J. (2006). Readiness for learning. In J. Bruner (Ed.), *In search of pedagogy* (pp. 47–56). London, UK, and New York, NY: Routledge, Taylor and Francis Group. (Reprinted from *The process of education* (1960), Cambridge, MA: Harvard University Press)

Christensen, C. (1992). Music composition, invented notation and reflection: Tools for music learning and assessment. *Dissertation Abstracts International, 53*(06A), 1834. (UMI 9231370)

Coleman, S. (1922). *Creative music for children.* New York, NY: G. P. Putnam's Sons—Knickerbocker Press.

Coleman, S. (1926). *First steps in playing and composing: A music book for children.* New York, NY: John Day Company.

Coleman, S. (1931). *A children's symphony.* New York, NY: Bureau of Publications of Teachers College, Columbia University.

Davis, S. G. (2005). That thing that you do: Compositional processes of a rock band. *International Journal of Education in the Arts, 6*(16), 1–19. Retrieved from http://ijea.asu.edu/v6n16/

De Lorenzo, L. C. (1989). A field study of sixth-grade students' creative music problem-solving process. *Journal of Research in Music Education, 37*(3), 188–200.

Dewey, J. (1967). *Democracy and education.* New York, NY, and London, UK: The Free Press, Collier-Macmillan Limited. (Reprinted from the original publication in 1916 by The Macmillan Company)

Dewey, J. (1990). *The school and society: The child and the curriculum* (Centennial. ed.). Chicago, IL: University of Chicago Press. (Reprinted from the original publication in 1900)

Education World. (1996). *State standards.* Retrieved from http://www.educationworld.com/standards/state/index.shtml

Gamble, T. (1984). Imagination and understanding in the music curriculum. *British Journal of Music Education, 1*(1), 7–325.

Gromko, J. (1996). In a child's voice: An interpretive interaction with young composers. *Bulletin of the Council for Research in Music Education, 128,* 37–58.

Guderian, L. V. (2008). Effects of applied music composition and improvisation assignments on sight-reading ability, learning in music theory and quality in soprano recorder playing. *Dissertation Abstracts International, 69*(11A). (ProQuest, formerly UMI, no. 3331120)

Guderian, L. V. (2009). Balance in structure and freedom when applying curriculum goals in general music education. *Illinois Association for Gifted Children Journal, 2009,* 68–69.

Guderian, L. V. (2011). *Music in the elementary classroom, K-6.* Lake Zurich, IL: LoVeeG Publishing.

Guderian, L. V. (2012). Music improvisation and composition in the general music curriculum. *General Music Today, 25*(3), 6–14.

Gurung, R. A. R., Chick, N. L., & Haynie, A. (2009). *Exploring signature pedagogies: Approaches to teaching disciplinary habits of mind.* Sterling, VA: Stylus Publishing.

Hickey, M. (1995). Qualitative and quantitative relationships between children's creative musical thinking processes and products. *Dissertation Abstracts International, 57*(01A), 145. (UMI no. 19614754)

Hickey, M. (2002). Creativity research in music, visual art, theater and dance. In R. Colwell & C. Richardson (Eds.), *The new handbook of research on music teaching and learning* (pp. 398–415). New York, NY: Oxford University Press.

Hickey, M. (2003). Creative thinking in the context of music composition. In M. Hickey (Ed.), *Why and how to teach music composition* (pp. 55–65). Reston, VA: Music Educators National Conference.

Kaschub, M., & Smith, J. (2009). *Minds on music: Composition for creative and critical thinking.* Lanham, MD: NAfME/Rowman and Littlefield Publishing.

Levi, R. (1991). Investigating the creative process: The role of regular musical composition experiences for the elementary child. *Journal of Creative Behavior, 25*(2), 123–136.

Loane, B. (1984). Thinking about children's compositions. *British Journal of Music Education, 1*(3), 205–231.

Mark, M., & Gary, C. (1999). *A history of American music education.* Reston, VA: MENC.

Miller, B. A. (2004). Designing compositional tasks for elementary music classrooms. *Research Studies in Music Education, 22,* 59–71.

Myers, D. G. (2004). *Psychology.* New York, NY: Worth Publishers.

National Association for Music Education (MENC). (1994). *National standards in arts education: What every young American should know and be able to do in the arts*. Reston, VA.

National Association for Music Education (NAfME). (2013). *Summary statement: What students should know and be able to do in the arts*. Retrieved from http://musiced.nafme.org/about/summary-statement-what-students-should-know-and-be-able-to-do-in-the-arts/

National Council for Music Composition. (2014). *Council for Music Composition – Executive Committee* Retrieved from http://musiced.nafme.org/about/societies-and-councils/council-for-music-composition-executive-committee/

Oakes, J. (1995). Normative, technical, and political dimensions of creating new educational communities. In J. Oakes & K. Quartz (Eds.), *Creating new educational communities* (Ninety-fourth Yearbook of the National Society for the Study of Education) (pp. 1–15). Chicago, IL: University of Chicago Press.

Partnership for 21st Century Skills (P21). (2002). *Our Mission*. Retrieved from http://www.p21.org/

Pitcairn, M. (2010). Brain research brings clarity to our instructional practice. *The Orff Echo, 42*(3), 20–24.

Pond, D. (1981). A composer's study of young children's innate musicality. *Bulletin of the Council for Research in Music Education, 68*, 1–12.

Regelski, T. A. (2004). *Teaching general music in grades 4-8*. New York, NY: Oxford University Press.

Reimer, B. (1989). *A philosophy of music education* (2nd ed.) Englewood Cliffs, NJ: Prentice-Hall.

Reimer, B. (2003). *A philosophy of music education* (3rd ed.). Englewood Cliffs, NJ: Prentice-Hall.

Resnick, M., & Rusk, N. (1996). The computer clubhouse: Preparing for life in a digital world. *IBM Systems Journal, 35*(3–4), 431–440.

Rogoff, B., Turkanis, C., & Bartlett, L. (2001). *Learning together: Children and adults in a school community*. New York, NY: Oxford University Press.

Rosenshine, B. (2012). Principles of instruction: Research-based strategies that all teachers should know. *American Educator, 36*(1), 12–19.

Scardamalia, M., & Bereiter, C. (1994). Computer support for knowledge-building communities. *Journal of Learning Sciences, 3*(3), 265–283.

Smith, J. P. (2004). Music compositions of upper elementary students created under various conditions of structure. *Dissertation Abstracts International, 65*(05A), 1713. (UMI no. 9315947)

Smutny, J., & von Fremd, S. (2004). *Differentiating for the young child*. Thousand Oaks, CA: Corwin Press.

Sousa, D. (2006). *How the brain learns* (3rd ed.). Thousand Oaks, CA: Corwin Press.

Stanford Center for Assessment, Learning and Equity (SCALE). (2013). *edTPA K-12 performing arts assessment handbook*. Stanford, CA: Pearson Education.

Stauffer, S. (2001). Composing with computers: Meg makes music. *Bulletin of the Council for Research in Music Education, 150*, 1–20.

Stephens, J. (2003). Imagination in education: Strategies and models in the teaching and assessment of composition. In M. Hickey (Ed.), *Why and how to teach music composition* (pp. 113–138). Reston, VA: Music Educators National Conference.

Strand, K. (2006). Survey of Indiana music teachers on using composition in the classroom. *Journal of Research in Music Education, 54*(2), 154–167.

Tomlinson, C. (1999). *The differentiated classroom: Responding to the needs of all learners*. Alexandria, VA: Association for Supervision and Curriculum Development.

Upitis, R. (1992). *Can I play you my song?* Portsmouth, NH: Heinemann.

Vygotsky, L. (1986). *Thought and language* (A. Kozulin, Trans.). Cambridge, MA: MIT Press. (Original work published in 1934)

Webster, P. R. (1987). Conceptual basis for creative thinking in music. In J. C. Peery, I. W. Peery, & T. W. Draper (Eds.), *Music and child development* (pp. 158–174). New York, NY: Springer-Verlag.

Webster, P. R. (1992). Research on creative thinking in music: The assessment literature. In R. Colwell (Ed.), *Handbook of research in music teaching and learning* (pp. 266–280). New York, NY: Schirmer Books.

Webster, P. R. (2002). Creative thinking in music: Advancing a model. In T. Sullivan & L. Willingham (Eds.), *Creativity and music education* (pp. 16–34). Twelve Oaks, CA: Sage Publications.

Webster, P. R. (2003). What do you mean, "Make my music different"? Encouraging revision and extension in children's music composition. In M. Hickey (Ed.), *Why and how to teach music composition: A new horizon for music education* (pp. 55–65). Reston, VA: National Association for Music Education.

Wiggins, J. (2003). A frame for understanding children's compositional processes. In M. Hickey (Ed.), *Why and how to teach music composition* (pp. 141–165). Reston, VA: MENC.

Younker, B. A. (1997). Thought processes and strategies of eight, eleven, and fourteen-year old students while engaged in music composition. *Dissertation Abstracts International, 58*(11A), 4217. (UMI no. 9315947)

12

FOSTERING CREATIVITY IN THE PERFORMANCE ENSEMBLE

Kate Fitzpatrick

IF YOU WERE to ask a member of general society who the most creative members of that society are likely to be, such a person would surely name artists, musicians, and dancers. If asked to name a creative musician, the same person would likely name not only great composers, such as Beethoven and Shostakovich, but also performers, such as Yo-Yo Ma or Wynton Marsalis. Performers are typically perceived as being creative, and the act of performing music, then, as being a creative activity. Yet, as stated by Graham, many typical school performance ensembles do not provide students with the opportunity to become directly involved in creative interpretation and decision making:

> Students are not trained to search for a spectrum of alternate approaches to the performance of a piece, a phrase, or even a single note. They are instead consistently directed in how to perform a selection in a manner selected by the teacher. The teacher's paradigm of the composition is treated as the only possible option....What is unfortunate is that the students are not directed and encouraged to move beyond this singular base, to see the range of historical interpretations that already exist, and to attempt to create in their mind a range of possible alternatives. (1998, p. 25)

Indeed, Webster (1990) stated that many people "misunderstand the nature of creative thinking in music. Many feel that the mere presence of performing groups and general music classes constitutes a commitment to 'creativeness' in the curriculum. They confuse the setting or the laboratory for creative experience with the experience itself" (p. 21).

The call for increased attention to creative thinking within the music class-room is not new. Indeed, in 1966, the Manhattanville Music Curriculum Project called for the centrality of creative thinking to all music classrooms (Pogonowski, 2001; Thomas, 1970, 1991), and, more recently, comprehensive musicianship approaches also have offered ways to integrate creative activities into the per-formance classroom (Austin, 1998; Grashel, 1993; Sindberg, 1998, 2006). Over the years, many authors have also called for a renewed focus on creative think-ing within the performance classroom (Ashton & Paynter, 1970; Paynter, 1972; Smith, 1979).

The National Standards for Arts Education have made the development of creative thinking in music education a priority, stating that "Every course in music, including performance courses, should provide instruction in creating, performing, listening to, and analyzing music, in addition to focusing on its spe-cific content" (Council of National Arts Education Associations, 1994, p. 42). It is important, then, for performance classes to become more comprehensive in their approach to music education.

If we as a profession do indeed value the development of every child's cre-ative potential and believe that a school-based performance ensemble ought to allow for such opportunities, then a contemplation of the issues pertaining to creativity in performance ensembles is in order. In this chapter, I will begin with a brief examination of the genre of musical performance and discuss how creativity within the performance setting might be achieved. I will then explore the ways in which the literature suggests students in school-based performing ensembles can become better engaged in creative thought within the rehearsal setting. Finally, I will examine the role of the conductor in fostering student cre-ativity and independence within the performing ensemble and will offer practical strategies that a practicing conductor-teacher may use to develop such a culture within his or her classroom.

IS PERFORMANCE A CREATIVE ENTERPRISE?

Webster defined creative thinking in music as "a dynamic process of alteration between convergent and divergent musical thinking, moving in stages over time, enabled by certain skills (both innate and learned), and by certain conditions, and resulting in a final product" (1989, p. 29). The movement between convergent and divergent thinking is key to the creative process, as the individual must first understand what is commonplace and expected within the music; choose other, more original possibilities; and yet still retain some sense of what is acceptable to the societal context. As a person creates, he or she draws upon prior knowledge to inform the process and produces a final product. This entire process takes place in a context, where environmental and societal conditions influence the act of creation.

Within the domain of music, many activities may be considered creative. Surely music composition, improvisation, analysis, and even listening can be considered creative musical acts (Reimer, 2003). Yet, is performance, which involves the re-creation of a composer's original work, creative? How does the performer engage in creative decision making through performance?

Creative thought in performance is engaged through the performer's interpretation of the musical work. Such an interpretation is not a complete reinvention of the piece, but rather a series of decisions that are based in a knowledge of convention (convergence) and a willingness to upset those conventions ever so slightly so as to create an emotional–physical response in the listener. If the performer strays too far from convention, the performance will be considered absurd or obnoxious, and yet, if the performer does not inject originality into his or her interpretation, the performance will be considered boring or uninspired. Thus, performance is a constant balancing act between convergent and divergent thought, and it is herein that performance involves creative thinking.

Still, the act of ensemble performance does not fit easily into existing models of creative thinking. For example, questions arise as one considers the group nature of ensemble performance and its relationship to the development or facilitation of creative thought. Reimer (2003) encouraged us to consider the intriguing dimension of "group creativity," yet few questions have been answered about the creative process within the group setting. What is the relationship between each individual's musical decision making and the group's? What is the nature of creative thinking in such a context? Do the "rules" of creative thinking in group and individual musical contexts differ? Future explorations of this topic might benefit from an examination of the literature on organizational learning (Choo, 1998; Rouse & Rouse, 2004). Similarly, the traditional teacher-directed nature of many performance ensembles forces us to consider the issue of locus of power and its effect on individual and group creative thought and decision making. How can divergency be promoted in a setting that historically has valued, above all, convergency? These and other questions deserve consideration in future research on creative thought in music education.

HOW CAN STUDENTS IN SCHOOL-BASED PERFORMING ENSEMBLES BECOME BETTER ENGAGED IN CREATIVE THOUGHT WITHIN THE PERFORMING ENSEMBLE?

A review of the literature on this topic reveals two strands of thought. The first focuses on how the creative musical activities of improvisation and composition can be incorporated within the performance classroom. The second focuses on how the performance experience itself can allow opportunities for creative thought.

Integrating Composition and Improvisation within Performance Classrooms

Authors that argue for the integration of composition and improvisation into the performance classroom claim that such integration has a twofold benefit: both to help students understand the process that composers and performers use to create the music that students traditionally perform and to involve students personally in the act of musical creation for its own sake (Kaschub, 1997). Many authors argue that a performance curriculum that does not include opportunities for composition and improvisation is similar to forcing visual artists to "paint by the numbers"— to reproduce someone else's work without ever being able to create one's own (Hickey, 1997); to "teaching sailing from a textbook and videotape without ever learning to tack with the wind in one's face" (Hickey & Webster, 2001, p. 22); or to "teaching a student to recite a poem or sing a song in a foreign tongue without teaching him the meaning of the words" (Bencriscutto, 1985, p. 22). Indeed, Priest (2002) worried that a performance class that focuses solely on notated music might exclude learners who understand music more aurally and who wish to create their own music rather than perform someone else's.

Several authors have described strategies for integrating composition into the performance classroom. For example, students can write warm-ups for the ensemble, discuss different compositional techniques utilized by the composers of their pieces (Hickey, 1997), and even create an original "group" composition (Hickey, 1997; Kaschub, 1997). Technology and new curricular materials provide another means for students to better investigate the compositions that they are performing and the compositional processes that were involved in their creation (Colgrass, 2004).

Although they perceive the development of creative thinking to be an important issue within their classes, many teachers feel that lack of time, scheduling difficulties, large classes, student overinvolvement, and lack of adequate teacher preparation deter them from providing creative music curricula (Mroz, 1982). However, specific strategies that teachers might utilize within their classrooms are provided in the literature. Guidance by the teacher is important to helping students compose within the performance classroom, as teachers must strike a balance between providing enough structure to enable students to compose while also providing enough freedom to allow them to explore their own rules

(Hickey, 2003). Specifically, the ensemble director needs to maintain an attitude that encourages creative thought by responding with excitement to a student's original music, encouraging creativity, offering positive reinforcements, encouraging risk taking, and demonstrating composition themselves (Hickey, 1997). The development of a supportive and nurturing classroom environment, then, is essential to the creative process. Such an environment is psychologically safe, contains many avenues for the exploration of sound, and allows for failure in risk taking (Hickey & Webster, 2001).

As for improvisation, the jazz ensemble provides an obvious venue for exploration, but other specialty ensembles, such as "Strolling Strings" (Gillespie, 1992) or vocal improvisation ensembles (Madura, 1997), may provide a rich setting for teaching improvisation to instrument families that are not typically included within the jazz ensemble setting.

Within the traditional large ensemble of a band, orchestra, or choir, teachers do not need to wait until students have sufficient performance experience to begin teaching improvisation. Indeed, successful improvisation is not related to level of performance ability (Wig, 1980). Teachers may have students learn the basics of improvisation during warm-up time, focusing on learning harmonic fundamentals (Bell, 2004) and even improvising on the warm-up scale (Hickey, 1997). The full ensemble can be taught to play or sing the harmonic background while individuals or even groups (Bencriscutto, 1993; Hickey, 1997) improvise. The twelve-bar blues and the blues scale might provide natural places to begin teaching improvisation (Bell, 2004; Hickey, 1997).

Fostering Creative Thought within Performance

Most of the scant literature that concerns creative thinking within the performance ensemble speaks to the inclusion of composition and improvisation within the ensemble. However, the sometimes narrow focus on these two musical activities as the locus of creative thought in music education tends to limit the discussion of how to address the creative process within other aspects of the musical experience. In addition to incorporating improvisational and compositional activities within the ensemble setting, it is important to consider the creative opportunities afforded by musical performance itself. As was previously mentioned, however, the group dynamics of the performance ensemble cause interesting questions to be asked. Reimer discussed this aforementioned special dimension of "group creativity":

> But within this reality of ensemble performance, creativity in a genuine sense is, I claim, achievable. The key to this claim is that no matter

how coordinated the playing and singing in groups must be, every performer can and should experience her or his contribution as one of individual selfness as integrated with the selfness of others....In the act of ensemble performance individuals "commune" in joint creativity, a self-combined-with-other-selves experience in which individuality and community are fused in service of original musical expression....So powerful is this experience in enhancing both the sense of self and the sense of self united with other selves as to change the inner lives of all who have been privileged to undergo it....Achieving this special dimension of creativity, I suggest, is the primary goal of ensemble performance. (Reimer, 2003, pp. 114–115)

How does one encourage such creative thinking within the performance classroom? Within performance itself, most authors focus on involving students in the interpretive decision-making process as the most direct avenue to encouraging creative thinking skills during performance (Graham, 1998). For example, Kraus (2003) suggested that providing opportunities within the large ensemble for students to make musical decisions can enhance the peak state of psychological involvement known as flow (Csikszentmihalyi, 1975).

Graham (1998) encouraged the incorporation of the following activities to promote creative thinking in the performance classroom: comparing different versions of performed examples (recorded), encouraging divergent thinking in approaching interpretive choice in performance, including students in the director's rehearsal decisions, encouraging individual creativity within the ensemble, encouraging creativity in phrasing, teaching toward a realization of the potential and limitations of music notation, and examining performance practices in music of diverse genres and cultures.

Hickey and Webster (2001) called this interpretive ability "aesthetic decision making" and encouraged such techniques as the "imagining" of sound as an avenue to creative thinking in the rehearsal (see also Reichling, 1990, 1992). Students may be asked, for instance, to imagine what sound would result if a melody were played by another section, or if the entire piece were played by a rock band. A teacher who is committed to promoting creative thinking could easily come up with other similar questions that would promote this type of thinking within the rehearsal.

Creative thinking in a rehearsal might be facilitated by the pieces that a director selects for performance. By selecting modern pieces that include such techniques as improvisation, chance occurrences, indeterminacy, or aleatoric events, students may be provided opportunities to make musical decisions during the course of a traditional rehearsal (May, 1976). To aid those students who are motivated beyond the rehearsal, directors may provide suggestions for individual creative projects that students may pursue individually (Garofalo & Whaley, 1978).

Even an ensemble such as the traditional marching band can be transformed into a creative experience. Indeed, Peterson (1993) discussed the creative nature of this medium, which combines music, movement, and artistic field design to create a complete sensory experience. Though normally the director designs and creates shows, the marching band ensemble can become a more creative experience if students are allowed to participate in the design of the entire program. Students can help design field charts, create compositions or arrangements, and choreograph specialized movements.

Although the literature provides some of the aforementioned suggestions as to how to both incorporate the activities of improvisation/composition within the school-based rehearsal and make the act of performance itself more creative for students, it seems important within this discussion to more thoroughly examine the role of the large ensemble conductor in fostering student creativity. As both the leader of the musical ensemble and the facilitator of learning within a school-based ensemble, the conductor/teacher plays an enormous role in either fostering or inhibiting opportunities for creative thought and decision making.

The concept of problem-based learning underlies many of the recommendations that follow. Within the framework of problem-based learning, students work together in a group setting to resolve complex, realistic problems under the guidance of a teacher (Allen, Donham, & Bernhardt, 2011; Spronken-Smith & Harland, 2009; Wood, 2008). When learning situations are designed around solving real-world problems (such as making appropriate musical decisions) rather than retaining facts (such as taking a test on musical terms), the role of the teacher shifts from "presenter of information to facilitator of a problem-solving process" (Allen et al., 2011, p. 23). With this framework in mind, the following section will provide practical strategies from the author's own experience for the development of creative thought and student independence within the rehearsal.

ROLE OF THE CONDUCTOR IN FOSTERING STUDENT CREATIVITY: PRACTICAL SUGGESTIONS

It is one of the great ironies of good conducting and teaching that, at times, the more we do to try to help our students, the more reliant upon us and the less independent they can become. Traditional models of conducting within the professional world have influenced the culture of the public school rehearsal environment, making most conductors of public school ensembles driven to lead their groups in a very teacher-directed manner. However, such a teacher-focused environment often leads to an ensemble culture that squelches individual opportunities for creative thought and divergent thinking in the classroom.

Despite our best intentions as educators, why does this often happen in school-based ensembles? Perhaps most importantly, many conductors of school groups often confuse a professional model of conducting with a public school model of teaching. As students, most of us observed collegiate or professional ensemble directors and witnessed a professional environment where the conductor is "decision maker" and the ensemble players are expected to turn the conductor's vision into a musical reality. Players at collegiate and professional levels are generally individuals who have decided to make a career out of music and thus come to the rehearsal with a different background, resources, and expectations than would a typical middle school or high school student musician. Many of us unknowingly take these models of rehearsal structure and locus of control with us into the public school music classroom and adopt them with our own students. Within a public school setting, however, it is important to remember that the goals of the performance ensemble are necessarily different. Students come to a rehearsal from many different backgrounds and with many different purposes, and, although one of our goals may be to prepare some of our students to play in collegiate and professional groups in the future, we must also remember that the focus of the public school setting is on fostering independence and democratic learning. Thus, our models of rehearsal structure and the locus of rehearsal control within our classrooms must be reconsidered.

Other ways we commonly squelch our students' creativity and independence from the podium are also important to consider. Oftentimes, we show students that we are intolerant of mistakes through the ways we respond when mistakes are made in our rehearsals. Besides promoting a hostile rehearsal environment, such an atmosphere also leads students to avoid risk taking, which is necessary for divergence of thought within a communal setting. If students are afraid to make mistakes, they will be afraid to try new things, which inevitably squelches their motivation to think (and play or sing) in creative ways.

We also tend to squelch creativity by taking a short-term view of success within our ensembles rather than a long-term view. This is due primarily to the nature of school ensemble performance schedules, which often involve multiple concerts and performing events in close succession, including contests and festivals at which both conductors and their ensembles are typically judged to be successful or not by judges, administrators, and community members. Such a high-stakes environment leads us to focus on "getting the notes right," prescribing exact parameters for joint musical expression according to our own vision for the piece of music being played, and neglecting to involve the ensemble in musical decision making for the sake of time. There is little we can do to change the competitive culture of many of our performance ensembles, but there is much we can do to change our own outlook on the rehearsal process. By fostering long-term student success rather than simply fixing mistakes when they happen, we establish a rehearsal culture in which students understand that it is their individual and group development that is prized most highly in our classrooms. By placing our own focus on the long-term success of our students, we may make choices regarding our daily curriculum that better benefit student development, if not the next concert or festival. In the short term, it is possible that students may not score as highly at festivals and contests. In the long term, however, such a focus on long-term success should inevitably lead to better achievement by our groups: "If at least some time were devoted to asking students to think in sound and make aesthetic decisions, the resultant earning about music would be so much more powerful that far less time would be required in subsequent rehearsals and classes to reach musical goals" (Hickey & Webster, 2001, p. 22).

Unfortunately, most of the efforts that we undertake to help our students succeed require enormous amounts of sheer will, strenuous effort, and determination on our part. Oftentimes, as conductors, we place ourselves in the position of being most responsible for the development of proper ensemble sound, expression, and technical development. We place ourselves in this position because we truly feel that our individual efforts will be noticed by students and will inspire them to put forth as much effort as we do. Unfortunately, many times our efforts have the opposite effect, as students "sit back" and allow us to do the "heavy lifting" while they lack an investment in the success of the ensemble. Thus, at times, *our* excess tension, frustration, and stress as conductors can in fact deprive students of *their* opportunity to become fully engaged, independent, and expressive musicians. It is important that we reconsider our role within our ensembles so as to better inspire students to become better invested in the rehearsal process.

How can we better facilitate student independence from the podium? Usually, the answer ironically lies in doing less and guiding our students to do more. We need to be facilitators of knowledge, not knowledge keepers. Here, I offer two practical suggestions of ways that we as conductors can better foster student independence and creativity within the ensemble experience.

Opening Up the Score

As the primary venue for creative decision making in performance settings is musical expression, we must find ways to allow our students to take a greater role in determining the ways that a piece of music might be shaped (Reahm, 1986). Within professional music ensembles, the decision-making "power" regarding musical expression lies primarily with the conductor, who then shares his or her vision with the rest of the ensemble and expects them to replicate his or her vision. Within a public school performance ensemble, the goal should be different, in that the director needs to make transparent the process of decision making to the group in a process that I call "opening up the score." Simply put, this means that we directly address moments of possible musical divergence with our students in a rehearsal.

We might, for example, discuss typical conventions of dynamic change in a traditional march style (convergent thinking) and discuss ways that we as an ensemble might subtly or dramatically alter these conventions so as to create excitement and surprise in the listener (divergent thinking). We might, as a group, try out different ways that we can do this according to ideas and suggestions of the group and may achieve consensus as to the musical decisions that we will make in performance. We may also find that we do not agree and may decide to perform this piece in different ways at different times according to different viewpoints. Either way, students become invested in the rehearsal process because their ideas are listened to and respected, and they are encouraged to think creatively about the music they are making rather than to simply follow directions.

Another technique we might employ is to ask students to compare different versions of recorded musical examples of the same piece of music, either on their own or in conjunction with a particular piece that we may be playing. By listening to and evaluating the many different ways that an ensemble can choose to interpret a piece of music, students understand that music is not a fixed set of instructions on a page, but rather they learn that they have the capability to make interpretive decisions according to their own insights.

Borrowing Chamber Music Techniques

Many of us have discovered the power of providing chamber music opportunities for our students. There is something powerful that happens when students take responsibility for their own music making with a group of their peers; previously uninvested students often take the lead in these small group settings as they are given more and more responsibility for their group's success. I do not think that it is a coincidence that such powerful musical moments often occur within these settings without the aid of a conductor. In many ways, students need opportunities to develop their own musical independence to become fully engaged as musicians. In the large group ensemble, we as conductors often stand in the way of this independence. What can we as conductors learn from chamber music settings that can improve our large ensemble rehearsals?

First, we need to refine our conducting gesture in such a way that we can better encourage the musical development of our students and stop serving as a metronome. Many of us have long heard this admonition from great conducting teachers over the years, but we continue to show every beat of the music in gesture because we feel that our students somehow need this security to stay together or stay in tempo. However, when we observe our students in chamber music ensembles, they learn how to stay together and how to maintain tempo together through a process of trial and error. Students in chamber groups have no conductor, and yet they are forced to maintain a sense of internal pulse and musical sensitivity that keeps the group together. Unless we provide students similar opportunities within our large group ensembles, they will learn to use us conductors as a "crutch" rather than developing these important musical sensitivities themselves. To better foster the independence of our students, we need to attend to the provision of "beats" sparingly within our rehearsals and instead work on attending to the musical line within our gesture. If, after all, we want students to be attentive to the higher-order skills of musical expressivity and creative decision making, we should model this as a focus within our conducting gesture and ask students to take more responsibility for the maintenance of internal pulse.

Another way we can better foster student musical independence and creativity by borrowing chamber music techniques is to actually step off the podium at times during rehearsal. When we mimic a chamberlike setting and ask our students to take total responsibility for the musical work, we empower them to recognize their own abilities and to be more bold in the musical decisions they make. For instance, we may decide to simply ask students to start and stop themselves, using the cues of breath or movement to coordinate their sound. I have found that students have a great deal of trouble doing this the first two or three times, but after several more attempts, I need not attend any longer to ragged entrances or exits as students become more personally invested in the process of starting and stopping their sound. We may also decide to step off of the podium during the times when it appears students need us the most: when tempo becomes an issue or when the music is lacking in dynamic contrast or expression. Instead of strengthening our metronomic conducting gesture to control tempo, we need to step off of the podium and demand that students take more responsibility for internal pulse. Instead of becoming desperately emphatic about leading the direction of a crescendo or shaping a musical phrase, we need to step aside and ask students to reconsider the musical decisions they are making. In each of these cases, stepping off of the podium and giving up control requires that we allow for multiple instances of failure on the path to success. We must allow students to try, to fail, to try again, and to continue the process until they are able to succeed individually. They can, after all, do so when working in small chamber groups, and so they can in a large group setting in which they are empowered to succeed independently.

These techniques can be adapted and shaped in various ways so as to address the individual needs of any ensemble. In my experience, what most often stands in the way of conductors fostering the musical independence and creativity of their students is the conductor himself or herself. It is difficult to let go; we are taught that the ultimate responsibility for our ensembles falls with us, and so it does. However, in a public school setting, our ultimate responsibility lies in helping our students become independent learners, and thus it is our responsibility to let go. I will never forget the first time that I completely "let go" as a conductor, when I had a group perform a challenging piece of music without me conducting at all. I stood on the podium on the afternoon of the performance with my arms down, had them stop and start themselves (at fermati and at the beginning and end of the piece), and placed all responsibility for musical expression in their hands. It was not a perfect performance—there were times when you could hear a slightly staggered pianissimo entrance after a fermata, for example—but to this date it was likely the most moving musical experience I have ever shared with an ensemble, as students were indeed making musical decisions independently and being creative. It is in the process of letting go that we can enable our students to find their own potential as musicians.

PULLING IT ALL TOGETHER

The role of the conductor in fostering an ensemble experience that encourages creative thought cannot be underestimated. In addition to the ways that an ensemble director can directly shape student opportunities for musical decision making in performance, there are also many ways that the creative activities of improvisation and composition can be integrated within the ensemble performance setting. Underlying these suggestions is a belief that the development of creative thought is essential to a student's complete musical education.

A shift to divergency in performance-based music education will require some adjustments on the part of the teacher (Webster, 2000), and the history and tradition of the conductor as decision maker certainly may hinder this effort. For the profession, issues of teaching creative thinking in performance will require that serious thought be given to the role of teacher education in such an effort. Teacher education needs to provide students with a firm philosophical grounding in the importance of creative thinking in all areas of music education, including performance. Such a philosophical basis will not be sufficient, however, if preservice and in-service teachers are not provided specific strategies for implementation of that philosophy, opportunities to observe practicing teachers successfully implementing creative thinking techniques, chances to practice such techniques in the field, and means for assessing student learning in this area. Obviously, such an effort will require a serious examination of the ways in which performance teachers are prepared.

The profession of music education has come a long way in its attempt to create more comprehensive learning environments for students. A renewed focus on creative thinking in our profession has led to important changes in the ways that music classrooms are structured. For students who participate in a large ensemble such as a band, orchestra, or choir, such an ensemble might provide one last opportunity to experience music in a formal setting. As a profession, then, we ought to better investigate how the performance classroom might nurture and develop their creative sensibilities. Should we wish to make the performance ensemble one in which conformity and assimilation are replaced by innovation and originality, such an undertaking is imperative.

REFERENCES

Allen, D., Donham, R., & Bernhardt, S. (2011). Problem-based learning. *New Directions for Teaching and Learning, 128,* 21–29.

Ashton, P., & Paynter, J. (1970). *Sound and silence: Classroom projects in creative music.* London, UK: Cambridge University Press.

Austin, J. R. (1998). Comprehensive musicianship research: Implications for addressing the national standards in music ensemble classes. *Update: Applications of Research in Music Education, 17*(1), 25–32.

Bell, C. (2004). Harmonizing and improvising in the choral rehearsal: A sequential approach. *Music Educators Journal, 90*(4), 31–36.

Bencriscutto, F. (1985). Develop creative musicians. *The Instrumentalist, 39*(10), 22–23.

Bencriscutto, F. (1993). Developing creativity through improvisation. *The Instrumentalist, 48*(3), 38–52.

Choo, C. (1998). *The knowing organization: How organizations use information to construct meaning, create knowledge, and make decisions.* New York, NY: Oxford University Press.

Colgrass, M. (2004). Composers and children: A future creative force? *Music Educators Journal, 91*(1), 19–23.

Council of National Arts Education Associations. (1994). *National standards for arts education: What every child should know and be able to do in the arts.* Reston, VA: MENC.

Csikszentmihalyi, M. (1975). *Beyond boredom and anxiety: Experiencing flow in work and play.* San Francisco, CA: Jossey-Bass.

Garofalo, R., & Whaley, G. (1978). Creative instrumental music projects. *The Instrumentalist, 32*(2), 42–43.

Gillespie, R. (1992). New possibilities: Strings are strolling! *Music Educators Journal, 79*(1), 23–24.

Graham, D. (1998). Teaching for creativity in music performance. *Music Educators Journal, 84*(5), 24–28.

Grashel, J. (1993). An integrated approach: Comprehensive musicianship. *Music Educators Journal, 79*(8), 38–41.

Hickey, M. (1997). Teaching ensembles to compose and improvise. *Music Educators Journal, 83*(6), 17–21.

Hickey, M. (2003). Creative thinking in the context of music composition. In M. Hickey (Ed.), *Why and how to teach music composition: A new horizon for music education* (pp. 31–55). Reston, VA: MENC.

Hickey, M., & Webster, P. (2001). Creative thinking in music. *Music Educators Journal, 88*(1), 19–23.

Kaschub, M. (1997). Composition in the choral rehearsal. *Music Educators Journal, 84*(1), 28–33.

Kraus, B. (2003). *Musicians in flow: Optimal experience in the wind ensemble rehearsal* (Unpublished doctoral dissertation). Arizona State University, Tempe, AZ.

Madura, P. D. (1997). Jazz improvisation for the vocal student. *Teaching Music, 4*(6), 26–28.

May, J. (1976). Independence and creativity in the choir. *Music Educators Journal, 62*(7), 54–57.

Mroz, R. (1982). Investigating curriculum planning practices for the cultivation of individual creative potentialities in secondary school instrumental music in selected school districts of Erie county. *Dissertation Abstracts International, 43*(2920A).

Paynter, J. (1972). Music and imagination. *Music Teacher, 51*(1), 11–12.

Peterson, S. (1993). Creativity and the marching band. *Music Educators Journal, 80*(3), 29–32.

Pogonowski, L. (2001). A personal retrospective on the MMCP. *Music Educators Journal, 88*(1), 24–27.

Priest, T. (2002). Creative thinking in instrumental classes. *Music Educators Journal, 88*(4), 47–51.

Reahm, D. E. (1986). Developing critical thinking through rehearsal techniques. *Music Educators Journal, 72*(7), 29–31.

Reichling, M. (1990). Images of imagination. *Journal of Research in Music Education, 38*(4), 282–293.

Reichling, M. (1992). Imagination and musical understanding: A theoretical perspective with implications for music education. *Quarterly Journal of Music Teaching and Learning, 3*(4), 20–31.

Reimer, B. (2003). *A philosophy of music education: Advancing the vision* (3rd ed.). Upper Saddle River, NJ: Prentice Hall.

Rouse, W., & Rouse, R. (2004). Teamwork in the performing arts. *Proceedings of the IEEE, 92*(4), 606–615.

Sindberg, L. K. (1998). The Wisconsin CMP project at age 21. *Music Educators Journal, 85*(3), 37–42.

Sindberg, L. K. (2006). *Comprehensive musicianship through performance (CMP) in the lived experience of students* (Unpublished doctoral dissertation). Northwestern University, Evanston, IL.

Smith, C. (1979). Technique versus creativity. *Choral Journal, 20*(3), 13–14.

Spronken-Smith, R., & Harland, T. (2009). Learning to teach with problem-based learning. *Active Learning in Higher Education, 10*(2), 138–153.

Thomas, R. (1970). *Manhattanville music curriculum program: Final report.* New York, NY: Manhattanville College of the Sacred Heart.

Thomas, R. (1991). Musical fluency: MMCP and today's curriculum. *Music Educators Journal, 78*(4), 26–29.

Webster, P. (1989). *Creative thinking in music: The assessment question. Access ERIC: FullText* (150 Speeches/Meeting Papers). Proceedings of The Suncoast Music Education Forum on Creativity (pp. 40–74). Tampa, FL: University of South Florida.

Webster, P. (1990). Creative thinking in music: Introduction. *Music Educators Journal, 76*(9), 21.

Webster, P. (2000). Reforming secondary music teaching. *Journal of Secondary Gifted Education, 12*(1), 17–24.

Wig, J. (1980). The effect of instruction in music composition strategies on middle school band students' ability to improvise melodies (Doctoral dissertation). *Dissertation Abstracts International, 41*(10).

Wood, D. (2008). Problem based learning. *British Medical Journal, 336,* 971.

Section Five

Evolving Roles

Why is it so difficult for us as conductors to relinquish some of our control so that students have input into their own decision making? Why should it be the rare occasion for students to be given voice within our rehearsals?

Kate Fitzpatrick

Part of the challenge is transcending in some way these notions of authority to a different kind of notion where the authority is still vested in the teacher in some way, but their knowledge manifests itself in a different kind of way than telling. Then teaching is not telling, but understanding what productive questions to ask.

Peter McCoy

13

REFRAMING LEADERSHIP AND THE MUSICAL EXPERIENCE

The Conductor as Servant Leader

Ramona M. Wis

PROLOGUE: THE LEADERSHIP QUESTION

THE CONDUCTOR OF a musical ensemble is a leader: the conductor starts and stops the music, gives interpretive and technical directives, makes decisions about programming, and manages countless administrative tasks that are a necessary part of running a musical organization. But while the conductor's role as a leader may be assumed, his or her approach to leadership and the quality of that leadership can take myriad realities. The conductor's beliefs about his or her job on the podium and the way in which these beliefs translate to his or her interactions with the musicians and the music are what make the ultimate difference in the musical product and, perhaps more importantly, the quality of the musical experience.

Historically, conductors of musical ensembles function largely as autocrats; they are the ultimate decision makers, the unquestioned experts making all the artistic and, often, administrative calls. This "top-down approach" characterizes the traditional model of leadership that has been part of our wider business culture for decades. Sometimes leaders move beyond an autocratic to a dictatorial style, beyond making all the decisions to enforcing those decisions in coercive or even tyrannical ways. As musicians, not only have we come to accept tyrants as a fact of our musical lives but also we even seem to endorse them; the folklore of the artistic diva, whether as a solo artist or as a conductor, seems to hold a kind of mysterious allure for us. If one is really brilliant, really artistic, and really important, then one must be *really* self-absorbed and demanding, right?

Not so. In recent years, a shift in leadership has occurred—in the philosophy, the approach, and, most important, the practices—and this shift is impacting leaders of musical organizations in significant ways. Changing from top-down, hierarchical thinking to collaborative decision making and leading by serving, conductors are reframing their leadership and, in the process, reframing the musical experience.

In this chapter, we will look at fundamental views and challenges of leadership, examine the approach to leadership known as servant leadership, and discuss ways in which applying a servant leadership mindset and practices to the conductor–ensemble relationship can significantly reframe the musical experience.

UNDERSTANDING LEADERSHIP: A PRIMER FOR THE CONDUCTOR

Leadership is a word so broad that it almost has no real meaning. We know leadership (good or bad) when we see it, but describing it in words is difficult and can lead to a limited, rather than a clarified, understanding. Yet for us to explore "reframed leadership," we need a starting point for our discussion.

Perhaps the best and simplest definition of leadership is John Maxwell's: "Leadership is influence—nothing more, nothing less" (Maxwell, 1998, p. 17). When we, as conductors, approach our leadership role as one of master influencer (rather than master dictator, master musician, or master administrator), we find an even greater opportunity to develop musicians' artistry, understanding, and emotive energy. When we are "of influence" rather than "in charge," we begin to see how our leadership talents can work hand in hand with our musical talents to provide a rich environment for growth and experience.

Understanding influence as our primary responsibility helps us to broaden our thinking of leadership beyond the administration of people and tasks. Indeed, we often confuse leadership with management, and while they are related, management is but a component of leadership—it does not constitute leadership in the fullest sense. Organizing rehearsals, people, repertoire, and concerts involves a long list of administrative details that must be handled competently if we are to be successful. But while managing is about efficiency and tasks, leadership is about innovation and people. Leadership researcher Warren Bennis put it this way:

The manager administers; the leader innovates.
The manager is a copy; the leader is an original.
The manager maintains; the leader develops.
The manager focuses on systems and structure; the leader focuses on people.

The manager relies on control; the leader inspires trust.

The manager has a short-range view; the leader has a long-range perspective.

The manager asks how and when; the leader asks what and why.

The manager has his eye always on the bottom line; the leader has his eye on the horizon.

The manager imitates; the leader originates.

The manager accepts the status quo; the leader challenges it.

The manager is a classic good soldier; the leader is his own person.

The manager does things right; the leader does the right thing. (Bennis, 1989, p. 45)

Influence is both broader and more powerful than authority. We may have the authority (i.e., the "right") to enforce our will because we hold a title—conductor, artistic director, professor, or teacher. But influence happens regardless of title: we influence people by who we are and what we do, by the strength of our character (or sadly, the lack of it), by the decisions we make, and by the way we relate to people. We should not assume that having authority automatically means we are a leader, if by "leader" we mean someone who creates an environment that moves people forward to reach their potential and the organization's artistic goals in a positive way.

Understanding leadership as more than autocracy, management, and authority is a critical first step for the conductor wanting to better understand his or her leadership role in a changing leadership landscape. That said, is there a need for leaders of musical organizations to change? The traditional top-down, directive model of conductor leadership, while not perfect, seems to work just fine. Why consider a different approach?

KEEP THE BABY, THROW OUT THE BATH WATER

Perhaps the most significant societal change that has impacted approaches to leadership is the rise of the "knowledge worker," a term coined in the late 1960s by management expert Peter Drucker. In contrast to manual workers, valued for their skill and efficiency, knowledge workers are valued for their knowledge and their ability to use it in diverse situations. Knowledge workers are not seen as subordinates, as manual workers are; they are not even usually viewed as "employees" in the traditional sense. Knowledge workers are considered "associates" who expect a good degree of autonomy, who focus on quality at least as much as quantity, and who are not likely to stay with one company for their entire career, in contrast to the "company man" of the first half of the twentieth century (Drucker, 1999).

Leading the knowledge worker is a different enterprise than leading the manual worker or the traditional employee. Instead of directing the workers in a clearly hierarchical system, today's leader understands his or her dependence on the unique abilities and knowledge of those he or she leads and is much more likely to involve them in decision making, while still maintaining his or her role as a leader. Drucker uses the conductor/orchestra relationship as an example of the way the leader and knowledge worker can function in harmony *if* the leader understands and respects the knowledge worker's contribution to the organization:

> Their relationship, in other words, is far more like that between the conductor of an orchestra and the instrumentalist than it is like the traditional superior/subordinate relationship. The superior in an organization employing knowledge workers cannot, as a rule, do the work of the supposed subordinate any more than the conductor of an orchestra can play the tuba. In turn, the knowledge worker is dependent on the supervisor to give direction and, above all, to define what the "score" is for the entire organization, that is, what are standards and values, performance and results. And just as an orchestra can sabotage even the ablest conductor— and certainly even the most autocratic one—a knowledge organization can easily sabotage even the ablest, let alone the most autocratic, superior. (Drucker, 1999, p. 20)

Many conductors today are still operating as though they are leading "manual workers"—people who have a particular skill that they perform with efficiency and according to the directives of the leader without any input, personal autonomy, or collaboration in creative decision making. As leaders, we need to recognize how wider societal shifts impact the environment of the organization we are privileged to lead, the musical ensemble. If the knowledge worker is being led differently today in a corporate environment, might this suggest a similar rethinking of the way we lead our own "knowledge workers"—musicians—in our musical environment?

The rumblings in the field say yes to this question. In their study of symphony orchestras, Jutta Allmendinger, J. Richard Hackman, and Erin V. Lehman asked questions about job satisfaction and compared responses with those of twelve other occupations and found:

> For general satisfaction, orchestra players ranked seventh of the thirteen. And for satisfaction with growth opportunities, they ranked ninth—just below federal prison guards (although I hasten to add that we studied a

very innovative prison) and just above operating room nurses and professional hockey players. (Hackman, 2005)

Why so unhappy? Is it the salary? The horrible working conditions? The terrible repertoire? Or is it something deeper? Seifter and Economy (2001) described the typical orchestral environment as follows, which might offer some insight:

> A conductor communicates with the more than one hundred musicians "reporting" to him by standing on an elevated platform and waving a stick of wood at them. This communication is essentially one-way since individual musicians rarely—if ever—express an idea or opinion to the conductor. Orchestral musicians are constantly required to conform, and they are usually denied an individual sense of accomplishment. For example, in a traditional orchestra, an important element of the job of violinist number 26 is to make absolutely sure that his bow flies off the strings of his instrument at precisely the same nanosecond as violinists number 25 and number 27. If he does his job well, violinist 26's immediate feedback (and reward) is to be ignored by the conductor altogether. Creativity, engagement in the process, and employee satisfaction don't really enter into the equation. (p. 20)

Could it be that musicians with a twenty-first-century knowledge-worker mindset yearn for something different than the long-standing tradition of a conductor-focused hierarchical pyramid? Seifter and Economy's study of the Orpheus Chamber Ensemble and its process of collaborative leadership indicates that a change may be called for:

> For double-bass player Don Palma, a founding member, a brief foray into the world of conducted orchestras proved to be an experience that he didn't soon wish to repeat. Says Palma, "I took one year off from Orpheus at the very beginning and went to the Los Angeles Philharmonic. I just hated it. I didn't like to be told what to do all the time, being treated like my only value was just to sit there and be a good soldier. I felt powerless to affect things, particularly when they were not going well. I felt frustrated, and there was nothing I could seem to do to help make things better." As a member of Orpheus, however, life is quite different. In Palma's words, "Orpheus keeps me involved. I have some measure of participation in the direction the music is going to take. I think that's why a lot of us have stayed involved for so long." (p. 26)

There appears to be a shift in thinking, an evolved view of the nature of the creative experience from the perspective of the ensemble member. Rather than doing little more than following directions on cue, many musicians today, in a knowledge-worker age, want to contribute in a deeper, more creative, more collaborative way than historical ensemble practices have allowed. Conductors of today's school or community organizations can verify that even young, inexperienced, or volunteer musicians wonder why they should robotically follow someone on the podium because he or she has a title when they, as the players or singers, are the ones actually creating the sounds and, therefore, have the intimate knowledge of and connection to the possibilities and the challenges involved in the music-making experience.

If musicians are going to have a deeper, richer engagement in the creative process, conductors must be willing to reconsider and, perhaps, reframe the roles of leader and performer. We can keep the "baby" of high-level musical performance while we consider throwing out the "bath water" of conductor-focused, directive approaches to creating that performance. This change depends on one important but critical shift in thinking: a shift from "me versus them" to "us"—a change from directing to facilitating and a willingness to reframe leading as serving.

This shift in thinking may be counterintuitive to our training in undergraduate music education and conductor preparation programs and to what we have personally experienced as members of ensembles. In his discussion on the "society of musicians," Bruno Nettl (1995) described the traditional music school environment as one in which conductors hold the ultimate position of musical power:

As conductors, professors receive the satisfaction of leadership in rehearsals (it is actually a dictatorial leadership that does not readily permit advice and consent) and also the glory that goes with public performance in which the conductor emerges as a member of a ruling class, receiving vastly more credit for the performance than the individual ensemble member. (p. 77)

Historically, conductors in music schools are trained to be excellent musicians, and then to be efficient managers of the musical ensemble (which usually means being "in control" of the musicians). This develops a "me in charge of you" mentality, which becomes intensified when we realize the added pressure of having our end product judged (we would like to think "enjoyed," but we know better) in real time in front of a watching world (an audience). Add a healthy dose of ego (not entirely a bad thing), and we have a view of leadership that makes it unlikely that we will trust musicians to make any decisions or provide input. And so we repeat the organizational practices we have witnessed our entire musical lives, practices that have now gotten us into a leadership predicament that can only be addressed by a change of heart and a change in our philosophy of leadership.

SERVANT LEADERSHIP: A PHILOSOPHY, A CHOICE

Not a new concept, the term *servant leadership* was coined by Robert K. Greenleaf in the latter part of the twentieth century. A retired AT&T executive, Greenleaf had a deep interest in managing, then leading, others and used his experience and explorations in the corporate world to begin what many would call a revolution in leadership thinking and practice. The most often cited quote by Greenleaf is his description of the servant leader:

> The servant-leader *is* servant first.…It begins with the natural feeling that one wants to serve, to serve *first*. Then conscious choice brings one to aspire to lead. That person is sharply different from one who is *leader* first, perhaps because of the need to assuage an unusual power drive or to acquire material possessions. For such it will be a later choice to serve—after leadership is established.…
>
> The best test, and difficult to administer is: Do those served grow as persons? Do they, *while being served*, become healthier, wiser, freer, more autonomous, more likely themselves to become servants? *And*, what is the effect on the least privileged in society; will they benefit, or, at least, not be further deprived? (Greenleaf, 1977, pp. 13–14)

The first challenge as we explore servant leadership is to recognize the negative connotations that may come with the word *servant*: images of servitude, of lower station or ability, or of being invisible, unmotivated, or incapable of leading. Being a servant, even when thought of in noble settings (as in "public servant"), is usually not something we aspire to in a contemporary, competitive, goal-setting society. But we can reconsider "serving" as a way of using our influence: using all of our talents, skills, opportunities, resources, experience, passion, energy, and personality *and* our titles or positions of authority to help move people forward in significant and meaningful ways.

Greenleaf's distinction between the role of servant and leader and the order in which the desires to serve and to lead manifest themselves within the leader is an important one according to Prosser. He believed Greenleaf's definition "captures the essence lying at the heart of the concept, namely that someone chooses to serve others and realizes that the best way to serve their needs is by becoming their leader. Therein is both the profundity and simplicity at the core of what it means to be a servant-leader: the term means a servant who leads" (Prosser, 2010, p. 7).

The second challenge in understanding servant leadership is getting past the limiting belief that it is "soft leadership," that serving others means giving them everything they want. But servant leadership is about giving others what they need, not necessarily what they want. This is tough leadership, knowing that to truly serve others means that we may need to challenge them to be more personally disciplined, more rigorous in the quality of their work, or more accountable. Servant leaders assess the situation, ask for input, and authentically listen to those they serve, but in the end they make decisions with the greatest benefit in mind, even when those decisions are not the most popular or the most personally comfortable for the leader. Programming simplistic or poorly arranged pop music, for example, might be a "want" voiced by musicians, but a wise servant leader can find a way to provide an experience that meets the real needs of the ensemble (variety, enjoyment, connection) without compromising artistic or educational goals. It's called servant *leadership* because we still have the responsibility for growing people even when they don't know what is needed to make that growth happen.

A third, and perhaps the most difficult, challenge is in understanding that servant leadership is not a to-do list, a "method," or a twelve-step program that can be followed like a map that will lead to a guaranteed final destination. Servant leadership is a change of heart, an evolution of one's personal leadership philosophy that has a bottom-line focus on *people* more than any other aspect of leading. "Getting to the level of servant organization requires a mind shift where the leaders see themselves differently, view the led differently and reshape their whole view of the purpose and meaning of leadership" (Laub, 2003, as cited in Prosser, 2010, p.26).

Prosser's research from many sources (2010, p. 32) further explains this point of view:

> As a result of this disposition, the servant-leader's primary focus is on the followers, not on the leader's personal interests or the organisation. Without doubt, the achievement of organizational objectives is seen as an essential outcome (Stone, Russell and Patterson, 2004)—servant-leaders do not live in a dream world, pretending that they can be oblivious to the harsh realities of the for-profit and not-for-profit sectors. However, their primary focus is on serving others. As a result of this, their principal motivation is to make life better for others, rather than for themselves (Keith, 2008).

Servant leadership is a way of being in the world, a philosophy that can be realized by different types of leadership personalities and styles, and with impressive results:

> In the end, being a servant-leader is not something you *do* but rather something you *are*. It is about creating the right environment to get the best out of people and unleash their true potential. Servant-leadership should not be misinterpreted as soft management—some of the most tough-minded leaders today are firm believers in and exponents of servant-leadership. Far from it, it is about effectiveness and there is clearly a need! (DeGraaf, Tilley, & Neal, 2001, pp. 27–28)

SERVANT LEADERSHIP IN OUR REAL CONDUCTING LIFE

What does servant leadership look like in the real life of conductors and their musical organizations? Despite the fact that servant leadership is not a method or even a prescribed "style" of leadership, there are identifiable behaviors and realities that will be seen in servant-led organizations.

Conductors who are servant leaders create an environment of **trust** with the musicians they lead. This means letting go of some of the control and trusting that musicians will want to accomplish the ensemble's goals and represent themselves and the organization at the highest level possible if led well. Servant leaders view musicians as people, not as "the first clarinet" or "soprano section leader." They acknowledge the performers' musical abilities, as well as their desire to be engaged in the decision-making process, and find multiple ways to involve the musicians in the rehearsal while still teaching and rehearsing efficiently.

Trust must work both ways. For conductors to be viewed as trust*worthy*, they need to be seen as consistent: consistent in their personal preparation of the music and the standards they set for excellence, consistent in holding people accountable, and consistent in their demeanor and approach to the ensemble and rehearsals. Conductors who are servant leaders do not become "other creatures" during concert week or in final rehearsals, lashing out at musicians with threats and belittling comments or with sarcastic remarks and guilt trips. Servant leaders may change their approach to the way they run the critical rehearsals before performance, even using autocratic or directive means to accomplish important goals when time is short, but this does not mean they have abandoned their servant leadership philosophy. Rather, it is precisely *because* a trust relationship has been built between leader and ensemble that the conductor can legitimately employ autocratic methods as a way of serving the ensemble at key points in the rehearsal process.

> It may sound shocking but servant-leaders can also be autocratic, if the need arises in their sincere and ethical efforts to serve others....It is not that they have become autocratic in nature, turning their back on everything they purport to believe—it is just that their act of service truly can be best delivered through a temporary engagement with autocratic leadership. (Prosser, 2010, p. 36)

Blanchard, Zigarmi, and Zigarmi (1985) supported the choice of a directive style (which may be thought of as an autocratic style) when "a decision has to be made quickly and the stakes are high" (p. 36). But this choice is made consciously, against a backdrop of a trust relationship that has been established between conductor and ensemble—ideally, a relationship that is characterized by routinely using a collaborative approach to reaching a mutual end goal.

Conductors who are servant leaders know themselves and their ensembles well and anticipate the challenges of bringing the details together; they realize there will be surprises, but they also plan well in advance, using their **vision** and **foresight** to construct a rehearsal environment that allows for musical exploration and musical accomplishment. Servant leaders set long-term goals, using input from those they lead, and articulate these goals often to keep everyone on track and aware of the bigger picture. Simply giving musicians a sense of "where we are" (not where *they* are) in the rehearsal process helps establish the momentum that can keep everyone aware of his or her personal responsibility toward the final performance. Articulating the group's vision also helps unify the ensemble, because it can provide a sense of purpose and remind them of why they are there. Regularly articulating the vision is also a method of assessment: *Where are we in the process? What do we need to do to get closer to our goals? What do we need to do before our next rehearsal?* Musicians can be involved in this assessment, giving them ownership and, therefore, greater responsibility for their part in accomplishing the ensemble's goals.

Conductors who are servant leaders use their vision as they plan rehearsals with a broader purpose than "getting through the first movement" or "fixing the notes on page 5." Each rehearsal is seen as a step toward not only developing an excellent concert program in the near future but also developing thinking, expressive, autonomous artists in the broader future (yes, even junior high students can develop into young artists if led with vision).

Related to vision is foresight, which servant leaders use to think through a series of events from beginning to end so they can make decisions, changes, or even tough choices early enough in the process to be effective. Greenleaf (1977) called foresight the "central ethic of leadership" and described it this way:

> The leader needs two intellectual abilities that are usually not formally assessed in an academic way: he needs to have a *sense for the unknowable and be able to foresee the unforeseeable.* Leaders know some things and foresee some things which those they are presuming to lead do not know or foresee as clearly. (pp. 21–22)

Foresight is a critical skill for conductors because it enables them to take action *now* to avoid problems that will likely occur, especially if past experience is ignored instead of used to help intuit the future. Why, when talking about a concert that will happen months from now, do we assume that we will be "running out of time" or that we will be "frantic" during concert week? Why are we *planning* to be out of time? If it is because we are always frantic during concert week, then we are not using our foresight to make different choices well in advance and, therefore, not repeat the pattern that has occurred in the past.

> Foresight demands that we have insight into people and process, into the art form at a creative (as well as a technical) level and that we have a keen sense of time. Foresight instructs pedagogy—pedagogy helps us when a challenge arises but foresight tells us the challenge is coming. Relying on foresight means we can plan ahead to create the best possible product because we can see, in advance, what is likely to happen with the process. (Wis, 2007, p. 38)

Because conductors who are servant leaders trust the musicians they lead and utilize their vision and foresight, they can rehearse and teach with the goal of **collaboration**. When we think of collaboration as "co-laboring," we are more likely to understand how to lead rehearsals as facilitators, working *with* the musicians rather than *above* the musicians. But a collaborative mindset demands strong leadership; a sense of knowing what will be needed by the musicians at any point in time; a commitment to constant re-evaluation, assessment, and pedagogical strategizing; and a keen sense of time in order to keep the group on track in a very real-world way. Collaboration is not the abdication of our leadership responsibility, but rather a different means of setting the tone and creating a mindset and environment for growth and exploration.

Collaboration does not mean every musical decision is up for a group vote (which would not only bog down rehearsals but also frustrate musicians, wondering if their leader has any vision or expertise to move the organization forward). Collaboration can be viewed as a continuum of rehearsal approaches that can be seamlessly woven among more traditionally directive styles of leading the rehearsal, always focused on what the ensemble needs at that moment in the musical exploration and learning process. For servant leaders, collaboration is a conscious choice to broaden the rehearsal to be more than skill development and technical corrections of the score; it is an opportunity to connect with the musicians on multiple levels and grow them for the long term.

At the simplest level of collaboration, servant leaders *share the thinking process behind the decisions conductors make.* The traditional diagnostic–prescriptive approach, where the conductor stops the ensemble to diagnose the problem and prescribe a solution, can be moved farther down the collaboration continuum if the conductor simply takes a moment to explain the thinking behind the "prescription." Rather than "Altos, round your vowel," conductors would take the time to say, "Altos, if you round your vowel that will not only unify the section sound but also help improve your intonation." Even that one change can make a significant impact on the performers' musical experience; while they learn to fix the technical problem, they appreciate being validated by a conductor who took the time to share his or her knowledge with them and help them learn skills for the long term, which they can apply in other situations.

Farther down the collaboration continuum is the act of *asking musicians questions* about everything from musical intent, to technical problem solving, to historical context, to even the most basic issues such as whether or not the choir can master the music from memory for the next performance. Here, conductors switch from "output" practices (prescribing solutions, providing rationales) to "input" practices; we *ask* the musicians to provide the missing information and steer the rehearsal in ways they perceive as appropriate and needed at that time. "What was the problem in that last line? Why did that transition falter? What else is in the score that we need to observe?" Involving ensemble members in their own musical destiny at every level possible demonstrates our trust but also charges them with responsibility. If we are going to create autonomous musicians, musicians who can apply their skill and understanding to other musical situations, then we need to give them the opportunity to be a part of this process and give them the responsibility of taking ownership of some of the decision making. Stopping the ensemble to ask questions creates an environment where musicians are always thinking *with* the conductor to create the best musical product and experience rather than waiting *for* the conductor to tell them what to do.

At the farthest end of the collaboration continuum is *delegating full responsibility* for rehearsing, learning, and decision making, as when musicians lead sectional rehearsals or chamber ensembles or help with the administrative aspects of the organization. But even at this far end of the continuum, conductors are still *leading* because they collaborate with musicians to ensure that the process of working on their own is successful and they act as mentors and musical resources as needed. Simply delegating responsibility without any preparation, resources, structure, or support can often be more of an exploration in ensemble frustration than in musical growth. As leaders, we need to ensure that the framework for success is in place before moving to the far end of the collaboration continuum.

Trust, vision and foresight, and collaboration are important indicators of the way in which conductors live out their commitment to servant leadership. But perhaps the greatest test of this commitment is in the way we use *persuasion*, rather than coercion, to accomplish a goal, manage the environment, and lead people.

While few would admit they use coercive approaches to lead others, many conductors use coercion as a means of getting what they want, even when what they want is viewed as important or admirable (a successful concert). Coercion can be subtle—sarcastic comments that are billed as "humor"—or more pronounced, such as threats to take away solos or chairs or to add more rehearsals (an interesting punishment—you were bad, so let's make more music...?). Coercion can be justified as "necessary" to whip the ensemble into shape, but servant leaders will first ask themselves what they could have done differently so there was no *need* to "whip them into shape." Better planning and programming? More effective teaching and rehearsing? Better use of time and stronger decision making on administrative matters? Conductors who are servant leaders will go through a checklist to determine how not to repeat the problem in the future because they realize coercive approaches damage morale and relationships and are likely to be needed again and again, every time the ensemble gets into the same crisis mode. Coercion never fixes a problem in the long term.

> Coercive power is based on fear in both the leader and the follower. Leaders tend to lean on coercive power when they are afraid they won't get compliance. It is the "big stick'" approach. It is an approach that few publicly support but may use, either because it seems justified in the face of other, bigger threats hovering over the leader or it is the expedient thing to do and seems to work at the time. But its effectiveness is an illusion. (Covey, 1990, p. 103)

Greenleaf agreed when he said: "The trouble with coercive power is that it only strengthens resistance. And, if successful, its controlling effect lasts only as long as the force is strong. It is not organic" (Greenleaf, 1977, p. 42).

Servant leaders attempt to use their powers of persuasion to move people. Persuasion, when viewed as passion with an openness toward and respect for others, can be a powerful force with positive, long-lasting results. Persuasion moves people for the right reason, focuses more on the important aspects of the musical experience, and preserves relationships in a way coercion never can. Covey described persuasion this way:

> *Persuasion,* which includes sharing reasons and rationale, making a strong case for your position or desire while maintaining genuine respect for followers' ideas and perspective; tell why as well as what; commit to stay in the communication process until mutually beneficial and satisfying outcomes are reached. (Covey, 1990, p. 107)

Servant leaders never give up persuading others to see the benefits of making appropriate decisions or acting in disciplined ways, always keeping an eye on the overriding purpose or mission of the organization and always reaching deep to the heart of the musicians to see life from their point of view. Understanding what moves musicians and what matters to them is critical to the conductor's ability to persuade musicians to practice their music or to approach their role in the ensemble in a dedicated way.

Admittedly, the line between strong persuasion and subtle coercion appears to be a fine one, but the determining factor is the conductor's motive and his or her desire to preserve the relationship among all members of the organization while still accomplishing important goals. Trusting the musicians, having and articulating a vision, and working collaboratively with them will go a long way toward persuading them (using positive means) and moving them in the right direction while not manipulating them (using devious means). Reality tells us that there will always be difficulties in working with some people, including strong-willed musicians who refuse to be persuaded by anything we say or do in our leadership of the ensemble. Dealing with challenging personalities, diva attitudes, or musicians who don't fulfill their obligations to the ensemble are all part of the conductor's job description. Servant leaders will do what they can to handle these situations with respect, but they will not be reluctant to hold noncompliant musicians accountable and, if necessary, make difficult decisions regarding their status in the ensemble.

> Letting the wrong people hang around is unfair to all the right people, as they inevitably find themselves compensating for the inadequacies of the wrong people. Worse, it can drive away the best people. Strong performers

are intrinsically motivated by performance, and when they see their efforts impeded by carrying extra weight, they eventually become frustrated. (Collins, 2001, p. 56)

Ultimately, servant leaders are viewed as having **character**, on and off the podium. Character, like excellent leadership, is something we recognize even if we find it difficult to describe in words. Character is demonstrated by a congruency of personhood—of behavior and word, of philosophy and action. Music is a profound means of expressing our personhood. To imagine that we, as conductors, can effectively manage two realities—the person on the podium versus the one off the podium—and expect that our musicians will be blind to this duplicity is only fooling ourselves. Even young students can tell when we are *acting* like we care about them and the music (manipulation) and when we are truly caring (authenticity).

Servant leaders grow in character with every leadership challenge they face. They consciously make choices based on their servant leadership perspective, trusting that they and their ensembles will benefit from these choices in the end. And when they do make mistakes, servant leaders acknowledge them, learn from them, and do their best to rectify the situation.

REFRAMED LEADERSHIP AND THE MUSICAL EXPERIENCE

Ultimately, a servant leadership environment has the potential to significantly enhance the musical experience for everyone involved. Reframing our conductor leadership to stand on a servant leadership philosophy can mean marked changes in everything from musical accomplishment and understanding, to engagement and morale, to a widespread commitment to taking ownership for one's part in the musical enterprise.

When conductors let go of some of the traditional autocratic approaches to leading the rehearsal and involve the musicians in ways that demand more than their technical compliance, they engage musicians in higher-order thinking skills, pave the way for long-term skill development and musical understanding, and allow for a deeper engagement with the music—all of which means a richer musical experience. Parncutt and McPherson (2002), in their research on teaching in the rehearsal environment, described the typical approach to leading rehearsals, as well as the results of the learning and experience that characterize this model:

While considerable proportions of rehearsal are spent in verbal activity and modeling, principally on the part of the conductor, little of it elicits higher order or conceptual thinking on the part of the performers. General music and ensemble classes generally involve students in lower cognitive processes, emphasizing mechanics of performance almost to the exclusion of the application and accumulation of musical knowledge and the abilities to think about music (Goodlad, 1983). Conductors' efforts appear to be weighted toward providing guidance on how to make corrections of presenting exact solutions, by saying things such as "you need more air" or "the percussion need to play softer." This limits opportunities for self-correction on the part of the ensemble through slight hints or scaffolding (Weeks, 1996). In these situations, ensemble members function much like simple machinery, rendering only specific responses to specific instructions about a specific point in a specific piece of music. (p. 342)

Reimer (1989) described it another way:

When performance group directors or classroom teachers are directing the music making of students but make all the decisions *for* them ("Trumpets, play those two measures louder," "Sing the beginning of the song with shorter notes," "Altos, you're getting that rhythm mixed up; do it like this," "Hold that trill longer, then fade out," and on and on forever), those *directors* are creating, but their students are surely not. The students have been forced to be artisans, used for making art but permitted no involvement in artistic creation. (p. 69)

The impact on performances can be dramatic when musicians feel a more invested part of the rehearsal, when they are not passive but active in the learning process:

The rehearsal atmosphere must be such that the combination of conductor persuasiveness and collaboration results in an ensemble that is responsive and receptive to the conductor's verbal and nonverbal behaviors. Indeed, performances appear to benefit when ensemble members feel a part of the learning process rather than functioning as passive recipients of information (Hamann et al., 1990). (Parncutt & McPherson, 2002, p. 336)

Conductors who choose a different approach to rehearsal can engage higher-order thinking skills and reap long-term benefits because musicians will be able to internalize skills and understanding and apply them to future learning:

Even though it appears that there is little encouragement of higher order thinking and the development of concepts in rehearsals, it would seem that planning and employing strategies to promote these throughout the rehearsal would be most effective in the long-term growth of performers and ensembles. Without these attributes, a conductor is condemned to reteach an idea every time a similar passage or concept is encountered, as opposed to musicians making connections cognitively and transferring knowledge and skills to new situations. More sophisticated performers have likely attained higher order music skills through inductive reasoning as a result of synthesis of many experiences; thus conductors of highly skilled ensembles are better able to attend to the performances that help make music rapturous. (Parncutt & McPherson, 2002, p. 333)

Do we have to wait to "make music rapturous" until we have an ensemble full of seasoned musicians, or can we choose approaches to leading the rehearsal that require musicians, at every level of ability and experience, to use more of their skill and knowledge to make connections, ultimately deepening their musical experience? Conductors who are servant leaders will make a conscious choice to deeply engage musicians because they know that their approach to leadership can make the critical difference between a technically correct performance and a deeply expressive and powerful musical experience, the latter marked by performing *with understanding*.

Engaged at a deeper, more meaningful level, musicians are more likely to feel committed to the ensemble's goals because they feel it is *their* ensemble, not the conductor's ensemble. This can result in higher morale and a sense of ownership, often evidenced by better rehearsal attendance, more cooperative attitudes, and a willingness to take on leadership roles. A dedicated ensemble is also an ensemble that can be held accountable at higher levels because they have a greater stake in the process and the product than when they are only viewed as fulfilling a limited role at the beck and call of an autocratic leader. They will press each other more and demand more of themselves and everyone in the ensemble because it is *their* ensemble and because they were allowed input into the process even in some limited way. Servant leaders avoid calling an ensemble "*my* band" or "*my* orchestra" precisely because they want to remind everyone (including themselves) who really has the ultimate power to be excellent. This fundamental shift in mindset and attitude is powerful and can have a ripple effect into every aspect of the ensemble's experience and artistic accomplishment.

And therefore, when one speaks about the feeling of power in the actual act of making music, the conductor has to understand what the nature of sound is: that he can change everything around it, but the actual sound, in the end, is made by the musicians. In an ideal situation, this will also keep the conductor's ego within bounds; and it will also give the individual musician in the orchestra the feeling that he is not just following orders, that he's not just an instrument for somebody else's feeling of power or determination, but that he's being very creative about it, too. (Barenboim & Said, 2002, p. 71)

OUR CHARGE AS CONDUCTORS WHO CHOOSE SERVANT LEADERSHIP

Embracing a servant leadership approach as a conductor does not mean compromising on artistic excellence or quality; choosing a reframed approach to leadership does not mean trading in our passion or desire for excellence in favor of some kind of rehearsal Shangri-La that feels nice but leads nowhere. That would not serve our musicians or our art.

With a servant leadership foundation, we reframe our quest for excellence. We focus on how we can influence people rather than use them, and we redefine the musical experience as a cherished opportunity to interact with people in a powerful and meaningful way toward the goal of an excellent public performance. Maestro Henry Charles Smith put it this way: "I really want most to tend to the musical business in a way that affirms and supports the musicians personally and artistically" (Helland, 2006, p. 363).

Choosing a reframed approach to leadership based on a servant leadership philosophy is just that—a choice. Ultimately, all leaders decide how to lead based on a deeply held set of beliefs and values and go out into the world to exert their influence in a way that is unique to them and the opportunities they have to lead others. Conductors have the opportunity for powerful leadership because we are not only working with people—their minds, their hearts, and their skills—but also working with music in all its expressive potential. *How* we use our opportunity to lead may just be one of the most important choices we have to make in our lifetime.

EPILOGUE: TOWARD A NEW REALITY

The path of servant leadership is an evolution of thought and practice, a change of heart that is continually challenged by pressures to be "practical" and by an ego that wants to be acknowledged as a capable leader who is also artistically accomplished. Thankfully, servant leadership does not require or endorse removing oneself from "real life." Servant leadership is about reframing "real life" and moving those we lead toward a new reality, one that can provide a deeper, richer, more meaningful musical experience and (not "or") a stunning musical end result.

If you are skeptical of a servant leadership approach and whether it "works," you are not alone. Most of us are skeptical about anything that sounds too good to be true. But I have seen time and again how servant leadership can magnify the impact we make as leaders from the podium: how it can fuel our creative output, deepen relationships, spark synergy, and give us all a more satisfying musical experience. Because servant leadership challenges us to be our best selves and attend to what matters most—people and, for conductors, the music—we can begin to see everything more broadly and more deeply at the same time. Being a conductor who aims to lead by serving is a decision we choose to make every day—truth be told, a decision we will struggle with some days—and one that continues to challenge, enlighten, frustrate, delight, and enrich our lives and the lives of those we are given to lead.

> The journey is never over; it continues as long as we live a life of awareness. But we are encouraged because as we move in the right direction we experience moments of wholeness—glimpses of an integration of self and others, gifts and expression, opportunity and accomplishment. We see what we *can* be—our ensembles, ourselves, our music—and we continue to move toward that goal with our eyes, minds, and hearts open to possibility. We keep looking for opportunities to lead from the podium in ways that serve, to be a conductor of character and a teacher with passion. Ultimately, what we find is not just meaningful work, but a meaningful life. (Wis, 2007, p. 171)

REFERENCES

Barenboim, D., & Said, E. (2002). *Parallels and paradoxes: Explorations in music and society.* New York, NY: Pantheon Books.

Bennis, W. (1989). *On becoming a leader.* Cambridge, MA: Perseus Books.

Blanchard, K., Zigarmi, P., & Zigarmi, D. (1985). *Leadership and the one minute manager.* New York, NY: William Morrow and Company.

Collins, J. (2001). *Good to great: Why some companies make the leap…(and others don't).* New York, NY: Harper Collins Publishers.

Covey, S. R. (1990). *Principle-centered leadership.* New York, NY: Simon and Schuster.

DeGraaf, D., Tilley, C., & Neal, L. (2001). *Servant-leadership characteristics in organizational life.* Indianapolis, IN: Greenleaf Center for Servant-Leadership.

Drucker, P. F. (1999). *Management challenges for the 21st century.* New York, NY: Harper Business.

Goodlad, J. I. (1983). *A place called school.* New York, NY: McGraw-Hill.

Greenleaf, R. K. (1977). *Servant-leadership: A journey into the nature of legitimate power and greatness.* Mahwah, NJ: Paulist Press.

Hackman, J. R. (2005). *Convocation address as cited in Sonorities, a news magazine of the* University of Illinois School of Music, Spring, 2007.

Hamann, D.L., Mills, C., Bell, J., Daugherty, E., & Koozer, R. (1990). Classroom environment as related to contest ratings among high school performing ensembles. *Journal of Research in Music Education, 38*(3), 215-224.

Helland, M. (2006) Maestro: Exploring the development of a servant-leader. *International Journal of Servant-Leadership, 2*(1), 351-376.

Keith, K.M. (2008). *The case for servant leadership.* Westfield, IN: Greenleaf Center for Servant Leadership.

Maxwell, J. C. (1998). *The 21 irrefutable laws of leadership.* Nashville, TN: Thomas Nelson.

Nettl, B. (1995). *Heartland excursions: Ethnomusicological reflections on schools of music.* Urbana and Chicago, IL: University of Illinois Press.

Parncutt, R., & McPherson, G. E. (Eds.). (2002). *The science and psychology of music performance.* New York, NY: Oxford University Press.

Prosser, S. (2010). *Servant leadership: More philosophy, less theory.* Westfield, IN: Greenleaf Center for Servant Leadership.

Reimer, B. (1989). *A philosophy of music education* (2nd ed.). Englewood Cliffs, NJ: Prentice Hall.

Seifter, H., & Economy, P. (2001). *Leadership ensemble: Lessons in collaborative management from the world's only conductorless orchestra.* New York, NY: Henry Holt and Company.

Stone, A.G., Russell, R. F. & Patterson, K. (2004). Transformational leadership versus servant leadership: A difference in leader focus. *Leadership & Organizational Development Journal,* Volume 25, No. 4, pp. 349-61.

Weeks, P. (1996). A rehearsal of a Beethoven passage: An analysis of correction talk. *Research on Language and Social Interaction, 29*(3), 247-290.

Wis, R. M. (2007). *The conductor as leader: Principles of leadership applied to life on the podium.* Chicago, IL: GIA Publications.

14

RECONSIDERING THE PERFORMING ENSEMBLE CLASS

AND THE ROLE OF THE CONDUCTOR/TEACHER IN

MUSIC EDUCATION

David S. Zerull

FROM MODEST BEGINNINGS in the nineteenth century as curricular classes in vocal music designed to teach singing, music education developed in ways that placed an emphasis on listening and the experience of music as important student outcomes. Music classes in music appreciation, choir, orchestra, and band evolved, with the growth of instrumental music especially widespread in the early twentieth century (Keene, 1982). As school band and orchestra programs proliferated, industries emerged to provide instruments, equipment, and services designed to support music education in a performance class style. Indeed, it was the music industry, and specifically music instrument manufacturers, that sponsored some of the first band competitions (Keene, 1982).

Since the latter part of the twentieth century, composers have produced music specifically for the school ensemble. A cursory examination of recent music publishing company catalogs reveals more than 750 new works, arrangements, and transcriptions for band alone. By all accounts, school band, orchestra, and choir seem to enjoy a popularity and prominence in schools that suggest a successful music education model, and untold numbers of students receive a music education that features performance of music in concert. The performance ensemble classes are taught by music educators who have become known as "directors," and the model of the professional conductor leading the ensemble has emerged as the basis for teachers of ensemble performance classes. To accommodate the demand for teachers, preservice teacher education programs continue to produce accomplished school band and orchestra directors who emulate their ensemble conductors and follow a model that results in public performance by the ensemble class.

THE MODEL

In countless middle and high school band and orchestra rehearsals, classes, or lessons, the routine is the same. Students warm up, tune, and begin work on a piece including correcting notes, rhythms, ensemble precision, tone, and the like. The results of these rehearsals are some of the most outstanding performances of musical literature composed for the ensemble. Anyone who attends a competition, festival, adjudicated educational event, or concert would be impressed with the quality of the ensemble. Middle school students, playing for just a year and a half, present performances where students display an ability to play a piece with good dynamics and sensitivity to musical line. High school performances are remarkable for their quality of performance in tone, facility, and musicianship. It certainly is a testament to the work that ensemble directors accomplish in a group lesson setting, a setting where many students do not study privately. It is obvious that making music in ensemble class is a worthy pursuit, goal, or mission, and it is accomplished daily, through performance of fine literature in a superior manner. So the question must be asked, if the results of the hours of practice and rehearsal in performance by our students are everything they should be, is there cause for concern? Is it not the desire of music education to develop to the fullest extent possible the capacity of every student to make and experience music? With such wonderful music making, are we not accomplishing our mission?

Perhaps there is some discomfort, because it is recognized that not all students in an ensemble are challenged or experiencing music in the same way. It is reasonable to suggest that the student learning and performing the baritone saxophone part may not engender the same learning as students playing other parts. Certainly the group performance is complete with all individual parts being played, but is the student's experience and learning commensurate with his or her colleagues'? More importantly, is the learning complete? It is here that two questions emerge in the consideration of conducting and performing in music education. Does the model of music education in ensemble performance classes provide for the full experience of music, and how complete can student music learning be given the constraints of the performance ensemble class model? In reconsidering the model of the performance ensemble class and the music educator as conductor, a brief exploration of musical experience will be presented. The act of listening in the musical experience and the musical listening and experience of a student performer will be explored. Suggestions for a more complete music education experience for our students will be presented that include a more prominent role of musical listening.

THE PURPOSE—BOTH MAKING AND EXPERIENCING MUSIC

As stated previously, the purpose of music education is to develop to the fullest extent possible everyone's capacity to make and experience music. In the secondary ensemble classes, we seem to have the "make music" part covered. As conductors, whether in rehearsal or performance, we daily guide our students to make music. The standard dictionary meaning of the word *conduct* is "to guide and to lead," from the Latin *conductus,* past participle of *conducere,* "to bring or lead together" (Webster's New Universal Unabridged Dictionary, 1983). In addition to leading and guiding students, many music educators recognize that making music entails more than "playing." These music educators are in the business of both educating and instructing. Educating, from the Latin *educere,* is "to draw out," or to pull out the "musical" in our students. We are fond of saying that music provides an outlet, or creative release, and an opportunity for self-expression. Of course, that is true and good, but it is unrealistic to think that "simply" teaching a student to play or sing makes him or her able to "express" in any meaningful way. Yes, the learning of scales, fingerings, and the proper articulation will provide the foundation, but consider the limitations. One cannot assert that simply having facility on an instrument constitutes musical education. There must be instruction. The other part of the "equation" is the instruction, from the Latin *struere,* meaning "to build." Music educators are to build up the knowledge and understandings that inform and lead to better performance. But can we take for granted that in the process of making music, we are providing for the experience of music? The experience of music is not to be taken lightly for a music educator who desires to develop the capacity of students to make and experience music. Reimer (1989) asserted:

> The experience of music as expressive form is the be-all and end-all of music education, for such experience is the only way of sharing music's aesthetic meaning. This indicates that musical experience itself should come first and last. The payoff of music education—the sharing of music's aesthetic meanings should be central, with all means focused toward that end and actually producing that end at every possible moment as learning proceeds. (p. 96)

This is a challenge to the serious music educator—the experience of music and sharing aesthetic meanings at *every possible moment as learning proceeds*. If music educators are to help students experience music and share aesthetic meaning, it is incumbent upon us to consider the notion of "musical experience" as it relates to the student engaged in performing in the ensemble class.

MUSICAL EXPERIENCE

The experience of music in performance is special. Performance is the production of sounds "in concert" with others to create a musical work of art. The intimacy with which the performer is involved with musical sound is singular in nature, with respect to both the performance of the piece and being in the moment. Each playing of a musical work is a new experience and has the potential to be both a profound and a pedestrian experience. In my career, the idea of musical experience has intrigued me and guided my involvement in music and music education, as I am forever searching for the answer to the question "How do I develop the capacity of my students to make and experience music?" There are two "profound" experiences with music that are illustrative of the thinking about the engagement of performers or makers of music with concert goers or listeners to music. These experiences are described next.

Vignette One: "The Rehearsal"

The high school band was rehearsing a section of a well-known piece of literature. While the group was not very good by most standards, and instrumentation was incomplete, the ensemble rehearsed the music with great intensity and concentration. After sections were taken apart and "repaired" and the balance and blend were adjusted, the time had come for a run-through of the music. A simple melody with an equally simple harmony was performed in an expert way. The rise and fall of the line, the dynamics, the phrasing—everything was as good as the group could play. At the end of the section, there was silence. Instead of the usual putting down instruments, adjusting seats, and even leaning over to say something to a stand partner, there was silence. Complete silence. And then the students said, in a hushed, respectful voice, "Can we do that again?" They were intensely moved by their performance as they were performing it. Their intimate involvement producing the sounds that came together as a musical whole went beyond making music to a depth of shared experience. In that moment, the students could not step back and simply hear the music, but they were a part of making it. Where was their focus? Were they focused on maintaining the right length of notes, listening to other players, adjusting pitch, maintaining balance, or any of a dozen things performers do when engaged in music making?

Vignette Two: "The Concert"

On another occasion, an outstanding professional orchestra performed a standard and well-known symphony. The audience was different at the moment; somehow, there was a sense of engagement, of intense connection to the sounds of the work. As the symphony came to a close and the final chord sounded, not a person moved. Instead of gathering coats and "dashing to the exits," the entire audience sat motionless and silent, seeming to want to prolong the "magic" of the moment. The long silence was finally broken by the near-simultaneous response of thunderous applause that broke out in the hall. The audience members had listened only and were "spectators" to the performance—not makers of it. The focus could have been entirely on the music without any distraction except those created in the mind of the listener to things unrelated to the music. Two musical experiences, similar, noteworthy, and memorable by their profundity, were felt in a corporate way by the individuals in the moment yet differently by what each person was thinking at the moment. It would seem that musical listening requires exploration.

MUSICAL LISTENING

Many have written about musical listening and the musical experience. To list the authors and their definitions or descriptions of musical listening and the musical experience would require pages of references. Fortunately, the Center for the Study of Education and the Musical Experience published a work that examined listening and musical experience in *On the Nature of Musical Experience* (Reimer & Wright, 1992). Focusing on the role of the listener, the book presented several important ideas concerning listening. The first is "that listening is foundational to musical experience" (Reimer & Wright, 1992, p. 231) and "that listening is the essential mode of musical experience..." (p. 234).[1] In describing the role of the listener, Blacking (1979) declared "that listening to music, like comprehending verbal language, is as much a creative act as making it" (p. 11). There needs to be an active involvement of the listener in the experience. The various authors whose works were explored pointed to an active process where meaning is grasped following perception of music to a "receiving mind" (p. 237). The mind of the listener is engaged not only as a receiver of sounds but also as the processer of those sounds who, perceives relationships in tones, expressive shadings, and (ultimately) forms, processing them in terms of musical memory and imagination. Listening is a complicated mental process, requiring the ability to attend to music and recognize and discriminate its elements. The critic, the composer, the instrumentalist, or the vocalist all perform a highly expert act of selective attention.... (p. 237)

In describing the mind of the listener, Langer (1953) described an "inward hearing" as "a work of the mind that begins with conceptions of form and ends with their complete presentation in imagined sense experience" (p. 137). Noting that it is a talent that must be developed, Langer related inward hearing to performance. "The mind hears, the hand follows, as faithfully as the voice itself obeys the inward ear" (p. 145). There seems to be agreement that in musical listening, there is need for attention or focus, and there seems to be a "creative" aspect to this listening. I have suggested that the engagement by the listener is a function of the musical imagination, and that the musical imagination is "where the personal musical experience and meaning is formed" (Zerull, 2006, p. 42). Johnson (1987) asserted that "there can be no meaningful experience without imagination, either in its productive or reproductive functions" (p. 151). He further described the "reproductive" function of imagination as supplying "all of the connections by means of which we achieve coherent, unified, and meaningful experience and understanding" (p. 151). My previous research (Zerull, 1993) explored the specific role of imagination in the musical listening experience. From this research, a framework of musical imagination was developed suggesting sixteen functions that seem necessary for the musical listening experience. The musical listening functions suggest a progression from the "simple" to the more complex (although simple does not suggest easy). Simple functions involve hearing sounds as music or a component part of music and recognizing and organizing these sounds including detecting form, The next functions engage musical memory, taking what is heard and holding it in the imagination for as long as necessary. More complex functions have to do with the role of musical imagination as the listener begins to act in response to that which is held in musical memory. Finally, at the highest functioning of musical imagination, meaning is created. What is of importance here are the functions that require memory and those that have to do with musical imagination as the listener begins to act in response to that which is held in memory. Reimer (1989) provided a wonderfully detailed description of what goes on in musical imagination in the creation of the musical experience:

The creative response...includes, in addition to the perception of expressive musical events and the reaction to perceived expressiveness, a constant recall and anticipation of musical events. The experience is marked by an absorption in the way music sets up expectations, deviates from expected consequences of events, satisfies musical implications. The experiencer not only perceives the melody in relation to its harmony, for example, but anticipates changes in the movement of the melody and the harmonic changes which seem implied. He feels the section coming to a close, the beginning of another, noticing the unexpected treatment of the movement toward the cadence, the expressive diversions, the sudden fulfillment, the much-expected new melodic idea but with a surprising carryover of harmony from the previous section.... He is in a real sense, creating along with the music.... There is a sense of "oneness" with the music.... (p. 129)

In a similar way, Hanslick (1957) wrote:

The most important factor in the mental process which accompanies that act of listening to music, and which converts it into a source of pleasure, is frequently overlooked. We here refer to the intellectual satisfaction which the listener derives from continually following and anticipating the composer's intentions—now to see his expectations fulfilled, and now to find himself agreeably mistaken. It is a matter of source that this intellectual flux and reflux, this personal giving and receiving, takes place unconsciously and with the rapidity of lightning flashes. Only that music can yield truly aesthetic enjoyment which prompts and regards that act of thus closely following the composer's thoughts and which the perfect justice may be called a pondering of the imagination. (p. 98)

Hanslick further called the pondering of the imagination "contemplation," suggesting that the experience of "beauty" or the aesthetic requires an imaginative awareness and process where one experiences a piece of music through "the voluntary and pure act of contemplation which alone is the true and artistic method of listening" (p. 97). Hanslick noted that one who is contemplating music is "following the course of the music" (p. 90), and he pointed out that "musical compositions belong to the class of spontaneous products of nature, the contemplation of which charms us without obligating us to enter into the thoughts of a creative mind, conscious of what it creates" (p. 91). Epperson (1967) summarized this thinking and noted that it seems that "imagination is the instrument of contemplation" (p. 119).

The notion of responding and constructing is a recurring theme in the writing concerning musical experience. Hindemith (1969) described the function of the receiving mind in a "co-construction" of the listener and composer via the performer:

> While listening to the musical structure, as it unfolds before his ears, he is mentally constructing parallel to it and simultaneously with it a mirrored image. Registering the composition's components as they reach him he tries to match them with their corresponding parts of his mental construction. Or he merely surmises the composition's presumable course and compares it with the image of a musical structure which after a former experience he had stored away in his memory. In both cases the more closely the external musical impression approaches a perfect coincidence with his mental expectation of the composition, the greater will be his aesthetic satisfaction. (p. 20)

Throughout the descriptions of musical listening and the function of the music imagination in contemplation is an implied sense of "objectivity," or what has been referred to as "psychical distance." Reimer (1989) explained that "aesthetic experience is 'disinterested'—not lacking in interest but lacking in concern about pragmatic outcomes" (p. 103). A person must "be sufficiently removed from practical involvement with the experience to be able to lose himself in its own, immediate power" (p. 103). Reimer further described aesthetic experience, and thus musical experience, as more than "detached recognizing or identifying"—but one where the person is "absorbed by or immersed in the expressive qualities being attended to, calling forth a feelingful reaction...to the perceived qualities" (p. 103). The notion of "objectivity" or "disinterestedness" in the musical listening experience leads to consideration of the role of the performer. Can one be fully removed from practical involvement, or is that involvement a component of the musical experience of the performer?

THE LISTENER AS LISTENER AND PERFORMER AS LISTENER

If the musical listening experience requires the engagement by the imagination with the sounds being heard, and if that process of contemplation happens while the music is performed, a natural question emerges: is a performer able to listen the same way a listener listens? Unencumbered with the instrument, an audience member may have complete focus on the sounds organized to be expressive and can co-construct or create the musical experience based entirely on the music as it is sounding. Ample descriptions of this have been given, and the role of musical imagination in that experience has been suggested. But what about the performer who is engaged in making the music? He or she is attending to the technical details of playing the instrument and performing the part along with the others. He or she is monitoring the dynamics, the balance, the blend, and the intonation while also making hundreds of minute adjustments with each note or musical passage. It is reasonable to ask if the musical focus and engagement necessary in the musical listening experience is possible while one is engaged in the demanding act of musical performance. There may be room for the argument that rehearsing and performing in ensemble performance classes may result in special or unique musical experience. If that is the case, special musical experience enjoyed by students in performance ensemble class may constitute more than enough justification for the singular pursuit of performance with ensembles.

THE PERFORMING ROLE

Reimer (2003) described musical roles and intelligences, positing that musicality may not be a general intelligence that manifests itself in various ways, but instead, the way a person is engaged in music may be its own intelligence. The role of the composer, performer, improviser, and listener should be conceived as a singular type of musical intelligence, and these persons may be categorized as "musical" because each is, in some way, thinking in music. According to Reimer (2003), the performer is involved in two dimensions of musical intelligence. The first dimension of musical intelligence is discriminating sounds to be made and making the sounds in performing the composition. Specific to performers, Reimer described a second dimension where

> performance intelligence is connected with the physicality by which sounds must necessarily be produced....Performance requires the conscious and controlled setting in motion of the physical energies required to produce desired sounds and to shape those sounds artistically....The involvement of the intelligent body—the body as the medium in which discrimination and connections are actualized—is requisite for all musical performance. (p. 223)

Perhaps it is the physical energies that might be the basis for the heightened musical experience? Athletes, amateur runners, and others engaged in physical activity often claim a "high" from being engaged in the activity. It is not difficult to see that the combination of physical exertion and manipulation of the musical material or sounds under the conditions of a group effort may contribute to a special and singular type of musical experience. An experience of this type can translate to many places—the rehearsal, the concert hall, the adjudicated event, or even the marching field. Moore (2000) developed the notion of the "physical" in performance, suggesting a kinesthetic connection that is not just in response to music, such as dance, but also in performance of music. Although addressing performance in the elementary general music classroom, she noted that "playing a musical instrument requires a keen sense of timing, understanding of the relationship of timing to energy, and comprehension of the importance of space" (p. 85). Applied to musical listening, Moore asserted that "movement then becomes an important factor in the internalization of various styles through immersion in them by active listening, including movement, as a helpful component" (p. 87). Reimer (1994) stated that "musical instruments provide the most extensive and intensive opportunity available to human beings to know within the body, through the body's activation of the acting, feeling, and thinking processes required to form sounds musically" (p. 12). Furthermore, a performer of any age "is given the opportunity to think musically in the mode of performance—the mode of musical knowing as physical creativity" (p. 12).

What sets the performing ensemble class apart from other classes is not only the "content" of the discipline but also the nature of the involvement in a physical way with the materials of the discipline. Sound, as produced by the instrument or voice, is more than the means of "learning about music." Sound production in the pursuit of creating a musical work of art is a main goal and feature of the ensemble performance classes. The special nature of the class makes it indispensible in school curricula that purport to educate the whole child. Few opportunities exist in other disciplines to experience the materials in the way students experience music in band, orchestra, or chorus. Performance provides special experiences and offers the motivation for pursuing opportunities to "make music." Performance in bands, orchestras, and choruses is an exacting and intimate way to get near the sounds. It is certainly a way to "think in" music, but as wonderful as the involvement with the sounds might be, is it possible that the very nature of performance limits the complete musical education? Does the model of teacher as conductor need to change to accommodate expanded expectations to teach beyond the skills and limited knowledge necessary to achieve fine performances?

THE QUESTION OF WHAT TO TEACH

The question of what to teach has consumed as much energy and effort as the question of how to teach music. Countless curricula have been proposed, and books, materials, frameworks, objectives, and standards have been developed. There seems to be agreement that "something" needs to be taught in music education, but as with many of the issues in music education focused on the creation, performance, and experience of music, we suffer from having an abundance of options and content to teach. In an effort to clarify music education curricular content, Gates (2000) summarized what is important in music study, including tonal development, rhythmic development, interpretive/expressive development, and process in music learning. Specifically, Gates contended that students should "evaluate musical validity from compositions and performances by self and others . . . analyze, evaluate, and produce music . . . and study music's many social, cultural, ethnic contexts" (p. 73). Davey (1989) summarized educational activity in the arts, suggesting that works of great quality should be the object of study as they "stimulate the imagination and are worthy of speculation and contemplation" and "that knowledge of a work, its compositional elements, structure, conventions, and expressive devices is essential to the process of interpreting, assessing, and integrating that work into life experience" (p. 111). Further, Davey asserted that the "development of the ability to engage in the formal analysis of art is not the proper end of education in the arts," that it is "but a means of explaining models of human experience" (p. 111). He concluded the summary of educational activity by noting that "through imaginative activity, involving both the cognitive and emotive mode, we are able to indwell the minds, and share in varying measure the experience and knowledge of others" (p. 111). Reimer (2000) addressed the nature of music education in the performance ensemble class, noting that "when performers have been helped to gain insight into the structure, context, significance, and relative merits of the music they are studying/performing, in addition to the technical facility to perform adequately, both musical understanding and the quality of performance are enhanced" (p. 188). Gates, Davey, Reimer, and others have provided clues to what needs to be done in the ensemble class to "teach beyond the notes." It seems that in addition to studying high-quality music, students must analyze, contemplate, evaluate, learn context, discover the structure, compare performances, listen to great music, and integrate this newfound musical thinking into their own musical world. This is a "tall order" for a traditional music ensemble class designed to provide for the development of performance skills in pursuit of musical performance.

A MORE COMPLETE MUSIC EDUCATION AND EXPERIENCE

There seems to be two areas that mark a more complete or comprehensive approach to music education in the ensemble performance class. The first is the acquisition of knowledge and understanding that are considered the "content" of musical study. The second is a listening component that provides for the expansion of the universe of music that students may experience.

Comprehensive Approach to Music Education

A comprehensive approach should be predicated on the fact that each student is capable of producing sounds with his or her voice or instrument and that material in the class is principally the sound. Certainly the conveyance facts or the learning "about" music is a necessary component, but this is a secondary approach to music education. In the comprehensive approach, there is focus on, and use of, sounds in the production of music and in the study thereof. The class has the potential to become a laboratory, where students can "experiment" with sounds. Presentation of material, for example, how harmonies work, is best accomplished by having the students play or sing the sounds rather than telling students about a specific harmonic progression. Students experience the sounds whenever possible. The creative conductor/teacher recognizes the potential of powerful learning that can take place as the students hear about harmony works and then "experience" how harmonies work. The "rehearsal" of the ensemble in the performance class becomes a laboratory as a result of the careful planning by the conductor/teacher. The process begins with careful consideration of the material to be studied. It is a critical first step to determine what the students are expected to know and be able to do following the completion of the study of a piece of music. This musical study of a piece must take place in the context of a greater plan that lays out what will be accomplished in a year or over the entire time that a student would be in the ensemble class. The design of the scope and sequence is central to the successful teaching, and adherence to the plan in everyday lessons is the key to making student learning in the ensemble performance class more complete.

Purposeful Inclusion of Musical Listening

The listening component of an ensemble class is obviously part of the ensemble class routine. Listening for technical details, tone, balance, blend, intonation, and other things is naturally developed in the course of the rehearsal/class. But there is another type of listening where students broaden their perspective and can plumb the depths of musical experience. Following Cook (1990), I suggest it useful to consider at least two "types" of listening. The first type is the kind of listening that is of practical value in the performance of music or "pedagogical listening." The second type of musical listening is "listening for experience" or the act of listening for musical gratification (Zerull, 2006). Pedagogical listening is that with which we are most familiar in ensemble rehearsal classes. Pedagogical listening includes attention to aspects of performance, such as balance, blend, and intonation, to name a few. A developed listening ability of this type is highly prized by our students in their effort to perform music at artistic levels. Of no less value should be listening for experience that requires the conductor/teacher to take responsibility for expanding the musical imagination and musical ear of the student. How does one go about engaging students in musical listening for experience?

The conductor/teacher interested in musical listening for experience must consider what music to experience and then devise a strategy or plan to engage the musical imagination of the students. With respect to music selection, what should inform our teaching is our music listening habits. Just as we require the nourishment of food and water to exist as human beings, as musicians, we are sustained daily by music to which we return time and time again. In addition, musicians revel in new discoveries, with a curiosity and desire to experience more and varied music. If conductor/teachers want students to develop curiosity and a desire to experience more and varied music, the conductor/teacher must first take responsibility for introducing music to students. It is critical that the conductor/teacher help students discover the wealth of music to be experienced and provide opportunities for learning how to experience music more fully. Lessons must be structured that involve musical listening or listening for experience and that develop the perceptual, memory, and response "functions" of students' musical imagination. In the rehearsal class, the conductor/teacher should provide time to listen to music, analyze music to see how the elements work together in creating the musical artwork, and, most importantly, provide opportunity for contemplation, or the "pondering of the imagination" mentioned earlier (Hanslick, 1957, p. 98). Why is this important? It is important because no matter what we believe or hope for our students in the pursuit of music and musical experience, our students will probably not continue to play after high school. Thus, it is imperative that during their school years, students develop their musical imagination. We must expand their capacity to hear and hold music in memory, make the comparisons, build expectations, follow the flow of the music, and create their personal musical experience. Our students must be imbued with a craving for more music than can ever be played in the school band or orchestra or sung in a choir. If we are to fulfill our purpose of developing to the fullest extent possible every student's capacity to make and experience music, then musical listening must be an important part of the performance class.

WHAT TO RECONSIDER?

In reconsidering the performance ensemble class model and the teacher as conductor of the ensemble in music education, it seems that what is at issue are the role of the conductor/teacher as listening guide and the role of the student/performer as listener rather than exclusive maker of music. For the conductor/teacher, there is the imperative to teach for the performance and provide the opportunity for music experience in performance that will bring musical satisfaction to students. There needs to be an acknowledgment that we are preparing our students for a "musical life" rather than a "musical existence" after high school. This "musical life" requires students to have a musical imagination and musical ear to fully experience the bounty of music available to them so that they may take or make the opportunity to discover it for themselves. In a sense, the conductor/teacher interested in providing a more complete music education does not think simply about the "next" student performance in developing the musical learning and experience for the class. The conductor/teacher considers where the students will be after the "final" performance. In the end, we certainly hope that our students leave high school with fond memories of music-performing experiences, but hope is no substitute for the confidence we should have that our students leave us with a keen musical imagination and sensitive ear to make possible the full experience of music in their lives.

NOTE

1. The following citations in this paragraph are all drawn from Reimer and Wright (1992) unless otherwise noted.

REFERENCES

Blacking, J. (1979). The study of man as music maker. In J Blacking and J. Kealiinohomoku (Eds.), The performing arts. The Hague, The Netherlands: Mouton.

Cook, N. (1990). Music, imagination, and culture. New York, NY: Oxford University Press.

Davey, E. (1989). The cognitive in aesthetic activity. Journal of Aesthetic Education, 23(2), 107–112.

Epperson, G. (1967). The musical symbol. Ames, IA: Iowa State University Press.

Gates, J. T. (2000). Why study music. In C. K. Madsen (Ed.), Vision 2020 (pp. 57–82). Reston, VA: MENC—National Association for Music Education.

Hanslick, E. (1957). The beautiful in music (G. Cohen, Trans.). New York, NY: Liberal Arts Press.

Hindemith, P. (1969). A composer's world. Gloucester, MA: Harvard University Press.

Johnson, M. (1987). The body in the mind. Chicago, IL: University of Chicago Press

Keene, J. A. (1982). A history of music education in the United States. Hanover, NH: University Press of New England.

Langer, S. (1953). Feeling and form. New York, NY: Charles Scribner's Sons.

Moore, M. C. (2000). The kinesthetic connection in performing and understanding music. In B. Reimer (Ed.), *Performing with understanding* (pp. 77–90). Reston, VA: MENC—National Association for Music Education.

Reimer, B. (1989). *A philosophy of music education* (2nd ed.). Upper Saddle River, NJ: Prentice Hall.

Reimer, B. (1994). Is musical performance worth saving? *Arts Education Policy Review, 95*(3), 2–13.

Reimer, B. (2000). An agenda for teaching performing with understanding. In B. Reimer (Ed.), *Performing with understanding* (pp. 185–201). Reston, VA: MENC—National Association for Music Education.

Reimer, B. (2003). *A philosophy of music education* (3rd ed.). Upper Saddle River, NJ: Prentice Hall.

Reimer, B., & Wright, J. (Eds.). (1992). *On the nature of musical experience*. Niwot, CO: University Press of Colorado.

Webster's new universal unabridged dictionary (2nd ed.). (1983). New York, NY: Simon and Schuster.

Zerull, D. (1993). *The role of musical imagination in the musical listening experience* (Unpublished doctoral dissertation). Northwestern University, Evanston, IL.

Zerull, D. (2006). Developing musical listening in performance ensemble class. *Arts Education Policy Review, 107*(3), 41–46.

Reconceptualizing Music Teacher Education

Our learning outcomes are not tied
to the teachers we are preparing,
but tied to the students that lie just
beyond them.

Michelle Kaschub

Innovative visions for a new model
of conducting and performing are for
naught if we neglect the important
role that teacher education can play in
helping future teachers reimagine the
possibilities that are available to them.

Kate Fitzpatrick

How do we amend teacher preparation
curricula to accomplish the goals
of heightened critical thinking
and reflective practice? How do we
find curricular space for these in
an overpacked teacher preparation
curriculum?

John Richmond

15

PRESERVICE MUSIC TEACHER PREPARATION FOR THE CONDUCTOR-EDUCATOR ROLE

Margaret H. Berg

HOW MANY OF us have had the opportunity to either work with or observe a middle or high school ensemble conductor who is respected and admired, not just by his or her peers and the local community for having established a strong program but also, and perhaps most importantly, by countless students who have participated in the ensemble program? Given the success of the instrumental music program established over several years of dedicated service, this teacher often serves another role of mentor to former students, teacher colleagues, and teacher candidates. In my experience, this is a person who applies a depth and breadth of musical knowledge to prepared rehearsals, which includes having an aural concept of the repertoire. At the same time, students' instrument-specific and critical listening skills develop as this teacher engages students in musical thinking. Musical thinking and risk taking are fostered through the use of questions and dialog mixed with constructive comments and persuasive statements that are respectfully delivered, sometimes in a gentle or humorous manner. The resultant learning, coupled with a rapport established both between the ensemble teacher and students and among students, contributes to personal, affective experiences of the music during daily rehearsals, as well as student appreciation for sustained attention. Admirable ensemble conductors cultivate relationships with ensemble members, students who often have varying reasons for participating in the ensemble. Rehearsals might be characterized as focused, playful, and joy-filled. Over time, a community of learners is established whose members assume various roles yet have a common purpose (Abril, 2012; Adderley, Kennedy, & Berz, 2003; Lave & Wenger 1991; Morrison, 2001; Wenger, 1999).

Various aspects of this description of a respected and admirable secondary ensemble teacher and his or her program are encapsulated in Yinger's (1990) metaphor of teaching as a conversation of practice. Like conversation, teaching and learning are jointly constructed and mutually negotiated. In effective teaching, a three-way conversation takes place between teacher, student, and place.

> A good teacher must co-labor with students (and with parents and with other educators) in a particular place with its particular patterns, traditions, and forms. The place, like other practical worlds, is organized on a number of levels: community, school, classroom, curriculum, activity, problem, story, etc. Knowledge and skill must be artfully adapted to the particular participants and context. The teacher's intelligence and action, like the farmer's and the poet's, must be situated and responsive. Understanding, meaning, satisfaction, and enjoyment—healthy learning—result when this is accomplished. (p. 83)

Practice, not to be confused with a musician's specific use of the word, is construed as teacher engagement in preparation, improvisation, and reflection, which "when healthy is participatory, unifying, and resonant" (p. 92). The improvisatory nature of teaching (Yinger, 1987) is evident when teachers engage in thinking out loud while solving a problem with students, trying different solutions, and weighing the pros and cons of each solution. Benedict refers to this as reciprocal teaching (Allsup & Benedict, 2008), which is a form of reflection in action (Schön, 1984). At the same time, the teacher observes students as they solve problems individually or with peers, which might happen through ensemble member dialogue fostered by the teacher (Johnson, 2011) or structured chamber ensemble rehearsals (Berg, 2008). Yinger encouraged us to consider the interactive, communal, and conversational activities of teaching, which are inherent in a definition of teaching as showing and demonstrating. Yinger's model provides a visual metaphor of Allsup's (2003) definition of democratic learning that includes dialogue, shared decision making, and collaborative learning between teachers and students as well as between students and students.

While I am hopeful that many of us have been inspired by teachers like the respected and admired ensemble teacher described at the beginning of this chapter, I would hazard a guess that many of us have either worked with or observed secondary ensemble conductors who would not be characterized as exemplars of Yinger's teaching as a conversation of practice metaphor—teaching that promotes a healthy learning environment—for a variety of reasons. Several writers (Countryman, 2008; Mantie, 2012; Wis, this volume) discuss the challenges faced, either from one rehearsal to the next or over the course of a career, of maintaining a healthy learning environment, given external pressures or lack of modeling. Secondary instrumental ensemble directors and programs have recently been criticized, with questions being raised about the hegemony of teacher-directed, authoritarian approaches used by many secondary ensemble teachers (Allsup, 2003; Allsup & Benedict, 2008; Countryman, 2008). Bartel (2004) suggested that the enactment of this approach is evident in a rehearsal model of "a teacher/conductor in front of a group of music makers controlling the starts and stops, correctly diagnosing problems, and effectively prescribing remedies to reach the goal of a flawless performance" (p. xii). Based in part on historically rooted tensions between the entertainment and artistic functions of school bands, the conductor yields musical insight, often through exacting standards that are repertoire focused rather than individual student development or community building focused (Mantie, 2012). Participation in ensembles whose directors are characterized as authoritarian results in re-creative rather than creative experience for students (Countryman, 2008; Reimer, 1989) and fails to develop student thinking or prepare them for lifelong engagement in the arts (Beckman-Collier, 2009). In fact, the long-term viability of school ensemble programs has been called into question (Kratus, 2007; Williams, 2011), although the teaching approaches associated with these critiques are likely not based on a model of ensemble teacher as conductor-educator.

CHARACTERISTICS OF A CONDUCTOR-EDUCATOR

Recent publications on conducting (Boonshaft, 2002; Morrison & Demorest, 2012; Wis, 2007), as well as transformational leadership (Bass & Avolio, 1994), describe the qualities and activities of the secondary ensemble conductor I've described in the first paragraph of this chapter whom I characterize as a conductor-educator. The Merriam-Webster dictionary provides several synonyms for the word *educate*, based on the Latin derivative of the word, *educere*, as well as the related word *educe*. Taken together, to educate means to rear, to lead forth, to bring out something that is latent, and to lead. The conductor-educator engages in all of these activities, figuratively and literally stepping off and on to the podium to lead from within or behind the ensemble and to lead from the front of the ensemble. The conductor-educator assumes various roles, which, taken together, demonstrate a more nuanced and broader conception of secondary ensemble conductors than the more narrow characterization of conductor as authoritarian, a characterization emerging from a limited definition of *educate*.

A conductor-educator leads rather than manages the ensemble, based on his or her vision for the ensemble, informed by student input. The conductor-educator is focused on providing a *musical* experience for the students. Wis (2002) characterized this conductor as a servant leader who "demonstrates a passion for *every* aspect of the experience: the music, rehearsals, musicians, and audience" (p. 20). (For a more thorough description of servant leadership, see Wis, chapter 13.) Battisti (2002) lists twenty-two characteristics of effective teacher-leaders that can be aggregated into Wis's (2002, 2007) servant leader categories of responsiveness, collaboration, persuasion, trust, vision, and character.

First, the conductor-educator considers his or her responsibility for creating a positive learning environment, which sometimes requires him or her to "take a step back" to reflect on curricular or instructional modifications that are needed to continue to foster this environment. This might also include discussions with students about repertoire selection. While Allsup and Benedict (2008, p. 166) suggested "a truly active encounter, one in which there is concern and care between parties, often finds teacher and learner in a horizontal space. Away from podiums and seating charts—away from 'the crowd,'" a conductor-educator is able to form relationships with students in the midst of ensemble rehearsals, albeit through sometimes moving off the podium to teach or using alternate seating arrangements. In addition, Battisti (2002) advocated for a conductor-educator encouraging and fostering community (e.g., student, parent, local arts organizations, politicians) involvement with operational aspects of the music program.

The conductor-educator can also promote the development of community within the classroom through the use of focused discussion during ensemble rehearsals that promotes the development of musical awareness and critical thinking (Rao, 1993), as well as through the use of various structured peer-assisted learning activities embedded in the rehearsal context (Johnson, 2013). Conkling (2000) noted the shift in authority base in an ensemble when members are expected to contribute their knowledge to solving musical problems as the conductor moves from the role of expert to architect:

> Whether functioning as an expert or as an architect, the conductor/teacher is no less a representative of mature musical knowledge and practice. When the conductor/teacher functions as an architect, however, musical understanding is conceived of as rich and multi-dimensional. Whereas the expert will want learners to understand that a piece of the choral repertoire is performed in a particular way, the architect will want learners to understand

how that practice came to be. Similarly, the expert will want learners to understand that music-making can be emotionally powerful, but the architect will want learners to understand why this is so. (p. 11)

A conductor-educator functions as an architect whose learning goals for students include the development of a deep understanding of our discipline, as well as music's unique potential for affective experience.

Given the various activities in which a conductor-educator is engaged, it can be challenging, especially for beginning teachers, to "see the forest through the trees." A unique, thoughtful response to Reimer's (1989) candid question about the purpose of our work ("Just what is it about my work that really matters?") can guide preservice music teachers toward a career that is deeply fulfilling, despite the inevitable challenges they will face. Boonshaft's (2002) analogy of creating a pearl during each rehearsal reveals one conductor-educator's response to Reimer's question rooted in a commitment to providing musical experiences for students that contribute to future performance goals and sustained motivation:

I believe that in every rehearsal we need to make one beautiful pearl. It's just this one little thing and it's perfect. I believe that when we rehearse, we need to give our students this beacon. It may be one chord, one release, or one measure. It can be something tiny. But it has to be as perfect as we are capable of achieving. If we can make one chord so beautiful that we can stop and say, "Listen, did you hear that? Play it again and listen to that. It's magnificent. It's gorgeous, did you hear how beautiful, resonant, rich and in tune it was?" (p. 11)

Boonshaft also articulated long-term goals for his students beyond a musical performance of a piece:

Of all the responsibilities we have as music teachers, our ultimate goal ... [is to] help students express, understand, deal with, share and find joy in their emotions, all of their emotions. Quite frankly, missing an accidental or playing an incorrect articulation is meaningless in the life of a child. Learning to express themselves freely can invigorate the lives of our students. To me that is all that matters. It is the reason we teach. It is the reason we conduct. It is the reason we are musicians. (pp. 137–138)

Ultimately, a teacher who we might characterize as a conductor-educator enacts the various principles of servant leadership described earlier, which can lead to vital ensemble rehearsals and programs. Our work as instrumental and choral music teacher educators, despite our various undergraduate curriculum frameworks and particular topics addressed in our methods and conducting courses, should be to foster the development of future music educators who are conductor-educators.

INFLUENCES ON PRESERVICE TEACHERS' RESPONSE TO BECOMING CONDUCTOR-EDUCATORS

Despite the best intentions of music teacher educators and current music teachers who both promote and embrace the vision of ensemble director as conductor-educator, there are several factors that contribute, either positively or negatively, to preservice music teachers' response to the concept of secondary ensemble conductor as conductor-educator. The next section of this chapter includes an introduction to three sociologically based areas of research that I've found to be particularly influential on preservice teacher response to the model of conductor as conductor-educator: (1) primary, secondary, and tertiary socialization; (2) occupational role identity development; and (3) preservice music teacher beliefs.

Primary, Secondary, and Tertiary Socialization

Primary socialization is a process that occurs prior to students entering universities as music education majors (Woodford, 2002). Given that primary socialization is based predominantly on the values communicated via one's family of origin during childhood, it is often not questioned and can be emotionally charged (Berger & Luckman, 1966), thus functioning as one's habitus (Bourdieu, 1993) or ideas about appropriate actions, values, and one's function in society (DeMarrais & LeCompte, 1999). Secondary socialization occurs during the years in which a person is in school prior to college—generally from kindergarten through high school. Tertiary or occupational socialization (Froelich, 2006) usually occurs when students are earning an undergraduate music education degree and are thus acquiring occupational role knowledge (Berger & Luckman, 1966), although one might argue that occupational socialization begins for some students during their high school years as a result of teaching opportunities and mentoring provided by their public school or applied studio teacher(s). During all three phases of socialization, prospective music education students internalize the roles and attitudes of both generalized others (Mead, 1962; Shibutani, 1967) and significant others (Berger & Luckman, 1966) through observation

and limited teaching experience. For music education majors, significant others might include family members, peers, and current or former precollegiate
teachers. Influential teachers might be teachers from other disciplines outside
of music, as well as various music teachers, including applied teachers, school
ensemble conductors, extracurricular youth orchestra and/or honor ensemble
conductors, drum corp teachers, and summer camp/festival directors.

In comparison with other education majors, the impact of family and former
private and public school teachers is more powerful and therefore more strongly
influences a preservice teacher's definition of professional norms (Beynon, 1998;
Cox, 1997; Duling, 2000; L'Roy, 1983; Roberts, 2000). Preservice teachers have
been found to identify with the role of music teacher before they enter college
(Beynon, 1998; Cox, 1997; Duling, 2000; Gillespie & Hamann, 1999; L'Roy, 1983;
Prescesky, 1997; Roberts, 1991), and therefore enter music education courses with
developing conceptions about how to teach. While some research has found that
preservice teachers are often socialized by family and teachers toward the role of
performer (Cox, 1997; L'Roy, 1983; Roberts, 1991), other research has found these
significant others to be a positive influence on a student's decision to pursue a
music education career (Isbell, 2008). In fact, Isbell (2008) found school teachers to be pivotal in initiating and sustaining interest in a music teaching career.
Also, Isbell (2008) found high school performances, rather than various teaching
experiences, to be most influential on the decision to become a music teacher.

Undergraduate students often need to reconcile approaches and ideas offered
by university faculty, ensemble directors, and practicum/cooperating teachers
with prior models provided by former high school ensemble and private teachers. Some research suggests that primary and secondary socialization models
may be more influential than tertiary socialization models (Cox, 1997). While
some research has found music education faculty to be influential on the decision
to continue studying music education (Isbell, 2008), other research has found
music education coursework to hold less influence on in-service instrumental
music teachers' planning, implementation, and assessment in comparison with
colleagues, college ensemble directors, and college applied instructors (Bauer &
Berg, 2001). Furthermore, over the course of a four-year degree program, students' philosophical beliefs have been found to remain stable, suggesting that
many students enter our programs with beliefs about music education that are
not necessarily altered by the alternative perspectives provided by music teacher
educators (Austin & Reinhardt, 1999).

Research on primary and secondary socialization alerts us to the reality that music education majors arrive at our institutions "prepared" through
their years of schooling, which includes hundreds of hours of observations of

and interactions with teachers—some of which the student considers positive and others negative or less exemplary. This "apprenticeship of observation" can lead to preconceptions about teaching and the nature of teachers' work (Lortie, 1975) that students need to be made aware of and examine. Sometimes, probing questions from a music teacher educator about prior ensemble director approaches can result in challenging conversations as students articulate both the strengths and limitations of approaches used by ensemble director role models, as well as assumptions they've held about the value of ensemble programs. Allsup and Benedict (2008) suggested that challenging conversations with students are rooted in problems of legitimacy and social history:

> "My band consistently won highest rankings at the state competitions, so why should I change my thinking about my own band program and my wind band conductor?" This unwillingness (inability) to confront their subjected role and to recognize their role in this community and to consider alternatives, including imagining or accepting a conductor who engages in practices that may be construed as not in control/abnormal, serves to reproduce the hegemony of the wind band program as social institution. (p. 163)

I've found it helpful, both to myself and to my students, to complete a life history trajectory assignment as a means for reflecting on pivotal life experiences and people that have contributed to our growth as musicians and the decision to pursue a music education degree. Given the strong influence of our students' prior teachers, we must take the conductor models they've observed into consideration, especially if the prior teacher has not demonstrated many of the characteristics of a conductor-educator. Furthermore, given the impact of habitus (Bourdieu, 1993) or worldview, which is primarily formed during primary and secondary socialization, it is important for preservice students to examine their conceptions of the role of the music ensemble teacher, including his or her contribution to facilitating ensemble members' musical experience. Given the potential impact of prior performance experience on the decision to become a music teacher, we might ask our preservice teachers to reflect on their prior ensemble performance experiences as a starting point for discussion about the role of the conductor-educator. Finally, given the variety of tertiary socialization influences, the music teacher educator needs to consider whether there is a connection between what preservice students are learning and observing in various instructional settings including classes, ensemble rehearsals, and applied lessons, a point I will elaborate on later in this chapter. If there is a disconnect, we might encourage our students to examine possible underlying causes for this disconnect.

Occupational Role Identity Development

Broadly defined, identity is "the imaginative view or role that individuals project for themselves in particular social positions, occupations or situations" (Woodford, 2002). For some writers, identity is socially constructed, a position that suggests that knowledge of self, others, and appropriate behaviors is based on previous experiences (Dolloff, 1999; Roberts, 1991). Wenger (2006) posited that an individual's identity is constructed through active participation in a community of practice, which also results in the continuous creation of a shared identity as a result of contributing to the practice of the community. (For a substantial review of various theoretical orientations to the construct of identity, see MacDonald, Hargreaves, and Miell [2002].)

Some writings on identity have used symbolic interactionism to explore socialization and occupational identity development among preservice music teachers (Isbell, 2008; L'Roy, 1983; Paul, 1998; Roberts, 2000). Symbolic interactionism theory is based on the premise that meaning arises out of the interactions between an individual and others through the use of such symbols or tools like language. To interpret the actions of others, the individual imagines how generalized and significant others perceive him or her (Berger & Luckman, 1966; Blumer, 1969; Mead, 1962). (For a more thorough description of this theory, please see Paul and Ballantyne [2002].) Research using this theoretical framework and Carper's (1970) work on occupational role identification has examined the relationship between self perception and inferred perception of the self from others vis-à-vis occupational role labels, reference group identification (Becker & Carper, 1970), and use of reference group gestures (Clark, 1972 Mead, 1962).

One of the first studies of preservice teacher occupational role identity development found that undergraduate students at one university had a relatively weak "teacher" or "band/choir director" role identity as compared to their "musician" or "performer" role (L'Roy, 1983). Roberts's (1991) ethnographic study of professional identity construction explored the impact of the university setting on undergraduate music education majors' identification as performers or musicians rather than music teachers. Woodford (2002) suggested that the emphasis on performance at universities and the social status afforded students based on their perceived level of musicianship may contribute to preservice teachers' developing professional identities being more closely aligned with their identity as musicians or performers rather than music educators.

Based on a large sample of students from a random sample of American institutions, Isbell (2008) found undergraduate occupational identity separated into three constructs: musician, self-perceived teacher, and teacher identity inferred from others. This finding suggests that the self and other facets of teacher identity appear to be more separate than they are with the musician identity, and it has implications for students' openness to receiving feedback on their teaching. Isbell also found that experiences associated with secondary socialization, rather than people, were a significant predictor of occupational identity.

Although beyond the realm of occupational role identity research, other writers (Conkling, 2004; Dolloff, 2007) have called for a more broadly defined conception of identity. Based on Clandinin and Connelly's (2004) concept of "personal practical knowledge," Conkling suggested identity is not fixed, but a narrative construction that changes and is reshaped based on the setting. Both Conkling and Dolloff spoke to the multiple identities held by teachers, and Dolloff speculates on the construct of occupational identity establishing a polemic view of identity:

> In this identity debate, it seems that we are concerned with "am I this?" or "am I that?". Placing identities in an either-or dyad assumes the role that we fulfill as a music educator can be narrowly and indisputably defined. In fact, we must bring all that we are to our role as music educators. (p. 3)

According to Dolloff, our work as music teacher educators should focus on helping our students "harmonize" the various subidentities they hold that contribute to their professional identities. Although beyond the realm of preservice music teacher education, some recent research (Bernard, 2005; Pellegrino, 2010) indicates that practicing music teachers who engage in music-making activities, both within and outside the classroom, view music making and music teaching as essential aspects of being a teacher, thus forming and informing their teaching and student learning. Participation in music making and teaching may be viewed as a complex duality whereby participation in both activities contributes to identity construction based on multimembership in various communities, thus promoting the development of an integrated identity (Wenger, 1999).

The findings from occupational identity research suggest that the role of musician or performer is one our preservice teachers seem to gravitate toward. Also, more recent research on preservice and in-service music teacher identity development frames music teacher identity as both multifaceted and changing. I'd like to suggest that encouraging our preservice teachers to both observe and "try on" the role of conductor-educator may be a way to bridge the potential conflict they may experience between their identities as teacher and performer. Recent research suggests that undergraduate music education majors enrolled in their first conducting course consider conducting to be synonymous with both teaching and performing (Johnson, 2009). This finding indicates conducting may be a viable means for preservice teachers to integrate teacher and performer identities.

Our students, though, would need to have some experience beyond learning the craft of conducting in order for them to realize the performancelike aspects of being a conductor. We might encourage students in both our methods and conducting courses to consider the performancelike aspects of Bernstein's (1965) description of preparation for a musical experience vis-à-vis conducting:

> The qualities that distinguish *great* conductors lie far beyond and above technique. We now begin to deal with the intangibles, the deep magical aspect of conducting. It is the mystery of relationships—conductor and orchestra bound together by the tiny but powerful split second. How can I describe to you the magic of the moment of beginning a piece of music? (p. 270)

In addition, we might bring discussion about role identity and identity development into our methods courses, perhaps asking students to define the role of conductor as a means for expanding their concept of the varied activities and goals of a conductor-educator. Since preservice teachers' identities are shaped by experience, it is important that they get an opportunity to observe and experience some of the unique aspects and activities of being a conductor-educator. This may require us to use available technology to set up observations of or interviews with teachers who live outside our region yet are models of conductor-educatorship.

Developing student awareness of occupational role labels—which often have associated meanings, values, and assumptions—can lead to expanded definitions of the ensemble teacher and his or her role, as well as the pivotal function musical experience holds for teacher and student. Also, it might be helpful to our current and former students to speak with public school teachers who have integrated music teaching and music making into their professional lives, thus helping students to recognize the possibility of merging subidentities that contribute to their professional music teacher identity (Pellegrino, 2010, 2012, in press). Finally, while some preservice teachers may engage in dualistic thinking (Perry, 1981), music teacher educators might challenge students to expand their focus, which is rooted in teacher identity conception, to include both teacher and student perspectives (Berg & Miksza, 2010; Fuller & Bown, 1975; Miksza & Berg, 2013). This broadening of focus, captured in Yinger's (1990) conversation of practice metaphor, also characterized as proximal positioning (Gholson, 1998), might enable secondary ensemble students' voices—both literally and figuratively—to become a part of the preservice teacher's conception of occupational role (Countryman, 2008; O'Toole, 1994).

Preservice Music Teacher Beliefs, Images, and Metaphors

In addition to the impact of socialization and occupational role identity, our preservice teachers also hold particular beliefs about teachers and teaching that inform their willingness, or not, to assume a role as conductor-educator once they earn a full-time public school teaching position. Wright (1991) suggested that beliefs and knowledge inform the social process of identity modification or transformation. Belief, if well reasoned, can serve as an organizing framework for curricular decisions and student interactions (Haefner, 1992).

The seemingly benign interview question "Where do you see yourself in five years?" might lead a student to reveal his or her beliefs about the roles of teachers and students, talent, motivation, and classroom management. Research provides evidence that the beliefs of preservice teachers strongly influence what they learn, how they learn, and their level of engagement in our music teacher education courses (Richardson, 1996). Thompson (2007) recommended several activities that require substantial reflection to encourage preservice music teacher shifts in beliefs about music teaching. Asking our students to construct visual images or metaphors, based on past student experiences or more recent preservice teaching experiences, is one way to make preservice teacher beliefs about teachers and teaching tangible (Dolloff, 1999). Dolloff found that conflicting beliefs and identities emerged with respect to students' visual representations of "the teacher you are" and "the teacher you would like to be."

It might be interesting to ask our students to construct visual images, metaphors, or cases of former and idealized ensemble directors as a means for exploring their beliefs about ensemble teaching. Such discussion could lead to further exploration of images or metaphors of a conductor-educator, which might then be compared and contrasted with previously created ensemble director images and metaphors. Furthermore, our students might benefit from tracking the development of teacher images and metaphors over the course of their teacher education program.

CURRICULAR INITIATIVES IN SUPPORT OF CONDUCTOR-EDUCATOR DEVELOPMENT

While the preceding discussion includes several suggestions for ways we might foster the development of conductor-educatorship in our instrumental and choral music education students, I'd like to end this chapter with a list of activities—some requiring curricular revision and others requiring modification to our existing courses—that might foster a conductor-educator approach to secondary school ensemble teaching.

- *Integrate methods courses, conducting courses, and/or field experiences*: Although this can create scheduling challenges, the integration of methods and conducting courses, either through a coteaching arrangement, guest lecture arrangement, or on-campus guest ensemble clinic, can help to foster a connection for our students between teaching and conducting. Some have been able to closely integrate a methods course and field experience, which can provide students with another example of a professional significant other (Robinson, 2001). This arrangement, as well as the inclusion of an on-campus guest ensemble clinic, can benefit all students as they are able to engage in structured conductor-educator activities under the guidance of teachers who ideally model this ensemble teaching model, a model that takes into account teacher and ensemble member experiences that impact identity construction.
- *Make planning and reflection transparent*: While our preservice students' and practicum teachers' schedules often do not allow for substantive postrehearsal debriefing, our students could learn more about effective conducting and rehearsals from such sessions. It might be helpful for students to schedule in advance several debriefing sessions over the course of a practicum experience where they speak with the observed teacher about their rehearsal plan and decisions made during the course of the rehearsal. While the level of performance will be substantially higher at the university, our students could also benefit from this same kind of discussion with college ensemble directors following a rehearsal in which they participated as a performer. Finally, we might make our methods course planning and decision making transparent to our students. It might be interesting to share examples with our students of how we utilize both our teacher and musician identities in our course planning, such that "the musician identity is part and parcel of our teacher identity, and infuses who we are and what we do, so the reverse is true" (Dolloff, 2007, p. 11).

- *Foster preservice teacher membership into the conductor-educator community of practice*: Defined as a social unit organized around a common purpose, a community of practice consists of members who regularly interact, share a common vocabulary, and learn from each other as they engage in an activity (Smith, 2005; Wenger, 1999). Members of the community exist along an experience-based continuum from novice apprentice to master. Apprentice knowledge and skill develop through a process of acculturation during social interactions with peers and more knowledgeable community members (Rogoff, 1990; Tharp & Gallimore, 1988), first in the form of "legitimate peripheral participation" through observation and limited activity (Lave & Wenger, 1991; Rogoff, 1995). Over time, apprentices assume increased responsibilities and varied roles in the community. Learning is configured through the process of becoming a full participant in a sociocultural practice. Preservice students can engage in various activities that will gradually introduce them to the conductor-educator community of practice, including peer-conducting activities (Bartleet & Hultgren, 2008); joint lesson planning with peers, graduate students, and/or practicum teachers (Feiman-Nemser & Beasley, 1997); and collaborative teaching experiences with graduate students who function as "near-peers" to undergraduate students (Berg, 2010). Students might also be introduced to varied ensemble rehearsal contexts that provide models of conductor-educatorship, including shorter-term collaborative learning activities (Conkling, 2000) or more extended peer-learning opportunities (Johnson, 2010, 2013). This introduction can occur through observation of these varied instructional contexts, as well as guest precollegiate school ensemble presentations during methods courses.

- *Develop a place-based perspective*: Learning the practice of teaching involves learning about place: "It involves learning in detail about other participants in practice, their lives, their histories, and their relations to one another" (Yinger, 1990, p. 90). Inherent in this learning is asking questions about whom, when, and where (Stauffer, 2012). Encouraging preservice teachers to ask these questions can foster the development of a place-based view of teaching, which includes taking into account various participants—from the local community, to school personnel (e.g., administrators, teacher colleagues, support staff), to parents/guardians, to ensemble members (including the students and the teacher)—and features of the teaching context (including local traditions, student backgrounds, and physical space characteristics). In addition to class discussions, various ethnographic activities such as classroom mapping, taking field notes, and teacher interviews can be incorporated into field-based observation assignments (Frank, Green, & Dixon, 1999; Miranda, Robbins, & Stauffer, 2007). Also, a placed-based view of teaching considers ensemble achievement and the development of independent musicianship (Morrison & Demorest, 2012). As a result, preservice teachers can learn to use rehearsal strategies where the teacher models individual practice (Prichard, 2012) and small ensemble rehearsal (Berg, 2008) activities during large ensemble rehearsals. In addition, since one goal of adopting a place-based view is learning how to take an insider or emic perspective, the activities mentioned earlier, along with other activities completed during student teaching, might help preservice teachers learn how to develop empathy for and rapport with students—a natural extension of holding a placed-based view of teaching and learning. These activities might include shadowing an ensemble student for a day (E. D. Long, personal interview, April 27, 2013), interviewing selected ensemble members, and attending school events in which one or more ensemble members participate.

- *Question assumptions while offering possibilities*: Embedded in preservice teachers' professional goals are assumptions about program quality (e.g., high contest ratings are the result of excellent teaching and are indicative of student learning) and legitimate repertoire (Allsup & Benedict, 2008). Using a dialectical, "this with that" approach to discussions (Jorgensen, 2003), students might be encouraged to view band, orchestra, or choir as a living tradition (2003) and therefore be encouraged to broaden their goals to also encompass student learning on various levels. On the day-to-day level, this might include soliciting anonymous student feedback (Zander & Zander, 2002) and/or student journal writing (O'Toole, 2003). Preservice teachers might also read about or observe ensemble conductor-educators using a comprehensive rehearsal approach that fosters students' personal responses to the music (Sindberg, 2012) and engages students in some decision-making opportunities like guided repertoire selection and/or contributing to the ensemble's musical interpretation through focused listening activities and/or whole-ensemble discussions (Brown, 2008; Johnson, 2011; Rao, 1993). On a program level, this questioning of assumptions might lead to the selection of a wider variety of repertoire, offering a greater variety of learning experiences in the ensemble context and in the total school music program and providing student leadership opportunities (Johnson, 2010).

- *Sustaining the conductor-educator vision during the teacher induction period*: The first three years of teaching can be challenging for our students in terms of applying what they have learned as a university student and integrating this learning into the specific cultural context in which they are teaching. How many of us have been saddened to learn that former students who seemed open to fostering conductor-educatorship in their ensemble teaching had reverted back to "teaching as they were taught" due to real or perceived performance pressures, as well as holding divergent perspectives from members of the school district's ensemble director community of practice? Some former students strive to approach their teaching as conductor-educators but, after several years of limited support from administrators, parents, and colleagues, leave public school teaching to pursue an alternate career in music that is more favorable to the conductor-educator model (Russell, 2008). It is possible for music teacher educators to support former students by providing district in-service or state conference workshops that encourage beginning teachers to form either school-based or virtual communities of practice (Berg & Smith, 1996). A process for sharing teaching videos might be modeled during the student teaching semester (Berg, 1997), thus providing novice teachers with a structure for continued dialogue with peer teachers or fostering the development of a new community of peers (Berg, 2012; Stanley, 2011) who are committed to creating a classroom environment and ensemble program that supports their development as conductor-educators.

POSTSCRIPT

Certainly, a teacher who functions as a conductor-educator utilizes teaching strategies that are more conversational and improvisatory in nature than prescriptive. The discussion that followed the set of papers on music performance at the Center for the Study of Education and the Musical Experience (CSEME) Twenty-Fifth Anniversary Celebration pointed to participants' research and teaching experiences where giving students the opportunity to be involved in making decisions in the context of the ensemble setting is crucial, although for many teachers this may require a philosophical and identity shift from authority to collaborator. We must recognize that this collaborative approach may stand in opposition to the professional conductor model, which may create a tension for teachers. However, models of more collaborative professional ensembles (e.g.,

Seifter and Eonomy's [2002] case study of the Orpheus Chamber Ensemble) have emerged and hold promise for a conductor-educator model being accessible at the precollegiate, collegiate, and professional levels.

Given that "the complexity of the interactions between teachers and students engaged in music performance instruction precludes simple answers" (Duke, 2000, p. 2), more complex models of the instrumental ensemble rehearsal space, which includes teacher, student, and place (as defined by Yinger, 1990), are needed. Tan's (2012) transcultural philosophy of instrumental music education, which uses pragmatic and ancient Chinese philosophies to "provide a cultural and artistic framework whereby students and teachers better themselves, society, and civilization" (p. vi), is one recent contribution. According to Tan, instead of engaging in "either-or" thinking (e.g., conductor as authority vs. "conductorless" programs), a model of interaction is needed to rebalance conceptions of what secondary instrumental music programs are and might be in the future.

At the same time, we must not take for granted that the large ensemble, particularly marching band, is a mainstay across our country, given the local interests of the community and significant resources needed to support large ensemble programs. Varied curricular offerings provide an opportunity for the industrious teacher to model conductor-educatorship in small and large ensembles whose repertoire may range from classical, to jazz, to world musics, to pop.

In her book *Transforming Music Education* (2003), Estelle Jorgensen suggested:

> Transforming music education enables music makers of all sorts to cross over between or collaborate with music makers from other traditions, just as it also promotes the transformation of those traditions themselves; it removes barriers and creates bridges of understanding between and among musics and those who make and take music, so that people can travel more easily between them. (p. 136)

Secondary ensemble conductor adherence to the conductor-educator model has the potential to transform school ensemble rehearsal tradition and, therefore, the ensemble experiences for all students who choose to participate in school ensemble programs. At the same time, if music teacher educators "begin with the end in mind" (Covey, 2013, p. 102), the end encompassing long-term goals for our collegiate students *and* their students, we can envision the wide-ranging impact of the conductor-educator model. We can look toward a future where we observe school ensemble rehearsals and performances, led by our former students, who are model conductor-educators. As a result of this enriching and inspiring experience, more students and secondary ensemble conductors will be truly engaged with music for a lifetime.

ACKNOWLEDGMENTS

This chapter is dedicated to E. Daniel Long, an orchestra conductor-educator who exemplifies "being a leader with students and among students, but not of them."

REFERENCES

Abril, C. (2012). Perspectives on the school band from hardcore American band kids. In P. S. Campbell & T. Wiggins (Eds.), *The Oxford handbook of children's musical cultures* (pp. 434–448). New York, NY: Oxford University Press.

Adderley, C., Kennedy, M., & Berz, W. (2003). "A home away from home": The world of the high school music classroom. *Journal of Research in Music Education, 51*(3), 190–205.

Allsup, R. E. (2003). Mutual learning and democratic action in instrumental music education. *Journal of Research in Music Education, 51*(1), 24–37.

Allsup, R. E., & Benedict, C. (2008). The problems of band: An inquiry into the future of instrumental music education. *Philosophy of Music Education Review, 16*(2), 156–173.

Austin, J. R., & Reinhardt, D. (1999). Philosophy and advocacy: An examination of preservice music teachers' beliefs. *Journal of Research in Music Education, 47*(1), 18–30.

Bartel, L. (1994). What is the music education paradigm? In L. Bartel (Ed.), *Questioning the music education paradigm: Research to practice* (Vol. 2) (pp. xii–xvi). Toronto: Canadian Music Educators Association.

Bartleet, B., & Hultgren, R. (2008). Sharing the podium: Exploring the process of peer learning in professional conducting. *British Journal of Music Education, 25*(2), 193–206.

Bass, B. M., & Avolio, B. J. (Eds.). (1994). *Improving organizational effectiveness through transformational leadership*. Thousand Oaks, CA: Sage Publications.

Battisti, F. L. (2002). *The winds of change: The evolution of the contemporary American wind band/ ensemble and its conductor*. Galesville, MD: Meredith Music.

Bauer, W. I., & Berg, M. H. (2001). Influences on instrumental music teaching. *Bulletin of the Council for Research in Music Education, 150*, 53–66.

Becker, H. S., & Carper, J. (1970). The elements of identification with an occupation. In H. S. Becker (Ed.), *Sociological work: Method and substance* (pp. 177–188). Chicago, IL: Aldine Publications.

Beckman-Collier, A. (2009). Music in a flat world: Thomas L. Friedman's ideas and your program. *Music Educators Journal, 96*(1), 27–31.

Berg, M. H. (1997). Student teacher video cooperatives. *Journal of Music Teacher Education, 7*(1), 16–22.

Berg, M. H. (2008). Promoting minds-on chamber music rehearsals. *Music Educators Journal, 95*(2), 48–55.

Berg, M. H. (2010). "Sampling from the mentoring buffet": A case study of mentoring in a middle school wind ensemble outreach program. Paper presented at the annual meeting of the American Educational Research Association, Denver, CO.

Berg, M. H. (2012). *Creating a music teacher professional learning community.* Clinic Presentation, Colorado Music Educators Association Conference, Colorado Springs, CO.

Berg, M. H., & Miksza, P. (2010). An investigation of preservice music teacher development and concerns. *Journal of Music Teacher Education, 20*(1), 39–55.

Berg, M. H., & Smith, J. (1996). Using videotapes to improve teaching. *Music Educators Journal, 82*(4), 31–37.

Berger, P. L., & Luckman, T. (1966). *The social construction of reality.* New York, NY: Anchor Books.

Bernard, R. (2005). Making music, making selves: A call for reframing music teacher education. *Action, Criticism & Theory for Music Education, 4*(2), 2–36.

Bernstein, L. (1989). Bernstein: The art of conducting. In C. Bamberger (Ed.), *The conductor's art* (pp. 270-274). New York, NY: Columbia University Press.

Beynon, C. (1998). From music student to music teacher: Negotiating an identity. In P. Woodford (Ed.), *Critical thinking in music: Theory and practice* (pp. 83–105). London, Canada: University of Western Ontario.

Blumer, H. (1969). *Symbolic interactionism: Perspective and method.* Englewood Cliffs, NJ: Prentice Hall.

Boonshaft, P. L. (2002). *Teaching music with passion: Conducting, rehearsing and inspiring.* Galesville, MD: Meredith Music.

Bourdieu, P. (1993). *The logic of practice.* Stanford, CA: Stanford University Press.

Brown, J. K. (2008). Student-centered instruction: Involving students in their own education. *Music Educators Journal, 94*(5), 30–35.

Carper, J. (1970). The elements of identification with an occupation. In H. S. Becker (Ed.), *Sociological work* (pp. 189–201). Chicago, IL: Aldine.

Clandinin, D. J., & Connelly, F. M. (2004). *Narrative inquiry: Experience and story in qualitative research.* San Francisco, CA: Jossey-Bass.

Clark. R. (1972). *Reference group theory and delinquency.* New York, NY: Behavioral Publications.

Conkling, S. W. (2000). Collaboration in the choral ensemble. *Choral Journal, 41*(2), 9–15.

Conkling, S. W. (2004). Music teacher practice and identity in professional development partnerships. *Action, Criticism & Theory for Music Education, 3*(3), 2–15.

Countryman, J, (2008). *Missing voices in music education: Music students and music teachers explore the nature of the high school music experience* (Doctoral dissertation, University of Toronto). Retrieved from ProQuest Dissertations and Theses. (Publication Number NR39801)

Covey, S. (2013). *The seven habits of highly effective people: Powerful lessons in personal change.* New York, NY: Simon & Schuster.

Cox, P. (1997). The professional socialization of music teachers as musicians and educators. In R. Rideout (Ed.), *On the sociology of music education* (pp. 112–120). Norman, OK: University of Oklahoma.

DeMarrais, K. B., & LeCompte, M. D. (1999). *The way schools work: A sociological analysis of education* (3rd ed.). New York, NY: Longman.

Dolloff, L. A. (1999). Imagining ourselves as teachers: The development of teacher identity in music teacher education. *Music Education Research, 1*(2), 191–207.

Dolloff, L. A. (2007). "All the things we are": Balancing our multiple identities in music teaching. *Action, Criticism & Theory for Music Education, 6*(2), 2–21.

Duke, R. (2000). Measures of instructional effectiveness in music research. *Bulletin of the Council for Research in Music Education, 143*, 1–49.

Duling, E. (2000). Student teachers' descriptions and perceptions of their mentors. *Update: Applications of Research in Music Education*, 19(1), 17–21.

Feiman-Nemser, S., & Beasley, K. (1997). Mentoring as assisted performance: A case of co-planning. In V. Richardson (Ed.), *Constructivist teacher education: Building new understandings* (pp. 108–126). Bristol, PA: Falmer Press.

Frank, C., Green, J. L., & Dixon, C. N. (1999). *Ethnographic eyes: A teacher's guide to classroom observation*. New York, NY: Heinemann.

Froelich, H. (2006). *Sociology for music teachers: Perspectives for practice*. Upper Saddle River, NJ: Prentice Hall.

Fuller, F., & Bown, O. (1975). Becoming a teacher. In K. Ryan (Ed.), *Teacher education, Part II: The 74th yearbook of the National Society for the Study of Education* (pp. 25–52). Chicago, IL: University of Chicago Press.

Gholson, S. A. (1998). Proximal positioning: A strategy of practice in violin pedagogy. *Journal of Research in Music Education*, 46(4), 535–545.

Gillespie, R., & Hamann, D. (1999). Career choice among string music education students in American colleges and universities. *Journal of Research in Music Education*, 47(3), 266–278.

Haefner, M. (1992). *Believe in yourself: A case study of exemplary music teaching* (Unpublished master's thesis). University of Cincinnati, Cincinnati, OH.

Isbell, D. (2008). Musicians and teachers: The socialization and occupational identity of preservice music teachers. *Journal of Research in Music Education*, 56(2), 162–178.

Johnson, E. (2009). *"Conducting is everywhere!": A case study of preservice music teacher occupational identity status in a first-semester conducting course*. Unpublished manuscript.

Johnson, E. (2010). *Peer teaching: Strategies for enhancing student ability, knowledge, and learning*. Presentation at the CMEA Clinic Conference, Colorado Springs, CO.

Johnson, E. (2011). Developing listening skills through peer interaction. *Music Educators Journal*, 98(2), 49–54.

Johnson, E. (2013). *The effect of symmetrical and asymmetrical peer-assisted structures on music achievement and learner engagement in the secondary large ensemble* (Doctoral dissertation, University of Colorado).

Jorgensen, E. R. (2003). *Transforming music education*. Bloomington, IN: Indiana University Press.

Kratus, J. (2007). Music education at the tipping point. *Music Educators Journal*, 94(2), 42–48.

Lave, J., & Wenger, E. (1991). *Situated learning: Legitimate peripheral participation*. Cambridge, UK: Cambridge University Press.

Lortie, D. (1975). *Schoolteacher: A sociological study*. Chicago, IL: University of Chicago Press.

L'Roy, D. (1983). *The development of occupational identity in undergraduate music education majors* (Unpublished doctoral dissertation). North Texas State University, Denton, TX.

MacDonald, R. A., Hargreaves, D. J., & Miell, D. (2002). *Musical identities*. New York, NY: Oxford University Press.

Mantie, R. (2012). Band and/as music education: Antinomies and the struggle for legitimacy. *Philosophy of Music Education Review*, 20(1), 63–81.

Mead, G. H. (1962). *Mind, self and society*. Chicago, IL: University of Chicago Press.

Miksza, P., & Berg, M. H. (2013). A longitudinal study of preservice music teacher development: Application and advancement of the Fuller and Bown teacher-concerns model. *Journal of Research in Music Education*, 61(1), 44–62.

Miranda, M., Robbins, J., & Stauffer, S. (2007). Seeing and hearing music teaching and learning: Transforming classroom observations through ethnography and portraiture. *Research Studies in Music Education, 28*, 3–21.

Morrison, S. (2001). The school ensemble: A culture of our own. *Music Educators Journal, 88*(2), 24–28.

Morrison, S.J. & S.M. Demorest (2012). Once from the top: Reframing the role of the conductor in ensemble teaching. In G. E. McPherson & G. F. Welch (Eds.), *The Oxford handbook of music education* (Vol. 1, pp. 826–843). New York, NY: Oxford University Press.

O'Toole, P. A. (1994). Redirecting the choral classroom: A feminist post-structural analysis of power relations in three choral classrooms (Doctoral dissertation, University of Wisconsin-Madison).

O'Toole, P. A. (2003). *Shaping sound musicians: An innovative approach to teaching comprehensive musicianship through performance.* Chicago, IL: GIA.

Paul, S. J. (1998). The effects of peer teaching experiences on the professional teacher role development of undergraduate instrumental music education majors. *Bulletin of the Council for Research in Music Education, 137*, 73–92.

Paul, S. J., & Ballantyne, J. H. (2002). The sociology of education and connections to music education research. In R. Colwell (Ed.), *The new handbook of research on music teaching and learning* (pp. 566–583). New York, NY: Schirmer Books.

Pellegrino, K. (2010). *The meanings and values of music-making in the lives of string teachers: Exploring the intersections of music-making and teaching* (Doctoral dissertation). Retrieved from Proquest Dissertations & Theses. (Publication No. AAT3429263)

Pellegrino, K. (2012). Becoming a music teacher: Preservice music teachers describe the meanings of music-making, teaching, and a tour experience. Paper presented at the annual meeting of the American Educational Research Association, Vancouver, Canada.

Pellegrino, K. (in press, 2014). Examining the intersections of music-making and teaching for four string teachers. *Journal of Research in Music Education.*

Perry, W. G. (1981). Cognitive and ethical growth: The making of meaning. In A. W. Chickering (Ed.). *The modern American college: Responding to the new realities of diverse students and a changing society* (pp. 76–116). San Francisco, CA: Jossey-Bass.

Prescesky, R. E. (1997). *A study of preservice music education students: Their struggle to establish a professional identity (Unpublished doctoral dissertation).* McGill University, Montreal, Canada.

Prichard, S. (2012). Practice makes perfect? Effective practice instruction in large ensembles. *Music Educators Journal, 99*(2), 57–62.

Rao, D. (1993). *We will sing!: Choral music experience for classroom choirs.* New York, NY: Boosey & Hawkes.

Reimer, B. (1989). *A philosophy of music education* (2nd ed.). Upper Saddle River, NJ: Prentice Hall.

Richardson, V. (1996). The role of attitudes and beliefs in learning to teach. In J. P. Sikula (Ed.), *Handbook of research on teacher education* (2nd ed., pp. 102–119). New York, NY: Macmillan.

Roberts, B. A. (1991). Music teacher education as identity construction. *International Journal of Music Education, 18*, 30–39.

Roberts, B. A. (2000). Gatekeepers and the reproduction of institutional realities: The case of music education in Canadian universities. *Musical Performance, 2*(3), 63–80.

Robinson, M. (2001). From visitors to partners: The evolution of a methods course. *Journal of Music Teacher Education, 11*(1), 21–26.

Rogoff, B. (1990). *Apprenticeship in thinking: Cognitive development in social context*. New York, NY: Oxford University Press.

Rogoff, B. (1995). Observing sociocultural activity on three planes: Participatory appropriation, guided participation, and apprenticeships. In J. Wertsch, P. Del Rio, & A. Alvarez (Eds.), *Sociocultural studies of the mind* (pp. 139–164). Cambridge, UK: Cambridge University Press.

Russell, J. A. (2008). A discriminant analysis of the factors associated with the career plans of string music educators. *Journal of Research in Music Education, 56*(3), 204–219.

Schön, D. (1984). *The reflective practitioner: How professionals think in action*. New York, NY: Basic Books.

Seifter, H., & Economy, P. (2002). *Leadership ensemble: Lessons in collaborative management from the world-famous conductorless orchestra*. New York, NY: Times Books.

Shibutani, T. (1967). Reference groups as perspectives. In J. G. Manis & B. N. Meltzer (Eds.), *Symbolic interaction: A reader in social psychology* (pp. 562–569). Boston, MA: Allyn & Bacon.

Sindberg, L. K. (2012). *Just good teaching: Comprehensive musicianship through performance (CMP) in theory and practice*. New York, NY: Rowman & Littlefield.

Smith, M. K. (2005). Communities of practice. *The encyclopedia of information education*. Retrieved from http://www.infed.org/biblio/communities_of_practice.htm

Stanley, A. M. (2011). Professional development within collaborative teacher study groups: Pitfalls and promises. *Arts Education Policy Review, 112*(2), 71–78.

Stauffer, S. L. (2012). Place, music education, and the practice and pedagogy of philosophy. In W. D. Bowman & A. L. Frega (Eds.), *The Oxford handbook of philosophy in music education* (pp. 434–452). New York, NY: Oxford University Press.

Tan, L. Y. C. (2012). Towards a transcultural philosophy of instrumental music education (Doctoral dissertation, Indiana University). Retrieved from Proquest Dissertations & Theses. (Publication No. AAT 3550904)

Tharp, R., & Gallimore, R. (1988). *Rousing minds to life: Teaching, learning, and schooling in social context*. New York, NY: Cambridge University Press.

Thompson, L. K. (2007). Considering beliefs in learning to teach music. *Music Educators Journal, 93*(3), 30–35.

Wenger, E. (1999). *Communities of practice: Learning, meaning, and identity*. Cambridge, MA: Cambridge University Press.

Wenger, E. (2006). *Communities of practice: A brief introduction*. Retrieved from http://www.ewenger.com/theory/

Williams, D. (2011). The elephant in the room. *Music Educators Journal, 98*(10), 51–57.

Wis, R. M. (2002). The conductor as servant-leader. *Music Educators Journal, 89*(2), 12–23.

Wis, R. M. (2007). *Conductor as leader: Principles of leadership applied to life on the podium*. Chicago, IL: GIA.

Woodford, P. G. (2002). The social construction of music teacher identity in undergraduate music education majors. In R. Colwell (Ed.), *The new handbook of research on music teaching and learning* (pp. 675–696). New York, NY: Schirmer Books.

Wright, J. E. (1991). *Belief systems and their influence on music experience* (Unpublished doctoral dissertation). Northwestern University, Evanston, IL.

Yinger, R. J. (1987). *By the seat of your pants: An inquiry into improvisation and teaching*. Paper presented at the annual meeting of the American Educational Research Association, Washington, D.C.

Yinger, R. J. (1990). The conversation of practice. In R. T. Clift, W. R. Houston, & M. C. Pugach (Eds.), *Encouraging reflective practice in education: An analysis of issues and programs* (pp. 73–94.) New York, NY: Teachers College Press.

Zander, R. S., & Zander, B. (2002). *The art of possibility: Transforming professional and personal life*. New York, NY: Penguin Books.

16

MUSIC EDUCATION

Relevant and Meaningful

David A. Williams

THE MUSIC EDUCATION profession in the United States has a fairly long and storied tradition. The model of the large ensemble performance established here, over one hundred years ago, has been the envy of music educators from other counties. This large ensemble model has, in fact, become synonymous with music education in schools, so much so that it is difficult for most music educators, as well as preservice music teachers, to consider anything other than the status quo. This model has served the profession well. However, as we move through the second decade of this century, concerns with school music enrollments that surfaced in the late twentieth century continue. At best, overall enrollment in the nation's secondary school music programs can presently be described as troublesome, and there is evidence the percentage of students electing to take music classes is dropping.[1]

As a result, many within the music education profession spend a considerable amount of time and effort trying to convince others of the importance of music through advocacy efforts. In the introduction to her chapter on advocacy in *The New Handbook of Research on Music Teaching and Learning*, Bresler (2002) suggested, "...the contemporary arena of school music often resembles a battleground, concerned with survival" (p. 1066). I worry we are now so busy advocating for what we do that we no longer pay enough attention to what it is we are doing. I would argue that the model of music education, that of the large performance ensemble based on Western European traditions, is now failing and will continue to fail as long as the profession remains blindly devoted to it.

Certainly there are schools where the traditional model is still strong and needs to continue, but just as certainly, there are schools in which it no longer makes sense to continue traditional instrumental and choral programs—and I would propose that there are actually more examples of the latter than the former. In fact, any school music program could benefit from including new and imaginative types of musical experiences for students, experiences many students not presently interested in school music programs would find both relevant and meaningful.

For the profession to make any real progress in the areas of enrollment and the development of lifelong musicianship skills for students, I propose we need to rethink both the nature of the music courses offered in schools and the makeup of our teacher preparation programs. I suggest the following matters be considered as we contemplate curricula and design new coursework for preservice teachers, so they might be better prepared to move the profession forward.

(1) **Student autonomy.** The large ensemble model places complete control in the hands of the teacher, a concept borrowed from professional orchestras where the conductor is in command and the main goal is excellent performance. In schools, where the main goal should be student learning, this model seems outdated in light of the wealth of research concerning constructionist learning theory and inquiry-based learning (Gardner, 1991; Papert, 1993). Such control over the classroom is important in the large ensemble model, though not necessarily conducive to the best student learning. While many school music programs involve solo and small ensemble experiences, which can allow individual students some level of control, these tend to be short-term extensions to the real business of the full ensemble. Green (1988) suggested that allowing students more autonomy over the learning environment can have positive effects on learning for life. New models of music education should allow control over the educational environment to be extensively shared inside the classroom by allowing students to experience self-directed learning, peer-directed learning, and small group learning as predominant aspects of the curriculum.

(2) **Musical/creative decisions.** In addition to control of the learning environment, the teacher in the large ensemble model is most likely making practically all the musical and creative decisions. In this educational design, students are most often reduced to technicians, simply carrying out the creative wishes of their music director. Again, educational research challenges this model (Campbell, 1998; Davies, 1994; Davis, 2005; Green, 2004, 2008; Marsh, 1995; Webster, 1992). While control of creative decision making is important for the large ensemble director, new models of music education would benefit from allowing students to learn from their own creative decisions. Additionally, students would benefit in

models where creative decision making plays a much more important role in the process of learning, where composing, arranging, and improvising are at least as important as performing and listening.

(3) **Formal concerts.** Following the professional model, school ensembles focus on public performance. The educational goal becomes performing an outstanding concert or obtaining an exceptional rating at a contest. In this model, the group result takes precedence over individual needs, and the evaluation of individuals is usually reduced to whether or not students can perform their part. The assumption that musical learning takes place through large group concert preparation is not documented. When the measure of success remains at the group level, there is no assurance that individuals within the group are developing musicality. New models of music education need to focus on individual students' musical learning where formal, public performance is significantly reduced, if not eliminated.

(4) **Class size.** Large performing ensembles are an important goal of the present model, and increasing class size is often a badge of honor for music teachers. Educational psychology suggests large class sizes are not educationally sound. Twenty students in a high school math class is almost always better than fifty. An eighty-member ensemble might look good from an advocacy standpoint, but not from an educational perspective. It is essential that new models of music education allow for reasonable class sizes where a music class of twenty should be considered preferable to a class of fifty. The issue we face is creating demand for a sizable total enrollment in music courses, but this enrollment doesn't have to be in one class.

(5) **Instruments.** School instrumental ensembles have employed the same instruments for over one hundred years. The string and wind instruments used in school ensembles were once popular in our society. Beginning in the 1970s, the use of these instruments began to decrease in general, and especially in youth culture, to the point where they have practically disappeared today. More students gain personal satisfaction and meaning from performing instruments that appeal and intrigue them, and new models of music education must make use of newer technologies and instruments that are of interest to students and are part of the culture in which they live. Larsen (1997) suggested that, in addition to a core of acoustic sound, we are now faced with "the musical reality of produced sound." She suggested, "We do not need to replace the basic standards but we must rethink the approach to music. We must rethink its core, and we must expand it to include the core of produced sound."

(6) **Musical styles.** Most music performed by school ensembles has become so esoteric that perhaps the only way to categorize it is "school music." Little of this

music has relevance to the lives of students outside of school. New models of music education must include a variety of musical styles and genres and should embrace popular styles, including cultural/ethnic considerations of interest to students. Many of these musical styles come with authentic learning and performance practices that are not well suited to our traditional large ensembles. Some schools might find an Afro-Cuban music course of great interest to students, while others could have success with classes based on Latin or Asian musics. Students at many schools could benefit from courses dealing with different popular music styles found in the United States such as rock, pop, country, or rap.

(7) **Traditional notation.** Large ensembles are bound to traditional music notation out of necessity, as rote learning in large groups is typically tedious and can slow learning to a crawl. Students involved with other musical styles and instruments function very well without the need for learning standard notational systems, and these musical involvements often lead to advanced aural skill development. In traditional music education, understanding notation skills is usually considered synonymous with music literacy. Literacy in music, however, has a much different connotation in the greater majority of musical genres throughout the world, and even in traditional forms of American musics including jazz and rock and roll. New models of music education could benefit from involving styles that emphasize aural development over written competence.

(8) **Lifelong skills.** In addition to some older research (Bergan, 1957; Casey, 1964; Hartley, 1996; Kruth, 1964; Martignetti, 1965; Rawlins, 1979; Solly, 1986), there is convincing empirical evidence that a very large percentage of students that begin participation in secondary school ensembles cease their musical involvements while still in school or soon after leaving high school. Aside from fond memories, there is little indication that traditional music education has much of an impact on musical life after high school for most students. Considerable thought should be given to the enhancement of lifelong musical skills when developing new models of music education. Most of the ways students experience music in our traditional classrooms are no longer significant parts of twenty-first-century musical life in the United States, especially within youth cultures. Students can't be expected to develop lifelong musical skills within a model of music education that is designed to prepare only a select few for a specific type of professional music making while ignoring the musical needs of the greater majority. Helping students find relevance between music study in school and their musical life outside of school will go a long way in the development of independent musicianship and lifelong learning.

(9) **Experience level.** Once a student has missed the entry point for participation in traditional ensembles, it is often difficult to break into the system

as a beginner. Few high school programs (especially instrumental) have serious options for students with no previous performance skills. New models of music education must not only allow but also encourage students to start music instruction at any grade level and place them into small group settings where students of varying abilities and experience can learn with, and from, each other.

(10) **Musical experience.** In traditional performance programs, it normally takes several years of practice and study to achieve a functional level on an instrument. Even with two full years of ensemble experience in a band or string class, students are not likely to have achieved a level of musicianship sufficient to sustain musical activity if they stop their in-school participation. Ideally, new models of music education need to help students reach a functional level of musicality within one year or less, allowing students who cannot, or choose not to, participate in school music classes for longer periods the opportunity to independently enhance their musicality.

I suggest that, used together, these ten experiences could be transformational for the music education profession, providing students who are not interested in traditional school music offerings opportunities they would find meaningful and relevant. These same opportunities would also be more likely to help students develop lifelong musicianship skills, even in cases where students could only participate for one school year or less. I want to be very clear, however, that these suggestions regarding a different model of music education are intended for new types of music classes and ensembles. I would think most of these ideas, if not all, would fail in traditional ensemble settings, and I would argue that our efforts will be more fruitful in considering new curricula instead of trying to redesign conventional classes and ensembles.

With consideration of these ten experiences, and to better prepare preservice music teachers, I suggest that three types of new courses be added to the undergraduate curriculum. First, to help them begin thinking deeply about music outside the Western canon, students should encounter a course devoted to the history and literature of blues and rock. While the majority of undergraduates already know of this music, most lack any real appreciation of the history, styles, and structure of popular musics, nor have they given much thought to how they might use these musics in classroom settings. This course would help students better understand musical styles, many with long, rich histories, which could play a valuable role in redefining K-12 music education programs.

Second would be a methods course, which would provide students a practical grounding in music education settings outside the traditional general, band, choir, and string programs. Such a course would focus on broadening musicianship and performance skills, enabling preservice music educators to develop competence in the areas of informal learning, creative thinking, systematic aural transmission, music technology, and popular musics. It would involve students with instruments typically not included in traditional music education programs, including electric guitar, bass, keyboard, drum kits, and digital instruments, and with popular musical styles including rock, pop, and rap. These methods courses must allow students to explore informal learning principles involving self-directed learning, peer-directed learning, and small group learning. Preferably, such a course would include a practicum component where students could see, and participate in, K-12 programs where nontraditional music offerings already exist. Additionally, there must be time for class discussion and consideration of the various issues involved in such a dramatic change to school music curricula.

Third would be a new ensemble course, in addition to the traditional large ensemble experiences. In this course, preservice teachers would divide into small ensembles and would apply concepts acquired in the new methods course. They would have extended opportunities to practice autonomous musicianship development and learning through aural-based practice. Contrasted to traditional ensembles, performance venues would differ significantly for these small groups. Performances in class for other students would occur often, but these might seldom include full rehearsed pieces. Rather, a performance might be just a few notes or beats learned by copying a recording of a favorite song. Performance might also occur through a YouTube video or with an impromptu concert in an area where students normally congregate.

Together, these new courses and ensemble experiences would allow preservice teachers to understand and participate in the way most popular musicians acquire their performing and musicianship skills. This is a methodology based on shared responsibilities among student-centered groups and acknowledgment for respect and value of students' preexisting interests, abilities, and preferences. Ideally, after taking the blues and rock history course, preservice teachers would be required to register for one or two terms of the new methods course and several semesters of the new ensemble so they would have sufficient time to develop skills and confidence in areas in which they most likely have little prior experience. Illustrative course descriptions for both the methods course and the ensemble are provided at the end of this chapter.

There are several issues standing in the way of including such changes in undergraduate teacher preparation programs, not the least of which is the traditional curriculum taken by most music education majors. Such curricula are normally stuffed full of coursework to the point where a music education degree generally has significantly more credit hours than other music degree programs. Simply adding additional coursework is problematic. While considering the redesign of music teacher education, I suggest that the aggregated components of the present music core need to be reduced to make room for new methods and ensembles. I would argue that developing musicianship in preservice teachers can be achieved in multiple ways and is not totally dependent on the traditional core. In fact, an overhaul of the typical core sequence for music education majors might be the most beneficial approach. This could include redesigned sections of music theory, history, and literature core classes specifically for music education majors and designed for the particular needs of K-12 music teachers. The idea that a single section of a core music course could meet the needs of students with diverse professional goals (performance, composition, education, etc.) seems flawed.[2] The same, no doubt, is true of ensemble experiences where music education students could benefit from involvement in ensembles with goals aligned more for individual musical development than group performance accomplishment.

It seems unlikely, from a practical perspective, that such an overhaul would be possible at most schools. Instead, achieving real change in K-12 music programs might necessitate decreasing current aspects of music education curricula. Targets for reduction could include the number of traditional music theory and Western European music history courses. Is it absolutely necessary for a music education student to complete a typical four-semester music theory sequence, or several semesters of Western European music history classes? I would argue that some number of these could be replaced by new music education courses as described earlier, including alternate methods and popular music history courses. Additionally, the prescribed number of semesters in traditional ensembles and in private might also be reduced and replaced with nontraditional ensembles like those described earlier. In all such cases, I would think growth of musical understanding and personal musicianship development could be enhanced. Additionally, students would find these changes in curriculum more meaningful and practically related to their future teaching experiences.

There are, no doubt, several variations on this theme of curriculum revision that could work at different institutions. I am convinced that the addition of new types of music education courses, combined with either a revamped music core or a reduction in the number of traditional core requirements, is necessary. We cannot allow the fear of change to keep us from examining the possibilities. Proposing such changes will take high levels of courage, determination, and resolve as there would certainly be widespread resistance from faculty in other areas of music. We have an obligation, however, to prepare today's preservice music teachers for the realities they will face in classrooms of the future. The issues of low K-12 music enrollments and the development of lifelong musical skills in students are of vital importance to the music education profession. Producing improvements in these areas will require significant change, both for teacher education programs and within the K-12 schools. Change is hard, but in this case it is a worthy struggle.

COURSE DESCRIPTIONS

Progressive Music Education Methods I

MUE 3xxx

Three Credit Hours

This course will provide students a grounding in methods for music education settings outside the traditional general, band, choir, and string programs. The course is intended to challenge students to engage in two modes of music learning that differ from notation-based instruction. These two modes are systematic aural transmission and informal learning, which together form the way most popular musicians acquire their performing and musicianship skills. This methodology is based on partnerships of students, shared responsibilities among student-centered groups, and acknowledgment by the classroom teacher for respect and value of students' preexisting interests, abilities, and preferences. In particular, student preference and knowledge become the primary starting points from which students expand outward into different musical styles, genres, and cultures. Topics may vary from semester to semester as new possibilities of music methods materialize. Potential topics include concepts of informal learning principles in music, development of creativity in music, theoretical principles of popular musics, computer and digital music technology, sound engineering and recording, multiple-arts approaches, and sound amplification. The course will include a combination of lecture, discussion, modeling, and hands-on activities such as singing, playing instruments, and moving. Students should wear clothing that is comfortable and allows freedom of movement. Additionally, some class sessions will include visiting artists and musicians. This is a paperless class. All course materials will be posted on Canvas.

Creative Performance Chamber Ensemble

MUE 3xxx

One Credit Hour (repeatable for credit)

This course will provide students opportunities to apply concepts of informal learning, gained through various coursework, in a nontraditional, student-directed, music education performance setting. The course is repeatable for a total of four credits. The course is intended to challenge students to engage in two modes of music learning that differ from notation-based instruction. These two modes are systematic aural transmission and informal learning, which together form the way most popular musicians acquire their performing and musicianship skills. This methodology is based on partnerships of students, shared responsibilities among student-centered groups, and acknowledgment by the classroom teacher for respect and value of students' preexisting interests, abilities, and preferences. In particular, student preference and knowledge become the primary starting points from which students expand outward into different musical styles, genres, and cultures. Students will be placed in ensembles of between four and seven students. Each ensemble will rehearse together a minimum of three hours per week outside of class meetings. Additionally, all ensembles will meet together, twice each week, in a seminar setting. All literature will be arranged and/or composed by members of the ensemble and both vocal and instrumental performance must be included. Additionally, ensembles are strongly encouraged to include aspects of various media, lighting, staging, dance, acting, and so forth and to work with students from art, dance, and/or theater. Each ensemble is to perform at least two public performances per semester. No ensemble should contain the exact same personnel for more than one semester.

NOTES

1. According to Florida Department of Education data, 16.45 percent of high school students were enrolled in music classes in 1985. This number dropped to 14.9 percent by 1995 and 11.67 percent by 2005. While this is just for the state of Florida, there is little to suggest such trends are not similar in other parts of the country.

2. For a compelling argument related to multiple music intelligences, see chapter seven of Reimer's *A Philosophy of Music Education* (2003).

REFERENCES

Bergan, H. A. (1957). *A study of drop-outs in instrumental music in five selected schools in Michigan* (Unpublished doctoral dissertation).Michigan State University, East Lansing, MI.

Bresler, L. (2002). Research: A foundation for arts education advocacy. In R. Colwell & C. Richardson (Eds.), *The new handbook of research on music teaching and learning* (pp. 1066–1083). New York, NY: Oxford University Press.

Campbell, P. S. (1998). *Songs in their heads: Music and its meaning in children's lives.* New York, NY: Oxford University Press.

Casey, G. J. (1964). *A study of instrumental music drop-outs of Moline (Illinois) schools* (Unpublished doctoral dissertation). Colorado State College, Fort Collins, CO.

Davies, C. D. (1994). The listening teacher: An approach to the collection and study of invented songs of children aged 5 to 7. In H. Lees (Ed.), *Musical connections: Tradition and change. Proceedings of the 21st world conference of the International Society of Music Education* (pp. 120–128). Tampa, FL: ISME.

Davis, S. G. (2005). That thing you do! Compositional processes of a rock band. *International Journal of Education and the Arts, 6*, 1–19.

Gardner, H. (1991). *The unschooled mind: How children think and how schools should teach.* New York, NY: Basic Books.

Green, L. (1988). *Music on deaf ears: Musical meaning, ideology, and education.* New York, NY: St. Martins Press.

Green, L. (2004). What can teachers learn from popular musicians? In C. Rodriguez (Ed.), *Bridging the gap: Popular music and education* (pp. 225–241). Reston, VA: Music Educators National Conference, National Association for Music Education.

Green, L. (2008). *Music, informal learning and the school: A new classroom pedagogy.* Burlington, VT: Ashgate Publishing.

Hartley, L. A. (1996). Influence of starting grade and school organization on enrollment and retention in beginning instrumental music. *Journal of Research in Music Education, 44*, 304–318.

Kruth, E. C. (1964). *Student drop-out in instrumental music in the secondary schools of Oakland, California* (Unpublished doctoral dissertation).Stanford University, Stanford, CA.

Larsen, L. (1997). *The role of the musician in the 21st century: Rethinking the core.* Plenary address to the National Association of Schools of Music National Convention. Retrieved from http://libbylarsen.com/index.php?contentID=226

Marsh, K. (1995). Children's singing games: Composition in the playground? *Research Studies in Music Education, 4*, 2–11.

Martignetti, A. J. (1965). Causes of elementary instrumental music drop-outs. *Journal of Research in Music Education, 13*, 177–183.

Papert, S. (1993).*The children's machine: Rethinking school in the age of the computer.* New York, NY: Basic Books.

Rawlins, L. D. (1979). *A study of the reasons for students dropping out of the instrumental music program of the Lincoln, Nebraska public schools* (Unpublished doctoral dissertation).University of Nebraska, Lincoln, NE.

Reimer, B. (2003). A philosophy of music education: Advancing the vision. Upper Saddle River, NJ: Prentice Hall.

Solly, B. (1986). *A study of attrition from the instrumental music program in moving between grade levels in Cherry Hill, New Jersey* (Unpublished doctoral dissertation). Temple University, Philadelphia, PA.

Webster, P. (1992). Research on creative thinking in music: The assessment literature. In R. Colwell (Ed.), *Handbook on research on music teaching and learning* (pp. 266–280). New York, NY: Schirmer Books.

17

"NO ACTUAL TEACHING"

Expanding Preservice Music Teachers' Imaginaries of Teaching

Teryl L. Dobbs

COURSE AND TEACHING evaluations are part and parcel of academic life, the underlying premise being that the feedback and comments will provide substantive, thoughtful, and usable information for improvement of pedagogy and course design, among other areas.[1] The narrative discourses in teaching evaluations take fascinating twists and turns, however, when students writing those same evaluations are preservice music educators, individuals who are learning to teach, and the subject of their responses is a seasoned educator who has weathered over twenty-five years in multiple music teaching venues. I am one of those seasoned music educators, and reading those course evaluations has consistently been an emotional challenge for me and to some extent I hope it remains so. Receiving and interrogating the texts inscribed on these evaluations is, for me, an experience that is multilayered and often humbling. In the case of my undergraduate preservice music educators who are taking their first steps as teachers and have yet to step into a classroom, their weighing in and critique of my teaching and pedagogy is illuminating and is also sometimes puzzling and frustrating. Regardless, I take students' comments seriously and enact adaptations in my courses in response, given that such tweaking enhances what the course is intended to do and meshes philosophically, theoretically, and pedagogically with what I desire to accomplish. Aside from my efforts at rationality, receiving an e-mail message stating, "Your course evaluations are available for your perusal" still causes me to break out in a cold sweat and have heart palpitations; butterflies flit in formation within the pit of my stomach. It is in this moment that I work to rein in my ego to empathize more fully with my undergraduate preservice students who, throughout the year, live in a world of double-consciousness, being simultaneously students and teachers in process.

During one particular semester, I again dug deep, trekked to the office where my course evaluations lived, and sat down to read them, notepad at the ready. Inscribed under the question "How does this professor's teaching compare to that which you have received in other coursework?" was the response, "No actual teaching…but mostly useful." What was *that* about? I searched the form for further elaboration and came up *bubkes*.[2] I was completely flummoxed and turned the comment incessantly over and over in my mind. My questions abounded: What did this student mean by inscribing, "No actual teaching" on a course evaluation form? What did this individual believe teaching to be? What were this student's beliefs and imaginaries about music teaching and becoming a music educator? What did this individual believe about the pedagogical model I had been enacting and embodying for the past semester? What was the message I was intended to receive? Clearly I bumped up against *something*, my sense of which were firmly established and closely cherished notions of what an instrumental music educator *was, does,* and *should be*. What I embodied, enacted, and presented pedagogically over the course of the semester apparently was not considered, believed, imagined, or, more problematically, valued as being *real* music teaching by at least one of my students.

This chapter, therefore, is a result of my musings and ruminations on the inscription "No actual teaching": an attempt on my part to sort out and interrogate the systems of belief that preservice music educators carry with them, particularly as they negotiate new ideas and ways of thinking that they encounter in praxial coursework. In doing so, I examine who our preservice teachers and their future students are, explore undergraduate preservice teachers' imaginaries and beliefs about teaching, and narrow my focus to those discourses and beliefs that swirl around instrumental music teaching, to which many of my own undergraduate students appear to cling tightly. Additionally, I discuss the students' spaces of resistance when confronted with the expectations, knowledge, and dispositions that socially and culturally contextualize musical actions and meanings. As we envision how music education will move forward in the twenty-first century, how it will be structured, what it will include (or not), and those who will be the field's teachers, scholars, and learners, accomplishing this vision ultimately depends on us—music teacher educators.

Like many of my colleagues in music teacher education, what I hoped to accomplish with this particular student cohort over the course of our time together was what I wish for all my preservice music educators: a partnership much like a *pas de deux,* one in which the students and I would collaborate in the reimagining of ourselves as instrumental music educators whose pedagogical practices were increasingly polymusical, holistic, culturally relevant/responsive, and socioculturally situated. I envisioned (and continue to envision) instrumental music educators who would cultivate dispositions and habits of mind necessary for building successful musical relationships in a twenty-first-century music teaching and learning space, such as openness, positive mutual regard (Rogers, 1969), an honoring of multiple diversities, and the ability to value and create feelingful human connections. What I have come to realize, however, is that the choreography for my dance partners was much more complex than I anticipated; where I zigged, the students zagged.

BACK TO THE FUTURE: TEACHER BODIES, STUDENT BODIES, AND WHY WE SHOULD CARE

Who are our preservice music educators? Who will be their students? Imaginaries and teacher beliefs are wrapped up within the corporeality of the body, and as a scholar and music teacher educator engaged in work at an increasingly selective school of music,[3] it is becoming quite clear to me just who is the more valued and valuable student body in competitive schools of music in the United States. As Julia Eklund Koza (2008) argued in her article, "Listening for Whiteness: Hearing Racial Politics in Undergraduate School Music":

> Stringent and restrictive notions of what constitutes musical competence, together with narrow definitions of legitimate musical knowledge, shut out potential teachers from already underrepresented culture groups and are tying the hands of teacher educators at a time when greater diversity, both perspectival and corporeal, is needed in the music teaching pool. (pp. 145–146)

From my own participation at undergraduate vocal auditions, I see that prospective students demonstrate ever-increasing performing abilities of music derived from the Amer-Eurocentric canon. Anecdotal conversations with students who have successfully auditioned for and have been accepted into selective schools of music reflect multiple examples of privileging, such as having had opportunities to study privately; having parents with enough disposable income and time to fund and travel to lessons; having abundant opportunities to participate in competitions, festivals, and recitals; and, not the least, having the financial wherewithal to afford professional-level musical instruments that sometimes requires the arranging of various types of loans, such as a second mortgage or line of equity taken against the family home.

While we faculty members purport to be listening for the *best* musicians in these auditions, which can be conceived fundamentally as gate-keeping exercises, we are also listening to a hidden agenda that is racialized, classed, and funded with social and cultural capital (Bourdieu, 1993). These future undergraduates, which include future music educators, performers, theorists, composers, and musicologists, embody and enact what sociologist Annette Lareau (2003) described as *concerted cultivation*: the end result of a set of middle-class childrearing practices whereby children's talents are cultivated in a calculated fashion through "organized activities, established and controlled by mothers and fathers" (p. 2). Our school of music undergraduates are more often than not the beneficiaries of an upbringing that advantages them in multiple ways. Winning an audition into a prestigious school of music not only signals that an individual is socially constructed as having certain culturally valued musical talents and abilities, but also that that individual has the advantages of certain funds of social and cultural capital: being fortunate to have parents who have the time, money, and additional means to cultivate a young musician's interests and capabilities. From this privileged pool of successful auditionees comes many of music education's future preservice music educators.

So just who comprises the body of educators in the United States and by extension, future music educators, including the elite group of preservice teachers with whom we work in highly selective schools of music? According to statistics compiled by the National Education Association in its report, *Status of the American Public School Teacher, 2005–2006* (2010), public school teachers identified themselves according to the following demographics:

- 87.3 percent were white;
- 5.5 percent were Black/African-American;
- 4.2 percent were of Spanish/Hispanic/Latino/a origin;
- .7 percent were each Native American/Alaska Native (First Nations) and Asian;
- .4 percent were either Native Hawaiian or other Pacific Islander;
- 70 percent were female;
- Minority teachers were less likely to be male than were white teachers;
- 50 percent of all public school teachers had a father having some college;
- 46.2 percent of all public school teachers had a mother who attended college.[4]

In contrast, the *Digest of Education Statistics 2008* issued in March 2009 (Snyder, Dillon, & Hoffman, 2009) presents data that by fall 2006, the student body enrolled in United States' public elementary and secondary schools identified themselves through an entirely different set of demographics from that of their teachers (p. 74):

- 57.5 percent were white;
- 17.1 percent were African American;
- 20.5 percent were of Hispanic origin;
- 4.7 percent were Asian/Pacific Islander; and
- 1.2 percent were First Nations (Native American/Alaskan Native).

The intersectionalities created by both poverty and disability paint this portrait as even more complex: the *Digest of Education Statistics 2008* (Snyder et al., 2009) determined that as of 2007, 16.5 percent of US children ages five to seventeen lived in poverty (p. 37). The *Americans with Disabilities: 2005—Household Economic Studies* (Brault, 2008) presented data that as of 2005, 54.5 million people in the United States—18.7 percent of its total population—had some level of disability. According to the same source, 35 million people in the United States, or 12 percent of its total population, had a severe disability, while African Americans and women exhibited a higher prevalence of disability than other groups (20.5 percent and 20.1 percent, respectively). Because of how disabilities are defined according to the *Individuals with Disabilities Education Improvement Act of 2004* (Public Law 108-446, 2004), these data are enormously difficult to disaggregate, but nonetheless, they give us an idea of how many children with disabilities compose the public school student body within the United States.

The disparity between the embodied student and the embodied teacher in the United States widens substantially when population projections come into play. By the year 2050, the *Population Projections of the United States by Age, Sex, Race, and Hispanic Origin: 1995 to 2050* predicts the following:

- Currently, people claiming Hispanic origin will make up the second-largest ethnic group in the United States; and
- by 2050, the United States' population will be 52.8 percent non-Hispanic white, 24.5 percent Hispanic, 13.6 percent African American, 8.2 percent Asian, and 0.9 percent First Nations (Day, 1996).

The preponderance of public school teachers in the United States, however, will be white, middle class, and female. In the preface to her seminal book, *The Dreamkeepers*, Gloria Ladson-Billings (2009) drew upon these data in her discussion of the rapidly changing demographics of United States' public schools:

Children of color constitute an increasing proportion of our students. They represent 30 percent of our public school population. In the twenty largest school districts, they make up over 70 percent of total school enrollment. Conversely, the number of teachers of color, particularly African American, is dwindling. African American teachers make up less than 5 percent of the total public school teaching population. (p. xvi)

What does this tell us and why should we as music educators care? Ladson-Billings's work and the data discussed previously inform us that the writing is on the wall: preservice music educators are facing and will continue to face the musical opportunities and challenges afforded to our field by a population of what curriculum theorist Bernadette Baker (2002) described as increasingly diverse *body-minds*. To teach in ways that honor their future students and to, as Beth Ferri (2004) urged, "[find] connections without erasing the differences" (p. 513), future music educators' thinking must evolve in relation to their understanding of the sociocultural situatedness of their students' musics. Whereas I acknowledge that there is diversity in whiteness, the burgeoning diversity in United States' public schools incorporates a student body that is rich in racial, ethnic, cultural, linguistic, religious, and economic diversity. Additionally, this student body carries with it multiple beliefs and constructions of ability, disability, gender, sexuality, and creativity, to name but a few. The musical diversity embodied by these music makers poses a vast set of possibilities for music education and its future music educators. It is now time (or past time) that both undergraduate and graduate students studying music education begin to think holistically about the field and the diverse body of music makers within their care, to broaden their constructions of themselves as music educators, and to interrogate their actions related to music making, music makers, and their wider sociocultural context. I argue that future music educators must interrogate their thinking about music, music makers, and their roles as music educators, as well as consider new ways of thinking about people and difference. But what of the invisible baggage that preservice music educators bring with them as they begin their professional journey, the belief systems that accompany them?

BAGGAGE AND HEAVY LIFTING: BELIEFS, PERSPECTIVES, AND ATTITUDES

As music teacher educators, we understand that the preservice teachers with whom we work come to us with sets of intact beliefs and a multiplicity of concerns grounded in personal history and experience: perspectives regarding knowledge, teaching, teachers, and students that are typically implicit and unarticulated. Dan Lortie (1975), in his seminal sociological study, *Schoolteacher*, observed that preservice teachers have already served an apprenticeship of sorts in their prior schooling, what he coined an *apprenticeship of observation* (p. 61).

These young people enter the profession experiencing what Lortie described as an "exceptional opportunity to observe members of the occupation at work" (p. 65); however, what preservice teachers know about teaching is for the most part intuitive and unproblematized (pp. 62–65).

Preservice music educators come to us having spent at least thirteen years observing classroom teachers and their own music teachers, both public and private, for similar amounts of time. In the case of our undergraduates who wish to teach general, choral, and instrumental music, most of them have spent in excess of eight years in public and private schools formally participating in a multiplicity of music-making experiences ranging from large ensembles, to musical theater, to performing solo and chamber works. However, these students were not only making music but also closely observing the music educator in charge of classes and rehearsals: in the case of large ensembles, the individual on the podium. During the time in which our students find themselves in our methods courses, they are typically required to participate in all sorts of ensembles, particularly in large conducted ensembles, thus continuing their close observations and absorbing the embodied and enacted discourses emanating from the podium.

Our future choral, band, and orchestra educators learn multiple lessons as a result of their inculcation into performance practices, such as who embodies the *proper* conductor, who makes musical decisions, what is *good* repertoire, what is musical talent and ability, and who belongs in the ensemble and who does not. These lessons, I argue, are but the tip of the iceberg. Additionally, preservice music educators absorb subliminal messages that surround music teaching and conducting from their experiences outside the university classrooms and rehearsal halls.

From their rich sets of musical experiences, preservice music educators arrive in our classrooms with hopefully not immutable but certainly robust beliefs about music, musical knowledge, music teaching, and their role as music educators/conductors. In his book, *The Maestro Myth*, Norman Lebrecht (1991) examined the origins and nature of the conductors' power (p. 11) and addressed the notion of the conductor as hero: a gendered, heteronormative, and raced construction of charisma and authority who, with no instrument but hands, creates sonic artistry and beauty via the *magical* control of the musicians arrayed before this individual. This is heady stuff, particularly if it is wedded to preservice music teachers' idealization of and identification with a particular music educator/conductor who was fundamental to their personal musical experiences. Lortie (1975) asserted that many of the respondents in his study linked their decision to teach with an influential teacher whose role was similar to that of the respondents, and that this influence was ongoing (p. 64). In both classroom discussions and informal conversations, my experiences are similar. Multiple students have shared with me their admiration for their high school ensemble directors, particularly if the students' experiences were positive and successful.

Preservice music educators also arrive in our courses as insiders to school; according to Frank Pajares (1992), most students see no reason to redefine their situation (p. 322) due to their previously successful school experiences. Through their own successful school music-making experiences and close observation of influential teachers, our preservice music educators' beliefs about music teaching are well established, tenacious, and resistant to change. Changing those beliefs is potentially threatening to our insiders, Pajares claimed, as it challenges their conceptions of identity and reality about school, the people in it, and the practices enacted there (p. 323), particularly those that might challenge their beliefs regarding the valorization of cherished musical behaviors and practices.

Diane Holt-Reynolds (1992) expanded upon this theme, maintaining that preservice students come to us "carrying prior knowledge about the concept of prior knowledge" (p. 326), what she described as *lay theories*. Lay theories represent the tacit, untutored knowledge that students develop over time through their lived classroom experiences; typically, these experiences lie dormant and unexamined (p. 326). Music education students are no different: they enter their professional teaching studies with an enormous amount of knowledge about schools, classrooms, music and music making, and how music *should* be taught, all based on their personal experiences. Additionally, they bring with them lay beliefs about "what works with students and therefore constitutes 'good' practice and with volumes of personal experiences in the form of narratives about teachers, teaching, classrooms, and subject-matter specific pedagogies" (p. 326). In essence, teacher education students and, by extension, music education students regard their robust sets of previous school and music-making experiences as *data:* they tend to reject new information and ways of thinking about teaching and learning as presented by their education professors when this information challenges their personal lay theories. Thus, our students tend to favor ideas and methods that mesh with their own experiences while opposing those that are less congruent with their beliefs about music learning and teaching.

This encounter between preservice teachers' lay beliefs and the professional theories presented in their teaching methods courses is sometimes a contentious one, as Holt-Reynolds (1992) discovered, resulting in a space of entrenched resistance on the part of the preservice teachers. Through in-depth interviews with undergraduate students engaged in a content-area reading methods course, she found that for the most part, the students' lay beliefs were remarkably robust, causing them to often reject their professor's professional and theory-based arguments for pedagogical change (p. 330):

> Each of these preservice teachers used their explanations of their own experiences as students in classrooms as data out of which to develop beliefs about how other students would react to particular teaching behaviors....When [the professor's] link between a teaching behavior and a student outcome failed to match the association each had already developed, each preservice teacher in this study questioned the validity of [their professor's] argument, not the validity of their own previously constructed premises. (p. 339)

The ramifications posed by preservice music educators' entrenched lay beliefs have the potential to be profound, particularly when these beliefs butt up against those espoused by music teacher educators who infuse their curricula with foci on creativity, diversity, and equity.

IT'S NOT JUST ABOUT TEACHING MUSIC: IT'S ABOUT TEACHING CHILDREN...ALL CHILDREN

Perhaps more troubling to me than their beliefs surrounding music teaching and pedagogy is preservice music educators' beliefs about the students within their care, particularly given that beliefs serve as mediators or filters of knowledge and action (Bandura, 1982, as cited in Pohan & Aguilar, 2001). In her review of the literature regarding preservice teachers and their beliefs surrounding cultural diversity, Cynthia Levine-Rasky (1998) noted that researchers and scholars have discovered that:

> It is prevalent among prospective teachers to persist in interpreting social difference and inequality through the lens of meritocracy in which success is directly related to individual achievement and talent irrespective of environmental or broader social factors such as racial discrimination, poverty, unequal treatment in public institutions, language barriers and other patterns of oppression. The effect of this orientation is justification of patterned, negative judgments and actions against children and their capabilities. (pp. 90–91)

Such ingrained biases are troubling for those of us working with future educators, and those of us in music teacher education must take pains to become aware of such baggage that burdens our students' beliefs and thinking. Maria Tatto (1996) maintained that the lay culture of preservice teachers is strongly ingrained in regard to their beliefs about teaching students from diverse backgrounds, particularly their perspectives regarding those students' sources of school success and failure. Cathy Pohan and Teresita Aguilar (2001) cited evidence that such beliefs "lead to differential expectations and treatment" (p. 160) of students and claim that personal and professional beliefs regarding diversity are positively correlated with each other (p. 175). Thus, we must take it upon ourselves to guard against the very real possibility of our preservice music educators' successful school music-making experiences serving as an obstacle that impedes their ability to teach empathically. What is needed as our field moves forward into the future is for music teacher educators to nurture within our students a sensibility that encourages and compels them to teach in caring solidarity those children from whom they differ in multiple respects. Speaking for myself, the last thing I want is for the future music educators with whom I work to somehow reinscribe multiple oppressions upon their students via musical experiences. Problematically, Tatto (1996) argued that beliefs on the part of preservice teachers are intransigent, even with the intervention of a multicultural teacher education focus (p. 175). However, research indicates there is hope that such beliefs can be shifted, if not entirely off the dime then at least to the edge of the dime. In a cultural diversity course in which the professors employed concept maps and surveys to explore preservice teachers' beliefs about culturally diverse students, Alfredo Artiles and Karen McClafferty (1998) discovered that their participants' beliefs indeed shifted positively. Their work informs us that as music teacher educators, it is incumbent upon us to enfold diversity issues within our own teaching, to challenge our students' systems of beliefs, and to structure this in ways that are processually supportive of our students' experiences. The caveat to this endeavor is that of the danger associated with deficit-centered thinking: Cynthia Levine-Rasky (1998) argued that by blaming preservice teachers for their deficit thinking, many analyses fail to contextualize preservice teachers' lived experiences as they negotiate their complex reality and lived experiences of social difference (p. 91), particularly the dialectical tensions that they experience between their own cultures and the objectives of equity education (p. 105). This is a thorny issue but nonetheless one from which we cannot shy away.

HEROES, BIOGRAPHIES, AND THE IMAGINARY OF CHANGE

Returning to the inscription "No actual teaching," this comment sticks with me, "churning my butter" to borrow a colleague's turn of phrase. As I continue to interrogate and problematize its multiple meanings, the steps to the discursive dance between my students and me begin to play out in bits of independent choreography. Where I assumed that I had partners who would dutifully collaborate in constructing a new dance, I instead realized that my partners were engaged in formulating their own interpretations of and creating steps to their own dances. I had not considered that the strength and cogency of their systems of belief would result in their creating such robust spaces of mental resistance. As I reflect, I intentionally structured this music praxis course, together with its attendant readings and engagements, as refracted through my own systems of belief regarding equity and diversity in music education. I found it imperative to immerse the students in the expectations, knowledge, and dispositions that socially and culturally contextualize musical meanings and actions. The climate I strove to create embraced student centeredness where knowledge was constructed and shared; a space that valued equity, collegiality, empathy, and divergent thinking; and a class during which diverse belief systems could be honored, explored, and expanded. As I continue to peel away the layers of meaning embedded in that inscription of "No actual teaching," I realize that to a degree, my dance partners were sometimes engaged in an entirely different set of steps, perhaps even those of an entirely different dance. In retrospect and considering my own beliefs about being student centered, that was as it should be; I needed to understand how to better negotiate their spaces of resistance.

There is the possibility that for this cohort of preservice music educators I was somewhat of a mismatch from the get-go. Rather than Lebrecht's (1991) mythical maestro hero, Lortie's (1975) idealized teacher, or Hollywood's Mr. Holland, my dance partners got me: a newly minted university professor who happened to be a woman of a certain vintage, hailing from her recent gig as an elementary and middle school music educator, someone who deliberately chose *not* to teach high school instrumental music; a middle-aged woman who pushed, prodded, asked hard questions, and expected the same in return; in sum, someone outside their known musical world, given their high school and current university experiences. I embodied and enacted a material alterity alien from my students' prior music education experiences.

In a chapter taken from *Stepping Across: Four Interdisciplinary Studies of Education and Cultural Politics,* "No Hero of Mine: Disney, Popular Culture, and Education," Julia Eklund Koza (2003) interrogated the discursive constructions of the "hero as solitary male music educator" in the Disney movie *Mr. Holland's Opus,* the antithesis of my embodiment. Mr. Holland goes it alone, makes all the musical decisions, and has all the musical answers, all the while exerting control over the musical minions gathered at the foot of his podium. His work is central to his life and identity; notwithstanding his irresponsible and reprehensible involvement with a female student, Mr. Holland is truly single-minded, toiling away in the isolation of his band room or study. He is the celluloid embodiment of Lebrecht's (1991) maestro myth, instrumental music's answer to another mythlike movie teacher hero, *Stand and Deliver's* Jaime Escalante. Sari Knopp Biklen (1995), in her text *School Work: Gender and the Cultural Construction of Teaching*, argued that the "idea of the heroic is so gendered as to be useless" (p. 3): what is constructed as heroic for a man in education is much different than that for a woman.

In addition to being gendered, I argue that the stereotypical archetype dwelling in some preservice music educators' unconscious is raced and typically gendered: in the Upper Midwest, few preservice music educators encounter high school band or orchestra educators who are not white males, particularly at the secondary level.[5] Further, this masculinist archetype reifies heteronormativity and classism. Lebrecht (1991) maintained that the maestro myth indeed plays to these tropes: "Given the prejudices of record companies and the predominance of middle-class values in concert life, blacks, women, and known homosexuals have been effectively shut out of the podium" (pp. 270–271). Thus, I argue that the high school band/orchestra director-hero that many preservice music educators unconsciously wish to emulate is that of a white, heterosexual male. This hero typifies the conservative (Biklen, 1995), so-called *good* band/orchestra director-educator. Young people desire to become *good* band, choral, or orchestra directors, and a *good* director selects *good* repertoire from within the Amer-Eurocentric canon, giving token nods to calls for musics that live outside it. This is a far cry from the experiences I provided (and continue to provide) in my courses: preservice music educators encounter a professor of embodied and enacted alterity, one who poses continual questions intended to unsettle and disrupt their ways of thinking about their closely held beliefs. For instance, a typical discussion might focus on the nature of instrumental music's repertoire, in which we interrogate the notion of what is good repertoire, why it is good, who gets to call it good, who selects it, who is reflected by this music, and, perhaps most troublesome, to whom does this belong. I rarely have the answers, but I consistently have plenty of questions.

My imaginary of what I hope to be a continual transformative tango with each cohort of preservice music educators involves the evolution of their thinking while at the same time honoring and affirming what they bring to our time together. I encourage them to consider different ideas, positionalities, and potentialities that will, I believe, expand their belief systems and thus their imaginaries about music, knowledge, music learning and teaching, music making, and children. Often, I ask them to consider themselves as agents of change and to interrogate their raced and socially privileged status within an elite school of music. This is a very tender subject, and I am often met with a good deal of initial resistance (coated with a veneer of midwestern politeness, for the most part) couched in terms of their lay beliefs (Holt-Reynolds, 1992). Sometimes, I am met with a weighted silence, which must be negotiated with caring perseverance. Such responses or lack thereof pose a particular set of dilemmas for preservice teachers in how they regard themselves and their biographies. Cynthia Levine-Rasky (1998) acknowledged, "It is rare for them to conceive themselves as classed and raced social actors moving within social worlds characterized by privilege and inequities" (p. 104).

In *Practice Makes Practice*, Deborah Britzman (2003) summed up this messy yet fascinating tango brilliantly, stating:

> We enter teacher education with our school biography. Teaching is one of the few professions where newcomers feel the force of their own history of learning as if it telegraphs relevance to their work.... [O]ver-familiarity animates the fantasy that no one can teach anyone to become a teacher; each must learn his or her own way. Theoretical knowledge of teaching is not easily valued and school biography matters too much. (p. 1)

Recognizing and understanding the power of preservice music educators' biographies is necessary to assist them in interrogating and understanding the expectations, knowledge, and dispositions that socially and culturally contextualize musical actions and meanings. In circling back to the inscription "No actual teaching," I am coming to grips with the notion that this individual's school biography and school musicking experiences served to create what Britzman maintained are cultural myths about the work and identity of a teacher (p. 223). "No actual teaching" speaks volumes about the cultural myths of music teaching, which merge with the fantasy of the band/orchestra director as hero: (1) everything depends on the (music) teacher, (2) the (music) teacher is the expert, and (3) (music) teachers are self-made (p. 223). These myths, as Britzman stated,

> authorize a discourse on power, knowledge, and the self that work[s] to promote the impossible desire of assuming the self to be capable of embodying a noncontradictory subjectivity and capable of asserting a form of control that depends upon the individual's unambivalent acceptance of authoritative discourse. Such a desire makes no room for the complications we live. (p. 223)

Britzman (2003) argued that learning to teach is a social process of negotiation, always in some state of becoming—"a time of formation and transformation. Of scrutiny into what one is doing, and who one can become" (p. 31)—and calls for a dialogic of teaching that "invites the possible" (p. 241). I contend that we employ our understandings of our preservice music teachers' complex and messy choreography of belief systems, lay theories, and cultural myths to continue to challenge and engage them in a transformative tango of possibilities. Not to challenge or engage our students in this manner ultimately means to tacitly allow them to teach as they were taught: accepting the status quo, reproducing an unjust society, and reinscribing sociomusical oppressions. It is time to negotiate a new set of dance steps as we envision and reimagine a holistic, culturally relevant, and socioculturally situated music educator, one who embraces equity and diversity and is attuned to the possibilities afforded by the challenges of living, teaching, and making music in a breathtakingly polymusical century.

NOTES

1. A version of this chapter was first presented as a paper to the May Day conference in June 2009.

2. According to the *Joys of Yiddish* (Rosten, 1996), *bubkes* is a scornful description of nothing, "something trivial, worthless, insultingly disproportionate to expectations" (p. 55).

3. See Bruno Nettl's (1995) ethnography, *Heartland Excursions,* for an insider study of the extant culture, practices, values, and folkways within a highly selective school of music.

4. My aggregations are based on disaggregated percentages, *Appendix B, Tabulation of Question Responses for Status of the American Public School Teacher* (2010), http://www.nea.org/assets/docs/2005-06StatusAppendixB.pdf.

5. Koza (2003) mined this data extensively, noting that instrumental music educators at the secondary level are overwhelmingly male. Data show that the teaching corps in the United States overwhelmingly identify themselves as white/Caucasian (National Education Association, 2010).

REFERENCES

Baker, B. (2002). The hunt for disability: The new eugenics and the normalization of school children. *Teachers College Record, 104*(4), 663–703.

Biklen, S. K. (1995). *School work: Gender and the cultural construction of teaching.* New York, NY: Teachers College Press.

Bourdieu, P. (1993). *The field of cultural production.* New York, NY: Columbia University Press.

Brault, M. (2008). *Americans with disabilities: 2005—household economic studies, current population reports.* Washington, DC: U.S. Department of Commerce Economics and Statistics Administration, U.S. Census Bureau. Retrieved from http://www.census.gov/prod/2008pubs/p70-117.pdf

Britzman, D. (2003). *Practice makes practice: A critical study of learning to teach* (Rev. ed.). Albany, NY: State University of New York.

Day, J. (1996). *Population projections of the United States by age, sex, race, and Hispanic origin: 1995 to 2050, U.S. Bureau of the Census, Current Population Reports*, P25-1130. Washington, DC: U.S. Government Printing Office. Retrieved from http://www.census.gov/prod/1/pop/p25-1130.pdf

Ferri, B. (2004). Interrupting the discourse: A response to Reid and Valle. *Journal of Learning Disabilities, 37*(6), 509–515.

Holt-Reynolds, D. (1992). Personal history-based beliefs as relevant prior knowledge in course work. *American Educational Research Journal, 29*(2), 325–349.

Individuals with Disabilities Education Improvement Act of 2004. (2004). Reauthorization of IDEA, PL 108-446, 108th Congress. Retrieved from http://idea.ed.gov/download/statute.html

Koza, J. (2003). *Stepping across: Four interdisciplinary studies of education and cultural politics.* New York, NY: Peter Lang Publishing.

Koza, J. (2008). Listening to whiteness: Hearing racial politics in undergraduate school music. *Philosophy of Music Education Review, 16*(2), 145–155.

Ladson-Billings, G. (2009). *The dreamkeepers: Successful teachers of African American children* (2nd ed.). San Francisco, CA: Jossey-Bass.

Lareau, A. (2003). *Unequal childhoods: Class, race, and family life.* Berkeley, CA: University of California Press.

Lebrecht, N. (1991). *The maestro myth.* New York, NY: Carol Publishing Group.

Levine-Rasky, C. (1998). Preservice teacher education and the negotiation of social difference. *British Journal of Sociology of Education, 19*(1), 89–112.

Lortie, D. (1975). *Schoolteacher: A sociological study.* Chicago, IL: University of Chicago Press.

National Educational Association. (2010). *Status of the American public school teacher, 2005–2006.* Washington, DC: NEA Research. Retrieved from http://files.eric.ed.gov/fulltext/ED521866.pdf

Nettl, B. (1995). *Heartland excursions: Ethnomusicological reflections on schools of music.* Urbana, IL: University of Illinois Press.

Pajares, M. F. (1992). Teachers' beliefs and educational research: Cleaning up a messy construct. *Review of Educational Research, 62*(3), 307–332.

Pohan, C., & Aguilar, T. (2001). Measuring educators' beliefs about diversity in personal and professional contexts. *American Educational Research Journal, 38*(1), 159–182.

Rogers, C. (1969). *Freedom to learn.* Columbus, OH: C. E. Merrill Publishing.

Rosten, L. (1996). *The joys of Yiddish.* New York, NY: Pocket Books.

Snyder, T., Dillow, S., & Hoffman, C. (2009). *Digest of education statistics 2008* (NCES 2009-020). Washington, DC: National Center for Education Statistics, Institute of Education Sciences, U.S. Department of Education. Retrieved from http://nces.ed.gov/pubs2009/2009020.pdf

Tatto, M. (1996). Examining values and beliefs about teaching diverse students: Understanding the challenges for teacher education. *Educational Evaluation and Policy Analysis, 18*(2), 155–180.

18

BUILDING BRIDGES TO SOLVE PUZZLES

Strategic Curriculum Design in Music Teacher Education

Michele Kaschub

A PUZZLE IS a problem that tests both inductive and deductive reasoning skills through challenging the perceptual capacities of the solver. Simple puzzles require piecing together individual elements to achieve a predetermined end, while puzzles constructed to allow for varied final configurations are considered to be more complex. Music teacher education sits firmly at the latter end of the spectrum.

Characterized by a nearly innumerable collection of pieces, the puzzle of music teacher education has arrived at the twenty-first century conspicuously devoid of its helpful box top cover. The pieces lie scattered with a few snuggly joined and others sitting near each other but disconnected. Still other pieces rest completely upside down with their intended contributions obscured by their current positions. Though shuffled and sorted in a variety of ways, very few straight edges emerge, and considerable difficulty befalls those attempting to discern the commonalities required to build the puzzle's boundaries.

In attempting to solve the puzzle of music teacher education, researchers have:

- questioned the wisdom and strength of external influences
  (Colwell 2006a, 2006b; Ester 2004; Forsythe, Kinney, & Braun, 2007; Johansen, 2008);
- considered possibilities for the overarching curriculum design
  (Asmus, 2000; Barry, 2008; Cutietta, 2007; Greher & Tobin, 2006; Hickey & Rees, 2002; Hope, 2007; Kimpton, 2005; Reimer, 2003; Rohwer & Henry, 2004; Wiggins, 2007);

- examined individual components within the curriculum
  (critical thinking: Barrett, 2006; Hanna, 2007; Killian & Dye, 2009;
  Willingham, 2008; philosophy: Bowman, 1998; Broomhead, 2004; Elliott,
  1995; Jorgensen, 2003; Reimer, 2003; Thompson, 2007; Woodford, 2005;
  research: Burton, 2004; Conway, 2000; Strand, 2006; Teachout, 2005b;
  socialization: Conkling, 2007; Teachout, 2007; Woodford, 2002; technology: Berg & Lind, 2003; Greher 2006);
- sought different teaching and learning spaces
  (community partnerships: Burton & Reynolds, 2009; Myers & Brooks,
  2002; Myers, 2003; Robbins & Stein, 2005; integration: Robinson, 2010;
  school-based partnerships: Strand, 2006; urban/rural: Benedict, 2006;
  Hunt, 2009; Kindall-Smith, 2006; Robinson, 2006);
- tried different vantage points
  (critical pedagogy/social justice: Abrahams, 2005; Allsup, 2007; Benedict,
  2006; DeLorenzo, 2003; Kaschub, 2009; Schmidt, 2005; Woodford, 2005;
  cultural awareness: Benham, 2003; Koza, 2008; Benedict & Schmidt,
  2007; lesbian, gay, bisexual, and transgender [LGBTQ] issues: Bergonzi,
  2009; Garrett, 2010; Hannahs, 2010);
- suggested hiding a few pieces in noncredited requirements in areas outside of the puzzle proper (Kimpton, 2005; Robbins & Stein, 2005); and
- called for additional puzzle solvers to join the fray
  (Circle, 2005; Ester, 2006; Hickey & Rees, 2002; Jorgenson, 2003; Kratus,
  2007; Teachout, 2005a; Williams, 2007).

Their observations and discoveries have been heard as both quiet whispers and heralded alarms of increasing fervor for the past decade.

A different type of action is now required. Having examined much of what the past and present have to offer, I believe it is time to set aside the idea of solving the puzzle by merely tweaking existing pieces or adding a few pieces to fill the cracks between heavily worn pieces. As stewards of music education's future, we can position ourselves as creators who bring vision to reality. We have the materials and tools needed to create a contemporary vision of music education with flexible boundaries. There is no rule that says that all of the old pieces have to be used as they are, or even at all. There is nothing to prevent us from reshaping, resizing, recoloring, or completely originating pieces. Therefore, we can use what we know about music and music education to consider exactly what it is we wish to achieve as we design a new picture of music teacher education.

This is not to suggest that further examination of our efforts is unwar-ranted, but to persist in documenting the faults of an existing system is to assume that such a system is still viable and fixable. Further, efforts that lead to the application of patches, plugs, and bandages to once fine ideas that we now label "problem areas" does a disservice to those who created our current programs—for surely their goal was to create a curriculum that suited the needs of the people it was intended to serve at the time of its creation. This begs the question "Can we truly say the same of our current music teacher education programs?"

In this chapter, I will describe the design of one particular "box top picture." I believe that the puzzle pieces can be linked in many ways and that the boundaries consist of some straight edges, pieces that reach out, and borders built to receive a variety of pieces assuming localized colors and shapes. I further acknowledge that the pieces needed to complete the puzzle were not found intact in other boxes, but were handcrafted to fit into their place or places with tools specific to their locale. Therefore, I do not suggest that this is *the* model to be adopted by the profession, but simply *a* model that may hold promise for others seeking to originate contemporary approaches to music teacher preparation.

KEY QUESTIONS

Many models of undergraduate curriculum are likely to emerge as music teacher education evolves. The unique character of each program indicates the overall health and growth potential of our diverse profession and the equally diverse populations that it is intended to educate. Yet, there remains room for some uniformity, even a need for certain elements of music teacher education to be shared so that the very concept of "music education" can exist.

To ascertain the principles that would guide our efforts, we began by asking the following questions:

- What do we believe about music teacher education?
- What are our institutional contexts?
- In what contexts will our students (future teachers) find themselves?
- What do our students need to know and be able to do for their students as they assume their first teaching positions?
- What do our students need to prepare them to meet the future?

These questions were first explored by the music education faculty and later brought to the attention of the full music faculty.

Beliefs about Music Teacher Education

In thinking about the state of our profession, quick agreement was found with authors suggesting that the profession has stagnated in practices adopted during the 1950s (Colwell 2006a, 2005b; Cutietta, 2007; Ester, 2006; Hope, 2007; Jorgenson, 2003; Kratus, 2007; Reimer, 2007; Williams, 2007). The evolutionary halt of the profession is often credited to factors including:

- Institutional barriers (policies and procedures for changing curriculum)
- Competing philosophies and perspectives (interdepartmental within music)
- Availability of resources (faculty, finances, scheduling, space, time, etc.)
- External bodies (local, state, and national accrediting agencies)
- Faculty personally and professionally defined by earlier missions

While other factors could be added to the list, these challenges, in sum, seem mere excuses for limited action. As Giroux (1992) and Gramsci (1971) have noted, real and lasting change comes from practitioners—in this case, those who practice music teacher education. The aforementioned impediments certainly influence music teacher education, but they have not, in and of themselves, prevented the delivery of an education that would prepare music teachers for contemporary and future contexts. We have done that by limiting the scope of our strategic efforts aimed at effectuating change.

Change has been approached through small, within-course adjustments to content or methods or the occasional addition of a course (Hickey & Rees, 2002). Attempts have been made to advance accrediting agency guidelines through the ongoing presence of music teacher educators focused on bringing about such change. However, our most significant challenge is not found in how we envision or package music teacher education; rather, it lies in our meager attempts to prepare teachers who can perceive needed evolution and actualize it in practice. *Our curricular failings find root in the absence of courses addressing philosophical inquiry and applied research at the bachelor's level.* Without these two tools, our future music teachers have little hope of meaningfully examining the implications of their actions in regards to their impact on the profession or their immediate impact on students.

In considering the need to prepare entry-level teachers to understand the ever-shifting "big picture," we decided to create a program that would develop specialists in music education (Asmus, 2000; Circle, 2005) rather than specialists in bits and pieces of music education (Cutietta, 2007). All teachers need to grasp the totality of what music education has been, what it is, and what it can become, so that future generations benefit from our offerings. To achieve this goal, all teachers need to be conversant in the five direct engagements of music—listening, singing, playing, composing, and improvising—and they need to be able to employ any engagement in any setting. They need to understand the philosophical import of each area while seeking to understand continuing evolutions as revealed in research and practice. Their ability to do these things underpins and influences their future actions as leaders of learning and can be accomplished through a curriculum that eliminates divisions in favor of a more timeless mission that focuses on *enacting current practices, with an eye toward the what's next, accompanied by a desire and determination to meet and shape the future.*

Institutional Contexts

The University of Southern Maine School of Music is situated within a college of arts and sciences at a state university. Enrollment within the school crests 180, with 160 undergraduate and 20 graduate students. Approximately half of the students are pursuing degrees in music education, and twelve to fourteen students are placed in professional internships each year.

The School of Music has eleven full-time faculty and forty-four adjunct/artist faculty. There are two full-time faculty in music education. Additional full-time and part-time faculty members teach single courses addressing conducting, woodwinds, brass, strings, percussion, piano, and guitar. We are additionally supported by a team of over forty mentor teachers who welcome our students as observers, allow them to lead entire classes or offer shorter activities within classes, and host our students during their professional internships.

Our teacher education programs are accredited through multiple bodies. The School of Music holds accreditation from the National Association of Schools of Music (NASM). Additionally, all teacher education programs at the university are linked through the College of Education and Human Development. These programs must adhere to the guidelines specified by the Council for the Accreditation of Educator Preparation (CAEP) and the Maine Department of Education (MDOE).

Our students are predominantly from Maine (70 percent) and have strong performance preparation upon arrival. They possess a range of informal listening skills but little to no prior experience in composition and improvisation. An ever-increasing number of incoming students have completed school-required service work under the guidance of middle or high school music teachers. Far fewer have experience with children in the K-5 settings apart from the occasional babysitting position.

Incoming students have a long history of being students but very little experience in the role of teacher. Many express great interest in teaching and credit that interest to their passion for music. However, it takes only a few questions to determine that students have thought in very limited ways about the role of teacher. Their knowledge of the profession and "teacher perspective" is limited to their observations and interactions with the handful, and sometimes not even that, of music teachers who have guided their development.

Our program is fortunate in that it is located in close proximity to rural, suburban, and urban schools. Our students can easily access a variety of teaching experiences with children of different ages, socioeconomic statuses, ethnicities, learning styles, languages, and many other factors. Teachers located near the university are sometimes "teachers of everything" and sometimes teachers with very narrow job descriptions. Our students can experience a day that ranges from a mix of classroom and ensemble teaching in K-12 to a day that is composed of six choral rehearsals back to back.

In addition to a wide range of school-based settings with supportive and welcoming practitioners, our students also have access to several high-profile arts organizations. The Portland Symphony Orchestra has a strong and ever-expanding educational outreach program, and Portland Ovations brings both seasoned and emerging artists to our area to present performances and interact with school children in workshop settings. In both cases, there exists reasonable opportunity to develop long-term partnerships featuring a variety of activities and engagements.

Practitioner Realities

Maine is a geographically midsized state with a small population spread from border to border. Only a handful of schools are considered to be urban, and all are situated within the southern half of the state. This leaves the vast majority of schools at a significant distance from arts centers. Teachers report that it is difficult to bring musicians into their schools or to transport students to concert halls to experience live performances.

Music teachers earn a certificate spanning K-12 music. While some authors have suggested that preparing K-12 music teachers is unrealistic (Cutietta, 2007; Rohwer & Henry, 2004), Maine and many other states have ample supply of rural K-12 everything jobs. These small-town positions are likely to include band and chorus at both middle and high school, general music PK-5 or 6, middle school exploratory courses, music theory or appreciation, guitar and keyboard classes, the fall musical, the spring cabaret, at least all the home games of the boys' and girls' varsity basketball teams, the Memorial Day parade, and a couple of local civic events. Of greatest concern is that students who complete music teacher education programs tracked for band, chorus, general music, or orchestra are insufficiently prepared for these positions. Unfortunately, teachers taking these positions are often insufficiently prepared to identify what they need to know to meet the needs of students whose interests lie beyond those of the single track for which the teacher was prepared.

Conversely, in more suburban and urban settings, music teacher positions are often more limited in scope. While the "all-choral" or "all-instrumental" jobs are nearly extinct, positions that are one-quarter or one-third ensemble balanced by offerings focused on music studies in areas other than performance are typical. Teachers are expected to be excellent classroom teachers and to mount remarkable public performances. This represents a significant shift in job expectations over the past decade. Moreover, teachers are interested in trying new things. Some have added guitar courses, popular music ensemble classes, or composition units (though still too often situated within theory courses). Others express the need to do something new so that they can connect to a greater number of students. Yet, these teachers are unsure of what to do and need help in determining exactly what will draw students through their classroom doors.

Regardless of whether they find themselves in rural, suburban, or urban settings, nearly half of our novice teachers accept positions requiring the completion of a master's degree within the first five years of teaching. While not yet a mandate of the state of Maine, an increasing number of school districts have added this requirement to their teacher contracts. In all cases, teachers must earn the equivalent of six credit hours every five years in order to renew their teaching certificates. Nearly all schools offer financial support to teachers seeking professional development, but teachers may find it difficult to access such opportunities in music unless they reside near one of the two university campuses offering music education courses. This often means that teachers complete credit hours in general education areas rather than in music specifically.

Music Educators Ready for the Present and the Future

Balancing the past, present, and future is a key component of music education. We deliver and maintain programs sprung from past traditions. We work in communities eager to hear bands, choruses, and orchestras filled with children who wish to participate in them. And yet we also have students who would rather do just about anything than be "stuck" in a band, chorus, or orchestra. They are simply drawn to different types of music or prefer musical engagements that are more individualized, don't require public performance, or perhaps incorporate different tools.

School administrators and school boards, like many community members, are perfectly content with the status quo. Rarely are administrators aware of the particulars of every subject offered within their school systems. They may not have sufficient understanding to appreciate the full breadth of what music has to offer. This is, in part, our fault and responsibility. These same administrators and school board members were most likely educated within schools that offered elementary general music, band, chorus, and orchestra. They may be troubled by decreasing ensemble enrollments or by the slim percentage of the total school population involved with music classes, but they have no other model to emulate. Administrators are forced to respond to what they observe—music's too frequent decline. Unless we offer a demonstrably better approach, school-based music education will continue to disappear.

We need teachers who can deliver instruction in elementary general music classrooms and middle/high school rehearsal halls. We need teachers who can tap folk instruments (guitars, keyboards, computers, smartphones), as well as teachers who can help students find their own generative voices in composition and improvisation. We need courses for students who wish to excel in performance with instruments not typically found in bands and orchestras. We need alternative ensembles. We need classes to expand and develop a broader range of listening skills. But even if music teacher educators were to build teachers specializing in each of these areas, school districts would still hire only one or two teachers and still offer very limited programs. So what is it that we really need? *Teachers who can bridge time-honored traditions with emerging practices and opportunities.*

Bridge Teachers

The Greek philosopher Kazantzakis (1883–1957) is attributed with pairing teachers and bridges. He suggested, "Ideal teachers are those who use themselves as bridges over which they invite their students to cross, then having facilitated their crossing, joyfully collapse, encouraging them to create bridges of their own." To expand music education within K-12 schools, we need teachers who can both carry tradition forward and institute new paths. This means that we need to create a curriculum that prepares teachers to engage students in singing, playing, composing, listening, and improvising in both classroom and ensemble settings, with a variety of tools and through techniques appropriate to the students' developmental capacities (Kaschub & Smith, 2009, 2013). Further, we need to acknowledge that while performance is a valuable platform for would-be educators, so too are the skills of listening and creating. We need to accept students into our music education programs and allow them to develop expertise in these areas just as we have traditionally accepted vocalists and instrumentalists.

In adopting this plan, we can prepare a new cadre of teachers who can competently lead a chorus and also guide the development of twenty composers working to create scores for movie shorts. We can help teachers learn to successfully coach three middle school string quartets during the first period of their day and then dash off to the high school to collaborate with the information technology (IT) teacher on *Phoning It In*—an integrated IT/music course where students study music and entry-level programming for mobile devices. These teachers will bridge music education from its limited but outstanding offerings in performance to its broader-based and more powerfully inclusive future.

Teaching of this nature springs from a breadth of understanding developed through the pursuit of deep learning. It requires an ever-evolving curriculum that allows preprofessional teachers to be motivated, invested, and increasingly autonomous in their learning and rewarded and energized through their teaching from the moment they begin their programs. It also requires music teacher educators to commit to meaningful change.

GUIDING PRINCIPLES

In reviewing the data gathered in response to our initial questions, we identified eight principles to guide our design efforts. Support for each principle was found within research literature addressing music teaching, learning, or teacher preparation. Elements related to content and teacher action within the principles were evidenced throughout and across music education in a variety of settings and grade levels. And lastly, each principle was found to be actionable; that is, each specifies a desired change that we believed we could affect within our curriculum.

The Principles

1. Every preprofessional music educator must develop personal experiential foundations in singing, playing, composing, improvising, and listening.

Almost every student who begins an undergraduate program in music education enters through performance. To expand the range of opportunities offered within school music programs, we need to prepare teachers to lead study in all direct engagements with music. Students draw far less on what we tell them than on what they have experienced. Therefore, it is critical that we create space in the curriculum for prolonged engagement in each direct experience of music.

To achieve this goal in personal musicianship, students are required to complete seven semesters of applied study in composition, on an instrument, or in voice. Students also participate in seven semesters of primary ensemble (band, chorus, composer's ensemble, jazz ensembles, or orchestra), four semesters of secondary ensemble, and a single semester each on chamber music, jazz ensemble/combo, and composers' ensemble. In the area of listening, students complete coursework including Multicultural Perspectives (world, jazz, and popular musics) and Music History Survey I & II (Western classical musics). They address analytical listening through the ear-training components of Music Theory & Eartraining I through IV that includes assignments in multitrack recording and entry-level digital mastering. Critical and diagnostic listening are also addressed in two standard courses: Choral Conducting and Instrumental Conducting. Composition and improvisation experiences are formally situated in applied lessons, jazz ensemble, composers' ensemble, and creative etudes in Theories I through III and heavily emphasized in Theory IV with a focus on the sonic language of the twentieth and twenty-first centuries. Projects include raps, songwriting, film scoring, and more. Students are also exposed to a breadth of musical literature through personal and ensemble performance and required recital and concert attendance.

2. Every preprofessional music educator must develop a personal philosophy of music education.

There is a difference between teaching as you have been taught and teaching mindfully (Ayers, 2010). For preprofessional teachers to understand the purpose for their coursework, they must first understand the nature and value of both music and music education (Reimer, 1989). Woodford (2002) suggested that "one of the first steps in any reflective or critical model of music teacher education is to make students' beliefs explicit so that they can be subjected to critical scrutiny" (p. 690). Inviting students to discover what they, their peers, and others believe about music and music education helps them develop an understanding of their earlier experiences in music while framing what they will learn in their program (Thompson, 2007). Further, the immersive nature of personal and protracted philosophical thinking (Broomhead, 2004) allows for the establishment of a social reference group (Teachout, 2007) in which philosophical exploration is expected and practiced.

Students begin their philosophical studies in Professional Foundations for Music Education, where they encounter the work of multiple philosophers and educational theorists and test their ideas against current practices and present-day political media. The groundwork laid in this course is then carried forward and developed in each of the five primary methods courses: Teaching Creative & Critical Listening, Teaching Vocal Music K-12, Teaching Instrumental Music K-12, Teaching Music Improvisation K-12, and Teaching Music Composition K-12. Students also research others' philosophies and test their own through their fieldwork in ProSeminars I through VII, as well as their two internships.

3. Every preprofessional music educator must be proficient in the basic conceptual content of the discipline of music.

Teachers need to have a strong command of the content of their discipline to effectively structure learning activities for others. Students enroll in four semesters of music theory and three semesters of music history/cultural studies as foundational experiences. Beyond these formal points of study, students encounter a wealth of music as listeners and performers in recital class, in ensembles, and through their own applied studies.

4. Every preprofessional music educator must develop the ability to design and implement programs in singing, playing, composing, improvising, and listening.

School music programs in the United States typically feature large performance ensembles to the near exclusion of other equally viable musical offerings (Williams, 2007). To expand music education's reach, future teachers need to be able to lead learning in a wide variety of contexts and settings suited to their particular situations. Once preprofessional educators possess foundational experience in singing, playing, composing, improvising, and listening, they are ready to situate their understandings within the role of teacher.

To be an effective leader of learning across the areas of direct engagement, students must be able to articulate a rationale for the inclusion of each engagement within a music education program. They must demonstrate an understanding of child development both broadly and in relation to each area specifically. They must also be able to design K-12 curriculum in each area, write lessons, create opportunities to learn, assess the acquisition of knowledge and skills, and evaluate the effectiveness of the programs they create.

To this end, students complete a series of five methods courses addressing singing, playing, composing, improvising, and listening. In these courses, students address traditional band, chorus, and orchestra issues and challenges but also participate in contemporary music ensemble experiences including rock bands and improvisation ensembles. They explore a variety of vocal music settings from solo pop singer, to bluegrass, to glee club. They learn to value traditional practices as they explore and challenge themselves—and their professors—to grapple with emerging opportunities and to harness new ways of engaging in music for educational purposes.

Students also complete supporting coursework to develop skills in piano, guitar, strings, brass, woodwind, and percussion techniques. Assessment and evaluation are both woven through these methods courses and addressed within the Research & Evaluation course.

5. *Every preprofessional music educator must demonstrate competency in creating and implementing opportunities to learn singing, playing, composing, improvising, and listening in classrooms and/or rehearsal halls (as appropriate) across grades K-12.*

Preprofessional music teachers need opportunities to practice what they have learned about music teaching through leading learning activities in school-situated environments. We find it difficult to imagine a college saxophone student arriving at a weekly applied lesson to listen to an instructor talk about the saxophone, outline theories of playing the saxophone, and describe what it is like to be in different types of ensembles without ever being asked to play the saxophone. Yet, music teacher educators are often guilty of the equivalent. Students need learning that is real and situated. They benefit from participation in a community of practice (Conkling, 2007) that draws together their personal experiences as musicians and teachers with their knowledge of materials and child development in a classroom where they are supported by experienced teachers and professors.

College students need regular opportunities to create and implement lessons in which they feel they impact student learning in meaningful ways. It is through these types of experiences that they determine their self-worth as teachers and gauge their potential contributions to the field of music education. It is important that opportunities to teach begin as "teaching etudes" with ample guidance and evolve into opportunities for preprofessionals to independently create lessons with broad freedoms. How creative a person feels when working on a project is the strongest and most pervasive driver of motivation, perseverance, and commitment to success (Lakhani & Wolf, 2005). Movement from semistructured to independent lesson design allows preprofessional teachers to enjoy a level of creativity that is motivating as it prepares the way for successful teaching autonomy (Pink, 2009).

Students find these experiences in seven semesters of ProSeminar. Students lead learning in a variety of settings, singly or as part of a team, a minimum of six to eight times per semester. Their encounters with students are further enhanced through coursework in Human Growth and Development and Teaching Exceptional Learners in the Classroom as offered through the College of Education.

6. *Every preprofessional music educator must demonstrate the ability to use critical reflection to improve teacher action and student learning.*

The ability to analyze teaching effectiveness in a manner that fosters improvement in future endeavors rounds out the curricular sequence of personal experience with music, guidance for teaching, and practice. Beyond teaching and thinking about the successful and challenging aspects of particular teaching episodes that they document in their ongoing web-based portfolios (Berg & Lind, 2003), students need to witness our critical reflection in action. We need to draw attention to teaching sequences within our own classes—the classes where their primary function is student—to highlight when our approaches were effective and when they were not. We need to think aloud and share why we are determining that one approach is effective while another less so. Students appreciate this type of honesty because it grants them access to the invisible "teacher think" that we ask them to develop.

In the assumption that we are "all learners and all teachers all of the time," we both model effective teaching practices and learn how our students are interpreting what they see of our teaching. Establishing this open environment is critical to the development of teachers who reflect critically on their own practice. It clearly demonstrates to preprofessional teachers that this type of thinking is not tied to course-writing assignments alone, but is a real and meaningful component of good teaching. We employ this strategy in all music education courses and ask our field-based mentors to do the same when they provide feedback to our students.

7. *Every preprofessional music educator must demonstrate an ability to design and execute independent learning as required of music educators.*

To prepare future teachers to adapt to music and music education's continual evolution, we must model a systematic approach to accessing and using new knowledge to further their teaching and their students' learning. We must "provide the fundamental theories" and "establish within each future teacher the skills, knowledge, and attitudes to be an on-going learner" (Asmus, 2000, p. 6). In doing so, we will enable our students to adapt, grow, and change as their students and the world around them shifts and evolves.

The ability to read, evaluate, interpret, apply, and conduct research within one's own classroom is a critical component of ongoing learning in the field of music education (Burton, 2004; Strand, 2006). Though often reserved for doctoral-level studies (Teachout, 2005a, 2005b), music educators need to develop such skills before embarking on their careers. Sending undergraduates into the workforce without the ability to understand research is evidence of malpractice at the hands of music teacher educators. If our students cannot read and interpret research studies and if they cannot understand how data was amassed and used to demand changes that marginalize the arts, then how can we hope that they will be able combat the loss of music from school curricular offerings?

To prepare students for these challenges, we have students concurrently enroll in their Pre-Professional Teaching Internship and Research & Evaluation courses. The teaching internship is half independent study and half internship. It is student designed, approved by an MUE faculty member, and then pursued by the student in collaboration with a field-based mentor working in the student's area of inquiry. The student's work is supported through the development of skills related to the use of research. Students learn how to pose a research question, complete a literature review, and outline a plan of inquiry. They may also undertake smaller research projects as part of their internship program. At the conclusion of this semester, all interns share what they have learned in a conference-style presentation for the full ProSeminar enrollment.

8. *Every preprofessional music educator must be able to engage in and contribute to a community of learners.*

Students consider themselves successful when others acknowledge their work and efforts. Their definition of success, however, relies heavily upon the relationship needed for others to know about their work. Teachout noted that "one of the most powerful socializing agents found in postsecondary institutions [is] the intimacy of one-on-one instruction" (2007, p. 26). Indeed, the relationship established within the private studio is one to be emulated. Students are less impacted by what we tell them in class than they are struck by the quality of the relationship that we build when our attention is focused solely on them as an individual.

In order to help preprofessional teachers find their identities as music educators, they need a curriculum of constant contact. We need to be with our students both in their classes and during their fieldwork. Beyond the relationships that they build with their professors and peer cohort, they need to establish professional relationships with practitioners. This is most easily accomplished through the establishment of ongoing partnerships.

Robbins and Stein (2005) described profitable partnerships as being site based (in schools, cotaught with professors, practitioners, and/or peers) or service based (in conjunction with arts organizations, with professional musicians and teachers). When such partnerships are created with practitioners who are up to speed with emerging ideas and models, novice teachers are less likely to follow the natural tendency to "teach as they were taught as school students." Partnerships can enhance music teaching and learning for all participants because they constitute a larger community composed of school-aged students, preprofessionals in music education, music teachers, music education professors, professional musicians, and arts organizations (Myers & Brooks, 2002). In all cases, attention to relationship formation and maintenance through mutually beneficial partnerships builds a strong foundation that can extend past program completion and into, and perhaps beyond, the early years of teaching. We begin this process in our ProSeminars, support it through coursework, extend it in the teaching internship, and further its growth through the final professional internship.

THE MUSIC EDUCATION CURRICULUM: KEY EXPERIENCES

The curriculum that resulted from this work is structured in such a way as to ensure that personal experiences with musical engagements in each area always precede courses addressing child development, teaching methods, and opportunities to practice music education. The curriculum also offers some courses concurrently so that materials and resources offered through faculty collaborations can be used in partnership with school-based mentors. While some traditional course titles were maintained to accommodate faculty who had lived with those titles throughout their careers, the content and collaborative and experiential nature of the courses vary significantly from prior offerings. Most notably, composition, improvisation, and listening gain equal footing with choral and instrumental methods courses, and all courses span K-12 in focus. These changes allow preservice teachers to develop an understanding of child development and curricular design as it unfolds across the five direct experiences of music from kindergarten through high school and beyond. To follow is a brief overview of some of the internal connections that allow students to experience, study, practice, and reflect throughout their program.

Curricular Threads

- Professional Foundations for Music Education and Human Growth and Development establish the philosophical principles and knowledge of the learner that underpin Teaching Creative and Critical Listening K-12, Teaching Vocal Music K-12, Teaching Instrumental Music K-12, Teaching Improvisation K-12, and Teaching Music Composition K-12.
- Multicultural Perspectives of American Popular Music and Jazz and Music History Survey I provide a content foundation for Teaching Creative and Critical Listening K-12. Music History Survey II continues this content development.
- Participation in a wide range of ensembles, both traditional and peer group–designed chamber music, provide foundational experiences

in collaborative and conducted ensembles and models to emulate in Teaching Vocal Music K-12 and Teaching Instrumental Music K-12.

- Conducted ensembles provide models for student work in Choral Conducting and Instrumental Conducting.
- Music Theory & Eartraining I through IV provide opportunities for students to develop an understanding of compositional practices as they have evolved to date. Students engage in many of the traditional activities in the study of music theory but also explore applications of those ideas in projects that include rhythmic and pitched raps, songwriting, film scoring, multitrack recording, digital mastering, and the use of a wide range of sonic resources and technologies for the purposes of original creation.
- Teaching Vocal Music K-12 and Choral Conducting, and Teaching Instrumental Music K-12 and Instrumental Conducting are offered concurrently. Faculty collaborate to share methods and materials across these courses to foster the development of rehearsal techniques and strategies that are directly linked to informed and responsive pedagogical practices.
- Brass, Guitar, Percussion, Piano, Strings, and Woodwind Techniques classes are spread across the program. In nearly all cases, middle school students are brought into these classes so that preservice teachers can practice their newly emerging teaching skills under the watchful eye of course instructors.
- Teaching Music Composition K-12 is offered concurrently with enrollment in the Composer's Ensemble so that students are actively engaged in a composition community as both composers and performers while they study composition pedagogy.

ProSeminar: Personal Experience and Theory Applied to Practice

In addition to traditional and expanded coursework, students participate in seven semesters of ProSeminar. The ProSeminar experience was designed to bring all MUE students together two to three times each semester to share in a community of teacher-learners, to explore emerging topics in music education, and to foster the idea of professional development through the hosting of speakers and participation in special programs. Most importantly, the ProSeminar experience was created to ensure field-based experiences for all music education students throughout their college careers. Six of the ProSeminar courses are tied to specific courses and partner with those courses to allow teachers and students to collaboratively shape projects that involve students teaching in K-12 schools. While projects may shift from year to year, a representative sample would include:

- ProSeminar I is partnered with Professional Foundations for Music Education. Preservice teachers are focused on developing their presentational skills and gaining a degree of comfort in classroom leadership. Projects include "I'm the Expert"—a five-minute presentation of any topic outside of music for which the teacher has expertise to share with peers; "Teams"—students work in teams to create a ten-minute presentation on any topic that interests them in music education; and "Bookscoring"—a fifteen- to twenty-minute lesson for K-3 students in which the teacher selects a children's book and facilitates students adding vocal and instrumental sounds (beyond sound effects) to enhance the value of the story.
- Due to university scheduling of core requirements, ProSeminar II exists without an MUE course partner. The main project of the course is "Listening Alive"—preservice teachers form chamber music ensembles, select a topic, and design a listening-based learning experience for students in K-8. The presentations are twenty to thirty minutes in length, involve solo and ensemble performance, engage listening activities on the part of the K-8 students, and close with a question-and-answer session. Preservice teachers take their "Listening Alive" lessons to at least three different schools and must adapt their lessons to fit at least two different age groups.
- ProSeminar III is tied to Teaching Creative and Critical Listening K-12. Preservice teachers develop a minimum of three lessons that are taught at the elementary, middle, and high school levels. Some lessons are taught individually while others are delivered with a partner. Team teaching allows for peer support but also for peer critique, which helps students develop reflective skills.
- ProSeminar IV works in partnership with Teaching Vocal Music K-12 and Choral Conducting. Preservice teachers develop singing-based lessons for grades kindergarten through two and grades three to four and observe and rehearse both middle school and high school choruses. Students also prepare and perform an informal concert where they select and prepare songs of their choosing from any genre to demonstrate personal vocal musicianship.
- ProSeminar V is unique in the ProSeminar cycle in that it also serves as a university core course in Ethical Inquiry, Social Responsibility, and Citizenship. Students engage in required core readings on ethics, conduct an independent study of a topic that intrigues them within music education, and complete a twelve-hour preprofessional internship with

a mentor teacher who is deeply knowledgeable about the intern's topic area. ProSeminar V is partnered with the Research & Evaluation course. Students conduct a detailed literature review of their ProSeminar V topic and then draw research and practice together in a twenty-five to thirty-minute conference-style presentation. All ProSeminar students attend presentations and complete detailed questionnaires addressing the presenter's knowledge of his or her topic, content, preparation, organization, presentation, and interaction with the audience. Students also observe and conduct middle school and high school bands in this semester.

- ProSeminar VI is partnered with Teaching Music Improvisation K-12. In this course, preservice teachers collaborate with their professor and a host school mentor to offer music lessons to students in grades five through eight. Lessons may be instrumental or vocal but include a wide range of improvisatory activities that are developed by the preservice teachers. Preservice teachers may also offer single-visit improvisatory activities in grades kindergarten through four or grades nine through twelve settings.

- ProSeminar VII joins with Teaching Music Composition K-12 to offer an eight-week Young Composers' Workshop for homeschooled students. The preservice teacher and professor design an eight-week curriculum based on the prior experiences and interests of the young composers. The professor leads the first day of the workshop and then the preservice teachers work in pairs to design the remaining workshop days. During collaborative projects, the preservice teachers are all actively participating within whole-class or small-group activities as composers equal to the young composers. Through these activities, preservice teachers gain firsthand knowledge of how young composers think and work, as well as experience in guiding the work of a community of young composers.

These ProSeminar experiences lead to the fifteen-week professional internship. As Maine certifies K-12 teachers in music, students split their internship hours between two schools. They teach at two of three possible grade spans (kindergarten through four, five through eight, or nine through twelve) and in both classroom and rehearsal settings. All students completing this curriculum have reported that the experiences of ProSeminars I through VII made the transition from college classroom to student teaching an easy one.

FINAL THOUGHTS

Evoking change where deeply entrenched practices exist requires creativity, ingenuity, commitment, and perseverance—and some would argue pain relievers and caffeine—because change typically arrives accompanied by naysayers, immense challenges, and the armed guard of the status quo. In too many situations, music teacher education is discussed and dissected as a decontextualized problem in need of unifying solutions. Yet, in practice, it is a contextualized problem fraught with diverse realities requiring multiple solutions. As the designers of music education's future, we should heed Hope's advice to create "customized solutions for local situations that reflect a common framework" (2007, p. 5).

The principles used to design the curriculum offered in this chapter are one possible model for the common framework to which Hope alluded. Inclusive of personal music experiences, philosophical foundations, musical understandings, supported teaching experiences within professional communities, and the tools to pursue continued learning, the principles are broadly applicable yet possess the malleability necessary to fit nearly any context.

Long after our curriculum work was completed, I came across an article in which the authors had written, "Most music education programs provide all-levels certification, meaning students graduate certified to teach in any area and at any level. To suggest that music education programs are actually able to achieve this goal effectively may be unrealistic" (Rohwer & Henry, 2004, p. 24). I humbly counter that the goal is only unrealistic if we approach the task in the same manner that we have for the past fifty years and expect the results to change. The best way to achieve what some term "impossible" is to look at the puzzle pieces in a different way. The pieces don't have to fit together to form a two-dimensional image like all the other pictures we have been shown. They can be artfully sculpted to construct a three-dimensional bridge anchored in tradition and extending to the future—and that bridge is just waiting for you and your students to build it.

ACKNOWLEDGMENTS

The author wishes to thank Douglas T. Owens, now F. Ludwig Diehn Endowed Chair of Instrumental Music at Old Dominion University, who contributed to the initial design and first year of implementation of this curriculum, and Steven Bizub, Assistant Professor of Music at USM, who worked with the author to implement coursework for the second through fourth years of the program.

REFERENCES

Abrahams, F. (2005). The application of critical pedagogy to music teaching and learning: A literature review. *Update—Applications of Research in Music Education, 23*(2), 12–22. doi:10.117 7/87551233050230020103

Allsup, R. E. (2007). Extraordinary rendition: On politics, music, and circular meanings. *Philosophy of Music Education Review, 15* (2) 144-154.

Asmus, E. (2000). Foundation competencies for music teacher education. *Journal of Music Teacher Education, 9*(5), 5–6. doi:10.1177/10570837000900202

Ayers, W. (2010). *To teach: The journey, in comics.* New York, NY: Teachers College, Columbia University.

Barrett, J. R. (2006). Developing the professional judgment of preservice music teachers: Grading as a case in point. *Journal of Music Teacher Education, 15*(2), 3–8.

Barry, N. H. (2008). The role of integrated curriculum in music teacher education. *Journal of Music Teacher Education, 18*(1), 28-38.

Benedict, C. (2006). Defining ourselves as other: Envisioning transformative possibilities. In C. Frierson-Campbell (Ed.), *Perspectives in urban music education* (pp. 3–14). Lanham, MD: Rowman & Littlefield Education.

Benedict, C., & Schmidt, P. (2007) From whence justice? Interrogating the improbable in music education. *Action, Criticism, and Theory for Music Education, 6*(4), 21–42.

Benham, S. (2003). Being the other adapting to life in a culturally diverse classroom. *Journal of Music Teacher Education, 13*(1), 21–32.

Berg, M. H., & Lind, V. R. (2003). Preservice music teacher electronic portfolios: Integrating reflection and technology. *Journal of Music Teacher Education, 12*(2), 18–23.

Bergonzi, L. (2009). Sexual orientation and music education: Continuing a tradition. *Music Educators Journal, 96*, 21–15.

Bowman, W. D. (1998). *Philosophical perspectives on music.* New York, NY: Oxford University Press.

Broomhead, P. (2004). The problem with music education philosophy for undergraduates. *Journal of Music Teacher Education, 14*(1), 20–26.

Burton, S. (2004). Where do we begin with inquiry-based degree programs? *Journal of Music Teacher Education, 14*(1), 27–33.

Burton, S., & Reynolds, A. (2009). Transforming music teacher education through service learning. *Journal of Music Teacher Education, 18*(2), 18–33.

Circle, D. (2005). Special issue: The future of music teacher education: Introduction. *Journal of Music Teacher Education, 14*(2), 3–4.

Colwell, R. (2006a). Music teacher education in this century: Part I. *Arts Education Policy Review, 108*(1), 15–27.

Colwell, R. (2006b). Music teacher education in this century: Part II. *Arts Education Policy Review, 108*(2), 17–29.

Conkling, S. (2007). The possibilities of situated learning for teacher preparation: The professional development partnership. *Music Educators Journal, 93*(3), 44–48.

Conway, C. (2000). The preparation of teacher-researchers in preservice music education. *Journal of Music Teacher Education, 9*(2), 22–30.

Cutietta, R. (2007). Content for music teacher education in this century. *Arts Education Policy Review, 108*(6), 11–18.

DeLorenzo, L. (2003). Teaching music as democratic practice. *Music Educators Journal,* 90(2), 35–40.

Elliott, D. (1995). *Music matters.* New York, NY: Oxford University Press.

Ester, D. (2004). Raising the standards: Music teacher education in a performance-based world. *Journal of Music Teacher Education, 14*(1), 34–38.

Ester, D. (2006). In search of the tipping point. *Journal of Music Teacher Education, 16*(3), 3–4.

Forsythe, J., Kinney, D., & Braun, L. (2007). Opinions of music teacher educators and preservice music students on the NASM standards for teacher education. *Journal of Music Teacher Education, 16*(2), 19–33.

Garrett, M. (2010). *Music education in the 21st century: The LGBT component of teacher training.* Paper presented at the conference for Establishing Identity: LGBT Studies in Music Education, University of Illinois School of Music, Champaign, IL.

Giroux, H. (1992). *Border crossings: Cultural workers and the politics of education.* New York, NY: Routledge.

Gramsci, A. (1971). *Selections from the prison notebooks* (Q. Hoare & G. N. Smith, Trans.). New York, NY: International Publishers.

Greher, G. (2006). Transforming music teacher preparation through the lens of video technology. *Journal of Music Teacher Education, 15*(2), 49–60. doi:10.1177/10570837060150020

Greher, G., & Tobin, R. (2006). Taking the long view toward music teacher preparation: The rationale for a dual-degree program. *Music Educators Journal, 92*(5), 50–55.

Hanna, W. (2007). The new Bloom's taxonomy: Implications for music education. *Journal of Music Teacher Education, 108*(4), 7–16.

Hannahs, L. (2010). *Out to in: A queer journey from college student to student teaching in the public school system.* Paper presented at the conference for Establishing Identity: LGBT Studies in Music Education, University of Illinois School of Music, Champaign, IL.

Hickey, M., & Rees, F. (2002). Developing a model for change in music teacher education. *Journal of Music Teacher Education, 12*(1), 7–11.

Hope, S. (2007). Strategic policy issues and music teacher education. *Arts Education Policy Review, 109*(1), 3–10.

Hunt, C. (2009). Perspective on rural and urban music teaching. *Journal of Music Teacher Education, 18*(2), 34–47. doi:10.1177/1057083708327613

Johansen, G. (2008). Educational quality in music teacher education: A modern project within a condition of late modernity. *Arts Education Policy Review, 109*(4), 13–18.

Jorgensen, E. (2003). *Transforming music education.* Bloomington, IN: Indiana University Press.

Kaschub, M. (2009). Critical pedagogy for creative artists: Inviting young composers to engage in artistic social action. In E. Gould, C. Morton, J. Countryman, & L. S. Rose (Eds.), *Exploring social justice: How music education might matter* (pp. 289–306). Waterloo, ON, Canada: Canadian Music Educators' Association/L'Association canadienne des musiciens éducateurs.

Kaschub, M., & Smith, J. (2009). *Minds on music: Composition for creative and critical thinking.* Lanham, MD: R&L Education—A Division of Rowman & Littlefield Publishers.

Kaschub, M., & Smith, J. (Eds.). (2013). *Composing our future: Preparing music educators to teach composition.* New York, NY: Oxford University Press.

Killian, J., & Dye, K. G. (2009). Effects of learner-centered activities in the preparation of music educators: Finding the teacher within. *Journal of Music Teacher Education, 19*(1), 9–24. doi:10.1177/1057083709343904

Kimpton, J. (2005). What to do about music teacher education: Our profession at a crossroads. *Journal of Music Teacher Education, 14*(2), 18–21.

Kindall-Smith, M. (2006). I plant my feet on higher ground: Music teacher education for urban schools. In C. Frierson Campbell (Ed.), *Perspectives in urban music education* (Vol. 2, pp. 47–66). Lanham, MD: Rowman & Littlefield Education.

Koza, J. (2008). Listening for whiteness: Hearing radical politics in undergraduate school music. *Philosophy of Music Education Review, 16*(2), 145–155.

Kratus, J. (2007). Music education at the tipping point. *Music Educators Journal, 94*(2), 42–48. doi:10.1177/002743210709400209

Lakhani, K. R., & Wolf, R. G. (2005). Why hackers do what they do: Understanding motivation and effort in free/open source software projects. In J. R. Feller, S. Fitzgerald, S. Hissam, & R. K. Lakhani, (Eds.), *Perspectives on free and open source software* (pp. 3–21). Cambridge, MA: MIT Press.

Myers, D. (2003). Quest for excellence: The transforming role of university-community collaborations in music teaching and learning. *Arts Education Policy Review, 105*(1), 5–12.

Myers, D., & Brooks, A. (2002). Policy issues in connecting music education with arts education. In R. Colwell & C. Richardson (Eds.), *The new handbook of research on music teaching and learning* (pp. 909–930). New York, NY: Oxford University Press.

Pink, D. (2009). *Drive: The surprising truth about what motivates us*. New York, NY: Penguin Group/Riverhead.

Reimer, B. (1989). *A philosophy of music education* (2nd ed.). Upper Saddle River, NJ: Prentice Hall.

Reimer, B. (2003). *A philosophy of music education: Advancing the vision* (3rd ed.). Upper Saddle River, NJ: Prentice Hall.

Reimer, B. (2007). Comprehensive education, comprehensive music education: A new vision. *Music Education Research International, 1*(1), 1–12.

Robbins, J., & Stein, R. (2005). What partnerships must we create, build or energize in K-12 higher and professional education for music teacher education in the future? *Journal of Music Teacher Education, 14*(2), 22–29.

Robinson, M. (2006). Creating and sustaining urban music education collaborations. In C. Frierson-Campbell (Ed.), *Teaching music in the urban classroom* (Vol. 2, pp. 139–152). Lanham, MD: Rowman & Littlefield Education.

Robinson, M. (2010). Preparing future teachers for work in an integrated curriculum. *Teaching Music, 17*(4), 60.

Rohwer, D., & Henry, W. (2004). University teachers' perception of requisite skills and characteristics of effective music teachers. *Journal of Music Teacher Education, 13*(2), 18–27.

Schmidt, P. (2005). Music education as transformative practice: Creating new frameworks for learning music through a Freirian perspective. *Visions of Research in Music Education, Special Edition*. Retrieved from http://www-usr.rider.edu/~vrme/

Strand, K. (2006). Learning to inquire: Teacher research in undergraduate teacher training. *Journal of Music Teacher Education, 15*(2), 29–42.

Teachout, D. (2005a). From the chair: How are we preparing the next generation of music teacher educators? *Journal of Music Teacher Education, 15*(1), 3–5.

Teachout, D. (2005b). From the chair: A call for action in music teacher education. *Journal of Music Teacher Education, 14*(2), 1–2.

Teachout, D. (2007). Understanding the ties that bind and possibilities for change. *Arts Education Policy Review, 108*(6), 19–32.

Thompson, L. K. (2007). Considering beliefs in learning to teach music. *Music Educators Journal, 93*(3), 30–35.

Wiggins, J. (2007). Authentic practice and process in music teacher education. *Music Educators Journal, 93*(3), 36–42.

Williams, D. A. (2007). What are music educators doing and how well are we doing it? *Music Educators Journal, 94*(1), 18–23.

Willingham, D. T. (2008). Critical thinking: Why is it so hard to teach? *Arts Education Policy Review, 109*(4), 21–32.

Woodford, P. G. (2002). The social construction of music teacher identity in undergraduate music education majors. In R. Colwell & C. Richardson (Eds.), *The new handbook of research on music teaching and learning* (pp. 675–694). New York, NY: Oxford University Press.

Woodford, P. (2005). *Democracy and music education.* Bloomington, IN: Indiana University Press.

Index

Adams, Bryan, 142
Adorno, Theodor, 36–37
African Americans, 298–299
Aguilar, Teresita, 303
Aguilera, Christina, 142
Albritton, R., 28–29
"Alice's Restaurant" (Arlo Guthrie), 97
Allmendinger, Jutta, 226–227
Allsup, Randall, 164, 262, 264, 268
Amabile, T.M., 196
American Recovery and Reinvestment Act
    (ARRA), 109
*Americans with Disabilities: 2005—Household
    Economic Studies,* 298
Amuah, Isaac, 103
Apple, M., 29
Art as Experience (Dewey), 16
Artiles, Alfredo, 303
"The Art of Collaboration: Promising
    Practices for Integrating the Arts and
    School Reform" (Nelson), 105, 118
Arts Education Partnership, 105
Arts Education Resources Initiative
    (Washington State), 118
arts integration approach to music education,
    107–108, 112, 118–122

Arts Propel project, 83
A+ Schools Program, 114
Asmus, E., 321
"Atom Heart Mother" (Pink Floyd), 97
"Austin" (Music Workshop participant), 53

"Bad Touch" (Bloodhound Gang), 142
Baker, Bernadette, 299
Bamberger, J., 47, 76, 78, 81
Barber, B., 35
Barenboim, Daniel, 239–240
Barrett, J.R., 186
Barrett, M.S., 176–177, 197–198
Bartel, L., 263
Bartlett, L., 56
Battisti, F.L., 264
Bauman, J., 172
The Beatles, 95–96, 142
Beethoven, Ludwig von, 69, 193, 205
Behne, K., 68–69
Bencriscutto, F., 208
Benedict, C., 150, 262–264, 268
Bennis, Warren, 224–225
Berg, Margaret, 7–8, 167
Berkley, R., 172, 174
Bernstein, Leonard, 271

Bieber, Justin, 98
Biklen, Sari Knopp, 305
Bizet, Georges, 53
Bizub, Steven, 327
Blacking, John, 14, 91, 247–248
Blair, D.V., 81
Blair, Tony, 33–34
Blanchard, K., 232
Blonde on Blonde (Dylan), 97
The Bloodhound Gang, 142
Bloom's Taxonomy, 183
Boal-Palheiros, G.M., 64, 74
Boonshaft, P.L., 265
Bowman, P.B., 145
Bowman, W., 14, 16, 20, 48, 146
Braddock Oaks Middle School, 169
Bradley, D., 146, 163
Bransford, J., 114
"Bread and Roses," 151
Bregman, A., 89
Bresler, L., 284
"bridge teachers," 316–317
Britzman, Deborah, 306–307
Broadbent, D., 89
Broomhead, P., 82
Brophy, D., 196
Bruner, Jerome, 48, 153
Bryk, A., 114
Buddha, 47
Bulgaria, 138
Bundra, Judy, 43
Burgess, A., 29
Burnaford, G., 119–120
Butler, A., 155–158

Campbell, P.S., 133–135, 145
Canada, 37–39, 129, 131, 135
Carmen (Bizet), 53
Carper, J., 269
Carter, Bruce, 6
Carterette, E., 91
Center for the Study of Education and the
    Musical Experience (Northwestern
    University), 9, 45, 276
chamber music techniques, 214–216
change
    in education policy, 109–110, 113–119
    in music education, 1–2, 9, 100, 149–151,
        153, 156, 164, 186, 217, 284–292, 301–302,
        312, 317, 327

in society, 2, 88, 140, 142, 298–299
Cherry, E., 89
Chicago Annenberg Challenge, 117
Chicago Public Schools Arts Magnet schools,
    115
Chicago Public Schools Fine and Performing
    Arts Magnet Cluster Program, 118–119
Chomsky, Noam, 30–32, 39
Christman, J., 26
Clandinin, D.J., 270
Clark, Frances, 16
Clarke, E., 92, 95
cocktail party effect, 89
Cold War, 36
collaboration
    among students, 57–58, 120, 156, 162–163,
        173–174, 185, 189, 191–192, 194–195, 215,
        262, 285, 291–292
    between arts teachers and external parties,
        5, 111–112, 116–122, 135, 145, 314
    conducting's facilitation of, 7, 226, 232–236,
        238–239
Collaboratives for Humanities and Arts
    Teaching, 117
Collins, Jim, 236–237
Colwell, R., 20
comparative perspectives, definition of, 140
The Composer's Datebook (NPR), 156
composition
    affect and, 15
    classroom technology and, 177–179, 208
    clubs for, 160
    computer and Internet applications
        for, 152
    constructivism and, 6, 154
    creative thinking and, 2, 149–150, 152–153,
        184–186, 189, 207–209, 216
    critical thinking and, 5, 153
    culturally responsive pedagogy and,
        155–158
    diversity and inclusion in, 5, 155–159,
        163–164
    eminent composers' practices and, 175–177
    environmental composition and, 161–162
    extramusical associations and, 171–172
    free composition and, 172–173, 178–179
    group instruction and, 173–174
    guitar classes and, 162–163
    music education and, 5–6, 149–164,
        169–180, 184–186, 188–189, 191–192,

194–195, 197–200, 207–209, 211, 216, 313,
315–316, 318–320, 323–324
notation programs and, 178, 180
obstacles to teaching, 6, 174–175, 184
performance and, 154, 158, 161, 174, 192,
194–195, 208
poetry and, 171, 193–195
SCAMPER process and, 171
social justice and, 5, 150–151, 155–156,
158–161
soundscapes and, 171–172
spatial elements of, 91
student-directed elements of, 149–150,
152–164, 171–173, 176–177, 186, 189, 192
tone matrix programs and, 179
virtual composers in residence and,
169–170, 177–180
concerted cultivation, 297
conducting
affect and, 15
Bernstein on, 271
chamber music techniques and, 214–216
choral conducting, 318, 325
coercion and, 235–236
community development within an
ensemble and, 264
conductor-educator model and, 263–266,
268, 270–278
definition of, 245
facilitation of collaboration and, 7, 226,
232–236, 238–239
facilitation of students' creative thinking
and, 7, 211–216, 221, 237–241
foresight and, 233, 235
instrumental conducting, 318, 324
leadership and, 223–224, 226, 228, 231–237,
239–241, 263–264, 304–305
listening and, 83
normative notions of, 300, 304–305
"opening up the score" and, 7, 213–214
persuasion and, 235–236
in professional ensembles, 214, 227
rehearsals and, 231–233, 237–239, 261–262,
264–265
secondary education settings and, 7,
261–264
servant-leader model of, 7, 231–237,
239–241
trust and, 231–233, 235–236
Conkling, S.W., 264–265, 270

Connelly, F.M., 270
Conservative Party (Canada), 38
Consortium on Chicago School Research, 117
convergent thinking, 196, 206–207, 214
Cook, N., 254
Copland, Aaron, 57–58
Coppelia (Delibes), 79
corporate media, 38–39
counterpoint, 90
course evaluations. See teaching evaluations
Covey, Stephen, 235–236, 277
Cream, 96
"Creative America" (President's Committee
on the Arts and Humanities report), 106
creative application pedagogy, 6, 185
creative thinking
composition and, 2, 149–150, 152–153,
184–186, 189, 207–209, 216
conducting's facilitation of, 7, 211–216, 221,
237–241
convergent thinking and, 196, 206–207, 214
divergent thinking and, 196, 206–207, 214
education reform and, 183, 206
group dynamics and, 167, 207
improvisation and, 2, 189, 207, 209–210,
216
marching bands and, 211
music education and, 6–7, 11, 81, 149, 174,
183–195, 197–200, 205–217, 254–256,
285–286, 289, 291
music listening and, 7, 72–73, 75, 207, 210,
214, 248–250
performance and, 6, 206–213, 217, 227
rehearsal and, 210–213
Cree students in Quebec, 129, 131
critical inquiry, 18–19
Critical Pedagogy for Creative Artists (secondary school music course), 160–161
critical thinking
composition and, 5, 153
democracy and, 27
music education and, 3, 20, 34, 36–39, 56,
155, 159, 264, 320
teacher training and, 259
Critical Thinking: What Every Person Needs
to Survive in a Rapidly Changing World
(Paul), 159
Cross, I., 92
culture, definitions of, 128, 130
Cutietta, R.A., 78

Darling-Hammond, L., 114
Davey, E., 253
Davidson, J.W., 71
DeGraaf, D., 231
Delibes, Léo, 79
Delorenzo, L.C., 158–159
democracy
    capitalism and, 28–32, 39
    equality and, 26
    freedom and, 26–27, 29
    moral agency and, 27
    music education and, 19–20, 25–33, 37–40
    neoliberal conception of, 27–31, 34
democracy, definitions of, 25
Democracy and Music Education (Woodford),
    26–27, 34
DeNora, T., 66–67
Dewey, John
    constructivism and, 47
    on education, 3, 16, 186–187, 189
    on experience, 3, 15–16
    on the public interest, 39
"Die Forelle" (Schubert), 53
Diehn, Ludwig, 327
Digest of Education Statistics 2008, 297–298
Dimova-Cookson, M., 26
"Dirrty" (Aguilera), 142
disability theory, 103
divergent thinking, 195–196, 206–207, 214
Dobbs, Teryl, 8, 103
Dollase, R., 69
Dolloff, L.A., 270, 272–273
Dreamkeepers (Ladson-Billings), 298–299
Drucker, Peter, 225–226
Duke, R., 277
Dunbar-Hall, Peter, 149
Dunn, Rob, 4, 11, 43, 79–80
Dworkin, Ronald, 39–40
Dylan, Bob, 93–94, 97

Economy, P., 227, 277
*edTPA K-&12 Performing Arts Assessment
    Handbook*, 183
educate, definition of, 263
"Education after Auschwitz" (Adorno), 36
educational management organizations
    (EMOs), 33–34
Education Group (educational management
    organization), 34

"Eine Kleine Nachtmusik" (Mozart), 79
Elder, Linda, 159
Elementary and Secondary Education Act
    (ESEA), 109
elementary education
    music and, 2, 5, 8, 50, 63, 149, 160, 170,
        188–189, 196–199, 252, 314, 316–317
    reform and, 8, 18, 30–31, 33–34
Elliott, David, 5, 14, 17, 130–133
Elluminate, 178
Empire of Illusion (Hedges), 36
England, 27, 32, 34–35
Enya, 193
Epperson, G., 249
equality, 25–27, 30
Escalante, Jaime, 305
"Have you ever really loved a woman?"
    (Adams), 142
Experience and Education (Dewey), 16
experience-distant concepts, 136
experience-near concepts, 136
Experience Sampling Method (ESM), 66

Fanfare for the Common Man (Copland), 57–58
far right political forces, 27–28, 31
felt pathways, 81
Ferri, Beth, 299
Fine and Performing Arts Magnet Cluster
    Program (Chicago Public Schools),
    118–119
Fiske, H., 15
Fitzpatrick, Kate, 6, 221, 259
formal listening, 74–75, 77
Foucault, Michel, 92, 97–98
Four Seasons (Vivaldi), 193
freedom, definitions of, 26
Freefall (Stiglitz), 30
French Canadian students in Quebec,
    129, 135
Fullan, Michael, 118

Gardner, H., 52
Gates, J., 253
Geertz, Clifford, 136–137, 143, 146n3
Ginnochio, J., 171
Giroux, H., 35, 312
Global Financial Crisis (2008-2009), 28, 30
Goals 2000: Educate America Act, 106, 109
Goldberg, M., 172

Graham, D., 205, 210
Gramsci, Antonio, 312
Great Depression, 36, 95
Green, L., 155, 174, 285
Green, T.H., 27
Greenleaf, Robert K., 229, 233, 235
Greher, G., 82
Gromko, J., 198
Gruhn, W., 71
Guderian, Lois Veenhoven, 6, 188
guitar classes, 162–163
Guthrie, Arlo, 97
Gutstein, D., 38–39

Hackman, J. Richard, 226–227
Haiku poetry, 193–195
Halpern, A., 91–92
Hanslick, E., 249, 255
Hargreaves, D. J., 64–65, 74, 84
Harlem (New York City), 95
Hedges, Chris, 36
Hendrix, Jimi, 96
Henry, W., 327
Hess, Frederick M., 110, 114
heterophony, 90
heterotopias, 92, 97–98
Hickey, M., 153–154, 171, 208–210, 213
Hindemith, P., 250
Hispanics, 298
Hitler, Adolf, 31, 36
Holmes Group Teachers for a New Era
    Initiatives, 117–118
The Holocaust, 36
Holt-Reynolds, Diane, 301–302
homophony, 90
Hope, S., 327

iChat, 178
improvisation
    affect and, 15
    constructivism and, 6
    creative thinking and, 2, 189, 207, 209–210,
        216
    jazz and, 209
    mindfulness and, 20–21
    music education and, 6, 180, 184–186,
        188–189, 193, 198–200, 207–211, 216, 313,
        316, 318–319, 323
    in teaching, 262

Indiefeed (podcast), 157
Individuals with Disabilities Education
    Improvement Act, 298
Integrating the Arts and Education Reform
    Initiative, 118
intuitive music listening, 70–78
iPods, 97–98
Iran, 138–139
Isbell, D., 267, 270
Italy, 136–137, 141–142, 144
Ivaldi, A., 66, 74
"I Wanna Hold Your Hand" (The
    Beatles), 142

James Bay (Canada), 129
jazz, 95, 163, 209
"Jimmy" (student in Virtual Discussions
    database), 136–137
Johnson, M., 248
Jones, P., 20
Joplin, Scott, 94
Jorgensen, Estelle, 19–20, 277
Jourdain, R., 97
Juslin, P.N., 67–68, 70

"Ka-Ching" (Twain), 142
Kant, Immanuel, 47
Kaschub, Michele, 8–9, 150, 153, 156, 160–161,
    171, 174, 259
Kazantzakis, Nikos, 316
Keith, K.M., 230
Kerchner, Jody, 3–4, 43, 50, 81
knowledge workers, 225–228
Koza, Julia Eklund, 296, 304
Kraus, B., 210
Kumashiro, K., 149–150
"Kutiman" (YouTube user), 98
"Kyle" (Music Workshop student), 53–54

Ladson-Billings, Gloria, 144, 298–299
Lamont, A., 65
Langer, S., 90, 248
Lao Tzu, 47
Lapidaki, E., 175–177
Lareau, Annette, 297
Larsen, Catherine, 5
Larsen, L., 286
Laukka, P., 67–68, 70
lay theories, 301

leadership
    character and, 237
    coercion and, 235–236
    conducting and, 223–224, 226, 228, 231–237,
        239–241, 263–264, 304–305
    contrasted with management, 224–225
    definitions of, 224
    foresight and, 232–233
    influence and, 224–225
    of knowledge workers, 226
    persuasion and, 236
    servant-leader model and, 224, 229–237,
        239–241, 264
    top-down style of, 223–225
Lebrecht, Norman, 300, 304–305
left political forces, 27
Lehman, A.C., 71
Lehman, Erin V., 226–227
Leonhard, C., 16, 37
Leslie speakers, 95–96
Let Them Eat Junk (Albritton), 29
Levine-Rasky, Cynthia, 302–303, 306
Levitin, D., 90
life music listening, 64–74, 79–82, 84, 137–138
"Like a Rolling Stone" (Dylan), 93–94
Lind, V., 155–158
listening. See music listening
"Listening for Whiteness: Hearing Racial
    Politics in Undergraduate School Music"
    (Koza), 296
listening literacy, 82–83
The Literary Mind (Turner), 93
Lortie, Dan, 299–301, 304
Los Angeles Philharmonic, 227
"Love Story" (Swift), 98
Lucas, T., 155–157

Ma, Yo-Yo, 205
Macedo, D., 26
The Maestro Myth (Lebrecht), 300, 305
Maine, public school system in, 314–315
Maine Department of Education (MDOE),
    313
Manhattanville Music Curriculum Project,
    206
Maple Leaf Rag (Joplin), 94
marching bands, 211, 277
Marcus, Lloyd, 31
Marsalis, Wynton, 205

Marshall, N.A., 65, 84
Mason, Lowell, 16
Maxwell, John, 224
McAllester, David, 138
McCarthy, M., 20–21
McClafferty, Karen, 303
McCoy, Peter, 221
McDermott, V., 89
McKoy, C., 155–158
McPherson, G.E., 237–239
"Melissa" (student in Virtual Discussions
    database), 137, 142
mellotron, 96
Merriam, A.P., 143–144
Meyers, D.E., 114
middle school education
    music and, 6, 63, 81, 161–162, 169–170,
        177–180, 212, 244, 261
    virtual composers in residence and, 6,
        169–170, 177–180
Miller, R., 47
Miniature Guide to Critical Thinking (Paul and
    Elder), 159
Minneapolis Public Schools FACETS program,
    114
Monahan, C., 91
monophony, 90
Montessori, Maria, 47
Montreal (Canada), 129
Moore, M.C., 252
Morgan, R., 91
Morin, F., 170–171, 174
Mozart, Wolfgang Amadeus, 79
Mr. Holland's Opus, 304–305
multiculturalism
    dynamic models of, 5, 132
    insular models of, 5, 132
    modified multiculturalism and, 132
    in music education, 5, 130–135, 146
musical experience
    conducting and, 8, 264
    fundamental components of, 1–2
    mainstream consumer music and, 29
    music education and, 16, 245–247, 255–256
    music listening and, 247–250
    performance and, 2, 34, 246–247, 251–252,
        290
    practice and, 17
    propaganda and, 29, 31, 36

musical maps. *See under* music listening
music education
  anthropological perspectives in, 136–137
  arts integration approach to, 107–108, 112,
    118–122
  classroom technology and, 177–180, 208
  class sizes and, 286
  commercial and popular music in, 29–30,
    32–35, 99–100, 162–163, 290, 315
  composition and, 5–6, 149–164, 169–180,
    184–186, 188–189, 191–192, 194–195,
    197–200, 207–209, 211, 216, 313, 315–316,
    318–320, 323–324
  context emphasis in, 133–134, 140, 146,
    150–151
  corporate partnerships and, 31–33, 35, 37
  creative thinking and, 6–7, 11, 81, 149, 174,
    183–195, 197–200, 205–217, 254–256,
    285–286, 289, 291
  critical thinking and, 3, 20, 34, 36–39, 56,
    155, 159, 264, 320
  culturally relevant pedagogies and, 144–145
  culturally responsive pedagogy and,
    155–158
  cultural values and, 139, 141–144
  decline in funding for, 30–31, 106, 111, 180
  democratic values and, 19–20, 25–33, 37–40
  diversity and inclusion in, 20, 53–55, 103,
    155–159, 163–164, 212, 296–299, 303
  ethnomusicology approaches in, 129,
    137–141
  improvisation and, 6, 180, 184–186,
    188–189, 193, 198–200, 207–211, 216, 313,
    316, 318–319, 323
  instrumentation and, 286
  learning community environments and,
    186, 189–192
  lifelong skills and, 287
  local music cultures and, 129–132, 141–146
  multiculturalism in, 5, 130–135, 146
  musical styles and, 286–287
  music listening and, 43, 45–47, 49–59,
    64–65, 78–81, 83–84, 174, 190–191, 193,
    195, 206, 210, 214, 243, 245, 254–255, 275,
    313, 316–320, 323–325
  outsourcing and, 34
  pan-cultural approach to, 134
  performance and, 16, 18, 21, 37, 51–52,
    57–58, 151–152, 205–214, 216–217,

243–246, 253–255, 263, 269, 284–286,
    288–289, 313, 316–319, 325
  pitch and, 89–90
  proseminars and, 320, 323–326
  reform in, 1, 8–9, 118, 151, 256, 273, 277,
    284–292, 310–312
  social constructivism and, 56, 59
  soundtracks for film clips and, 81–82
  spirituality and, 20–22
  standards and, 37, 106–108, 118, 120, 184,
    253, 286, 290
  student autonomy and, 285
  student collaboration and, 57–58, 120,
    156, 162–163, 173–174, 185, 189, 191–192,
    194–195, 215, 262, 285, 291–292
  student decision-making in, 285–286
  sustainability and, 21
  traditional notation and, 287
  at urban schools, 5, 106–107, 110–112, 119,
    150, 154, 160–162
  utilitarian values and, 16, 34
  world music pedagogy and, 129, 131–135,
    138–139, 145–146
Music Educators National Conference
    (MENC), 17
  See also National Association for Music
    Education (NAfME)
musicianship, definition of, 151–152
music listening
  affect and, 65–66, 72–73
  behaviorism and, 3, 46
  cognitive responses and, 72–75, 78, 88
  cognitive science and, 4, 46–47, 52, 71, 92
  constructivism and, 3–4, 47–48, 59, 71
  contemplation and, 249–250
  contexts' role in, 4, 15, 48, 51, 56, 65, 67–68,
    70–74, 96 (*See also* music listening,
    spaces for)
  creative thinking and imagination in, 7,
    72–73, 75, 207, 210, 214, 248–250
  disinterestedness or objectivity and, 250
  diversity and inclusion in, 4, 43, 51–52
  emotion and, 64, 66–70, 72, 75
  as ensemble director, 83
  everyday life and, 45, 63–74, 78, 137–138
  extramusical responses and, 72, 75
  felt pathways and, 81
  focus and, 76, 78, 248
  formal modes of, 4, 74–78

music listening (*Cont.*)
 headphones and, 97–98
 Internet and, 4, 84, 96–98
 intuitive modes of, 4, 63, 70–78, 83
 kinesthetic responses to, 72–73, 75, 92, 252
 life music listening and, 64–74, 79–82, 84, 137–138
 listening for experience and, 255
 listening literacy and, 82–83
 live performances and, 82, 94–95, 98, 137
 lyrics and, 93–94, 97, 142
 meaning making and, 73
 melody and, 97
 mental representation and, 71–73, 78
 multisensory responses and, 48–54, 57–59, 72–73, 80
 musical experience and, 247–250
 musical maps and, 49, 51, 53–54, 56–58, 79–81
 by musical performers, 250–251
 music appreciation model of, 63–64, 243
 music education and, 43, 45–47, 49–59, 64–65, 78–81, 83–84, 174, 190–191, 193, 195, 206, 210, 214, 243, 245, 254–255, 275, 313, 316–320, 323–325
 past experiences and, 71–72, 74–75, 250
 pedagogical listening and, 254–255
 popular music and, 66
 psychoacoustical elements of, 88
 radio and, 4, 95, 137
 school music listening and, 64–66, 74–75, 82, 84
 segregating sounds and, 89
 self-identity and, 65–66
 skill development and, 49–50
 spaces for, 4–5, 88, 92–101
 spatial differentiation and, 89–92, 95–96
 spirituality and, 94
 stage development theory and, 46
 student-directed forms of, 4
 temporal space and, 93–94
 tonal aspects and, 90–91
 wipe-out phenomenon and, 76, 78
Music Manifesto educational initiative (England), 32–33, 35, 37
The Music Manifesto: More Music for More People, 32
Music of the World's Cultures (Nettl), 139–140
Music Workshop class (Kerchner), 53–58
Musikerleben, 68–69

Myers, D.E., 114

"Nadine" (student in Virtual Discussions database), 141–142, 144
Nagel, Thomas, 26
National Association for Music Education (NAfME), 17, 37. *See also* Music Educators National Conference (MENC)
National Association of Schools of Music (NASM), 313
National Council for Music Composition, 184
National Standards for Arts Education (1994), 45, 106, 109, 206
National Standards for Music Education, 184, 200
Navaho, 138
Neal, L., 231
Nelson, A., 105, 118
neoliberalism, 27–31, 34
Nettl, Bruno, 138–141, 143, 228
New Handbook of Research on Music Teaching and Learning, 284
New Orleans (Louisiana), 95
Nirvana, 65, 76
Noblit, G., 114
No Child Left Behind Act (2001), 109
"No Hero of Mine" (Koza), 304
Norman, R., 26
North, A.C., 64–67, 84
Northwestern University, 2–3, 9, 45
Noteflight, 178

occupational role identity development, 269–272
O'Neill, S.A., 64, 66, 74
On the Nature of Musical Experience (Reimer and Wright), 247
orchestra performers, 226–227
Orpheus Chamber Ensemble, 227, 277
Orwell, George, 39

Pajares, Frank, 301
Palma, Don, 227
Parncutt, R., 237–239
Paul, Richard, 159
Mr. Perez (middle school teacher), 161–162
performance
 affect and, 15
 composition and, 154, 158, 161, 174, 192, 194–195, 208

creative thinking and, 6, 206–213, 217, 227

felt pathways and, 81

improvisation and, 209

music education and, 16, 18, 21, 37, 51–52, 57–58, 151–152, 205–214, 216–217, 243–246, 253–255, 263, 269, 284–286, 288–289, 313, 316–319, 325

music experience and, 2, 34, 246–247, 251–252, 290

participatory emphasis in, 6

physicality of, 251–252

teacher-directed elements of, 207

persuasion, 235–236

Peters, Valerie, 5, 103, 141

Peterson, S., 211

philosophy

definitions of, 13

feminism and, 17

of leadership, 224, 229–240

music education and, 3, 9, 15–22, 37, 70, 88, 158–159, 177, 186–188, 217, 277, 312, 318–319

Piaget, Jean, 46, 71, 187–189

Pink Floyd, 97

Pitcairn, M., 185, 199

Pohan, Cathy, 303

policy churn, 110–111, 122

popular music

lyrics and, 93, 97

melody and, 97

music education and, 29–30, 32–35, 99–100, 162–163, 290, 315

music listening and, 66, 142

Population Projections of the United States by Age, Sex, Race, and Hispanic Origin: 1995 to 2050, 298

Portland Ovations, 314

Portland (Maine) Symphony Orchestra, 314

Practice Makes Practice (Britzman), 306–307

praxialism, 17

President's Commission on Arts and Education, 117

President's Committee on the Arts and Humanities, 106

Priest, T., 208

primary socialization, 266–268

privatization, 33–34

Project AIM, 114

Prosser, S., 229–230, 232

The Public and Its Problems (Dewey), 39

Quebec City (Canada), 129, 135

Quesada, M.A., 132

"Race to the Top" (federal education initiative), 109

radif (repertory of Iranian music), 139

ragtime, 94

Rao, Doreen, 11

Rauscher, F.H., 71

Rawls, John, 26

recorder (instrument) education, 6, 188–189

reform

curricular redesign and, 9, 18, 100, 119–120, 151

in music education, 1, 8–9, 118, 151, 256, 273, 277, 284–292, 310–312

neoliberalism and, 28–29

school-based management and, 109

shared decision-making emphasis in, 115

teacher professional development and, 113–117

at urban schools, 108–113, 119, 122

Reimer, Bennett

on conducting, 238

on creative thinking, 167, 207, 209–210, 248–249

on "disinterested" nature of aesthetic experience, 250

Elliott and, 17

on interconnectedness of musical process, 15, 83

on musical composition, 185, 196

on musical experience, 245, 248–249

music defined by, 14

on music education, 16, 31, 245, 253, 265

on music listening, 247, 249, 252

on performance, 251

on research, 9

on varieties of musical intelligence, 151, 185, 251

relativism, definition of, 140

Rice, T., 138

Richmond, John, 259

Robbins, J., 322

Roberts, B.A., 269

Rockefeller Foundation, 117

rock music, 95–96. See also specific artists

Rodriguez, Carlos Xavier, 4–5, 100

Rogoff, B., 56

Rohwer, D., 327
Rüsenberg, M., 69

"Sad Eyed Lady of the Lowlands" (Dylan), 97
Sager, R., 91
Said, Edward, 239–240
SCAMPER (Substitute, Combine, Adapt
    or Add, Magnify, Put to other uses,
    Eliminate, and Reverse or Rearrange),
    171
Schmidt, P., 150
Schön, Donald, 17, 48
school music listening, 64–66, 74–75, 82, 84
Schoolteacher (Lortie), 299–300
School Work: Gender and the Cultural
    Construction (Biklen), 305
Schopenhauer, Arthur, 47
Schubert, Franz, 53
Schwandt, T., 128
Science, Technology, Engineering and Math
    (STEM) education, 18, 29
secondary education
    music and, 2, 5, 8, 50, 63, 149, 160–161,
        170, 212, 244, 246–247, 261–263, 266–267,
        277–278, 284–285, 290–291, 300–301, 314,
        316–317
    reform and, 8, 18, 30–31, 33–34
secondary socialization, 266–268, 270,
    300–302
Seifter, H., 227, 277
servant leadership, 224, 229–237, 239–241, 264
"Shine On You Crazy Diamond" (Pink
    Floyd), 97
Shostakovich, Dmitri, 205
Silver, E.A., 115
Skype, 178
Sloboda, J.A., 66, 74
Small, C., 14, 45
Smith, Henry Charles, 240
Smith, Janice, 5, 153, 167
Smith, M.S., 115
social justice, musical composition and, 5,
    150–151, 155–156, 158–161
Song of the Day (Minnesota Public Radio),
    156–157
Sousa, John Philip, 94
Southeast Center for Education in the Arts
    (SCEA), 119–120
Special Research Interest Group (SRIG), 17

Spector, Phil, 95
Spinning Wheels: The Politics of Urban School
    Reform (Hess), 110
Stand and Deliver, 305
standards
    creative thinking and, 183
    education reform and, 108–110, 112–113,
        118, 183
    music education and, 37, 106–108, 118, 120,
        184, 253, 286, 290
    National Standards for Arts Education
        (1994) and, 45, 106, 109, 206
    National Standards for Music Education
        and, 184, 200
    neoliberalism's emphasis on, 28–29
Stanford Center for Assessment, Learning
    and Equity (SCALE), 183
"The Star Spangled Banner," 96
Status of the American Public School Teacher,
    2005-2006, 297
Stein, M.K., 115
Stein, R., 322
Stepping Across: Four Interdisciplinary Studies
    of Education and Cultural Politics, 304
Stiglitz, Joseph, 30
Stokes, W.A., 47
Stollenwerk, H., 69
Stomp performance group, 191, 200n1
"Storms out of Africa" (Enya), 193
Strand, K., 184
stride technique of piano playing, 95
Strolling Strings Ensemble, 209
students in United States
    demographic profile of, 8, 297–299
    disabilities among, 298
Swanwick, K., 133, 135
Swift, Taylor, 98
symbolic interactionism theory, 269

Tan, L.Y.C., 277
Tarrant, M., 65
Tatto, Maria, 303
Teacher Education Accreditation Council
    (TEAC), 313
teachers. See also conducting
    beliefs about students among, 302–303
    beliefs about teaching among, 272, 295,
        299–302, 304–306, 314
    "bridge teachers" and, 316–317

"conversation of practice" with students and, 262–263

demographic profile of, 8, 155, 296–299

facilitation of student creativity and, 211–216, 221

improvisation and, 262

mentoring and, 261, 265

music education training and, 5, 19, 32, 36, 88, 99–100, 108, 110–112, 163–164, 217, 228, 244, 259, 266–277, 288–290, 295–297, 300–307, 309–327

occupational role identity development and, 269–272

place-based perspectives and, 274–275

professional community-building among, 114–116, 118–119, 274, 322–323

professional development and, 113–117, 119, 121–122, 315

research capacities of, 321–322

shared decision-making among, 115, 118

teaching evaluations, 8, 294–295

Teachout, D., 322

"Tea Party Anthem" (Marcus), 31

tertiary education

music and, 5, 19, 32, 36, 88, 99–100, 108, 110–112, 163–164, 217, 228, 244, 259, 266–277, 288–290, 295–297, 300–307, 309–327

reform and, 35

tertiary socialization, 266–268

Thatcher, Margaret, 33–35

Thompson, L.K., 272

Tilley, C., 231

total personal musicianship, 99–100

Transforming Music Education (Jorgensen), 277

Turkanis, C., 56

Turner, M., 93

Twain, Shania, 142

University of Illinois, 16

University of Southern Maine School of Music, 8–9, 313–327

Urban Professional Development School (PDS), 114–115, 117–119

urban schools

accountability emphasis at, 109

arts integration and, 108

demographic diversity at, 110

musical composition and, 150, 154, 160–162, 169

music education at, 5, 106–107, 110–112, 119, 150, 154, 160–162

"policy churn" at, 110–111, 122

reform and, 108–113, 119, 122

teachers in, 115

virtual composers in residence at, 6, 169

user-generated content (UGC), 98

utopias, 92, 97–98

Vancouver Winter Olympic Games (2010), 37–38

vaudeville, 94

Vaugeois, L., 154–155

"Victor" (student in Virtual Discussions database), 142

"Victorio" (student), 64–65, 76

Villegas, A.M., 155–157

Vivaldi, Antonio, 193

Volk, T.M., 132

Vygotsky, Lev, 48, 81, 187–189

Wade, B. C., 14–15

Walker, R., 132, 134

Washington State Arts Commission, 118

Webster, P.R., 196, 198, 205–206, 208, 210, 213

Wenger, E., 56, 269

"We Shall Overcome," 151

"Where Have All the Flowers Gone," 151

Wiggins, J., 172

Williams, David A., 8

Williamson, S.J., 64–65, 76

Winter Olympic Games (2010), 37–38

Wis, Ramona M., 7, 233, 241, 264

Woodford, Paul, 3, 11, 269, 318

Woody, R.H., 63–64

world music pedagogy (WMP), 131–135, 138–139, 145–146

Wright, J., 247, 272

Yinger, R., 262–263, 272, 274

Younker, Betty Anne, 3, 20, 153–154, 197

YouTube, 97–98

Zerull, David S., 7

Zigarmi, P. & D., 232

Zimmerman, M., 46, 48–49

Zinn, Howard, 26

Printed in Poland
by Amazon Fulfillment
Poland Sp. z o.o., Wrocław